A Green History of the Welfare State

Environmental problems – particularly c   ᴄhange – have become increasingly important to governments and social researchers in recent decades. Debates about their implications for social policies and welfare reforms are now moving towards centre stage. What has been missing from such debates is an account of the history of the welfare state in relation to environmental issues and green ideas.

A Green History of the Welfare State fills this gap. How have the environmental and social policy agendas developed? To what extent have welfare systems been informed by the principles of environmental ethics and politics? How effective has the welfare state been at addressing environmental problems? How might the history of social policies be reimagined? With its lively, chronological narrative, this book provides answers to these questions. Through overviews of key periods, politicians and reforms the book weaves together a range of subjects into a new kind of historical tapestry, including: social policy, economics, party politics, government action and legislation, and environmental issues.

This book will be a valuable resource for students and scholars of environmental policy and history, social and public policy, social history, sociology and politics.

Tony Fitzpatrick is a Reader at the University of Nottingham, UK.

Routledge Explorations in Environmental Studies

Peak Energy Demand and Demand Side Response
Jacopo Torriti

The Green Economy in the Gulf
Edited by Mohamed Abdelraouf and Mari Luomi

Ecology, Sustainable Development and Accounting
Seleshi Sisaye

Environmental Change and the World's Futures
Ecologies, ontologies and mythologies
Edited by Jonathan Paul Marshall and Linda H. Connor

Environmental Adaptation and Eco-cultural Habitats
A coevolutionary approach to society and nature
Johannes Schubert

Complexity and Creative Capacity
Rethinking knowledge transfer, adaptive management and wicked environmental problems
Kelly Chapman

Contemporary Perspectives on Ecofeminism
Mary Phillips and Nick Rumens

Culture and Conservation
Beyond anthropocentrism
Eleanor Shoreman-Ouimet and Helen Kopnina

The Governance of Sustainable Rural Renewal
A comparative global perspective
Rory Shand

Disasters and Social Resilience
A bioecological approach
Helen J. Boon, Alison Cottrell and David King

Fairness and Justice in Natural Resource Politics
Edited by Melanie Pichler, Cornelia Staritz, Karin Küblböck, Christina Plank, Werner Raza and Fernando Ruiz Peyré

Environmental Justice in India
The National Green Tribunal
Gitanjali Nain Gill

Socioeconomic Evaluation of Megaprojects
Dealing with uncertainties
Edited by Markku Lehtonen, Pierre-Benoît Joly and Luis Aparicio

High Speed Rail and Sustainability
Decision-making and the political economy of investment
Edited by Blas Luis Pérez Henríquez and Elizabeth Deakin

Rawls and the Environmental Crisis
Dominic Welburn

A Green History of the Welfare State
Tony Fitzpatrick

A Green History of the Welfare State

Tony Fitzpatrick

LONDON AND NEW YORK

First published 2017 by Routledge

2 Park Square, Milton Park, Abingdon, Oxfordshire OX14 4RN
711 Third Avenue, New York, NY 10017

Routledge is an imprint of the Taylor & Francis Group, an informa business

First issued in paperback 2018

British Library Cataloguing in Publication Data
A catalogue record for this book is available from the British Library

Library of Congress Cataloging in Publication Data
Names: Fitzpatrick, Tony, 1966– author.
Title: A green history of the welfare state / Tony Fitzpatrick.
Description: Abingdon, Oxon ; New York, NY : Routledge, 2017. |
Series: Routledge explorations in environmental studies
Identifiers: LCCN 2016042583 | ISBN 9781138781887 (hbk) |
ISBN 9781315769547 (ebk)
Subjects: LCSH: Great Britain–Social policy. | Welfare state–Great
Britain. | Environmental policy–Social aspects–Great Britain. |
Great Britain–Politics and government–1945–
Classification: LCC HN390 .F57 2017 | DDC 306.0941–dc23
LC record available at https://lccn.loc.gov/2016042583

ISBN: 978-1-138-78188-7 (hbk)
ISBN: 978-0-367-03018-6 (pbk)

Typeset in Goudy
by Wearset Ltd, Boldon, Tyne and Wear

What remains conjectural is whether this concern for the quality of the human environment ... is leading (or will lead to) a reappraisal and a rethinking of the role of social welfare in our societies.

Richard Titmuss, International Conference on Social Welfare, 1972

'It's a poor sort of memory that only works backwards,' the Queen remarked.

Lewis Carroll, *Through the Looking-Glass*, 1871

Contents

List of abbreviations   viii
Acknowledgements   x

Introduction   1

1 Made of coal and surrounded by fish: 1945–51   10

2 A final farewell: 1951–55   27

3 An impenetrable fog: 1952–64   42

4 Upheavals: 1964–70   60

5 Crises of power: 1970–74   77

6 The party is over: 1974–79   95

7 The soul of a marketplace: 1979–87   113

8 Venus in capitalist furs: 1987–90   131

9 The long shadows: 1990–97   149

10 New dawn, new politics, new Britain: 1997–2001   169

11 Fixing the planet: 1997–2005   190

12 Crashing and burning: 2005–10   210

Conclusion   229

References   242
Index   267

Abbreviations

BMA	British Medical Association
CDM	Clean Development Mechanism
CEGB	Central Electricity Generating Board
CND	Campaign for Nuclear Disarmament
CO_2	carbon dioxide
CPRE	Campaign for the Protection of Rural England
CSA	Child Support Agency
DEFRA	Department of the Environment, Food and Rural Affairs
DETR	Department of the Environment, Transport and the Regions
DHSS	Department of Health and Social Security
DoE	Department of the Environment
EAPs	Environmental Action Programmes
EC	European Community
EEC	European Economic Community
ERM	Exchange Rate Mechanism
ETS	Emissions Trading Scheme
EU	European Union
FoE	Friends of the Earth
FSA	Financial Services Authority
GDP	Gross Domestic Product
GHGs	Greenhouse Gases
GPs	general practitioners
IMF	International Monetary Fund
IPCC	Intergovernmental Panel on Climate Change
JSA	Jobseekers Allowance
LA21	Local Agenda 21
LEAs	local education authorities
MDGs	Millennium Developments Goals
NGOs	non-governmental organisations
NHS	National Health Service
NOx	nitrogen oxides
NUM	National Union of Mineworkers
OECD	Organisation of Economic Co-operation and Development

Ofwat	Office of Water Services
OPEC	Organization of Petroleum Exporting Countries
PFI	Private Finance Initiative
ppm	parts per million
QUANGO	quasi-autonomous non-governmental organisation
RSPB	Royal Society for the Protection of Birds
SDP	Social Democratic Party
SEA	Single European Act
SERPS	state-earnings-related pension
SO$_2$	sulphur dioxide
UNEP	United Nations Environment Programme
VAT	Value Added Tax
WTO	World Trade Organization
WW2	World War Two

Acknowledgements

Many thanks to Chris Pierson, Carolyn Snell and Ian Gough. Particular thanks to Robert Page who practically copy-edited the thing and suggested several important publications I had missed. My thanks also to Margaret Farrelly and others at Routledge with whom I have interacted over the years.

Introduction

If we are to address environmental problems successfully we must ask questions about the suitability, resilience and effectiveness of our economic, political and social institutions. Given the extent to which it has been woven into the fabric of modern societies many of those questions will concern the welfare state: to what extent might existing social policies either help or hinder us in responding to environmental challenges?

One way of casting light on this topic is to explore history. That is because the laws, rules, social networks and organisations, inequalities, social cultures, norms and practices of the past are transmitted by and through us into the future. Our inheritance shapes our present-day capacities, such that we never face the future without reference back to the failures and successes of what came before.

All of which implies that in thinking about environmental challenges there are some key questions we must direct towards the history of social policies:

1   What relationships between the environmental and social policy agendas have emerged?
2   To what extent have social policies and the politics of welfare reform deliberately informed and been informed by the principles and values of environmental ethics and politics?
3   How effective has the welfare state been at helping to deal with environmental problems in the past? On that basis, to what extent can it assist policymaking in the future?
4   What does this critique add to our understanding of the history of social policies?

Let's go through these one by one so that we can understand what this book is doing and saying.

Question 1: *What relationships between the environmental and social policy agendas have emerged?*

Previous work suggests that the relationship has been weak (see Fitzpatrick, 2014a). Perhaps we take nature to matter only intermittently and when things

go severely wrong, e.g. because of destructive weather, at which time we intervene by mopping up the damage and repairing what has been broken, e.g. flood
victims are rehoused. Otherwise, nature's sustainability has largely been something we take for granted. A weak relationship is thus an *ex post* one: so far as
nature is concerned, social policies are *compensatory* and *reparative*.

If this portrayal is accurate the consequences are potentially dangerous.
Environmental scientists and campaigners have long insisted that nature and
society are symbiotic and densely interdependent; each resonates in the other
through a complex series of intermeshing, feedback loops. The risk of a weak
relationship is that, given their centrality within modern society, social policies
have helped to *produce* environmental problems as much as they have helped to
resolve them. They are compensating for and repairing problems that they have
in part created.

The chapters to come will suggest that the post-1945 welfare system has
indeed embodied a weak relationship. Take three key events. First, the flooding
and London smog of 1952–53 was a wake-up call to a welfare state government
that supposedly took the wellbeing of its populace as its primary responsibility.
Second, the growing awareness of pollution in the 1960s and acid rain a decade
later demonstrated how nation-states were increasingly interlocked. Third,
awareness of climate change and the effects of Greenhouse Gases (GHGs)
would build from the late 1980s onwards, highlighting the extent to which economics and societies would have to change in the twenty-first century. In each
case, as I will illustrate, the British government was slow to act in general and
slow to understand a need to build longer-term synergies between environmental and social policy agendas. At each stage there has been a welcome evolution in government thinking, but these have rarely been as ambitious, rigorous
and effective as the evidence warranted. The principal stages within this weak
relationship will be tracked at the ends of chapters and summarised in the
Conclusion.

Question 2: *To what extent have social policies and the politics of welfare reform
deliberately informed and been informed by the principles and values of environmental
ethics and politics?*

What accounts for that weak relationship? A lack of conscious effort, presumably, taking different forms at different times. In the 1950s and 1960s it may
have been overconfidence, a sense that post-war reforms were so robust that the
framework for any future challenges was already in place. Neither Left nor Right
recognised that environmental problems were so important they necessitated
any grand rethinking of what each already believed to be true. Later, amid fears
of national decline in the 1970s and 1980s, governments tended to hunker
down by prioritising short-term, domestic needs. Left and Right both thought of
the economy as being detached from its natural foundations. Britain gained a
reputation as the 'dirty man of Europe'. The hints of a determinate *ecosocial*[1]
policy and politics would emerge in the late 1990s but New Labour's progress

was tentative and uneven. Here too, evolving trends will be tracked at the ends of chapters and summarised in the Conclusion.

Question 3: *How effective or ineffective has the welfare state been at helping to deal with environmental problems in the past? On that basis, to what extent can it assist policymaking in the future?*

Yet as the following chapters will also show, there are respects in which embryonic forms of environmental policies were key to post-war welfare reform and policymaking. For instance, the Attlee government initiated the framework in town and country planning that was more or less intact 65 years later. The Clean Air Act in 1956, the world's first Department of the Environment (created in 1970) and New Labour's quality of life agenda also represent interesting developments. We will explore each and determine the extent to which they are examples of good practice. A summary is provided in the Conclusion where we address the additional question of whether the existing welfare state is fit for ecological purpose.

Question 4: *What does this critique add to our understanding of the history of social policies?*

Given what has been said already it may seem that a green perspective has little to add to existing histories. So how should we proceed? Rather than identify ways in which natural ecosystems have influenced the development of modern capitalism and democracy (Clapp, 1994; Hughes, 2006) or investigate the impact of welfare states on the natural environment, two assumptions have guided my thinking.

First, while vital and interesting both these approaches might take us too far away from standard social policy histories. I suspect it is necessary to revise and expand the analytical horizons of such histories rather than starting with an entirely fresh sheet of paper. This is because, second, I doubt that a green society could or should reinvent its social policies from scratch (for a justification see Fitzpatrick, 2014a). Consider three possibilities:

1   One or more of the existing models of state welfare that already exists, or has existed in the past, is compatible with and facilitative of a green society. We just have to work out which.
2   There is no extant welfare model consistent with the likely needs and goals of a green society, but there may be disparate elements which are compatible and from which a new model could be constructed. Our job is to identify and encourage mutually reinforcing synergies between social and environmental policies.
3   A green society would have to adopt a radically different form of social organisation. We therefore ought to abandon orthodox approaches to social policy and start afresh.

Which of these is most persuasive? If social policies and policymakers have already drawn upon environmental principles and practices, have been sensitive to environmental impacts and invited the participation of green groups into the policy process then the answer is more likely to conform to (1), or at least rest somewhere between (1) and (2). But if policies and policymakers have neglected and even been hostile to environmental issues then the answer arguably shifts more firmly towards (2) and perhaps beyond it to (3).[2] We therefore need to start from where we are. Only by first conjoining social policy literatures and debates with environmental ones can we see whether they are allies, strangers or enemies. Only then will we have a better idea on how to proceed (see the concluding chapter).

All of which adds up to both a more or less ambitious agenda than is normally presented in social policy histories (e.g. Timmins, 2001; Lowe, 2005; Glennerster, 2007). This is why what follows is offered as a framework for further thinking, research and debate. My aim is to suggest where, why and how a green critique directs new light onto the history of post-1945 British social policies, but not to replicate the kinds of details already available in other, more mainstream accounts. The chapters to come will not pursue every plot twist in every story.

In trying to outline this new framework I have kept things theory-lite.

Does history always move at a glacial pace or in punctuated spurts? Are we the prisoners of the past or are we always free to escape its texts and write new pages? Is history the unwinding of some inner dynamic or has it no given direction, no fixed destination? All important questions, no doubt, but not ones essential to the account which follows.

Nor is this book particularly concerned with explanatory models of policymaking and state/market relationships, nor with how the connections between social policy and the environment should be theorised (for introductions to the subject see Fitzpatrick, 2011a, 2011b, 2014a). Nor has it been my intention to design a green society as a benchmark against which to judge, retrospectively, the actions (and non-actions) of governments.

I have not wanted to compose a philosophical treatise or a social blueprint, in other words. Instead, my work is much more preliminary than this, more grounded and inductive in that I have sought to gather data and learn a few basic lessons from a broad range of events, developments and issues.

Clearly, then, the book goes beyond an 'administrative' conception of social policy as that primarily dealing with the legislation, implementation and delivery of publicly-funded, welfare services. Its conception is broader than this. Social Policy is here considered as *an interdisciplinary and interdepartmental field of governance, which is concerned with the collective production and distribution of public goods and social resources that are intended to improve social conditions by addressing social problems and/or enhancing individual and social wellbeing.* The book therefore deals with the tapestry of society, economy, environment and government, with particular reference to the welfare state.

'Environmentalism' is here used in a general sense, too: that which is concerned with ecological sustainability and social-natural interdependencies.

In technical language, sustainability implies that 'throughput' (the economic system's inward flows of resources and outward flows of waste) should not exceed the regenerative and absorptive capacities of natural ecosystems (Daly, 2007: 72–3). The natural world has limits to the amount of resources that can be extracted and the amount of pollution it can absorb.

Ecological systems[3] are therefore more vulnerable than we often appreciate and human activities should be organised accordingly. We should not extract or pollute beyond the planet's capacity to cope. We must be the stewards of nature's resources, applying an ethic of responsibility that respects the value and worth of that which we use and affect. For instance, renewable resources should be replenished and non-renewable ones should be used if and only if we are fully sensitive to the consequences of that use. Economic growth and social development should be sensitive to and consistent with the requirements of sustainability.

Furthermore, the natural environment is an interconnected web of organisms. The currents of this web are complex, fluid and tightly interwoven, such that changes ripple across those entanglements in ways that are difficult to predict but which may often be profound. This 'ecoweb' therefore consists of interdependent relations. The 'environmental commons' – the atmosphere, oceans, ecosystem, etc. – do not belong to us, nor can they be parcelled into units of private property. Humans are just one element of those dense intersections (Urry, 2011). We are social *and* natural beings; animals who have recently developed rapidly due to their capacity to form complex social communities. Those communities have altered the natural environment considerably and in ways that have become increasingly destructive and risky during the fossil fuel era.

We therefore possess responsibilities, which are both wider and deeper than are normally acknowledged in mainstream political debates. The greater the power we wield the greater our moral obligation to do so with sensitivity and empathy towards those affected by our actions. Ecological responsibilities imply principles of preservation, care, stewardship and equilibrium across multiple dimensions of space (re nonhumans) and time (re future generations).

How should we fulfil those responsibilities? Environmental policies do not exist in an ideological vacuum. Any diagnosis is grounded in a range of political and moral ideas and ideals. Therefore, while adopting a reasonably open approach there is an ideology about which I will be particularly critical. My assumption will be that at the very minimum we need to re-regulate capitalism, direct it towards ecological ends and distribute the burdens and benefits of the resulting social transition fairly. Since it may seem I am loading the dice from the offset, let me justify my reasoning at greater length.

The deregulated capitalism,[4] which has dominated since the early-mid 1980s has produced neither ecological sustainability nor social fairness.

For example, economics textbooks typically tell us that free markets are by far the most efficient mechanism for the allocation of scarce resources

(Anderson & Leal, 2015). They tell us that by freeing people from the state, e.g. allowing them to keep more of their income by reducing tax rates, social positions begin to reflect merit, hard work and personal desert. And they tell us that deregulated economies provide a space for entrepreneurs to design and implement innovative goods, services and manufacturing processes, including those needed for a sustainable society. On this view, a society both green and just must be a free market society rather than one based upon egalitarianism, state ownership, regulation of the economy and a large, thriving public sector.

But the reality of free markets is somewhat different[5] (Sandel, 2012: Marquand, 2013: 77–83).

- People are not the straightforward preference-maximisers that the text-books imagine. Consumers have multiple – often conflicting – preferences. Short-term desires frequently loom larger than long-term ones and without collectivist intervention long-term preferences may remain unsatisfied, e.g. people fail to save for retirement without a system of compulsory savings. And people do not always obey the dictates of economic rationality for three reasons. First, humans are frequently driven by impulses, emotions, instincts, habits and prejudices. Second, social circumstances often constrain what we can do, think and value. (Mullainathan and Shafir (2013) highlight the extent to which scarcity engenders behaviour that creates *more scarcity*.) Finally, there are many non-economistic values and aspects of life to which an ethos of consumption, preferences and self-interest do not apply.
- Public goods – those things that individuals cannot supply for themselves – require communal action to overcome the limitations of individualism, i.e. collective action problems, in which individuals unintentionally create undesirable states of affairs.

    Furthermore, consumers typically possess less knowledge about the good or service they purchase than those providing it; and so the more an exchange occurs in a deregulatory context the more dependent the consumer is on the professionalism and good sense of a provider who is seeking to maximise profits. Dissatisfied consumers have recourse to the law when contracts are broken, but this is often burdensome and can require both considerable resources and resourcefulness. Besides, healthy economies depend upon relations of trust that underpin contractual exchanges and relationships. By allowing relationships between individuals to be dominated by impersonal contracts, self-interest and profit-motives, free markets easily undermine the trust relationships upon which economies depend.
- Also, my capacity to fulfil a want depends upon how many other people with the same desire have a purchasing power which exceeds mine. In short, those who can outbid me will be ahead of me in the queue. By and large those at the front of the queue tend to monopolise resources and opportunities in ways that entrench their advantages and my comparative disadvantages. Free markets therefore embody relations of socioeconomic

power, i.e. they rely upon and exacerbate inequalities since, by definition, a free market implies the absence of measures to correct market outcomes. In short, free markets are freer for some than they are for others. Free markets constrain those who lack the power to take advantage of, and flourish within, them. To those who have will be given more.

- And markets create externalities where that which is produced by an exchange is not factored into that exchange (Fitzpatrick, 2014a: 82–4, 155–6, 180–4). While some externalities create benefits many are negative. My desire for low-priced chocolate may create jobs (positive externality) but could also keep the living conditions of those who harvest the cocoa (negative externality).

  Factoring negative externalities into prices requires more deliberation, regulation and coordination than free market defenders identify. Prices must be higher than the 'market clearing' rate set by desires that will be typically insensitive to environmental and social contexts. For such contexts are often invisible to individualised purchasers who, because they are individualised, may not have a great motivation to factor fairness into their calculations and exchanges. As consumers we all too willingly succumb to self-interest by free riding on the disadvantages of others.

- Finally, the era of free markets has been one characterised by the retrenchment of the welfare state, the advance of corporate governance and the rise of a new state which is usually more interested in the monitoring, surveillance and control of individuals than it is in social justice and the regulation of economies. Private capital has both floated away from its national moorings *and* increasingly started to colonise those public services and public spaces that are central to national identity and social wellbeing. Frequently, governments now see their role as making their workforces – their human capital – disciplined and compliant enough to attract flows of inward investment.

  The gap between those who wield political-economic power and those who are subject to it is now wider than it has been since the nineteenth century. The ideology of free markets has captured many political parties, to varying degrees. Anger and apathy collapse into one another along a cycle of disempowerment as (global) capitalism now increasingly displaces (nation-based) democracy. The freedom to shop has accompanied a surrender of other freedoms.

In short, free market proselytisers misread human motivation, lack understanding of the social and moral context of human action, are insensitive to power asymmetries and inequalities and neglect how the effects of their own reforms even undermine liberty by fusing the over-powerful state with anti-democratic corporative governance.

None of which should lead you to believe that this book will treat the period from 1945–79 as the apotheosis of western civilisation, followed by a descent into a new dark ages once the ideology of free markets re-emerged from the shadows into which they slunk in the 1930s. My antipathy to that ideology aside, the book tries to be open-minded about the successes and failures of each era. As indicated above, its method is inductive.

After all, the welfare state was decades in the making and was made by many across the political stage: social liberals, *noblesse oblige* conservatives, social democrats and democratic socialists, feminists, and no doubt countless others. The 'post-war settlement' was a messy compromise in which lots of people found something they liked and other things they disliked but felt they could live with. This being the case a 'green welfare state' would surely also have to attract support from a wide constituency too.

A few more minor points before we start.

First, I have tried to make the book as readable as possible, in the tradition of narrative history. The chapters are chronological (charting the major changes in government) with one or two overlaps the justification for which should be clear as we encounter them. Terminology is kept to a minimum and when it cannot be avoided I have tried to make it as user-friendly as the relevant debates permit.

Second, this book is both a sequel to an earlier one, *Climate Change & Poverty* (Fitzpatrick, 2014a), and its prequel.[6] While finishing that publication it became clear that I needed an account of how we got to where we are. However, you do not need to have read the earlier book.

Third, little is said about the pre-1945 period. In many respects Victorian reforms constituted the first great era of ecosocial progress. In waging their battles 'against squalor, poor housing, dirty water, sewage, ignorance and, ultimately, germs' (Halliday, 2007: 1–2) the interactions of the social and the natural were clear. Those who felt otherwise were increasingly on the back-foot as the state took over functions previously reserved for philanthropists, entrepreneurs, charities, friendly societies and commercial firms (Halliday, 2007: 26–7, 34, 215–18). It would therefore be instructive to compare the 1945–2010 period with an earlier one of similar duration, e.g. 1845–1910. The task must wait for another time, however.

Fourth, given the weak relationship I have hypothesised between the domains of social and environmental policymaking, the risk this history runs is that of having to tell discrete stories that can on the surface seem disconnected. How do you relate a history of something that doesn't really exist yet?! The narrative adopted below is one in which by rearranging and juxtaposing some key tiles we build up a mosaic of intersecting components: economics, party politics, government action and legislation, welfare reforms and environmental issues. The approach is therefore one that weaves the environment and social policy into a new tapestry, which I hope both experts and beginners will find instructive.

Finally, most of the following chapters will conclude by addressing two of the key questions with which we began. *What relationships between the environmental and social policy agendas have emerged? To what extent have social policies and the politics of welfare reform deliberately informed and been informed by the principles and values of environmental ethics and politics?* We will then be in a position to answer the third question at the very end of the book.[7]

The book is therefore about restoring some of the dead branches of the past that we have pruned away (Fischer, 1970: 135), unconcerned as they tumbled towards the forest floor before being lost from sight; forever now part of a dead undergrowth the living tread upon but rarely notice. This restoration is important because those missing branches and leaves are as much a part of the history that made us as the legislative acts and the institutional reorganisations upon which conventional policy histories concentrate. And so once we recognise how vast and how dense the forest really is we may picture our forebears on an immense, always fluctuating landscape, assaulted by monstrous storms they could barely see, surrounded by forces and powers they could barely touch, battling sometimes with and sometimes against nature in struggles that only endured until they were dissolved and poured back into the universe, into their second and final eternity of silence.

Notes

1 The 'ecosocial' is used as a blanket category, which denotes understanding and operationalising (1) the social dimensions of what are typically held to be natural events and processes, and (2) the natural dimensions of what are typically held to be social events and processes. An ecosocial welfare system would be one that weaves social policies and environmental policies together.
2 It is possible that even if policymaking has not drawn upon environmental principles we have somehow stumbled upon a welfare system ideally suited to the ecological challenges we face. I am assuming that such a coincidence is unlikely, however.
3 I will use 'environment' and 'ecological' interchangeably.
4 Often called 'neoliberalism' but for reasons I won't bore you with I dislike the term and will avoid using it.
5 This is a schematic summary only. Of course, totally free markets are rare. What we are really discussing are 'minimally-regulated markets'. Chapters 7–9, particularly, offer a more detailed overview of the relevant market reforms, including how the deregulation of markets frequently accompanies the reregulation of people to suit economistic (frequently corporate) imperatives.
6 For a summary see Fitzpatrick (2014b).
7 The one dealing with the relevance of a green critique to social policy history will not recur. You have either been broadly persuaded or not by the above justification.

1 Made of coal and surrounded by fish
1945–51[1]

The weather had turned bitterly cold again, as if spring was reluctant to settle. But Tuesday, the radio announced, would be warm and sunny, though with some possibility of thundery showers in the afternoon. Peter Clarke, on the first of his two days off school, was astonished at how correct this proved to be and assumed that all weather forecasts would be similarly accurate. After all, this was the first weather report he had ever heard because it was the first one broadcast in six years. Forecasts, the authorities had feared, might aid the enemy.[2]

Sheffield accountant George Taylor noted how becalmed that Tuesday – 8 May 1945 or Victory in Europe day – felt (Garfield, 2005: 21–2). Driven in by the rain after a morning in the garden, he listened to the celebratory broadcasts on the radio. Yet George took days to remove the blackout material from around his home. Fearing it may be needed again he stored it in the loft, "ready for the next war". The tinned chicken, saved since 1941, was a disappointment. The tinned sausages, unopened since 1940, were only a little better.

George's ambivalences and disappointments would be echoed by others. On hearing of Churchill's crushing defeat in the July 1945 election the Catholic conservative Evelyn Waugh took a curious pleasure in the thought that a new Dark Age was about to descend (Hastings, 2002: 495). Ten months later the socialist George Orwell (1998: 286) would report that public attitudes towards the Labour administration were favourable though "every kind of privation seems more irritating because there is no war to justify it":

> … and though the deeds of the new government are perhaps somewhat uninspiring, there is no competing ideology in sight. The Conservative Party is bankrupt of ideas…. All it can do is to yap against 'state interference' and 'bureaucracy', which the ordinary person may slightly dislike but far prefers to economic insecurity.

So once the flags were taken down, once the dancers had staggered home and detritus from the street parties swept away, what kind of country did those like Peter Clarke and George Taylor find themselves in? What was it becoming?

It has become common in recent years to offer a street-level view of the period. The publication of diaries and of Kynaston's (2007) *Austerity Britain* allows us to walk among and overhear the everyday hopes, misunderstandings, prejudices, resentments and anxieties of ordinary people. These offer a necessary corrective to Leftist nostalgia: of a triumphant community striding arm-in-arm into a socialist future (e.g. Last, 2008: 32–3, 50–1, 63–4, 98, 124–5). The 1949 film *Passport to Pimlico* portrays a community spirit that both supports *and yet also* sticks two fingers up to the rule-making visions of Whitehall bureaucrats. But we must be wary of resetting the gauge too far in the opposite direction, of allowing the noise of the crowds to drown out the sense that something *had* changed and changed for the better. In other words, we should resist an altern-ative conservative myth in which plucky Brits resent and resist the new era of state bureaucracy (Green, 1993).[3]

For the welfare state was never some monolithic entity. True, post-war reformers frequently shared similar ideals. True, the initiatives of 1944–48 represent a significant new chapter in our national story. And, true, there was a wider pro-reform constituency than those eager to shoot down the thesis of a 'post-war consensus' like to imagine. But the welfare state was not parachuted suddenly into a nation of ration books and George Formby. Its roots stretch back into the nineteenth century and, indeed, some of its finest moments would post-date the 1940s by decades. Similar systems, whose roots had also been growing for generations, were springing up in other countries (Judt, 2005: 73–7). It was what it remains: a diverse, multifaceted, contested and yet integral part of modern social, political and economic development.

Similarly, although Addison (1994: 4; also Kynaston, 2007: 39–46) notes a political shift to the Left during the early 1940s, we should tread carefully here too (Weight, 2003: 84–91). A Mass Observation report suggested that one in three had changed their political views as a result of the war (Calder, 1992: 292; also 136–9, 289–94). But changed from where to where and by how much? Conservatives can propose that because Labour's landslide was overturned as early as 1951, no real revolution in the British character occurred. Yet the Left can observe that Conservatives were only trusted with power again once they committed to a continuation of post-war reforms (see Chapter 2). Such a Left-leaning hegemony depended not on a few election-time speeches but on a momentum that had been building across decades (Calder, 1992: 572–83). The woman dining at the Savoy Hotel, who on hearing the result of that July elec-tion pronounced, apparently without a trace of irony, "But this is terrible. They've elected a Labour Government, and the country will never stand for that!" was only dimly aware of the nation she'd been living in all her life (Jef-freys, 1998: 45). But, then, the country we live in is always partly a country of our imaginative hopes and fears, of the inward as much as the outward gaze.

For the time being, then, victory lay with those who saw in the Beveridge Report of 1942, or the Labour Party manifesto of 1945, a hazy image of a better nation (Harris, 1997: ch. 16; also Calder, 1992: 525–45). Who can disparage those moments of euphoria?

Keynes's revolution

The nation's most prestigious economist was perhaps a bit less euphoric than the VE crowds. John Maynard Keynes had once imagined a future that an exhausted Britain in 1945 seemed a long way from building.

If his 1930 essay, 'Economic Consequences for our Grandchildren', is a guide then Keynes (2009) yearned for a capitalism that pushed beyond itself, becoming so prosperous and fair that society would no longer need it. A world of abundance would eventually bid farewell to all the acquisitive, rat-racing and bootstrap-pulling sanctimony that made capitalism a necessary but hopefully temporary evil. In the meantime capitalism must be reengineered, he proposed. State intervention during downturns was necessary to stimulate activity and consumption and get the economy moving again.

As such, though a Liberal who expected a Conservative victory, and surprised at the Labour landslide, Keynes agreed to serve as chief economic advisor to the new Chancellor of the Exchequer, Hugh Dalton (Skidelsky, 2003: 790).

For there was work to be done on problems that transcended party lines (Tomlinson, 1997: 25–9). Facing a huge current account deficit, Britain was in trouble. Lend-Lease – which covered 60% of Britain's cumulative trade deficit during the war – was due to end in August, leaving it with the problem of paying for dollar imports when its capacity to produce and sell goods was severely depleted: imports were at 60% of their pre-war level but exports were only at 30% (Dell, 2000: 128–38). Keynes called this balance of payments problem a 'financial Dunkirk'. Loans would be forthcoming from the USA, but only on terms that further shifted the balance of economic power westwards across the Atlantic (Marquand, 2009: 123–5).

Yet even against this difficult background, old conventions were being overturned because of years of experience. Keynesianism became the new orthodoxy because the Great Depression had made free market assumptions undesirable, because the war had made them unnecessary[4] and because the power of its economy meant the USA could happily pay lip-service to Keynes' proposals for a regulated international monetary system, even as it was rejecting most of them (Boughton, 2002). Keynes articulated the gap in capitalist thinking which the retreat from free markets left behind. With so much pent-up demand and so many controls already in place (including on prices and imports) a return to the free market totems of the 1930s was never likely.

Thus the commitment to full employment was one the Labour government stuck to resolutely (Grieve Smith, 1997: 42–9, 56–62). Between 1945–51 UK unemployment averaged at 1.9%, compared to 13.1% between the First and Second World Wars (Hennessy, 1993: 126–9).[5] Anything less would have shot the government's credibility and political support to pieces – though we could speculate on how steadfast it would have remained if faced with a less sympathetic USA government.

Without full employment the country could probably not have afforded the expansion in welfare services that occurred at the same time as the balance of payments problem was being corrected.[6] The price paid was a continued lack of growth in personal consumption – by 1950 this had risen by just 6% (Addison, 2010: 12). For now, the government reasoned, the needs of the country must override the needs of consumers for well-stocked shelves. But this would be bearable, it expected, due to a growth in the social wage. The social wage is the total value of all those services provided free, or subsidised, by the state; and which can therefore be said to boost most people's disposable income since otherwise they would have to pay user-charges for such services. The social wage, therefore, hopefully, made continued austerity and rationing easier to live with. And it worked. By 1950, exports had risen by 77% and imports by only 14%, easing the trade situation considerably (Grieve Smith, 1997: 56). Labour would pay a political price, though, for continued personal hardship at the general elections of 1950 and 1951.

But Labour's resolute attachment to full employment was also due to a moral stance. This was a case of fundamental principles and values, deriving from the suspicion that free market capitalism is inherently wasteful, sacrificing human lives in the pursuit of profits and dividends (Tawney, 2004: 33–7). Full employment embodied the solidarities, communalisms and mutual sacrifices which the Left had championed since long before the Second World War, symbolised by memories of the Hungry Thirties and the lingering shadows of the workhouse and poorhouse. Nor were moral arguments confined to the Left. Beveridge's social liberalism made a moral case for full employment, defining this at a level lower than even Keynes thought the economy could bear (Harris, 1997: 440–3; Skidelsky, 2003: 714).

Very quickly, then, Keynesianism became *the* model of post-war economics and its central moral justification and economic objective was the maintenance of full employment (Kynaston, 2007: 432–99). The welfare state was more than just a continuation of the warfare state. By underpinning state welfare, few reforms enabled a shift away from pre-war, free market capitalism as effectively.

Keynes and nature

What, from a green perspective, could be wrong with any of this?

Daly (2007: 56) observes how, for Keynesians, growth meant expansion in output and so a concomitant increase in the use of natural resources. Keynes may have dreamed of a future society of steady-state abundance, but he proposes no mechanism to bring it about. He appears simply to assume that capitalism would be self-limiting because we (or our descendants) would eventually have our materialistic desires satiated. As such, one of history's greatest economists, the man who helped to tame capitalism, fundamentally misunderstood the capitalism he helped to tame:

> … Keynes saw a real possibility that was simply rejected by the growth obsession, to which, ironically, conventional 'Keynesian economics' has itself contributed substantially.
>
> (Daly, 2007: 119)

Along similar lines, E. F. Schumacher (1973: 19–27), who had unsuccessfully urged Beveridge to a more radical politics in 1943, argued that, though well motivated, Keynes' division between means and ends lacked credibility. How can rapacious capitalism lead to harmonious abundance for all? The vices we employ today will inevitably affect what happens tomorrow and no intermediate mechanism – not the invisible hand nor the regulatory state – can ensure otherwise. Focused exclusively upon investment, savings, consumption and national income, Keynes was writing in and for a mass, industrial society that was increasingly abstracting itself from nature. Natural resources were seen simply as another input into the production process.

If these critiques are fair the result is this. Though in 1945 the description would have puzzled most, Keynes was the economist for the next, regulatory phase of fossil fuel-based, carbon-intensive capitalism.

Churlish? Perhaps. Who could deny that full employment was desirable? And as a member of the Bloomsbury Group of writers and artists, Keynes could not be insensitive to the aesthetic qualities of nature. But an economy cannot be powered on aesthetics, he must have thought. What mattered were the resource inputs nature supplied. Besides, as a movement of the industrial revolution the Left had long been committed to a labourist, productivist approach. No Red-Green politics would emerge for another 30 years or so.

All of that said, it was not as if alternative ideas were unavailable to Keynes and his Labour Party followers. Though disparaged by Keynes, Marx incorporated nature more fully into his economic thinking, such that capitalism represents a 'rift' in the exchange of matter between humans and nature (Foster *et al.*, 2010; Dean, 2014). And John Stuart Mill (1970: 169–70), one influence on Keynes's 1930 essay, had characterised landowners as enjoying increased wealth "independently of any trouble or outlay incurred by themselves" and he used this to justify a taxation on the value of land since this accrued from "the general circumstances of society" rather than from "working, risking or economizing".[7]

Nor was Keynes oblivious to such arguments. In the *General Theory* he observes that rentiers benefit from scarcity in capital the same way that landowners benefit from scarcity in land:

> But whilst there may be intrinsic reasons for the scarcity of land, there are no intrinsic reasons for the scarcity of capital.
>
> (Keynes, 1954: 376)

The solution to the latter being "communal saving through the agency of the state".

Now, short of colonising other planets and moons, yes, land is indeed scarce in a geographical sense. But Keynes skips over the extent to which the *value* of land is *not* a constant and, like capital, changes according to the unearned and undeserved hoarding of the relatively few. Why he refused to build the insights of Marx, Mill and George into the heart of his economics is a mystery. Perhaps he simply thought that addressing the problem of capital scarcity is the sufficient condition of all else.

Does it matter? Yes (Fitzpatrick, 2014a: ch. 8). Recent housing poverty has resulted from property booms fuelled by a scramble for the best property in a crowded island where millions of acres are owned by just hundreds of families and organisations. Those booms have also fuelled urban sprawl and unsustainable housing densities. Therefore, like capital, the value of land is determined by rent-seeking behaviour and politically manufactured scarcities.

Keynes therefore seems to imagine that his post-capitalist society will come from ending the scarcity of capital alone, without appreciating the natural substrate upon which our economies rest (Henderson, 1981). By not following the lead of predecessors like Mill and George, he therefore helped to dig an intellectual hole in social democratic notions of value and ownership, which persists to this day, e.g. Skidelsky and Skidelsky (2012: 132–44) are fairly hostile to environmentalism. No wonder Daly and Schumacher felt there was something hollow about Keynes' hopes for a capitalism that creates its own post-capitalist terminus.

We can only speculate. By making society-nature interactions more visible, by respecting nature's intrinsic value and not regarding its resources as just another input into the production process, would more people have connected the dots between diverse environmental issues (smog and pollution, flooding, car dependency, pesticides, the unsustainable use of fossil fuels and other resources) more readily? Would we have been more prepared for the news that carbon emissions threatened runaway global warming?

Nature in the raw

But if Keynesianism rendered nature invisible there were other aspects of Labour's traditions for which this was less true.

If in the 1940s you spoke casually to a stranger about 'nature' what would they have taken you to mean? The ground beneath your feet? The air above you? Animals? The weather? The countryside? Probably. And they may have made a leap to something else. Some would even have uttered the term 'raw materials'.

In Britain, the imperative to collectively own and control nature's matter was most closely associated with the nationalisation of coal, steel, gas and electricity (Hennessy, 1993: 100–4, 203–8).[8] Take what was perhaps the central issue, one captured by Orwell (1962) perfectly. The British Empire had been built on coal such that, though they seemed oblivious to the fact, the playing fields of Eton owed their wealth and power to the underpaid, overworked, unseen and unheralded miners beneath its surface. Coal dust ran through the veins of the labour movement. The pits were de facto nationalised during the war and public ownership had been Labour policy since the 1920s. Since manufacturing industry *was* coal, since you couldn't control the one without the other, nationalisation duly followed in 1946.

Similar developments occurred elsewhere (Kynaston, 2007: 136–42, 316–24). The electricity industry was nationalised in 1948, the gas industry a year later as was (most controversially) iron and steel. The expectation was clear. If Imperial power and labour power flowed together then once the workers took control they could change Britain and, through Britain, the Empire and, through the Empire, the rest of the world. The impulse to control and pacify the forces of nature therefore derived from a need for security, solidarity and for the popular control of the raw materials that had made the Empire tick (Brivati, 1997: 139–42).

Labour's conception of society-nature relations in 1945 was thus fairly straightforward: government, on behalf of the British people, would nationalise the raw materials of Empire, share the wealth out fairly and so occupy the commanding heights needed to dispel the insecurities and uncertainties of war and capitalism alike. So, yes, as a matter of hard-headed economics, nature was a store of resource inputs. Speculation about its intrinsic value was suitable only for the allotment, the drawing room or the philosophy seminar. Nature was very much seen through the lens of productivism, economic growth and the dignity of the working man (those who worked on and with nature). But there was at least an element of distributive justice to Labour's vision.

There is an ambiguity here, then. On the one hand, for Keynesians nature was just an input into the production process; on the other, across the labour movement more generally it (as 'raw materials') had a more tangible and symbolic presence. The ambiguity arguably manifested itself in a peculiar way. Environmental reform would constitute an important plank of the 1945–51 government's achievements and yet has been barely recognised as such in retrospect, in part because – compared to founding the National Health Service (NHS), insurance benefits, full employment, education reform, etc. – it seemed disconnected from the Keynesian revolution.

We return to this point shortly. Let's first go back to the beginning of post-war social reorganisation.

Social reform

Arising from the tides of post-war economic growth and the accompanying faith in controls and planning (Tomlinson, 1997: 235; Kynaston, 2007: 143–70, 278–86; Morgan, 2011: 135–6), the main pillars of post-war social policy are well known and can be stated briefly:

1944 Education Act
   Creation of primary and secondary schools in every local authority, the abolition of fees in state schools and the school leaving age was to be raised to 15 and then 16.
1945 Family Allowances Act
   Provided £0.25 per week, funded by the Exchequer, for each child after the first regardless of parents' means.

1946 National Insurance Act
  Covering the entire population, this established flat-rate benefits in exchange for flat-rate contributions. These included sickness and unemployment benefits, retirement pensions, maternity and widows' benefits, a guardian's allowance for orphans and a death grant for funerals. The separate Industrial Injuries Act extended the insurance principle to accidents at work.

1946 National Health Act
  Implemented a national healthcare system in 1948, mainly from taxation, free at the point of use with free registration with a GP. Most hospitals were effectively nationalised.

1948 National Assistance Act
  Formally abolished the Poor Law and established a system of supplementary, means-tested allowances; a 'safety net' for those who were not eligible for, or had exhausted their entitlement to, insurance benefits.

At the time, Rowntree and Lavers (1951: 49) observed that while such legislation could not guarantee that unemployment would not lead to poverty, it had "substantially reduced the amount and the severity of the poverty that would be consequent on unemployment".

Yet if the basic *ethos* of welfare was clear in other respects, especially in its *implementation*, it remained less so. For instance, as Minister for Health, Bevan was the great centraliser, arguing that a truly universalistic, national service had to be centralised since local authorities lacked the capacity to control the voluntary hospitals. (Even here, though, Bevan's approach was "steeped in concessions" (Morgan, 2011: 216).) But as Minister for Housing, Bevan was the great *decentraliser* (Addison, 1985: 59–60). Local authorities remained dominant and regulation was tempered by a knowledge that home ownership had long been a British obsession.

Many within the Labour government would have felt similarly pulled in multiple directions. Centralisation and decentralisation, welfare experts and welfare users, national priorities and local autonomy, state ownership and popular ownership all – somehow – needed one another. How could they be brought together coherently?

For the most part, faith was invested in 'the state' and in Labour now being so dominant politically that it would have time to work out the finer details later. Having won the war, wasn't there enough evidence that the state could 'win the peace' too? The state was entrusted by many to manage and keep a lid on society's conflicting tendencies. But what must have seemed reasonable in the 1940s would eventually leave British social democracy economically, politically, socially and philosophically exhausted several decades down the line (see Chapter 6).

In fact, a sense of fatigue had set in even by the end of the 1940s. To some extent this was because many of the leading players had been in government for a decade, years of violence, turmoil and uncertainty unlike any the country had experienced since the seventeenth century. It was also because many believed that the most important reforms had been achieved. Tony Crosland would articulate this perspective just several years later (see Chapter 4). Once you have achieved your dream, he intoned, you'd better start living in the here and now rather than pushing socialist ideals into an always unobtainable future. In the late 1940s Labour looked at itself and found divisions between those who wanted to press on and abolish capitalism once and for all and those 'revisionists' who wanted to consolidate (Dell, 2000: 160–2; Kynaston, 2007: 535–41). At the moment of its greatest victory the wounds that would help keep the party out of power for much of the 1951–97 period were already beginning to bleed.

It was the revisionists and consolidators on Labour's Right who were initially ascendant. In part, this is because the 1940s welfare state was always an "austerity product of an age of austerity" (Tomlinson, 1997: 261, 281). According to Pugh (2010: 287), welfare services rose from what was already 34% of central expenditure in 1937 to just 40% in 1950. In other words, social spending was as secondary as domestic spending to the needs of exports and of industry. Therefore, by the end of the 1940s key Labour ministers were persuaded – on limited evidence – that the horizons of redistribution had been reached already, such as the new Chancellor Stafford Cripps (Radice, 2008: 175). For Labour's Right, the moral argument was no longer sufficient. Social justice could only be delivered by higher economic growth and productivity. Decades before anyone had heard of 'human capital', the new test of welfare reform would be its contribution to economic efficiency. This was a key aspect of post-war welfare from its very inception.[9]

A forgotten environmentalism

All of which must make it sound as if the post-1945 government was as oblivious to environmental needs as it's possible to be. An obsession with growth, national efficiency, productivity and exports? Not quite what Schumacher, Daly and many of the other Greens we encounter in this book have had in mind.

Yet in some respects the 1945–51 administration was more ecologically sensitive than many of its successors. It is even tempting to regard the relevant legislation as a defining plank of post-war reform (Addison, 2010: 28–32), albeit one which has been largely forgotten, that has left an enduring and mostly successful legacy (Fitzpatrick, 2016). Forgotten in part because there was no distinct Sixth Giant to slay, no ongoing ecological crisis for Beveridge's biblical language to identify or for Keynesian economics to target.

So, what we can now rearticulate in ecological terms was, at the time, folded into other forms of discourse. For instance, although back in the late 1940s food subsidies were redistributive, they were also an instrument of macroeconomic policy because the Labour government retained them in order to justify holding down wage claims (Tomlinson, 1997: 253, cf. 268). Food was part of the social wage and by 1950 those subsidies were costing as much as the NHS.

To access that 'forgotten environmentalism', then, we must access other histories, that of housing and planning in particular.

Communities needed to be rebuilt as a result of 'blight and blitz' (Hasegawa, 1999: 140–1). The residue of too many slums was still disfiguring too many cities, and parts of the country had been devastated by bombs. And the spirit of the age said that communities *could* be rebuilt, by planners, architects and others belonging to the scientific-managerial classes who would be unleashed by government (Hasegawa, 1999: 142–4).[10] New estates, suburbs and city centre developments would integrate the community spirit of old into a comprehensive design, it was anticipated.

And how to relieve urban congestion while protecting the countryside? Here, too, planning and control were the maxims of the day. Protect the countryside through National Parks and Green Belts, it was thought, while channelling urban expansion, industrial growth and transport infrastructure on and around the 'new towns' (Wood & Carter, 2000: 420–1; Kynaston, 2007: 29–37, 159–67). The New Towns Act of 1946 and the Town and Country Planning Act of 1947 were the culmination of the ideal that a peacetime society could be as directed towards determinate goals as a wartime economy (Sheail, 2002: 41–5, 62–72).[11]

In truth, ambitious plans for radical reconstruction were diluted as economic realities bit and due to the lack of a national planning system. By the 1950s people's short-term desperation for a 'house anywhere' began to override the longer-term principles and methods of planning (Hasegawa, 1999: 149–59). Still, for a time, reconstruction and idealism went together. As others have observed, the new towns harked back to the Garden Cities tradition of Ebenezer Howard (Taylor, 1998: 23).

How successful were those Acts? As some Conservative critics appreciate, they prevented the kind of ad hoc, free-for-sprawl that had prevailed between the wars and to which the New Towns legislation was in large part a response (Clapson, 2005: 62–3, 69–70; cf. Corkindale, 2001). Scathing about so many government blunders, King and Crewe (2013: 10) refer to the 1947 Act as "so successful that most people now have probably never heard of it". Despite this, the wartime and post-war level of faith in planning would come to appear anachronistic and worth forgetting as the "successes of planning have been overlooked" (Addison, 1985: 72). Ironically, always an urban-centred party, the 1947 Act has been pretty much erased from Labour's memory too! For within the overall success there was a notable failure that stabbed at the heart of Labour's wish to socialise wealth.

Socialising the land

What the 1947 Act did was to bring all development under control by subjecting it to planning permission, with powers given to county councils overseen by a Ministry of Town and Country Planning. By July 1951 "all areas were to have development plans indicating the areas allocated to the main uses, the main transport routes, minerals areas, woodlands, green belts, reservoirs, and means of water supply and sewage disposal" (Rydin, 2003: 19). With the exception of agricultural development, all development was to be subject to control and permission.

Thus, landowners were granted rights only in the *current* use and value of their land; developers were to pay a development charge of 100% of the increase in the value of the land resulting from its development – this charge was known as the 'betterment levy' (Cullingworth & Nadin, 2006: 23; Cullingworth *et al.*, 2015: 26–7). The rationale here is simple. Beforehand, if development was likely on a piece of land its market price would increase, making its acquisition inevitably more costly. Speculation made it expensive to acquire land for development since the speculation would itself raise the value of that land! A 'betterment' in the value of land – at least those resulting from planning per-mission – should therefore pass to the community, it was argued, rather than the landowner. All land would exchange at the existing use value only "taking no account of the increase in value associated with the proposed development" (Rydin, 2003: 20).

The 100% betterment levy would, it was hoped, end land speculation and make it comparatively more profitable to use land rather than hoard it. Land would remain (mostly) in private hands but the right to develop it was effect-ively nationalised. (Those who, as a consequence of this, were effectively denied a right to develop their land could claim from a compensation fund if this denial led to demonstrable hardship.)

All of which constitutes an element of state welfare rarely commented upon in the standard histories: like health, education, and so forth, land was being viewed as a public good,[12] one that should be taxed with the resulting proceeds redistributed to the community on an equitable basis. Why was this attempt to capture land value not better known, then? Blundell (1994; cf. Lowe, 2005: 252–3) cites several flaws with the legislation itself.

First, the sheer complexity of the Act made it difficult to administer, creating anomalies and unintended side effects. Second, most increases in land value were from causes other than development so that a betterment charge could not be levied and proceeds to the community were lost. Third, what mattered were buildings and other improvements rather than the potential value of the land itself or the natural resources it contained. Similarly priced plots of land could therefore attract different charges because they were being used differently. Finally, those refused the right to develop their land often withheld it from sale, preferring to sit tight and not sell at 'present-use value', so *increasing* hoarding and speculation.[13]

As a result, inconsistencies and overzealousness in interpretations of the rules – as well as a general sense of unfairness and confusion – dominated the head-lines and the reform never gained a place of affection in the British people's mind. By so closely identifying the principle of redistribution with the interests of everyday communities, the betterment levy was particularly vulnerable to a backlash by property developers and their political apologists. This element of the 1947 Act was therefore repealed by the Conservative government in the early 1950s. By contrast, and while they had their critics, both new towns and planning controls *did* 'take root' in British society.

There is a further reason. The Labour Party never really fought for its own levy. Town and country planning was regarded as a "wretched little backwater" (Baroness Sharp, quoted in Pimlott, 1985: 578). Though on the retirement of Lewis Silkin the Ministry was given to the former Chancellor and though Dalton gave the subject his best enthusiasm, his political capital was on the wane and there is no mention of the levy in his memoirs (Dalton, 1962: 351–6). Even less interested in land taxation than land planning (see below), the party backed away from its own reform. Since the expectation was that redistributive justice would come mainly through jobs, housing and the social wage, the levy could be safely dropped – as would happen again decades later (see Chapters 4 and 6).

A fundamental error lay in the separation of departmental responsibilities for housing from those for town and country planning – and Silkin was denied a cabinet level seat. Bevan already had his hands full with health reform. What sense did it make to give him the housing portfolio too? Yes, many health problems derived from the appalling state of British housing conditions. But this, if anything, should have inspired what was years later called 'joined-up policy', rather than trying to cram too much under the same ministerial roof. With health and housing already on his plate a third dish (town and country planning) was initially separated from housing. Attlee finally made the ministerial and departmental connection in 1951, by which time it was too late.[14] Labour had only a few months left in office. Consequently, as we will see, the Conservative governments of the 1950s found it much easier to marketise land use and therefore house building than they did healthcare, social security, employment policy and the like. It all added up to the mother of missed opportunities for Labour.

Conserving the past

There is an additional consideration. When it came to social reform Labour in 1945 was ideologically dominant. The same could not be said about the environmental sphere, with Labour hesitant to disrupt a de facto truce, which characterised a lot of the campaigning about the countryside and so reluctant to shape others to its will. Take the main environmental organisations of the time as an example.

Stevenson (2003: 192) identifies a "group of fast-growing organisations and pressure groups" as the central inspiration for the legislative programme which shaped policy after the war in terms of agriculture, conservation, countryside access and urban planning.[15] Many clubs and associations dedicated to rambling, cycling and hosteling sprang up from the late nineteenth century onwards as people sought weekend escapes from the maddening crowds of the cities (Taylor, 1997: ch. 4; Byrne, 1997: 129–30). Equally, rural inhabitants didn't necessarily want those maddening crowds parked outside their houses and fields.

In many respects, it was those excursions of urban populations into the country-side which, against a background of urban expansion, fears of economic decline and rural poverty, prompted anxieties about 'invasion' and the erosion of the picturesque, timeless qualities of the country.

What we now call the conservation movement was therefore a reconciliation of two needs: the need for greater access to the countryside and the need to pre-serve that into which greater access was to be granted. Prior to the war it was non-governmental organisations that promoted this agenda, foremost among which was the National Trust and the Council for the Preservation of Rural England.

Though he does not justify the distinction, Stevenson (2003: 203) regards such organisations as part of a 'powerful lobby', whose diverse groups often found shared causes, rather than a 'movement' per se. His insistence is curious since Stevenson highlights the extent to which, by lacking an all-encompassing ideological identity, those organisations frequently shared a common sense of direction and mobilised opinion accordingly. The urgency and passion of those causes were often articulated in terms of political principles and values (Left vs Right, city vs country, past vs present) *while also being removed* from the realms of trench warfare that characterised so much political activity. They allowed the expression *of* the political without a sense of political partisanship.

In any event, Stevenson's overall analysis seems correct and, indeed, this convergence upon some shared notion of the common good was nothing new. Hardly a Marxist, Octavia Hill – earlier doyen of the Charity Organisation Society and a co-founder of the National Trust – had urged collaboration between the Trust and Society for the Protection of Ancient Buildings, founded by William Morris in 1877 (Darley, 1990: 306).[16] There was a kind of 'apolitical politics' to all of this, therefore. People frequently agreed on the ends even though their motivations and underlying principles could be widely divergent (Stevenson, 2003: 204–6).

Which is to say that the ruralism, which flourished between the wars, spanned the political spectrum. For the Right, the attraction of nature lay in a patriotic reaction against mass society and liberal modernity; its organic qual-ities contrasting with what they saw as the Left's impersonal rationalism. Bald-win's conservatism appealed to a kind of tranquil nostalgia that saw the countryside as the repository of national memory.[17] For liberals, land reform was more about opposing the vested interests of landlords. For socialists it carried echoes of the radical romanticism of Cobbett, Shelley and early Wordsworth in which rural workers are viewed as the real – yet unheralded – heroes of British history. In terms that would have been recognised by Morris, G. D. H. Cole argued that rural wellbeing and the beauty of the countryside went together (cited in Stevenson, 2003: 200).

Driven by non-governmental organisations, then, a political convergence on the merits of town and country planning had begun to emerge by the late 1930s and was set in stone by a wartime ethos, which sought the widest possible appeal to national interests. 'We are fighting for our common inheritance', was effectively the clarion call of the 1942 Scott Report, which, like the more famous Beveridge Report, saw post-war imperatives as a continuation of wartime ones (Taylor, 1997: 273).

As the party that would initiate post-war reform, the Labour Party tradition-ally favoured land nationalisation but this had been gradually replaced through-out the 1930s by a 'softer' focus on control and planning which could leave the structures of ownership largely untouched. The party's increasing support for the National Trust (Stevenson, 2003: 210) allowed it to preserve support for the idea of the public good without having to contemplate nationalising land with the enthusiasm it later displayed when nationalising the actual raw materials (especially coal), which could be found on and within the land.[18] Land value taxation fell away from Labour's reform programme as economic and social benefits increasingly dominated its thinking. Social justice vis the land was to come from a distributive levy rather than from popular ownership.

In short, a large degree of legislative consensus towards the countryside occurred because Labour turned away from its former radicalism. As it said in the 1945 manifesto:

> Labour believes in land nationalisation and will work towards it, but as a first step the State and the local authorities must have wider and speedier powers to acquire land for public purposes wherever the public interest so requires.[19]

Planning rather than ownership or extensive taxation was therefore central to the 1947 Town and Country Planning Act, with much of the countryside remaining in private hands:

> ... the countryside had become part of a consensus which spanned the political spectrum and drew heavily upon a group of national voluntary associations, which were themselves representative of a wider network of local voluntary effort.
>
> (Stevenson, 2003: 210)

And just as non-governmental organisations had inspired a non-partisan form of politics, so this broad consensus would help to leave countryside interests at arms-length from the daily barricades of political governance. Little surprise, as such, that the betterment levy was not at the forefront of the Labour govern-ment's thinking or reform efforts.

As the first post-war government, then, Labour wanted to preserve and build upon that sense of national togetherness through a statism that sought inclu-siveness. Titmuss (1950: 506) put it well; since German bombs didn't discrimi-nate, efforts to repair society had to include all communities:

> ... by the end of the Second World War the Government had ... assumed and developed a measure of direct concern for the health and well-being of

the population which, by contrast with the role of Government in the nineteen-thirties, was little short of remarkable.

In terms of economic policy (reorganising industry, nationalising key utilities) and social policy (universalising welfare services and meeting the needs of the working-class) that inclusiveness was one that Labour could easily dominate since that was where its support was located. But when it came to land and countryside, an existing consensus, and the fact that support for a Labour government and socialism was weaker in rural areas, inspired Labour to step more carefully. Here, the inclusivity was defined more by others. Knowing it already had some big fights to pick there were other fights that Labour sought to avoid. Substantial land reform was one of these. Added to various administrative errors – the initial separation of housing from town and country planning, and the fact that the latter was regarded as a backwater – constructed a fault-line between the social and the environmental aspects of government policymaking.

Key questions

What relationships between the environmental and social policy agendas have emerged? To what extent have social policies and the politics of welfare reform deliberately informed and been informed by the principles and values of environmental ethics and politics?

From the very beginning there was a split between the social and environmental aspects of post-war governance. Nature was all but invisible to Keynes, though for the labour movement the nationalisation of a raw material such as coal held symbolic as well as economic importance. Some of the government's greatest successes did lie within an embryonic environmental policy (the new towns and rural planning controls) but, as noted above, there was a blunting of its socialising radicalism and an administrative divide in departmental responsibilities.

As such, we cannot identify much crossover between the policy domains at this time. The departmental divide meant that the sphere of housing was split between (a) the need to build houses, and (b) urban–rural interrelationships. These two aspects of 'the social' were disconnected, in other words. Any recognition of a wider network of social–natural interrelationships ran a distant third, then. Pollution was not yet widely constructed as a social problem and there would be no 'politics of pollution' until the 1970s at least. There would be natural disasters (a London smog in 1948 may have killed 300 people) but there was no sense of government having to reflect upon its notions of wellbeing and state responsibility beyond what had already been achieved vis health, education, income protection and so forth. So, the social and environmental spheres were intellectually as well as organisationally separate.

Some legislative and organisational rethinking would occur in the mid-1950s (see Chapter 3) but no intellectual revaluation until the end of the 1960s (see

Chapter 4). Overall, then, environmental issues would thus tend to fall between the cracks of government departments. That between-the-cracks framework would not be addressed until 1970 and then again in 1997.

In short, from the outset post-war reforms were characterised by a disjunction between the social policy programmes of reformers and that of an environmental politics which was, nevertheless, already present in embryonic form. Recognition of environmental problems would begin to build, accompanied by an understanding of the social causes of those problems, but environmental policy was always playing 'catch-up'. Successive governments may have failed to weave the social policy and environmental policy agendas together because, in part, the starting-line for the race was already very uneven.

We will begin to see how and why this story played itself out from Chapter 3 onwards.

Notes

1 In a speech in Blackpool, 24 May 1945, Aneurin 'Nye' Bevan said "This island is made mainly of coal and surrounded by fish," reported in the *Daily Herald* the day after.
2 www.weather-banter.co.uk [accessed 14 November 2013]
3 Beveridge regretted that the state crowded out too much of the voluntary sector, but he also acknowledged the need for national schemes and universal provision to drive away the last vestiges of the Poor Law (Zijderveld, 1999: 34–5).
4 Ferguson (2008: 205–11) is at least partly correct to regard the welfare state as a continuation of the warfare state into peacetime.
5 We should also remember that this was really full time *male* employment, dependent upon female workers being displaced; 400,000 women left the labour market in the 12 months to July 1946 (Walsh & Wrigley, 2001: 1).
6 Indeed, Keynes was instrumental in helping Beveridge cost his proposals and so head off criticisms that they were unaffordable (Harris, 1997: 399–404; Skidelsky, 2003: 708–11).
7 There were also the similar, well-known ideas of Henry George.
8 Keynes was not enamoured of Labour's drive towards nationalisation.
9 Note the title of a 1948 Labour Party pamphlet: 'Production: the Bridge to Socialism'.
10 Some public involvement in plans for post-war reconstruction was initiated, though with limited impact on the actual implementation phase (Larkham & Lilley, 2012). Ultimately, the top-down approach was too top-heavy (Hasegawa, 1999: 148, 156).
11 We should also note the National Parks and Access to the Countryside Act of 1949. There was also the 1951 Rivers (Prevention of Pollution) Act: "An Act to make new provision for maintaining or restoring the wholesomeness of the rivers and other inland or coastal waters of England and Wales in place of the Rivers Pollution Prevention Act 1876". See www.legislation.gov.uk/ukpga/Geo6/14–15/64/contents [accessed 13 March 2014]
12 Both in the sense of the common good and in the sense noted in the Introduction: those goods that individuals cannot supply for themselves alone: parks, national defence, policing and (though this is where ideological battles over social policy centre) national systems of healthcare, income protection, social care, housing and education.
13 Blundell concludes that all a betterment levy does is siphon off some of the value of the land at any one point in time. It would be better to levy a tax on all land values

regardless of its state of development. The activities of the landowner are one thing, but what also matters are factors such as soil fertility, minerals, proximity to towns and relevant infrastructures, and the social and ecological needs of the community.

14 It initially remained the Ministry of Town and Country Planning and then became the Ministry of Local Government and Planning in January 1951, finally taking over the housing portfolio.

15 Though moderate, traditional and anthropocentric in outlook – aiming "to conserve the environment as an area for human beings to enjoy" (Nehring, 2005: 395) – these constitute an early manifestation of a Green Movement.

16 Morris would not convert to Marxism for another few years but the Society was always dear to him and he always dedicated time to it.

17 On the far right were organicists like Rolf Gardiner, co-founder of the social association and enthusiast for hiking, nudism, folk dancing and voluntary labour camps. For an overview of Gardiner's significance to British environmentalism, especially its Right wing, see Jefferies and Tyldesley (2011).

18 And in Octavia Hill, the Trust had in at least one of its co-founders someone who expressed distaste for commercial interests and for the restrictions ordinary men and women who wanted to visit the countryside faced (Darley, 1990: 297–8). Enough of this chimed with Labour's values.

19 www.politicsresources.net/area/uk/man/lab45.htm [accessed January 2015]

2 A final farewell
1951–55

"It may well be a blessing in disguise!"

Churchill had flown back from the Potsdam Conference for the 1945 election results. The previous night he had awoken suddenly with a premonition that all was not well. By noon, nighttime fears had become daytime miseries: the Conservative Party had been wiped out. How could the British people have repaid their leader this way? Winston was sardonic about his wife's (slightly self-serving) attempt to be optimistic. "At the moment," he replied sourly, "it seems quite effectively disguised" (Gilbert, 1992: 855).

More was ending than Churchill's residency in No. 10, though. The necessity of making shared sacrifices and common cause would continue to have appeal for a little longer, but the political and social differences that the war had largely supressed would resurface before long. On 28 May Churchill had made a tearful farewell speech to the Coalition cabinet. A few days later he was accusing his former Labour colleagues of wanting to impose a socialist Gestapo on the British people (Gilbert, 1992: 846–7; Ramsden, 1995: 76–7).

A man who so often resolved his contradictions by embracing them, Churchill was instrumental both in bringing that era to an end while overseeing and preserving one of its greatest legacies: the welfare state.

The Gestapo overreaction was more than just the usual stagecraft of professional politicians. Churchill, a man of exuberant surfaces, seems to be describing something entirely alien to himself in his famous observation of Soviet Russia as "a riddle wrapped in a mystery inside an enigma".[1] Yet the description also reads like history's shortest autobiography. Here he is, then. The neglected son who seeks praise from the now dead father who neglected him; the young journalist-soldier whose best stories are about himself; the heir to privilege who is elected to parliament from working-class Oldham; the defender of free trade who clings to Empire; the social reformer who wages war against workers; the disgraced Cabinet minister who regains himself by fighting on the Western Front; the defector from Conservatives to Liberals and back to Conservatives again; the democrat who understands the allure of dictatorship; the sentimentalist who is a political warrior. Churchill's Gestapo references *were* him, in all of his glory and stupidity. Churchill wrapped and rewrapped surfaces around himself constantly.

Was that the secret of his appeal? That you could see in him what you wanted to see? If so, it's a quality that helped make him the best possible Prime Minister at the worst possible time. His contradictions were as multiple as those of a nation that in 1940–42 needed direction and unity. But as party leader the Churchill of 1945 reminded people of a past that the future might all too easily resemble. For in 1945 the Conservative Party was too distrusted by too many. No longer able to speak a language of both nation and party (Ramsden, 1995: 84), Churchill surrendered valuable ground to those he feared now understood this new Britain better than he. To Labour would fall the task of preserving national unity for a while longer, forging it across a particular set of social institutions.

It was around social policy that many of these battles revolved (Hennessey, 1993: 75–8). Churchill had made encouraging noises in 1942 on publication of the Beveridge Report. After all, Churchill had helped pioneer Liberal welfare legislation years earlier, in 1908–11 (Havardi, 2010: 44–50). But other conservatives disagreed (Hennessey, 1993: 84). The Chancellor, Kingsley Wood, warned that a Beveridge-based system represented an open-ended commitment that the country could not afford. Better to earn before you spend rather than the other way around (Barnett, 1995: 130; Charmley, 2008: 139–40).

There was already an efficiency counterargument to the Chancellor's position available, dating back at least to the Boer War. Namely, that unless you spend money on keeping your workforce healthy, educated, comfortably housed and free from insecurities you won't earn as much money as Wood's 'good housekeeping' model of economic management assumed. But too few Tories invoked that counter-argument and so the Conservatives seemed, at best, to equivocate over the Report and they suffered for it accordingly (Childs, 2001: 17).

Churchill himself was pulled in different directions, too. As his daughter, Sarah, warned, the noises he made in the 1945 election were discordant. It was at her urging that the younger Churchill briefly re-emerged – the Churchill who had pioneered national insurance and labour exchanges – allied to a new recognition of the need for health and housing reform (Gilbert, 1992: 847). But if that was the case then why paint your opponents as Stalinists in waiting? Because they wanted to nationalise a little bit more of the economy than you? Not exactly where the Bolsheviks began in 1917, is it? So every time Churchill shouted 'Gestapo!' enough of the electorate heard the leader of a party of privilege, which wanted the next 20 years to be a re-run of the 1920s and 1930s (Ramsden, 1995: 79–80). Thanks but no thanks.

Whose nation?

The modern Tory Party had been forged by Disraeli (1981) who by acknowledging social divisions – two nations – found a language, which to this day stands as a sign that the Conservatives have a 'one-nation' social conscience (Ramsden, 1995: 221–2; Walsha, 2003: 69–71; Seawright, 2005: 70–6; Garnett

& Hickson, 2009: 29–31; Dorey, 2011: ch. 2). Yet the heroine in *Sybil* turns out to be the long lost daughter of a toff. Disraeli's 'one nation' is forged by the poorest identifying with, and subordinating their interests to, the richest.

Perhaps, decades later, it took time for the Tories to reconcile themselves to post-war realities because here, briefly, society's currents ran in the opposite direction. Effectively, in 1945 Labour performed the Disraelian trick in the opposite direction: the two nations were to be reconciled by using a distinct proletarian accent, though in tones soothing enough to reassure enough of the middle-class.

But once the reconciliation had been effected (Bale, 2012: 69–74), the slogan of 'one-nation conservatism' could serve as a welfare state update of Disraeli's 'Tory democracy' (Walsha, 2003: 88).[2] For a while, it would be called the 'middle way' as noted below and in the next chapter. By championing Keynesianism, planning and social ownership, Labour demonstrated a willingness to align economic and social policies around a new egalitarian commitment to social wellbeing. Yet for the Tories, from 1951–79, economic policy and social policy were more likely to pull against one another. This tension would actually serve them well with an electorate sceptical about going any farther down the collectivist road. But it also gave the party a difficult task: how to reconcile humane, one-nation instincts with the ingrained impulse to create sound financial conditions and balanced budgets? Take the case of the man who ushered in the 1944 Education Act: R. A. Butler.

In some respects, Butler's struggles were a more sedate version of Bevan's (Garnett & Hickson, 2009: 23–5). But where Bevan stuffed doctors' mouths with gold, Butler had to stuff the churches' mouths with prayers and religious instruction to get his legislation through (Glennerster, 1995: 58–63). Butler thus created the initial stage onto which debates that would preoccupy governments for the next seven decades could step: academic vs. vocational needs, local vs. national control, comprehensive vs. selective admissions.

Initially praised by almost everyone, the 1944 Act would come to be criticised. It does not appear to have affected the relative social mobility of working-class children very much, and may even have worsened it in some respects (McKibbin, 1998: 260–9). And in failing to resolve the above issues it bequeathed to posterity a sometime poisonous legacy (McCulloch, 1994: 45–62). Yet given the conservative forces Butler faced, thwarting radical reform may have been the inevitable price to be paid for achieving any reform at all (Lowe, 2005: 208–14).

And that was as far as a political tactician like Butler could comfortably go. As Chancellor, a few years later, Butler would try to swing the pendulum back towards a free market model of capitalism (see below). Ditto the rest of the party. The notion of comprehensive social engineering was, quite simply, alien to conservative thinking, still as suspicious as Burke had been of abstract rationalisms (Oakeshott, 1991: 11–35). So while some reforms, like education, could be supported the idea of doing too much too fast was simply anathema to conservative inclinations.

The two conservatisms

How should we conceptualise all of this?

At least two tendencies are visible within the modern Conservative Party (Kirk, 1985; cf. Honderich, 2005).[3] There is, first, the *market voice*, which whispers constantly that 'markets can do no wrong', which may also be code for 'the existing distribution of wealth is perfectly fair'. This is the voice of *homo economicus* in other words. Humans are self-interested beings seeking the most reward for the least effort and the best society is therefore that which allows self-interest to flourish through the coordinating mechanisms of the market's 'invisible hand'. The job of government is to protect and preserve an economic landscape in which economic investments, profits and contracts can flourish.

The second, *social voice* suspects that markets make better servants than they do masters. Here, society is regarded as an organic web of potentially fragile connections. Individuals are inherently flawed and imperfect. To some extent, markets may enable those flaws to be transmuted into virtues. But markets are not immune to human folly; commercial interests may become corrupt, debase social life and loyalties, and direct resources away from other important activities. A patrician distaste for the 'cash nexus', for the grubby business of money-making and conspicuous consumption was often a palpable motivation. The job of government is to nurture that social web, intones this voice, even if this means restricting the scope and power of markets.

These voices relate to one another in a number of ways, often as warring partners in a turbulent marriage.[4]

In the latter part of the nineteenth and early part of the twentieth centuries – let's call it phase 1 – those tendencies coexisted within the framework of Empire (Viereck, 2006: 41–5). British-dominated markets were to be the masters of colonial peoples. But at home things were different. The post-1867 recognition of trade union rights, followed by the right to strike and improvements in working conditions, implied that market power must give way – at least partially – to political power. The Tory Democracy promoted by Disraeli sought to integrate the working-class, as 'little imperialists', into the Victorian order.

During phase 3, from the 1970s onwards, an automatic-pilot form of economics became ascendant (Friedman & Friedman, 1980: 13; see Chapter 7). Where Adam Smith had once asked 'how can we make capitalism moral?', now the assumption was that whatever free market capitalism did *was* moral by definition (Smith, 2013). It follows that whatever produces limited government is ethical. Economics is what matters, was the refrain, and the welfare state would just have to be reformed accordingly.[5]

It was during a brief intervening period, from the late 1940s to the mid-1970s, that the two voices perhaps established a greater degree of harmony than either before or since. This was phase 2. The tension described above, between economic and social policies, would be apparent but not to the point where a break with Keynesianism and the planned, regulated mixed economy was seriously contemplated. Not yet, anyway.

State welfare was a target for both tendencies during phase 2 conservatism (Green, 2002: 273–7). The market voice disliked it for soaking up resources that could be directed more productively, and profitably, through the private sector; the fear being that state services would create expectations for unsustainable levels of future taxation, spending and government meddling. The social voice disliked its centralisation, its confusion of 'public' and 'state', its usurpation of civic virtue (neighbourliness, charitableness), its vision of government as a busy little engineer always finding something new to tinker with.

Yet each voice also found enough about the welfare state to like and therefore support. By stabilising the economy and ensuring decent levels of demand it could provide a basis for sound, long-term investment. Only the most idiotic free marketeers imagined that the 1929 crash and subsequent depression were caused by an *over*-regulated capitalism! Keynes had been no revolutionary. He wanted to make capitalism work *better*. On the social side of things, state welfare promised greater fairness than *laissez faire* markets could provide – a genuine reconciliation between classes whose social and economic circumstances were otherwise so disconnected.

Phase 2 support was also inspired by memories of recent social conditions, i.e. the rude awakening some on the Right had experienced in the 1930s and 1940s (Marquand, 2009: 169). For Hogg (1947: 149) it is,

> … a complete perversion of the Conservative viewpoint to suggest that [they] adhere slavishly to any particular *status quo*, or that they are in the least complacent in the face of poverty.

Hogg's (1947: 259) Disraelian brand of big tent conservatism could thus accommodate itself to the moderate socialism implemented after 1945 while claiming that Tories had been in favour of Beveridgean and Keynesian reforms all along![6]

For phase 2 conservatives, then, a genuinely new partnership between haves and have-nots was needed. Churchill's influence was instrumental here. As a pragmatist who remained receptive to new ideas and new circumstances even quite late in life, Churchill's peripatetic wanderings and glorious inconsistencies were what the country needed as much in the early 1950s as it had in 1940. The socialist mother would withdraw and hand the child, the welfare state, over to the conservative father.

So, yes, from 1951–64 successive Tory administrations would always seek to curtail spending, lift the lid on private providers and divorce 'public' from 'state' (Kynaston, 2009: 252–3). The 'one-nation' group of backbench MPs were more right-wing than either their title or their initial 1950 declaration of intent seemed to warrant (Green, 2002: 242–4; Walsha, 2003: 94–7; Seawright, 2005: 76–8; Hickson, 2005a: 184–5; Page, 2015: 37–9). But this does not mean we should try to read phase 2 conservatism as a simple offshoot of its phase 1 predecessors or as a simple preface to its phase 3 successors (Dorey, 2011: 84; also Garnett & Hickson, 2009: 36). The conservative welfare state was a child with its own political identity.

Social reforms

So had the socialist-baiting Churchill remained the National Father beyond July 1945 the welfare state may never have been born; but the welfare state may never have survived had he not been its nursemaid six years later.

True, the Prime Minister of 1951 was not the spry leader of old. Seventy-seven years of age, distracted, barely interested in social policy anymore and suffering several minor strokes, Churchill was effectively being pushed to one side by 1953 (Ramsden, 1995: 270–4). Yet he set the tone for the new administration, and all Tory governments to follow for the next two decades. Many of his Cabinet appointments were depressingly atavistic (Bale, 2012: 74–5). But he also appointed a few young pups, including one-nation men like Harold Macmillan (Ramsden, 1995: 245; Gilmour & Garnett, 1997: 76–8; Morgan, 2001: 113–14; Hennessey, 2007: 196–9; Kynaston, 2009: 43).[7] Much of this was due to Churchill's political antennae – and the fact that he was more interested in foreign affairs anyway.

But it took more than the humiliation of 1945 for conservatives to turn away from their former selves (Garnett & Hickson, 2009: 26–9). As we see in the next chapter, a middle way conservatism had been formulated years earlier, inspired by genuine compassion, pragmatism and a certain loathing for *laissez faire* markets (Ramsden, 1995: 152–3). This would be *the* philosophy of phase 2: the post-war ascendancy of the middle way is what made adaptation to key aspects of Labour's programme less traumatic than many Tories had feared. A commitment to a welfare state did not entail commitment to welfare *collectivism*. Most existing state interventions could be supported without compromising opposition to any further, socialistic interventions. You could support some social equality without being a socialist egalitarian.[8]

In short, middle way conservatism was a reinvention of one-nation Tory Democracy. Older and in failing health he may have been but the Churchill of 1951 saw what the war leader of 1945 had not.

Lucky timing

Equally true, it was also a matter of luck, or at least of good timing (Bulpitt & Burnham, 1999: 9–10; also Tomlinson, 2005: 562–5).

Compared to how things had stood six years earlier, by 1951 the economy had come a long way and was in rough health. But many worried that the green shoots were only barely managing to poke through the soil. Was it perhaps time to reach for some pre-Keynesian solutions?

The following year the new Chancellor, Butler, advocated that the pound should be floated and sterling allowed to find its 'natural level', rather than depending upon Britain's gold reserves (Gilmour & Garnett, 1997: 62–5; Morgan, 2001: 120–2; Hennessy, 2007: 199–217; Kynaston, 2009: 73–6). Butler acknowledged that this would probably lead to higher unemployment and rising food prices, but felt that Britain's deteriorating financial reserves required it

(Garnett & Hickson, 2009: 32). The proposals were defeated, partly because of technical arguments, partly because the economic climate improved, partly because of the need to defend sterling,[9] but mostly because Conservatives were fearful of being seen to take the country backwards:

> A Disraelian cohesion, fortified by favourable economic circumstances, dominated the public mood.
>
> (Morgan, 2001: 122)[10]

By 1953 the international trade situation had improved and Britain was well placed to take advantage of it.[11] As the first stirrings of economic prosperity and consumer affluence began – both of which the Conservatives were quick to claim credit for – the conviction was that the country could afford the required social expenditure *and* cut taxes (Ellison, 2011). Middle way conservatism had found its maxims: increases in spending are legitimate *only if* they are subject to stringent controls; tax cuts are justified *only if* public services – especially those on which the middle-class depend – are not threatened.

Butler's proposals therefore went back into the drawer and his reputation as the third 'B' in the welfare architecture – behind Beveridge and Bevan – was thereby secured. The years 1951–55 were therefore ones largely of consolidation (Raison, 1990: ch. 3; Morgan, 2001: 116–18; Page, 2015: 42–4), though the desire to slash expenditure, create more space for private providers and emphasise user choice, i.e. service charges, loomed large within the Tory Right (Garnett & Hickson, 2009: 60–4).

The conservative welfare state

The NHS was a particular thorn (Ramsden, 1995: 265–6). But though some advocated a counter-revolution, which would first reset the healthcare clock to before 1948, political considerations prevailed. The NHS was clearly popular with Tory-leaning voters (Raison, 1990: 19; Kynaston, 2009: 625–6). As Mass Observation diarist, Nella Last (2008: 131), said in 1947:

> I rejoice to think a time will come when women like me, too well off for charity and not well off enough for nursing home treatment, will be looked after in illness and operations.

The thorn had thus been left there by many potential Tory voters with a simple message: tread carefully (Kynaston, 2009: 73). Better, therefore, to take owner-ship of the health system (Ramsden, 1995: 166–7, 185–6). Give it a conservative face. Then you could nip and tuck in the name of improving services rather than cutting them for the sake of cutting. User charges in the NHS *were* enacted but remained fairly minimal.

The degree of agreement and cooperation in education has rarely been matched since (Sandbrook, 2005: 420–5); cooperation, note, between a

Conservative national government and local education authorities that were largely Labour controlled (Lowe, 2005: 215–17). The quarter century after 1951 would see spending on education double as a percentage of public expenditure (Lowe, 2005: 205).

Things were also fairly quiet in terms of the benefit system. Some doubts were voiced about the long-term viability of social security expenditure, but these would not become politicised until the 1960s.[12]

As indicated in the last chapter, it was in the area of housing that the Tories would feel most able to place their particular stamp on post-war reforms. The new government removed restrictions from the private housing market but it was recognised that the private sector could not deliver on the Conservative's election promises alone: 300,000 new homes per year (Ramsden, 1995: 172–4, 255–7; Jones, 2000: 117). Hitting that target meant that the amount spent on each house went down, an emphasis on quantity which, its critics alleged, meant compromising on the quality of the new houses constructed (Campbell, 1987: 163). Living space would become smaller as a result (Glennerster, 1995: 76–7). Overall, though, even in the housing sector there was no major counter-revolution. Controls on land use remained in place, albeit with some changes we note shortly.

By the 1955 election, then, overall social expenditure, as a percentage of Gross Domestic Product (GDP), was more or less where it had been in 1951 (Lowe, 1999: 351–3; Clark & Dilnot, 2002: 10–13). Spending on health and housing went down; that on social security and education went up (Hennessy, 2005: 217–21). The one major change came with the ending of food rationing and subsidies, which meant that (with the exception of school meals and school milk) food was no longer seen as a social service (Raison, 1990: 32–3). Yet this barely mattered to the electorate. The Conservatives were no longer seen as an anti-welfare state party. Another election victory beckoned.

Consensus?

Did all of this add up to a consensus (Morgan, 2001: 118–19; Sandbrook, 2005: 64–6; Charmley, 2008: 156–64; Matthijs, 2012: 69–72)? Well, as social scientists are fond of pointing out, it depends on your point of view.

In terms of political geography and rhetoric there was no consensus. By the 1951 election the country was split between Labour North and Conservative South. The language of blame and retribution, which peppered manifestoes and speeches continued to be vituperative. Even mild-mannered Attlee went so far as to accuse Churchill of being a puppet of press magnate Lord Beaverbrook (Williams, 1961: 8–9); though no one equalled Bevan's remark that the Conservatives were "lower than vermin" (Foot, 1975: 235).

Yet the reconciliation described above *was* real. Even in the midst of its 1950 manifesto, when it spoke liberally of the 'Socialist deception', the Tory Party had learned its lesson and was pledging to improve and take ownership of, rather than reverse, much of what had happened in the previous five years. Intellectually, this was an era of social democratic domination and the cleverer

Tories knew it (Judt, 2005: ch. 11). Though the word 'Keynes' is not found in the manifesto, the Tories were committed to maintaining buoyant levels of demand.

Of course, 'consensus' was often a retrospective accusation thrown at post-war politicians by the resurgent Right (accusing middle way conservatives of giving in to socialism) and Left (seeing the welfare state as serving capitalist ideology). There is no consensus about consensus, in other words. Instead, it may be best to refer to a post-war *settlement*, one which emerged from a temporary convergence of values and ideas, whose highpoint was 1951–79 and whose legacy has lasted much longer. The politics of the next six decades began in the early 1950s, then. Labour was fearful of being seen as fiscally irresponsible; the Tories were fearful of being seen as social Neanderthals. The tempo and rhythms would change, especially in the 1980s, but the underlying mood music would not alter that much.

Tories and nature

Where do environmental issues fit into all of this?

Wasn't the Conservative Party the natural party of, well, nature? Traditionally, love of country and love of countryside found expression in each other. As Prime Minister Stanley Baldwin (1927: 6–7) put it, "England is the country, and the country is England". With much of the urban working-class being drawn to labourism, the Conservative's terrain was equally obvious: the leafy suburbs, the villages, the shires, the fens, the farms, the dwellings of the landed gentry. It was in the 1950s that geographical divisions in political allegiances became entrenched, with Conservatives the party of the South, Midlands and rural areas, and Labour the party of Scotland, the north and urban areas (Ramsden, 1995: 218, 230; Curtice & Steed, 1986: 212).

But nature for conservatives is not just the rolling hills, it is also that which 'holds' and 'fixes' (Scruton, 2013). The reasoning goes like this. We are inclined by nature to bow towards that which is superior: God, Authority, Family, Church, History, Country, Empire. Nature reminds us of the timelessness of things; it is the essence that underpins, giving structure and regularity to the everyday, to the social world itself. We are immutable, cast in forms determined elsewhere by forces forever unknowable to us. Nature wants you to be a hard working Anglo-Saxon Christian who loves his country, obeys traditions and expects obedience from wife and children. Wasn't it just common sense that those who assert any number of radical doctrines, e.g. equality of the sexes and the races, were offending the natural order? No, only blood and breeding equip a man for government. Edmund Burke, the guru of modern conservatism, described the aristocracy as the "great oak that shelters a country" (Burke, 1960: 377). Inequalities are natural. As a small-c conservative Nature is surely a Conservative voter too!

The countryside was, then, a source both of national identity and existential security. The market voice saw land as a source of wealth; for the social voice, land expressed the spirit of the national community, one that had to be protected from those who disrespected it, including the usurer and the developer. Churchill's famous words from 1909 on land ownership articulated not a conversion to socialism but a need for the nation to symbolically and physically endure (italics added):

> Unearned increments in land are not the only form of unearned or undeserved profit, but they are the principal form of unearned increment, and they are derived from processes which are not merely not beneficial, but positively detrimental to the general public.... Roads are made, streets are made, services are improved, electric light turns night into day, water is brought from reservoirs a hundred miles off in the mountains – and all the while the landlord sits still. *Every one of those improvements is effected by the labour and cost of other people and the taxpayers.* To not one of those improvements does the land monopolist, as a land monopolist, contribute, and yet by every one of them *the value of his land is enhanced.* He renders no service to the community, he contributes nothing to the general welfare, he contributes nothing to the process from which his own enrichment is derived ...[13]

Environmental policies

In line with its social and economic accommodation to Labour's political dominance, given the conservative preference for order and continuity it is no surprise that the environmental policies of the 1951–55 administration were largely about consolidation – while making some additional room for the private sector and for class-based interests.

In the election manifesto of 1950[14] the Tories promised an end to food subsidies. Should this lead to price rises then compensations would be paid: "larger family allowances, pensions and other social benefits, and ... reductions of taxation". Nationalisation of land was opposed and planning was to be made more flexible and less bureaucratic. But while they pledged to "drastically change" Labour's 1947 Act they thought to review and revise its most contentious aspect – the betterment levy – rather than abolish it altogether. Barely more than 18 months later, the 1951 manifesto was a short and simple reiteration of its predecessor.

Once back in government, four Tory initiatives stand out (O'Hara, 2012: 133–5).

First, the new government took advantage of existing legislation in order to manage the dispersal of population and industry away from overcrowded urban centres. As Macmillan's housing boom began so peripheral estates were beginning to mushroom, cities beginning to overspill again and fears soon arose that the pre-war splurge in urban growth was being repeated. Since the 'new towns' could not supply all needs, the 1952 Town Development Act enabled the expansion and redevelopment of existing ones (Rydin, 2003: 27; Kynaston, 2009: 55–6).[15]

The Conservative counties fought against what were often Labour controlled cities for control of the countryside (Cullingworth & Nadin, 2006: 25). For a Conservative national government – wanting new homes and a revived private market, but cognisant of where its electoral interests lay – the tensions were acute. To some extent it could side with the counties in prioritising the need for good quality agricultural land but, over time, the baby boom and the growth of car ownership (and thus the need for new roads) would only increase those tensions.

Second, the principle of a green belt (land protected from development) was extended.[16] Subsequently, where the 1947 Act *invited* local authorities to include green belts in their development plans, a 'green belt circular' of 1955 went further in its *encouragement*, the effect of which was to make green belts a more permanent feature of local planning. The aim was to contain urban sprawl and preserve the countryside, historical villages and towns (Cullingworth *et al.*, 2015: 403–6).

Third, key elements of the 1947 Act were preserved, namely the discretion local planning authorities had been given to make decisions regarding land use proposals in terms of a generalised development plan – locally designed, subject to public inquiry and signed off by a Whitehall minister. There was to be no return to pre-1947 zoning which effectively gave power to developers so long as they developed land according to the usage for which it had been designated (Cullingworth & Nadin, 2006: 18, 108–9).

Fourth, much of this was designed to remove what conservatives saw as the shackles from around the ankles of the private sector. Therefore, despite the promise of the manifesto – and regardless of what Churchill had said in 1909 – the betterment levy *was* abolished.[17] Cullingworth and Nadin (2006: 197) argue that "it is probable that the Conservative government's plans for private building would have been jeopardised by it". The Town and Country Planning Acts of 1953 and 1954, "re-established market value for most land market transactions but existing use value continued to determine compensation on compulsory purchase" (Rydin, 2003: 29). Allowing acquisitions of land by public authorities to remain at the 'existing use value' was a compromise designed to protect public finances.

It meant that by 1954 there were two values for land: that derived from the open market and that from public authority purchases (Cullingworth & Nadin, 2006: 198). This literally was a 'mixed economy' and the two values quickly diverged. Indeed, by reducing supply, planning restrictions themselves led to an *increase* in market values. With those whose land was subject to planning controls only able to sell at a price markedly below what its market value would otherwise have been, resentment and frustration resulted. The compromise continued until 1959 when a further Town and Country Planning Act re-established open market value as the basis for *all* transactions (Rydin, 2003: 29). Rather than market transactions being constrained by public goods, as enforced by the state, the emphasis shifted to market processes contextualising and constraining state activity.

Did such reforms work? Cullingworth and Nadin (2006: 28) regret the end of the betterment levy, seeing it as a "vital piece of the planning machinery":

> Planning is therefore essentially a servant of the market.... This change, made in the 1950s, is far more fundamental than the high profile changes made under the Thatcher regime.

But at the time Conservatives patted themselves on the back. The target of building 300,000 new homes per year was exceeded without despoiling the shires and the villages. In its 1955 manifesto the Party even sought to colonise the Left's traditional concern with social deprivation:

> There has been only one full-scale slum clearance drive in British history, and that was when Conservatives were in office in the late thirties. Now, under Conservative Government, there is going to be another. We shall root out the slums at an increasing pace, and aim to rehouse at least 200,000 people a year from them. People are already benefiting from the repair, improvement and conversion of the older houses in which they live. They should remember that the Labour Party voted in Parliament against the Act which gave recent impetus to this work.[18]

Slum clearance resumed in the mid-1950s and rose to its pre-war peak (Cullingworth & Nadin, 2006: 27).

A new prosperity

In the early 1950s, then, the domains of both social policy and environmental policy were characterised by a sometimes-uneasy amalgamation of public and private.

A similar blend was manifested in broader cultural values and social habits. As rationing ended so a new consumerism began to emerge, but it was a consumer ethos that often yearned for sameness in shared public spaces. Keeping up with the Joneses meant copying them, acquiring what they had acquired. Rising disposable incomes meant regular holidays, but often to places that resembled the places you'd left: crowded seaside beaches, package holidays and hi-de-hi holiday camps. Places containing 'people like us'.

The story has been told many times (Benson, 1994; Sandbrook, 2005: ch. 4; Hennessy, 2007: 520–1, 534–41). In the 1950s a significant shift occurred in social habits: we went shopping. As economic growth picked up again, as American popular culture dominated, as the working-class became more affluent and as technologies became domesticated ('labour saving devices'), so what you bought became as central to personal identity and social relations as what you did for a living. Supermarkets, commercial television, teenagers, pop music, new fashions, annual holidays and other recreational activities, all became integral to the meaning and the look of civil society.

This was also about economics. Consumerism was a way of keeping money circulating through the economy's veins. The new consumerism was thus another tool in the economist's toolbox, along with social policy. If consumers spent too much, for instance, taxes and insurance contributions could be increased so that some spending is deferred to the future. But because cutting social expenditure is politically difficult – unless it is targeted on the poor, where the electoral ramifications are minimal – the welfare state may be a weak mechanism of stabilisation. Critics blamed it for contributing to Britain's 'spend, spend, spend' mentality, taking resources away from investment and technological innovation (Barnett, 1995; Ferguson, 2014).

What, from a green perspective, should we make of the new consumerism? Cahill (2002a: 8–10; 2002b) highlights the extent to which the 1950s initiated social practices that in time would become unsustainable: high levels of energy use, waste, valuable resources being depleted to feed the luxuries of the affluent and the affluence-chasers. It would be clear by the end of the century that we could no longer consume with the reckless abandon of previous decades.

For some, this message of sustainability echoed the anti-consumerist instincts of those on the Left for whom consumerism denotes a distraction from more important business: revolution, social justice, world peace, and so forth (Hannigan, 2011: 49–52). Consumerism is either an elitist sleight-of-hand, a means of getting wage slaves to desire their submission; or it represents a reminder of a 'world we have lost': a materialist, selfish replacement for communal solidarities (Hoggart, 2009). The workers were interpreted as being embourgeoised and so subject to new, subtle forms of regulation.

As such, given that we are devouring so much of the Earth's resources in a constant effort to maintain social status, to allow corporations to make profits, to manufacture new desires, to relieve ourselves from the stresses of modern life (overwork, underemployment and consumerism itself, of course), then this is not simply a question of what we do. Values and attitudes matter too. And if we do, indeed, need freeing from the seductions of consumerism then it is legitimate to appreciate how and why the gilded cages we endlessly flit between were first assembled.

But context is everything. Those in the 1950s who had lived through years of depression, war, austerity and rationing should not be the objects of retrospective censure. They surely deserved TVs, washing machines and cars as long-delayed rewards and as a welcome promise that their children would experience a more prosperous life. Furthermore, we should be wary of reproducing the haughty disdain of cultural conservatives. We need to consume less. But we will only consume less by consuming *better*, and that means appealing to the pleasurable, gift-giving elements of consumerism, in which people do things for and with others based around an ethos of needs, even as we reject its more desperate, addictive, selfish qualities. Green consumption need not treat 'consumerism' as a dirty word, so long as (like certain appliances) this is a consumerism that knows when to switch itself off.

I don't propose to return to the Introduction's key questions yet. The thesis of this chapter is that by accepting much of what Labour had done from

1945–51, the Tories were instrumental in forming a post-war settlement that would remain more or less intact until at least 1979. So although there would be greater emphasis after 1951 on the private sector, market values, controls on public expenditure, and so forth, neither social policies nor environmental policies would undergo major changes. The points made at the very end of Chapter 1 can therefore continue to stand.

But our overview of the period remains incomplete. We have yet to review events which would begin to shift attitudes and practices about the connection between the social and the ecological, however slowly. To this, then, we now turn.

Notes

1 Radio broadcast made on 1 October 1939. See Toye (2013: 29); many thanks to Robert Page for recommending Toye's book.
2 Though the phrase was associated more with Randolph Churchill (Walsha, 2003: 70). Many thanks to Robert Page for alerting me to Walsha's article.
3 Green (2002: 279) characterises them, though slightly differently, as libertarian and paternalist.
4 The usual caveat applies. The following categories are heuristic and indicative only. Walsha (2003: 72, 94–5, 103) observes that the reputation of 'one-nation' thinking as the decent face of Conservatism was acquired once Thatcher became dominant.
5 It quickly became commonplace to regard this as an ideological resurgence of the nineteenth century. But that association was always purblind. For every self-help Social Darwinist there were many serious minded thinkers within Victorian conservatism. Milton Friedman never wanted to be the new Thomas Carlyle or Benjamin Disraeli. Friedman's project was to barge through the crowd of moral philosophies and settle upon economic doctrines that depend upon a few simple premises about human behaviour and a few quasi-mathematical equations.
6 Marquand (2009: 118, 147) gives too much credence to this self-serving lament (cf. Marwick, 2003: 28; Todd, 2014: 143–4).
7 Macmillan's appointment to Housing seemed like a slight initially but this was a new department that Churchill saw as the most important of the social services (Jones, 2000: 102–3). Given Conservative election promises it was rapidly obvious how important Macmillan's performance would be to public perceptions, and thus the future fortunes, of the party.
8 Dorey (2011: 107–8) highlights the extent to which the 1950s established the most egalitarian period in British history with a narrowing in the distribution of wealth between rich and poor.
9 This partly explains why 1950s conservatives wanted to maintain high, expansionist levels of public spending (Ellison, 2011). The reasoning goes like this. Growth depends upon demand. Demand is maintained through public and private spending. Too much private spending, though, risks sucking in imports and compromising sterling's position vis-à-vis the dollar. Robust demand therefore requires high but controlled levels of public spending.
10 Nigel Lawson would later claim that had Butler's reforms been implemented, Thatcherite adjustment to the economy would have been unnecessary; a reading with which Bogdanor (2011) seems to concur. However, this view neglects the extent to which Thatcherism was as much a political, ideological and moral project as an economic one.
11 Cruelly, had Attlee hung on and not called the 1951 election it's possible that Labour could have claimed credit for the new affluence.

12 Note, though, that Bridgen (2006) highlights the extent to which the continuity between Labour and Conservative administrations was due to a Treasury-dominated view that the Exchequer's role in financing pensions should be considerably lower than Beveridge had originally envisaged. Both governments wanted the system to be financed mainly through contributions, with taxation playing a modest role only.

13 www.progress.org/banneker/chur.htm [accessed 7 March 2014]

14 www.politicsresources.net/area/uk/man/con50.htm [accessed 22 March 2014]

15 Not until the late 1950s would a second generation of new towns be permitted. However, by then the ideals of the 'garden city' had long been forgotten and a reaction set in against dispersing people to what could be soulless, low density, outlying estates with few amenities and poor transport. Modernism would come to imply a 'new urbanism' and 'high-rise brutalism' (Kynaston, 2015: 128–9, 293–4, 446–9, 677–9).

16 It was first applied to London in 1935.

17 See Macmillan (1969: 420–7). Macmillan's (1969: 422) central justification is that it had been "a mistake to turn a Planning Act into an engine of taxation", but while he defends the principle of taxing an 'unearned increment' he does not indicate what might or should have replaced the levy.

18 www.politicsresources.net/area/uk/man/con50.htm [accessed 22 March 2014]

3   An impenetrable fog
1952–64

On 4 December 1952 a high pressure system was spreading slowly towards the south east of the country (Clapp, 1994: 43–52; Thorsheim, 2006: ch. 10; also Mayor of London, 2002: 3–9). Londoners venturing outdoors that Thursday noticed how much colder, damper and calmer the air was compared to the day before. By midnight the wind velocity was practically non-existent and in the hours that followed many sections of the Thames Valley experienced a 'temperature inversion'. Cold air near the ground became trapped by warmer air above and was unable to move sideways because of a lack of wind. London was now becalmed and would remain so for four days. Already, river traffic had ceased on the Thames due to a heavy fog. This thickened even more overnight and as the city awoke it quickly clotted with smoke and soot from car exhausts, domestic chimneys and industrial stacks.

The perils of air pollution had been noted as far back as 1273 (Sanderson, 1961: 236). In the nineteenth century many Victorians were proud of their dirty air. Wasn't it a sign of progress and prosperity (Wise, 1968: 38–9)? Besides, everyone burned coal, the reasoning went, so how can you change the habits of an entire society and economy? Improvements were made from 1880–1920 but then stalled and London's streets were still reminiscent of the Victorian pea-soupers (Clapp, 1994: 37–9, 54–5, 68; Kynaston, 2007: 400–2). The advent of the motor car had added another lobby to those opposed to change.

It wasn't until 1946 that a committee appointed by 'Manny' Shinwell recommended a comprehensive shift to smokeless fuels, but its report spoke of a timescale of several decades and the government neglected to act even after a fatal smog hit London in 1948. People should be free to burn what they wish, the Ministry of Fuel and Power insisted, and if industry can save costs by using lower-grade fuels then atmospheric pollution was a price worth paying (Wise, 1968: 55–60). The next Conservative government displayed the same attitude.

By Friday morning 693 square miles across Greater London were shrouded in smog that had the ph. of battery acid (McCormick, 1989: 72; Sheail, 2002: 247–9). Around noon someone passing through Trafalgar Square noticed that the top of Nelson's Column was disappearing into the mist (Wise, 1968: 96). By the evening, district nurses had treated twice as many respiratory cases as on the previous day, ambulance calls had increased by a third and the death rate in

London had shot up by 50%. Yet government, media and public opinion in general seemed as becalmed as the weather. Peasoupers were as British as Sherlock Holmes.

Dr Brian Williston had already tried unsuccessfully to wake the authorities up to the silent disaster that was upon them (Wise, 1968: 102–7). One of London's Medical Officers of Health, the doctor's office overlooked a small garage owned by a young man called Amberson who was often out of doors repairing someone's motor. By mid-afternoon Williston was seriously concerned with reports from GPs of breathing difficulties among patients with chest and throat problems. Returning through the streets to his office he suddenly noticed that his hands and collar were black with soot. Later, making observations from the roof, he saw that black clouds of smoke from a nearby chimney stack were flowing not upwards but down towards the ground! Yet his efforts to alert County Hall to the dangers of all this came to nothing. On Saturday evening he heard that, having gone to bed around noon, complaining of tiredness and a burning throat, Amberson was dead (Wise, 1968: 127–30).

On Saturday visibility was even worse than before (Wise, 1968: 116–17, 133, 143–5). Heathrow was closed as, effectively, was the Thames; inter-city and underground trains were running much slower than normal; some bus services had closed and drivers struggled to get anywhere. And the colder it became the more coal people burned to stay warm. Sulphur dioxide was, officially, 3–12 times higher than normal. In truth the pollution was so bad that instruments were malfunctioning and some estimates put the amount of smoke in London's air as being 54 times higher than on an average winter's day.

By Sunday the death rate was four times higher than normal. Monday press reports made much of the unusual conditions, but noted its adverse effects mainly in relation to prize cattle at Smithfield (Wise, 1968: 151–4). That upwards of 2000 people had died, and tens of thousands more made seriously ill by the smog, was not something that widely registered. By mid-December a further 2000 deaths had been attributed to the smog. *The Lancet* would estimate 4700 casualties in total, though more recent estimates go as high as 12,000 (Bell *et al.*, 2004; Thorsheim, 2006: 167–70). It wasn't until Tuesday the 9th that the weather system began to shift, the air clear and London return to something approaching normality.

Yet complacency and passivity did *not* shift, not right away. Nature can be brutal, but what can you do? That only two weeks earlier the government had been urging a hard pressed nation to save money by burning low grade – and highly polluting – 'nutty slack' was quietly forgotten (Thorsheim, 2006: 161–2).

It was known as 'Low Z' and was first noticed on 29 January 1953 (Pollard, 1978: 20–6; Baxter, 2005). A depression had broken away from a low pressure area north of the Azores and was moving towards Europe, deepening as it travelled. As it lunged down the North Sea gale force winds picked up and, on 31 January, the car ferry *Princess Victoria* was hit. She struggled, she buckled, she sank. One hundred and thirty-two lives were lost.

The worst flood in almost a century was now hitting the east coast of Britain (Sheail, 2002: 219–21; Kynaston, 2009: 257–90). The combination of low pressure, a high tide and strong winds building up a wall of water (a 'surge') was to kill over 300 people in Britain (and 1800 in the Netherlands), damage 24,000 homes, cause 32,000 people to be evacuated, affect over 1000 miles of British coast and leave 160,000 acres below sea water, rendering much of it unusable for years. For many, the night of Saturday 31 January was the worst night of their lives.

It was the combination of winter cold, the suddenness of the surge, the darkness, and the lack of warning that did it (Pollard, 1978: 34–6, 46–7, 66–8). The Mansers of Canvey Island were not well off. Two adults, nine sons and one daughter somehow squeezed into a cramped bungalow. At 12.30 am the family awoke to find the water already up to their waists and it was rising with every second. Standing on furniture was no good as it either broke or floated away. Soon the sea was lapping at the faces of adults and older children desperately trying to keep youngsters and babies above the water. Smashing through the ceiling they tried to gain as much elevation as possible, though not everyone could make it up. By daybreak they were exhausted and it would be many more hours before everyone was rescued. Except that not everyone could be. The three youngest children had died of exposure.

The night's horrors contained many moments of surrealism – riding a huge wave a bungalow smashed into a train – and even the comedic:

> In Felixstowe, a surprised resident ... ventured downstairs when the water had retreated to find two pigs in his front room, sitting at either end of the settee.
>
> (Pollard, 1978: 81)

But for the most part it was horror played out in dark hours of loneliness, silence and helplessness, punctuated by occasional, unanswered cries for help.

The national government did not cover itself in glory (Pollard, 1978: 79–80; cf. Thorpe, 2011: 284). Only a coordinated effort could synchronise volunteers, supply provisions and resources for rescued families, direct repair efforts, restore amenities, pump out water trapped between flood banks and recover the dead bodies of animals and humans. Local councils did their best, but where was Harold Macmillan's housing and local government department? Well, it was practically closed on Sundays and only on 2 February did the government galvanise itself into something resembling action. Having failed to learn any lessons from a flooding in March 1949 (then the worst in 65 years), no contingency plans seemed to be in place. By the time central government acted most of the initial rescue efforts were over. Churchill made one of his tearful, 'national character' speeches to the Commons[1] and later promised that the government would match the relief fund set up by the Lord Mayor of London. But according to Pollard it reneged on the deal to the tune, by 1956, of over £5 million – worth well over £100 million in today's money.[2] Emergency grants from the relief fund were permitted, but only on terms that strongly resembled a means-test (Pollard, 1978: 99). It was not Churchill's finest hour.

The insurance industry did not cover itself in glory either (Pollard, 1978: 97–8). So severe had it been, much of the damage could not be assessed using typical methods. Evacuees found themselves pursued by insurance agents demanding premiums for policies that would not pay out for months. And, of course, many of the poorest households had inadequate insurance or none at all. The Mansers had to borrow money to bury their three children after their company attributed the deaths to an 'Act of God'.

Only donations from the general public and the actions of voluntary organisations corresponded to what simple humanity would suggest was a proper response. Thirteen-year-old Christopher Manser would remember local people donating clothes from which they had not troubled to remove money, cigarettes, diaries, and so forth (Pollard, 1978: 89). The trouble was that once the media spotlight sweeps away people's attention so often turns elsewhere too. Those affected by disasters need the long-term help and attention that government cannot necessarily provide in full but which it must underpin. Only reluctantly did the government introduce a billeting subsidy for homeless families, one that turned out to be fairly inadequate, covering lodging but not food (Pollard, 1978: 96). If you were in need, said the Ministry for Housing and Local Government, you could apply to the National Assistance Board. It was not Macmillan's finest hour, either (Kynaston, 2009: 257). Christopher's father never worked properly again due to ill-health.

So two major disasters had struck the country within the space of two months, yet initial media responses were as inert as those of the government.

During the smog *The Manchester Guardian* concentrated on crime, transport problems and cancellations to sporting and cultural events.[3] According to Thorsheim (2006: 163–4) newspaper reports during the smog said nothing about its health effects, preferring the romantic images of a ghostly, transformed London. Things were not much better weeks later. Baxter (2005: 1302) records that on Sunday 1 February, most newspaper reports concentrated on the sinking of the *Princess Victoria*. True, access to the stricken areas would have been limited, but given the severity of a storm powerful enough to sink a ferry it is puzzling that on the Sunday itself the media appeared to be as somnambulant as the government. Television was rudimentary at the time and none of the local radio stations broadcast at night. An emergency radio network was quickly set up by amateur radio operators and provided a vital service for days (*Yorkshire Post*, 2013).

Did the inertia of the media shape that of the government, or was the former inert because there was little urgency from the latter? Were the horrors of war so recent that two more catastrophes still seemed commonplace? Was there a fatalism about natural disasters that conceived them as unavoidable features of human life?[4] It's easy to speculate yet difficult to say, but if we treat the media as a barometer of public opinion then no one seemed to be clamouring for change. Not at first.

Cleaning the air

But once the smog's mortality statistics had sunk in, aided by comparisons with the cholera epidemics of the previous century, which suggested that at its height the smog had been deadlier, a shift in media and public opinion did occur. Reluctantly and gradually, the UK government travelled in the same direction.

In the weeks following the smog the response of Macmillan's department and that of the Department of Health continued to be as woeful as during the days of the disaster itself (Sanderson, 1961: 243–52; Thorsheim, 2006: 165–7; Mayor of London, 2002: 11–15). Previous governments had failed to act too but, in the wake of over 4000 deaths (according to contemporary figures) and at a time when the state possessed extraordinary powers, attempted excuses quickly become threadbare (Thorsheim, 2006: 170):

> Delayed reaction to the fog can be attributed in part to the time needed to assemble and analyse mortality statistics, but it also resulted from the ruling Conservative Party's attempt to escape blame for the tragedy and to avoid being pressured into stricter controls on air pollution.
>
> (Thorsheim, 2006: 165)

It was two Labour MPs who repeatedly called for a public inquiry, only to be met with obfuscation by Macmillan (Wise, 1968: 163–4). Government is doing all it can, officialdom publicly declared, while secretly worrying about the costs to the economy of cleaning the air. Things began to shift only once the economic costs of doing nothing became obvious. The National Smoke Abatement Society made some headway with a report suggesting that the smog had cost London approximately £10 million (over £200 million in today's money). Twenty-five thousand more claims for sickness benefit were received in December 1952 than in December 1951 – a number that does not include those outside the labour market and so not entitled to claim such benefits.

As public opinion shifted the government finally agreed to set up an interdepartmental committee, though for many months the assistance it received from the Ministry of Housing and Local Government was zero (Wise, 1968: 165–6). Wanting to be seen as doing something the Minister of Health announced that 'smog masks' would be available on the NHS (Sanderson, 1961: 246). Its final report in November 1954 recommended the elimination of black smoke from all chimneys, regulation of industry, the production and distribution of smokeless fuels and the creation of smokeless zones. Several Labour and Conservative backbenchers agreed to support a Private Member's Bill. There was some prevarication by the government, unsettled by a report in *The Economist* warning that legislation would give the state Gestapo powers to enter people's homes. But the bill was eventually rendered superfluous by a government promise to accept the committee's recommendations.

The subsequent Clean Air Act became law in 1956 (Wise, 1968: 168–75; Thorsheim, 2006: 180–4) and levels of smoke and sulphur dioxide in the atmosphere began their decades-long decline (Mayor of London, 2002: 16). By the late 1960s coal smoke had reduced by 60% in urban areas, with household use falling by one-third (Thorsheim, 2006: 188). That the fatalities of several days of London smog in 1962 numbered just a few hundred was attributed to the Clean Air Act.[5]

Defending the coasts

The country had also been criminally unprepared for the floods. The government surmised that the absence of a proper early warning system had been crucial and so established a stop-gap system until something more permanent could be designed and implemented. To that end it also established a Departmental Committee on Coastal Flooding, tasked with considering causes, future risks and possibilities of recurrence, the adequacy and cost of sea defences, as well as possible warning systems. This "formed the foundations of government policy on coastal flooding for the remainder of the twentieth century" (Baxter, 2005: 1307; Lumbroso & Vinet, 2011: 1326–7).

It was in the committee's report, for instance, that the possibility of constructing a Thames flood barrier was first raised. As contributory factors the committee pointed to the lack of a warning system (cited as a major cause of the loss of life), to neglected sea and river defences (and uncertainty about who was responsible for them) and to the pressures on housing following the war. Many cheap, substandard houses had been constructed in vulnerable areas, sometimes extremely close to the sea. It ruled out as prohibitively costly measures to offer comprehensive defence against all forms of tidal surge, and recommended that the most valuable properties and land be protected. Otherwise, it said, early warning systems should combine with measures to remove people from vulnerable areas and curtail irresponsible developments on low-lying plains and near coasts.

The subsequent strengthening of coastal defences would use the height of the surge as a benchmark against future occurrences. However, Baxter (2005: 3009–10) notes that this may have led to complacency in the years that followed, with the coastal population rising by 30–90% in some places in subsequent decades.

There was arguably another form of complacency, one harder to pin down. Many of the dead were low income households reliant on the cheap housing, which was vulnerable to tidal surges. Terrible, but the disaster happened at a time when many thought that poverty was being defeated. With some places now protected against the kind of surges, which – according to contemporary understandings – only occur once a millennium, what else was needed but occasional updates to equipment and procedures? In short, did the country take its eye off the ball by imagining that future floods could be dealt with effectively and that the social conditions allowing social vulnerabilities to compound natural vulnerabilities were being eradicated?

This is admittedly speculative. Yet since Gordon (2012: 133–4, 137–8) notes how much more at risk lower income households are to sea flooding, with much less capacity to cope and recover from its effects, Baxter's (2005: 3010) conclusion that the 1953 flood's impact on British society was limited and of short duration may well be correct.

Environment and government

How might we understand such developments in the context of the times?

First, there was as yet no such thing as 'environmental policy' as a distinct arm of government responsibility and discourse.[6] The quality of the air was a concern secondary to the needs of industrial policy and of homes still dominated by coal fires – gas and electric fires were spreading slowly. The patriotic association of 'hearth and home' still prevailed (Hennessy, 2007: 117–21). Nor had Britain's coastal defences – so long geared to military needs – been reorganised yet. Notwithstanding the new emphasis upon planning, the urgent need for housing in the wake of the war is what drove many of the haphazard, coastal developments that would be overwhelmed by the surge. In 1953, responsibility for maintaining sea and river fortifications was confused. Thus, natural events occupied discrete silos within distinct government departments. So far as nature was concerned, the notion of joined-up thinking was still decades away.

Second, the UK government had been reactive and to some extent obstructive. An earlier attempt to establish a volunteer emergency communications service had been rejected in 1950. The dangers of smog and air pollution in general had been known for centuries[7] yet policy seemed little more advanced than in the days of Edward I, i.e. when pollution increases you temporarily ban the thing causing it until things improve. To call this a 'lag' between identification of the problem and formulation of a long-term solution would be, how shall we say, an understatement! But it could have been worse. Had things turned out a little differently – had Gerald Nabarro M.P. not been allowed to introduce the bill that finally kicked the government into acting – then there may have been no Clean Air Act in 1956. The USA did not introduce one until 1970.

Third, there was an extremely weak integration of social policy with what, in retrospect, we can see as the beginnings of post-war environmental policies. The connection should have been strongest in the housing sector. If inspired by social justice and applied wisely, planning would surely keep people away from flood-prone areas. Yet, as intimated above, this was not to be the case. What of health? If in December 1952 you found yourself hacking and coughing then the doors of a health service, free at the point of use, were open to you. But you didn't want to be hacking and coughing in the first place did you? The Clean Air Act is a good example of a preventative healthcare measure, though it was also an isolated example in an economic system where the welfare state is often better at cleaning up a mess than at preventing the mess from appearing in the first place. And how should we account for the treatment handed out to the grief-stricken Mansers or those reliant upon an inadequate billeting subsidy? Was this due to confidence that the country's new-fangled benefit system could cope with all contingencies? Or was it illustrative of the holes in the system; holes through which the most vulnerable were allowed to tumble?

That said, social policy and these embryonic environmental policies at least belonged to the same paradigm: that collectivised, tax-funded, state-centred action was the most appropriate response. Government bureaucracies had been slow to move in December and January, and this certainly cost lives and caused avoidable suffering. But despite the misgivings of some on the political Right – *The Economist*'s Gestapo warning causing a brief political wobble – I can find no one who was arguing for a free market solution to air pollution or storm surges. Resolving problems and restoring wellbeing was now seen as primary government responsibilities. And if the state was slower to understand the social contributions to natural disasters at least now, by the mid-1950s, there were signs it was finally waking up.

At a more philosophical level, therefore, what both sets of policies incorporated was an understanding that an individual's powers are limited. But rather than this inspiring a fatalism, it motivated the widespread belief that, via the state, the social community could do what individual men and women could not. If the economy downturns then there are limits to what get-up-and-go, sock-puller-uppers can do to avoid unemployment. But the state, most now accepted, can and should create the conditions for full employment. Similarly, though we cannot control the movements of weather systems we *can* affect whether such systems lead to a fatal smog or to the low income occupants of cheap housing being swept into oblivion. Lurking behind the Clean Air Act is a belated recognition that natural disasters are not so natural after all and are so much more disastrous through their interaction with malfunctioning social contexts and institutions.

In many respects, then, the triumphs and errors of the age go together. The Clean Air Act epitomised the fact that government now stood at the centre of a collective attempt to ensure personal and social wellbeing. Yet there was a continued lack of forward thinking and we will witness one effect of this in Chapter 6.

Because those triumphs and errors go together it is no great surprise that they are embodied in the towering political figure of the period.

The middle of the way

There was no great epiphany. From dark and muddy trenches he would help semi-articulate comrades stay in touch with wives and parents back home; and once he'd finished reading them, books would be passed on to other soldiers. There was something within him that sympathised with those less advantaged than himself. Years later, seeking a political career, he seriously toyed with the idea of joining the Labour Party, but it was the Conservatives who provided the first opportunity and so he joined them instead. Yet, he continued to ponder on switching parties and for a long time yearned for a centrist party that would attract the best talents from Left and Right. That's why he briefly considered joining Mosley's New Party and as late as 1946 lobbied, naively, to change the name of the Conservatives to the New Democratic Party.

But Harold Macmillan was destined to make waves wherever he ended up. That inner compassion was made of a steely conviction that things needed to change drastically. As early as 1927 he co-authored a pamphlet, which advocated a mixed economy, collective bargaining, industrial councils and workers' representation (Thorpe, 2011: 85). Another publication recommending planning earned the highest praise from the doyen of free market economics, Friedrich Hayek: he hated it (Thorpe, 2011: 111). For anyone even vaguely on the Left of politics Hayek's status as an ideological canary in the mine was already assured by the 1930s, i.e. if he keeled over with apoplexy then you must be doing something right. But most Conservatives agreed with Hayek: Macmillan was obviously unsound. Bit of a Bolshevik, perhaps?

In 1938 Macmillan sealed the reputation that would eventually allow him to mould the Conservative Party in a new image, with the publication of *The Middle Way* (Ritschel, 1995). There was nothing startlingly original about this work. It deferred to Keynes and called for a planned economy that would reconcile public and private, labour and capital, collectivism and individualism. Many people on the Left were saying the same thing. *The Middle Way* only seemed revolutionary to a Conservative Party that was still walking backwards into the future, its eyes yearning towards an ever-receding past. Two decades later, Macmillan's book would be seen as the bible of one-nation conservatism, as their heir to Disraeli.

Macmillan spent much of the 1945 election anticipating defeat, therefore. We need a programme of social reform, he politely informed Churchill (Thorpe, 2011: 237). Churchill recognised Macmillan's talents but never really forgave him for being right.

Nonetheless, the Churchill of 1951 trusted Macmillan with what both men saw as the most important aspect of the social services: housing (Hennessy, 2007: 493–5; Kynaston, 2009: 53–60).[8] It was Macmillan who scrapped the betterment levy, who gave local authorities greater powers to repair or replace existing stock and who delivered greater freedoms to private builders (Thorpe, 2011: 283–5). And by exceeding their stated annual target of 300,000 new homes it was Macmillan who in 1953 enabled the Conservatives to cross that symbolic Rubicon and gleefully kick the water back in Bevan's face. It was also Macmillan who skilfully camouflaged the fact that building through the public sector was not being cut back as drastically or as rapidly as the Conservatives were pretending (Jones, 2000: 115–16).

Prime Minister

This success set the template for Macmillan's occupancy of 10 Downing Street (Sandbrook, 2005: 79–96; Hennessy, 2007: 376–87, 546–7). As far as the welfare state was concerned it was a further period of consolidation and stability (Raison, 1990: ch. 4; Page, 2015: 49–57).

The most significant new structure during Macmillan's tenure was the 1959 National Insurance Act. To date, flat-rate contributions had funded a flat-rate pension, in part due to Beveridge's insistence that contributions be low enough to be affordable by the lowest paid worker. But in addition to fears that the resulting pension income would be inadequate there was the worry that over time the value of state pensions would fall relative to private pensions. Reform was broadly supported by Left and Right (Pemberton, 2012). The Act therefore introduced a 'graduated pension', which basically raised the social insurance contributions workers paid in order to top-up their state pension provision with extra credits. It turned the state pension into a modest earnings-related scheme in which the basic tier was supplemented with a 'second pension'.

Elsewhere, it was business as usual for Macmillan's government. Education spending was rising rapidly, in large part due to the baby boom, which, by the late 1950s, necessitated an expansion in educational places (Lowe, 2005: 215–18). But the 1959 Crowther Report and the 1963 Newsom Report both expressed misgivings with the existing, tripartite system in which educational attainment was still largely a reflection of parental circumstances. Education was continuing to fuel social inequalities. By 1963, half of all Local Education Authorities were planning to introduce comprehensive schools (see next chapter).

The NHS was also allowed a continued period of consolidation. By the end of Macmillan's time in office, though, pressures for change were mounting (Lowe, 2005: 190–5). Between 1956 and 1963 the contribution of the national insurance fund to the funding of the NHS almost tripled, while the contribution made by taxes fell by 10%. Capital expenditure began to soar under the Conservatives who initiated a modernisation and rationalisation of hospital facilities that would last from the early 1960s to the early 1970s.

Elsewhere, though, there was a distinct scaling back of Labour's reforms (Weiler, 2000). Housing remained a priority, but less emphasis was given to council housing, owner-occupation was encouraged and the 1957 Rent Act loosened controls on private sector rents. The argument against rent controls was that they demotivated landlords and so stifled the market. Why bother improving a property if you can't benefit from those improvements by raising the rent? But the counterargument was that market forces lead to rent increases – disadvantaging the poorest – and give more power to unscrupulous landlords bullying the powerless. The Rachman controversies began under Macmillan's watch (see Chapter 4). But once the market genie was out of the bottle getting him back in would prove to be impossible. By the late 1960s it was clear that without rent controls the gap between low incomes and rents would have to be bridged through some kind of 'housing benefit'.

But such changes occurred within the framework of the post-war settlement and did not amount to its demolition. Even those Conservatives who did not share Macmillan's one-nation convictions had not forgotten the lessons of 1945. And there's the irony. As Labour dug more and more foxholes on the opposition benches, the better to conduct a civil war with itself, the more opportunity the Tories had to change things. Yet ideological power and momentum still somehow favoured the Left because that was the price the Conservatives had paid in order to return to government in the first place.

And the longer the Conservatives remained in office the more their own legacy hindered their freedom of movement. Voices demanding more space for markets, profits, user charges and private companies were audible but not yet dominant (Bale, 2012: 99–100). In the late 1970s, free market liberals like Thatcher thought that to defeat socialism they would first have to defeat those conservatives they interpreted as quasi-socialists. That is the reason Macmillan came to occupy a role in Right-wing thinking – as a betrayer of the true faith – that would disrespect his actual status and legacy.

At the time, however, Macmillan was king of all he surveyed. His famous quote – 'you've never had it so good' – came to symbolise the self-satisfied affluence of late 1950s Britain. In fact, Macmillan was warning *against* complacency and in favour of the continued need to reform economic and social systems if the gains made were not to be lost again (Hennessy, 2007: 559–64; Thorpe, 2011: 392, 405).

This would come to imply a strategy of 'fine tuning' and corporatism in which government would enable employers and workers to decide, first, how to create growth by raising productivity and then how to share the resulting wealth out equitably (Green, 2002: 175–86). Fine tuning would come to imply an incomes policy in which wage rises are controlled through industrial agreements so that increases in earnings did not become self-defeating because of inflation. Macmillan maintained that a balance could be struck between deflationary economics on the one side and inflationary growth on the other (Morgan, 2001: 170–6). Economic management required a brake, an accelerator and the wisdom to know when *and when not* to use them.

Macmillan therefore successfully faced down those who maintained you could only defeat inflation by slashing public spending (Kynaston, 2015: 101–11, 522–4). But those voices would only be kept quiet if the alternative strategy worked. It did, for the time being (Sandbrook, 2005: 360–71, 515–25). What would eventually take the wind out of Macmillan's sails was de Gaulle's intransigence over Britain's application to join the Common Market (Morgan, 2001: 220–1; Weight, 2003: 325–38; Sandbrook, 2005: 526–39).

The grandfather of environmentalism?

Yet Macmillan the decent chap who 'got' the welfare state and compelled other conservatives to 'get' it too, was also the Macmillan who was condemned by some for his response to the environmental catastrophes described above.

In his diaries from the period Macmillan (2003a: 198) refers once to the smog: "Another lovely day in the country, with impenetrable fog in London". And there is no mention of subsequent discussions in the Commons and of the stonewalling by Macmillan's own department.

Regarding the floods, the diary seems to confirm what was noted above, that the government did little until Monday 2 February, 36 hours after the waters hit. But, even now, Macmillan the politician is hard at work:

> … the Socialists will certainly try to exploit the position. Morrison suggested that we had cut expenditure on sea defences – which is untrue. We cut expenditure on sea erosion. But a cliff may crumble without letting in the sea!
>
> (Macmillan, 2003a: 210)

He does not specify how many 'safe crumbling cliffs' are needed as a percentage of 'total crumbling cliffs' to maintain this distinction between sea defences and sea erosion. Macmillan (2003a: 211–12) subsequently records his victory over the Socialists and notes satisfactorily that at least they now "seemed rather ashamed of themselves". The inadequacy of the billeting allowance (that it only covered lodging) is lost to him and the notion that the Lord Mayor's Fund be distributed on the basis of entitlement, rather than charity, is rejected in order to defend the principle of insurance. Macmillan (2003a: 214) makes his point with reference to ICI and Unilever. The implications for affected individuals like the Mansers are ignored. Overall, Macmillan gives the government full marks for handling the floods "expeditiously and effectively", with dissenters condemned for being politically motivated.

Thus the Macmillan who triumphed by defining and overseeing the centrist, welfarist politics of the period was the same man who embodied the errors of the age. Even after the Clean Air Act, he saw the natural environment as little more than a matter of day-to-day management and political strategising.

There are two further respects in which the period, and Macmillan's tenure, gave birth to the green politics of the future, however inadvertently.

Marching for peace

For the most part, anti-nuclear protests were protests against 'the bomb' (Byrne, 1997: 95–6). True, not everyone opposed to the bomb was necessarily opposed to nuclear energy; just as not everyone opposed to nuclear energy had to oppose the bomb. Nonetheless, the differences between these distinct but complementary technologies were not always drawn in the context of a Cold War that threatened annihilation. You couldn't make an atomic bomb without creating large amounts of uranium 235 in a reactor (Rhodes, 1988: 496–500, 547–9).

Britain's first atomic bomb detonated just two years after the first reactor at Windscale, in Cumbria, achieved critical mass (Hall, 1986: 25). The first fusion bomb was exploded in 1952 by the USA, with the Soviets following suit in 1953; in 1954 the Bikini Atoll hydrogen bomb spread radioactive fallout around the world; and in 1957 people looked nervously upwards because the launch of Sputnik seemed to herald an imminent weaponisation of space.

And it was in Britain that what is still one of the world's worst nuclear accidents occurred (Hall, 1986: 58–64). On 7 October 1957 the physicist in charge of the no. 1 plutonium-processing pile at Windscale was given a false reading by incorrectly positioned thermometers. He therefore decided to heat the core and, as a result, one of the fuel rods was set on fire. The temperature continued to rise for days and there seemed nothing technicians could do to bring it down again. By 10 October radioactivity outside the reactor was reaching unacceptable levels. By now, the pile was on fire and, on 11 and 12 October, water was used to extinguish it – a high-risk option since water poured on molten metal could have shattered the reactor.

Because iodine 131 had been detected in samples of milk, by 14 October a ban on all sales of milk extended across 500 square miles: two million litres would be destroyed. The government did not rule out evacuation of the area. Rumours and fears about the safety of water and livestock spread rapidly, fuelled by a lack of warnings, consultation and transparency and, following the accident and William Penney's report into it, a patrician sense that it was in the national interest for the nation's people not to know certain things about their nation. It was deemed more important to hide the embarrassing details from the USA (Macmillan, 2003b: 65–9).[9]

This was hardly surprising. The nuclear programme had not been developed in a glare of publicity or public discussion (Hall, 1986: 25–31). The 1945 Labour leadership kept their atomic programme in the shadows, away from the media, Parliament and even most of the Cabinet (Hennessey, 1993: 261–72).[10] Driven by power politics ('isn't this the kind of thing that a great country should be doing?') as well as energy needs, the panic and paranoia which erupted in the late 1950s was entirely understandable. Nor did Windscale change much. It was Prime Minister Harold Macmillan's decision not to publish the Penney Report in full, one that he was nervous about but probably felt was vindicated when there was no public outcry (Macmillan, 2003b: 71).[11] That Macmillan had also been Minister of Defence in 1954 when the decision was made to build Britain's hydrogen bomb raised the suspicions of many that government was so committed to nuclear bombs and reactors that it didn't much care about the risks of either.

So fears about nuclear accidents and a nuclear arms race energised a suspicion that the 'establishment' was disdainful towards ordinary people. It wasn't just the technology, it was the sense that the village elders and betters were making decisions at a distance and with patrician disregard for those they governed. Attlee and Labour? Macmillan and Conservatives? It didn't seem to make much difference. So where else had protestors to go when the main political parties not only agreed with one another but slunk off into the shadows to do so? Where else but outside parliament?

In short, launched in 1957 the Campaign for Nuclear Disarmament (CND) pioneered the kind of coalitions and extra-parliamentary activities that would outlive the heyday of CND itself (Morgan, 2001: 178–82; also Morgan, 2007: 210–13). CND was not just anti-bomb but also a receptacle for all sorts of Cold

War anxieties in which there were no hard and fast lines between those who were anti-nuclear, pro-peace and anti-establishment (Kynaston, 2015: 123–7). This is also why, as a form of moral as well as political protest, CND's example prefigures the 'new left' of the 1960s (Mattausch, 1989: 10–14).

And Mattausch (1989) highlights the extent to which CND drew large parts of its membership from the welfare state. In short, some of Attlee's children were less than happy with some of Attlee's legacy. Health, education and social work professionals were comparatively well paid, well educated and willing to swing their middle-class elbows in the direction of Whitehall. As such, CND anticipates an association between the welfare state, middle-class angst and a peace movement that would by the 1970s inspire and, to some extent, morph into the green movement. So although few in the 1950s would have worried that nuclear power was feeding people's addiction to energy – and thus to fossil fuels – by the 1970s and 1980s this kind of anxiety consolidated an association between the anti-nuclear movement, the peace movement and what had come to be called the green movement. The line leading to the latter began in the 1950s under Macmillan's watch.

The axe

A second respect in which Macmillan's government inadvertently shaped the future was through its transport policy. Namely, its failed assumption that public transport would become residual and its refusal to consider the future of road, cars and buses in unison (Addison, 2010: 138–44; Cullingworth *et al.*, 2015: 483).

Beneath the surface of a welfare state collectivism and top-down governance the elements of a possible alternative future were beginning to gather. Few items symbolised this cultural shift better than the car. Though one family in five owned a car in 1939 because of rationing the private car virtually disappeared during the war. In 1951 just 14% of households owned a car or van (about four million licensed vehicles); by 1962 these figures had doubled (Department for Transport, 2011). In 1959 the first full-length motorway opened and, with vehicle running costs still comparatively low, the open road was yours (Zweiniger-Bargielowska, 2005: 229–30). By the early 1960s car ownership had more than recovered its pre-war peak and was on a rapid upward trajectory (Zweiniger-Bargielowska, 2005: 239).

So while car ownership wasn't new it *felt* new; it felt like this was the future. The more other parts of life were regulated the more important it seemed to cling to private freedoms. And with each regulatory step – speed limits, parking meters, yellow lines, the breathalyser, seatbelts – governments knew that these would have to be seen to assist the motorist and not penalise him. Cars were becoming an Englishman's castle on wheels (Root, 2000: 448–50; Sheail, 2002: 182–91).

Where did this leave the more communal, collective modes of transport? Yes, a train could travel faster but try meandering down country lanes on them.

Management systems were ossified. Investment was low. Road haulage was denationalised in 1953, after which trains often failed to compete with lorries and vans over small-to-medium distances.

Yet in the mid-1950s the Tories proposed to revitalise the railways with a plan that was breathtakingly ambitious, expensive, long-term and one which emphasised the railways as a public good (Wolmar, 2007: 276–80; Buttle, 2008: Chs 4 and 5). Transport was still seen as part of the mixed economy; privatisation would not be on the agenda for decades.

Unfortunately, the plan lacked cohesion and effective lines of control and responsibility. It created too little of what was needed (speed and connectivity) and too much of what wasn't (marshalling yards and poor headlines). The problem wasn't with planning per se, but with the continued British insistence on using a patchwork of technologies, decision-makers and routes that worked against one another. And once a bad decision was made it was locked into a system so interdependent its consequences could ricochet back and forth for years, inspiring more bad decisions down the line. The railways would eventually stand as a symbol of national ineptness and decline. By 1960 the tap labelled railway expenditure was pouring water straight down the plughole. So what was needed? Not more water, surely?

It's not as if line closures began with Beeching (Buttle, 2008: ch. 6). Indeed, some of the conservationists we encountered in Chapter 1 cut their campaigning teeth on opposition to earlier closures. The tracks were more than geographical connections, they were connections of and across history.[12] But in 1962, Britain still had 17,500 miles of track and almost 7000 stations. Time to reduce the tap's flow and reach for a plug. Macmillan's transport minister, Ernest Marples, was so pro-road that his company built them and Marples it was who appointed Richard Beeching with a simple remit: get the railways into profit. The 'public good' aspect of the railways was thus the first victim; all talk of transport integration ceased[13] and commercial imperatives were foregrounded.

The 'Beeching cuts' is a phrase that still resonates for older Britons, usually with regret. Beeching found that while several lines made a profit in terms of passengers and/or freight most did not cover their costs and that, in general, waste was endemic throughout the network. He proposed that a third of all stations and lines be closed and thousands of coaches scrapped. Bus services could connect those towns and villages no longer accessible by branch line. And, of course, more people were buying and travelling by cars anyway. By the early 1970s, one third of lines and nearly half of all stations had closed. In effect, this was the slash-and-burn marketisation with which the country would become familiar in decades to come; though occurring within a system that remained in public ownership.

Did the finances support Beeching's case? Not quite (Wolmar, 2007: 282–7). Beeching failed to account for the hidden advantages of rail (the fact that roads are most effective when rail takes up the strain) and the hidden disadvantages of roads (negative externalities like congestion and an increasing car-dependency that disadvantages those on lower incomes).[14] The railways did not achieve profitability even after the cuts and their *social* value simply occupied no part of Beeching's cost-benefit model.[15] Trains were now seen as a business first and a public service second. Ironically, as cars became more popular, people would pour on to the roads and find not open-topped freedoms but jams, pollution and rising running costs. The race to the suburbs was on. Britain's lose-lose auction began here. More roads would have to be built to supply the demand and the declining state of public transport would push people onto those roads to over-demand the supply (Fitzpatrick, 2014a: 150).

So, while Macmillan's government retained the railways in the public sector, Beeching's approach brought a subtle shift in priorities from public to private[16] – one that prefigured a central characteristic of government thinking in the 1980s and beyond. The long-term effect was to displace the railways from national affections, leaving a space into which the pollution-spewing car was more than happy to drive. By the 1990s, the reductions in GHGs, which Britain was achieving, were being partially counteracted by its addiction to private vehicles and continued underinvestment in public transport (Fitzpatrick, 2014a: 169–71). Much of this began with Macmillan.

Key questions

What relationships between the environmental and social policy agendas have emerged? To what extent have social policies and the politics of welfare reform deliberately informed and been informed by the principles and values of environmental ethics and politics?

The London smog and the Great Flood awoke the nation to the social dimensions of what had previously been seen as unpredictable acts of nature. And now that government was held accountable for preserving and enhancing social wellbeing it was less easy to absolve itself from responsibility. After all, the Victorians had fought cholera, typhoid, smallpox and the like by building sewers, improving healthcare and implementing inspections of factories, food and water supplies.

The Clean Air Act was a worthy successor yet it would never have happened without concerted action by many nowhere near the government benches. Therefore, an economy-first ethos still reigned and 'social needs' perhaps identified in this instance with the 'needs of industry'.

What also reigned (as Macmillan's own diary reveals) was day-to-day management, political manoeuvring and the desire for short-term newspaper headlines. The ex-Minister of Housing, Macmillan, is to this day praised by his supporters for the quantity of houses he built and attacked by his critics for their quality (see Chapter 2). Less commented upon are the long-term consequences of their geographical location. Because construction costs are lower, even after the 1953 flood house building would persist on flood plains and on reclaimed marshland, especially when it came to low-cost housing. One reason lay in the pressures on housing stock; another in the fact that housing was the one aspect of state welfare the Conservatives were eager to deregulate.

So even after 1956 the interrelationship between society and nature continued to be perceived as weak and incidental, with policymakers still conceiving their respective policy domains as having fairly residual and minimal implications for one another. The departmental silos, which had characterised the 1945–51 period were still in place. Welfare services like healthcare and income protection were treated as reactive, necessary as a means of helping to cope with disasters *once* they had happened.

Even the Clean Air Act was preventative only to a limited extent. It arguably led to long-term complacency about vehicle emissions, invisible pollution (the fine particulates which affect respiration and circulation) and, as we see in Chapter 6, sulphur dioxide (Thorsheim, 2006: 192, 199–200). Even here, then, systematic, forward-thinking connections between environmental problems and healthcare were not being made. Indeed, might the 1956 Act, allied to the development of what was held to be clean energy (nuclear power), have even led policymakers to believe that a key healthcare problem (air pollution) had been solved, facilitating a shift from rail to road in transport policy?

Notes

1 http://hansard.millbanksystems.com/commons/1953/feb/19/flood-disasters   [accessed 12 August 2014]
2 The nearest I have come to confirming this is the 1960 acknowledgement from Keith Joseph, then Parliamentary Secretary in the Ministry of Housing and Local Government, that £3 million from the fund had been "unused". See www.theyworkforyou.com/debates/?id=1960-11-11a.1406.0#g1429.1 [accessed 6 May 2014]
3 www.theguardian.com/theguardian/from-the-archive-blog/2012/dec/05/great-smog-london-1952-archive [accessed 7 May 2014]
4 Even in our age of instantaneous news the federal government's response to the 2005 New Orleans floods was criminally slow.
5 http://static.guim.co.uk/sys-images/Guardian/Pix/pictures/2012/12/4/1354639229081/Smog-in-London-death-rate-001 [accessed 1 June 2014]
6 The measures we reviewed in Chapters 1 and 2 had been thought of more in terms of countryside and rural policy.
7 Hennessey (1993: 88–9) reports how many British buildings were grainy black from smog and soot. It took until the 1960s to clean some of them.
8 Macmillan was initially reluctant to take the job but came to see it was a way of promoting his personal and political agenda.
9 Hennessey (2007: 538) describes Macmillan as exuding "a fog of benevolent paternalism". In terms of his approach to nuclear power the fog was a bit less benevolent. As Penney's report came shortly after negotiations in Washington over nuclear cooperation and it is clear from his diaries where the PM's mind was.
10 The Commons had no knowledge that (in today's money) over £2 billion was spent, to the astonishment of the new PM, Churchill, in 1951.
11 You keep something secret and when most people understandably remain ignorant of those secrets you interpret this as a justification of secrecy! Macmillan also concealed other incidents, such as an earlier escape of strontium 90 from Windscale (Morgan, 2001: 180).

12 See the 1962 film 'John Betjeman Goes by Train' at www.eafa.org.uk/catalogue/76 [accessed 15 June 2014]
13 Attlee had sought to combine rail, roads, waterways and docks.
14 And we might add negative externalities like fossil fuel dependency and, of course, pollution with consequent impacts on health. True, environmental economics was hardly flourishing in the early 1960s, but this does not absolve policymakers entirely given the examples of the 1952 smog and the subsequent Clean Air Act.
15 For diverse assessments of Beeching's long-term impact see Gourvish (1986: 401–30), Loft (2001), Wolmar (2007: 286–7), Buttle (2008: 292–3).
16 The success of British Rail's InterCity programme in the 1970s depended upon it offering passengers things that cars could not, like tables for businessmen to work on (Wolmar, 2007: 288–94).

4   Upheavals
1964–70

Was it a good election to lose or not?

Labour in 1951 had reason to look at the electorate and react as Churchill must have reacted six years earlier: ungrateful buggers. We inherit a severely bankrupt country following the worst conflagration in history. We repair the nation's finances, create full employment, build a welfare state, help establish a United Nations, help to reshape Europe and defend it against the USSR, begin to shed the bunting of an Empire that colonised peoples will no longer tolerate, and this is the thanks we get? Not everything has gone right but when does it? You threw us out because a few things are still rationed?[1]

Then again, perhaps defeat wasn't so bad after all. The party's senior figures had been in high ministerial office for 11 exhausting years. In the 1951 election Labour had actually received more votes than any political party in history up until that time; the Conservatives were still distrusted and their majority slim. So four or five years in opposition mightn't be so terrible.

Yet lurking beneath the surface were a series of tensions that were about to erupt and help keep Labour out of office for 13 gruelling years (Dell, 2000: ch. 9, 282–300).

There was the inevitable inquest into the reasons for defeat (Childs, 2001: 25). How had things turned around so quickly? In the 1950 election, the Labour landslide of five years earlier was almost entirely washed away as they returned to government with a majority of just five seats. This was partly because of boundary changes and a new postal vote facility. But the country had polarised. Labour support in its working-class heartlands approved of its record; the middle-classes much less so (Marquand, 2009: 123–5; Todd, 2014: 165–9). Middle-class households often liked Labour's social reforms but didn't trust the parent to raise the child.

Some opprobrium was directed towards Attlee (Harris, 1995: 484–94), who was not so fatigued that he wanted to retire and hand over to those who might have reenergised the party's fortunes. After 19 months another election was called and this time it was Labour which sounded tired, intolerant and out of touch. The Conservatives benefited from the death throes of the Liberal party but some blamed Attlee for clinging on, while bowing to royal pressure and calling the 1951 election too early[2] (without having consulted anyone).

But how much difference would a new leader have made in easing the social anxieties of Tory-inclined voters? For its critics the Labour government had moved both too quickly (towards a semi-socialist state) and not quickly enough (to end rationing, especially). Yet it's not clear what else the government could have done given its core support and its 1945 mandate. In 1945 Labour represented the future and, through a combination of muddle, bravery and good fortune, had largely delivered (Hennessey, 1993). But those six years also left the party bereft of an obvious future direction.

Did the electorate sense an uncertainty within the governing party? Was it fearful of those now spending their time hunting around for more, ever smaller things to nationalise? What about ending the exhausting queues for life's necessities? Wasn't life meant to be fun? Wasn't it better to have a steadying conservative hand on the wheel?

Effectively, Labour had been defeated by its own greatest victory as its forward momentum crashed into a wall that, adapting a term favoured by Marquand (1991), can be called the 'progressive dilemma': the ideals which brought you into politics inevitably become diluted by the battles for power and influence that politics involves. So, should you modify or even abandon those ideals or not? By 1951 Labour had learned how to govern but not how to cope with its own record in government and so how to reflect and renew. So, this wasn't just a question of Left versus Right, though that certainly mattered too (Jeffreys, 2004). In the late 1940s the Keep Left group of MPs presented themselves as the conscience of the party, more so than a leadership which, they thought, had become sullied by the inevitable compromises of ministerial office (Hennessy, 1993: 333–8). Add in the usual personality clashes, plus stinging memories of Ramsey Macdonald's 'betrayal' of 1931, and it was a recipe for a bloodletting. Might a larger election defeat that year actually have saved it from subsequent self-indulgence and complacency?

It was around nationalisation that many of these tensions erupted (Morgan, 2011: 249–56; Ellis, 2012: 51–4). Although nationalised industries were far more successful than most newspapers cared to pretend (Kynaston, 2015: 516–18) there were those who warned against equating socialism to state nationalisation, especially at a time of rising affluence and consumer identities. For the Keep Left group, on the contrary, socialism meant economic planning, control and so extensive social ownership.

Which group was closest to the truth? Neither of them, unfortunately. Wherever the line was being drawn the underlying model of public ownership barely changed (Marquand, 2009: 132–3). It was all so very *top down* and centrist; services and industries being run *for* people rather than *by* them. Even socialists like Laski and Cole favoured nothing more than some worker representation on public boards (Morgan, 2011: 248). And what about the needs of the economy in 10, 15, 20 years' time? How do you cope with U.S. domination? With a shrinking Empire and an expanding Europe? What about relations between management and trade unions? Is the state sufficiently enabling? Where are your research and educational resources to be directed? These conversations were barely happening because Britain still perched at the apex of a vast empire, enjoying the continuing momentum of its glorious past. In retrospect, the similarities between Labour's various groupings loom as large as the disagreements.

And these questions were only one element of the progressive dilemma that Labour now faced. How should those who regard capitalism as problematic try to reorganise and run it? How do you socialise something that resists principles of social accountability and responsibility? How do you redistribute the power of the powerful without becoming a new power elite yourself? How do you facilitate altruism, community and cooperation in a system based upon self-interest, individualism and competition? All too often, the British Left has turned away from serious reflection. All too often, its values (solidarity, equality, universalism) has been so relentlessly at odds with its practices (internecine accusations of betrayal, heresy and apostasy).

Civil war

Before long, Labour's divisions resolved themselves around two figures who, throughout the 1950s, squared off against one another in a battle to shape the future: Bevan and Hugh Gaitskell (Brivati, 1997: 149–50; Dell, 2000: 192–200).

That the Keep Left group transformed into 'Bevanites' is no surprise (Morgan, 2007: 143–7, 159–64; Foot, 1975b: 140–2). In addition to the sheer force of his personality Bevan had been at the frontline. He had proved that you could dance the ministerial dance, knowing when and how to compromise, without diluting your principles (cf. Campbell, 1987: 165). But Bevan didn't offer blueprints of social and economic transition. His 1952 book *In Place of Fear* speaks of a "changed relationship" between workers and management in the nationalised industries but also acknowledges it will take time, patience and ingenuity to break down antagonisms (Bevan, 1978: 128–9). But here again is the progressive dilemma. The transition to socialism takes much more time than socialist governments in a democratic and capitalist society have usually possessed (Wright, 2010: 311–20).

The Gaitskellites were really Croslandites (Dell, 2000: ch. 10, 402–7; Plant, 2004a: 109–13). Published in 1956 Crosland's *The Future of Socialism* remains one of the most influential books ever published by a British MP. There has occurred, insisted Crosland, a genuine transfer of economic power from the 'business class' and management to the state and trade unions, with more wealth now flowing to workers in the form of wages than would once have seemed possible (Crosland, 1956: 21–41). Equality now has to mean not only the fair distribution of wealth, but a moral, social and cultural equality; less a rearrangement of 'property relations' and more a society in which your possessions matter less than your status as a citizen (Hickson, 2004a: 121–4). Education, thinks Crosland, will be central.

Crosland himself was never a serious contender for Labour leader. It would fall to Gaitskell to make the practical case for Crosland's 'revisionism' (Kynaston, 2015: 415–23).

All of which underscores the ambivalent attitude of Labour to post-war social policies. In 1951 only dogmatists would refuse to see the welfare state as arguably its greatest victory to date. Whether you were a Bevanite or a revisionist, it was a step in the right direction surely. Yet even if this was the case, there was no consensus or even clear idea of the way forward. If it was a stepping-stone to socialism then what should the next step be? Or, if the revisionists were correct in believing that what mattered now was good management, how did this differ from what middle way Tories were doing?

Bevan and Gaitskell would eventually achieve a personal and political rapprochement, but the broader damage was done. Labour had ultimately wrongfooted itself.

Assisted by the deaths of Bevan in 1960[3] and Gaitskell in 1963 the factions would pummel each other into a truce that, with some exceptions, would last until the 1980s. The so-called rediscovery of poverty in the mid-1960s (see below) assisted that truce. If one of the welfare state's key objectives, the eradication of deprivation, remained to be fulfilled then Labour still had a purpose and sense of direction. And on that, surely, its Left and Right could agree.

The truce was embodied by a figure whom neither side loved very much, but with whom both decided they could live (Marquand, 2009: 194–8).

Harold

When in July 1941 his former employer asked him to come back and work on a new project the 25-year-old Harold Wilson did not hesitate. He said no. Wilson was a hard worker but his employer managed to surpass him in discipline and daily routine (Harris, 1997: 351). Wilson was interested in facts and data but his work as a Research Fellow had often been grindingly dull. Besides, his employer had been habitually domineering, rude and arrogant to an extent that few young men would have tolerated. So Wilson declined. And in declining he missed the opportunity to contribute to – and forever be associated with – what came to be known as the Beveridge Report (Pimlott, 1992: 62–76). Many years later, as Prime Minister, Wilson would claim that he had educated Beveridge about the role insufficient demand played in creating unemployment – a claim we should treat sceptically (Pimlott, 1992: 64).

Would a contribution to *Social Insurance and Allied Services* have changed Wilson's life? Probably. It might have diverted him away from politics, or it might have given his political career such a boost that his later climb through the ranks would have been more direct, making him less of the corkscrew opportunist he became.

He marched out of the Cabinet in 1951, supporting Bevan's objection to Gaitskell's rearmament programme and its implications for the NHS, i.e. the introduction of prescription charges (Hennessey, 1993: 415–20; Brivati, 1997: 113–23). He then drifted to the Right (Brivati, 1997: 308).[4] Had he not possessed principles no-one would have looked twice at Wilson. But without the ducking-and-diving he might not have become the unity figure he seemed to so many and which the party needed following its civil war (Pugh, 2010: 322–4). For the Left, Wilson's past association with Bevan continued to matter; for many on the Right he was enough of a revisionist to recommend him above Jim Callaghan (too inexperienced) and George Brown (too drunk). Who else in the 1963 leadership contest could have garnered support from both Tony Crosland on the Right and Michael Foot on the Left (Pimlott, 1992: 254–60)?

So Wilson promised both party and country a new start (Dell, 2000: 300–18, Chs 12 and 13). Invoking an economy reinvigorated by the 'white heat of the scientific revolution' was a typical Wilsonism; it sounded great but what did it mean? It didn't matter. The Tories had floated the economy on hot air so why not Labour too?

More consensus

For in truth there was a great deal of continuity between Macmillan's Britain of 1962 and Wilson's in 1965 (Grieve Smith, 1997: 65–77; Marquand, 2009: 178–81, 201–3). The Tories had flirted with planning, creating the National Economic and Development Council (Sandbrook, 2006: 171, 175–7). Wilson's own faith in planning was undimmed.[5] Scientific expertise would direct research and technological development, economic expertise would direct investment strategies and at the apex of it all would be a government reaping the benefits. Given how discredited planning has been since the 1980s it is important to remember that in the mid-1960s many still looked – whether nervously or admiringly – towards the USSR whose promise to leave the West behind was symbolised by one triumph after another in the space race. This was still the era of regulated capitalism (Judt, 2010: ch. 2).

Wilson's National Plan was meant to guide fiscal and monetary policy; and while some public ownership was required the Plan was meant to oversee the entire economy and so make wholesale nationalisation unnecessary (Thompson, 2006: 58–61). In contrast to France – where large parts of the system of governance, and even the private sector, where invested in planning – the UK's Department of Economic Affairs was fairly toothless, however (Thompson, 2006: 68–9). Treasury domination continued. It was planning without real power (Morgan, 2011: 228, 233–4).

The government also sat at the apex of industry, supposedly able to bring employers and unions together for the greater good and achieve that fine balance between braking and accelerating which Macmillan had desired (see last chapter; Dorey, 2006a). But it didn't work out that way and the British economy now took on the lurching, 'stop-go' quality that would characterise it for years to come (Callaghan, 1990: 196–202; Morgan, 2001: 242–6, 262–6, 279–81, 298–305; Childs, 2001: 122–4, 133–6, 141–4). The economy overheats so you press the deflationary brake (spending cuts, tax rises, wage squeeze). Then, to get things moving again, you inject money back into the economy – which duly overheats and requires another deflation.

Ideally, an incomes policy should leave households with enough spending money to buy the economy's goods without overheating anything. But someone wasn't playing ball. The media and government blamed unions for demanding what they saw as wage rises the economy could not afford; unions and the Left complained that the government was using wages to manage the economy and had nothing to say about profits and dividends (Dorey, 2006b: 81–2; Morgan, 2007: 243–7; Pugh, 2010: 343–4; Todd, 2014: 284–9). Furthermore, the government's need to control conflicted with the unions' tradition of 'free collective bargaining' and resentment towards statutory measures (Morgan, 2001: 252; Thompson, 2006: 70). The view of Wilson and Barbara Castle that the union cause would be served by greater self-discipline did not go down well and their 1969 White Paper, *In Place of Strife*, was defeated (Dell, 2000: 383–90; Sandbrook, 2006: 720–8; Morgan, 2007: 255–8).[6]

To all this was added pressures on sterling, which Wilson attributed not to economics but politics: international bankers putting pressures on a socialist government, though they allowed Tory administrations to get away with murder (Thompson, 2006: 55). Whether an earlier devaluation would have worked is something still debated, but bad memories of a 1949 devaluation loomed large (Sandbrook, 2006: 89–91; Pugh, 2010: 333–4). It boosted your exports but it looked bad politically. Wilson's eventual devaluation was delayed so long that the economic benefits were minimal, and the government got hammered in the press, leaving the UK still dependent on IMF and US loans (Dorey, 2006b: 85–6; Sandbrook, 2006: 416–29; Thompson, 2006: 67). A sense of post-imperial humiliation set in.

Was Wilson's Europe strategy a genuine change of direction or a desperate sticking plaster for the above dilemmas? It didn't matter. The UK's application to join the European Economic Community (EEC) was vetoed by de Gaulle, just as it had been in 1963 under Macmillan (Morgan, 2001: 272–3; Childs, 2001: 140–1).

All of which fuelled a feeling of decline. For years to come, whenever conservatives sought to justify market liberalisation the subtext was, 'You don't want to return to the 1960s, do you?' Was this fair (Dorey, 2006d: 361–6)? The average rate of growth from 1964–70 was 2.2%. But this was less than Britain's main competitors and the country's share of world trade declined by one-third between 1960–70.

Was this Wilson's fault or was it the inevitable adjustment Britain had to make now that the empire was over? Already by 1960 the UK's share of world trade was half what it had been in 1900. Of course Britain was going to find itself overtaken by others, particularly the USA. In fact, in crucial respects Britain had been lagging behind since 1870 (Mathews *et al.*, 1982: 20, 31).[7] There was much that Wilson could and should have done better but Britain's economic problems were endemic, the result of decades' refusal to invest and reorganise the financial and industrial sectors.

Social reforms

And jobs were still aplenty: 1964–69 unemployment averaged at 2% per annum, something that boded well for the welfare state. For Labour, there was a proud legacy to protect.

First, housing. The Tories had attacked rent controls as distortions of market forces, as restricting the private rented sector. Now, in the 1960s, Perec Rachman was the worst of the crooked landlords who terrorised and bullied his tenants into relocating so that their homes could be 'decontrolled' and re-let at a massive profit. The Rachman scandal and its association with the Conservative Party was a key reason why Edward Heath would later refer to the 'unacceptable face of capitalism'. And even aside from the antics of landlords, there are other factors that may keep a household attached to a property beyond their means: access to jobs, local amenities, family, friends and other vital social networks. Labour therefore took steps to strengthen tenants' rights and ensure 'fair rents'. The 1966 Rating Act directed rent rebates towards those in need.

In healthcare, second, growth in the numbers of hospitals was ongoing and funds were released to improve the GP-patient ratio. Prescription charges were first abolished but then reintroduced in 1968.

Third, no aspect of the Wilson government's reforms left a more controversial legacy than that of education (Dorey, 2006c: 267–74). Circular 10/65, issued by the Department for Education, whose minister was Tony Crosland, called on all local authorities to submit proposals for establishing non-selective 'comprehensive schools'.

Crosland (1956: 208, 233–5, 268–74; cf. Jay, 1962: 248–52) had made his objections to selection plain. You could probably not eliminate all the socio-economic advantages and disadvantages conferred by birth, but the job of social institutions was to give it a bloody good go. Equal educational opportunity was insufficient since this could imply nothing more than making the entrance exam to Eton fairer, when it was the very existence of temples of privilege like Eton which was the problem: perpetuating segregations and unequal social conditions (Kynaston, 2015: 217–47). The comprehensive principle, therefore, was about much more than the operation of schools and local education authorities (LEAs), it was about equal citizenship and social status.

If this was social engineering it was engineering 'from below' (Timmins, 2001: 241). Comprehensives dated from the late 1950s with many middle-class parents horrified to find their cherubs failing the '11-plus' and facing a less than privileged future (Kynaston, 2015: 234–44, 548–50). Crosland's defenders delighted in pointing out that more comprehensive schools would be created later during the tenure of future Education Minister, Margaret Thatcher, than under anyone else.

For the Left, the comprehensive revolution did not go far enough. Whatever they may have been called, some schools were little more than the old 'secondary moderns' which took those pupils who were less academically gifted. A latter-day Gaitskellite like Roy Hattersley (2004) repeatedly observed that the comprehensive principle was never given a chance, hamstrung by social inequalities and the middle-class tendency to barge their way to the front of whatever queue is available.

For many on the Right, Wilson's government was the beginning of everything that became terrible in British society: permissiveness, lack of discipline, trendy progressiveness, Bolshevik teachers, liberal relativism (Cox & Dyson, 1969; Marwick, 1999: 499–502; also Morgan, 2001: 255–62 and 2011: 236–7). The Black Reports of the late 1960s and early 1970s would anticipate the later tone of the radical Right for whom state education resembles a Pandora's Box: a receptacle to which you can attribute all the evils of the world.

Finally, improving income security was also a priority for Wilson's government. Earnings-related benefits and contributions were introduced to cover unemployment, sickness, industrial injury and widows' benefits. National assistance was replaced with a new, means-tested Supplementary Benefit. This, though, accompanied a 'wage-stop'. If your earnings were below the level normally provided by such benefits then, if made redundant, your entitlement would be lowered accordingly. The rationale was to prevent the low paid from quitting their jobs and signing on to receive the Supplementary Benefit. That Labour saw as the solution for low pay not 'higher pay' but 'lower benefits' did not bode well.

The cumulative effect of all this was to increase the numbers reliant on means testing to 7.7% of the population by 1970 (Lowe, 2005: 157). A key principle of the Beveridge reforms – the eventual abolition of means testing – had been abandoned (Jay, 1962: 224–9; Webb, 2000: 568–71). It was in order to sweeten this bitter pill that the government tried to simplify benefit administration and emphasise the rights of claimants. Yet the social security system now started to exhibit the paralysis which would characterise it for the next 50 years; where attempts to hammer away a dent in one part of the system only manage to create dents elsewhere.

Such was the argument of what came to be called the 'poverty lobby'. Its intellectual leader, Peter Townsend, would spend the next 40 years arguing in favour of a renewed effort towards social justice (Walker *et al.*, 2011). It was in 1965 that Townsend published *The Poor and the Poorest* with Brian Abel-Smith. The notion that post-war affluence had provided no automatic solution to deprivation shattered the complacency of many. Families with children were especially vulnerable and the Child Poverty Action Group was established in 1965 – followed by Shelter and other campaigning organisations in the years to come. The idea, popularised by Townsend and others, that poverty is relative, i.e. that you are or are not poor relative to the standard of living of others, would be rejected by many on the Right (Alcock, 2006: 64–70). But the poverty lobby also made some on the Left uneasy. If the welfare state had not worked as well as originally thought then what should the solution be?

Renewing the left

For the 'New Left' the answer was simple, at least in outline. The rediscovery of poverty could inspire renewed critiques against a capitalism whose injustices and exploitations were so deep that well-intentioned welfare institutions were incapable of reaching them (Kenny, 1995; Sandbrook, 2006: 530–3; Kynaston, 2015: 423–8, cf. 745–6; for a discussion of the New Left's influence on ecosocialism see Wall, 2010: 95–9).

However well-intentioned, therefore, welfare state capitalism was a *dead end*! It wasn't only injustice in the distribution of resources it was the elitism, the fact that people's lives were being governed so very far from the places where those lives were actually lived. The welfare state was a system for the administration of things and the administration of people because under capitalism, the New Left argued, *people* are made to resemble *things*. So, what do you do when democracy becomes identified with, and submissive to, state-managed capitalism? You go back to the grassroots and back to the streets (Sandbrook, 2006: 534–45).

True, most people didn't man the barricades. As Sandbrook (2006: xvii) observes, people in the Swinging Sixties were much the same people who had been around in the Unswinging Fifties. But this does not mean they were not breathing the same social atmosphere. You might not know the meaning of hegemony but it's just possible that journalists, songwriters, clothes and graphic designers, film and TV directors did.

And there were various places where that atmosphere thickened so that it was impossible to ignore. Following the diminution of CND after 1963 other outlets for activism would appear. Vietnam was one. Anti-war protests in Britain were nowhere near the scale of their counterparts in the USA but, as noted in Chapter 3, the UK's peace and anti-nuclear groups were if anything more firmly established. Such activism also intermingled with new student protests and grievances (Marwick, 1999: 632–42).

Britain was not involved in the Vietnam War but the government refused to condemn it (Pugh, 2010: 336, 341–2). In fact, at a time when Britain's economy was looking fragile, Wilson risked a lot by keeping Britain militarily neutral (Pimlott, 1992: 391–4). Leftist objections to Wilson were therefore juvenile; as if his job was to lob rocks at the American Embassy in Grosvenor Square. But they did symbolise an increasing distance between Labour – and by extension the labour movement – and what came to be seen as the 'new social movements' (Callaghan, 1990: 206–9; Morgan, 2001: 292–8; Childs, 2001: 146–7).

We should not overemphasise the gap between party politics, centred on the state, and the 'movement politics' of civil society (Wall, 2010: 134–6). It was the Wilson government which legislated on divorce and equal pay, while facilitating the legalisation of abortion and abolition of the death penalty (Childs, 2001: 155–6; Pugh, 2010: 336–7). Marwick (1999: 689) also highlights the contributions made by female trade unionists in Hull and Dagenham. And while these new movements were critical of certain aspects of the post-war settlement they were largely egalitarian and pro-welfare state (Rowbotham, 1997: 340–8). These groups were not a new constituency, then; they consisted of people who had belonged to the old constituency but who were now raising their voices to demand greater power, freedom, respect and opportunity.

Nonetheless, there was a clear gap between, say, the women's movement and a male-dominated labour movement. Similar considerations applied to other, new demands for social rights along the lines of ethnicity, disability and sexuality. Labour was in a bind, therefore. The intelligentsia might welcome diversity and what came to be called 'identity politics', but many of the party's supporters were cultural conservatives, fearful of what rapid social change means for economic security, social solidarity and post-imperial national identity. So, the same party that restricted immigration (with the 1968 Commonwealth Immigration Act) would also introduce the 1965 and 1976 Race Relations Acts, which, for all their flaws,[8] challenged the populist racism of Enoch Powell (Morgan, 2001: 284–7; Childs, 2001: 147–50).

Pimlott (1992: 487, 564) is therefore no doubt correct. It is unfair to traduce Wilson when his government's record is one of a liberalisation that it either engineered or facilitated, including the legalisation of homosexuality and a general shift away from censorship (Dorey, 2006d: 380). Wilson the human corkscrew was largely successful in navigating not only the traditional divide between Labour's Left and Right but also the other upheavals and schisms that the 1960s initiated.

A new environmentalism

Gender, race, disability, sexuality. Where was the natural environment in all of this? Marwick (1999: 17, 81–7, 249–50, 442–54) makes a welcome attempt to insert environmentalism into the political bloodstream of the 1960s (for a US perspective see Rome, 2003). There were various key incidents, which stood as mounting evidence of the ecological cost of growth and affluence.

For instance, in March 1967 the world's first supertanker, the *Torrey Canyon*, ran aground off the Scilly Isles, spilling 50,000 tons of crude oil into the sea (18,000 reached the coast) (Sheail, 2007). Across 140 miles of Cornish coastline 15,000 seabirds were killed and the first iconic image of environmental catastrophe – a bird struggling to walk let alone fly, its plumage glued with oil – entered public consciousness. The disaster awoke Britain to the dangers of pollution, with real effects on government (see below).

There were also more positive images. In December 1968 the first spaceship to orbit the moon, Apollo 8, captured a picture of the Earth as the craft emerged from the far side of its lunar orbit. The resulting image – Earthrise – is one of the most reproduced photographs in history. The notion of 'spaceship Earth' caught on (Boulding, 1966). Though the planet looked fragile against a backdrop of cosmic darkness its real vulnerability came from human irresponsibility.

As Sandbrook (2006: 639–40) highlights, such images (both negative and positive) boosted the conservation movement, led to numerous pressure groups and organisations, and opened up a division between old and new wings of environmentalism (see next chapter).

Academic research was also beginning. In 1967 Mishan (1967: 148–52) analysed the costs of economic growth in terms of resource depletion. Because it involves the pursuit of private affluence and personal desires, he said, consumerism loses sight of the public good. We are in a permanent state of dissatisfaction, erroneously believing that the disease (the view that more material goods will eventually bring happiness) is really the cure. Mishan's critique chimed with the Leftist argument of Galbraith (1984) that private affluence so often accompanies public squalor – views echoed in the 1968 Presidential campaign of Robert Kennedy. As early as the 1940s, Kenneth Boulding (1949) had argued that satisfaction comes from the capital stock and not from either additions to it (production) or subtractions from it (consumption).

All of which signalled the beginnings of a new branch of economics: ecological economics. Green political philosophy was also in its infancy (see the final chapter in Leopold, 1949), though future luminaries like Murray Bookchin were constructing its foundations with sometimes breath-taking speed (Biehl, 1997: 7–8).

A Noisy Spring

But it was two books in particular which would become seminal reference points. Both focused not on events – like smogs, floods and oil spills – that kill rapidly, but on a serious of slow processes and catastrophes that were ultimately more invidious.

In 1962 Rachel Carson published *Silent Spring*. Though powerful as a philippic against the pesticide industry, Carson's polemic struck a nerve because of the links she articulates between nature, ecological harm, human needs, personal behaviour and social practices. She could thus appeal to conservationist groups who were concerned with particular issues, while stressing the futility of any conservationism that disavowed a critique of broader economic and social activities (Lytle, 2007: 200–4). Who has contaminated the environment?

> The decision is that of the authoritarian temporarily entrusted with power; he has made it during a moment of inattention by millions to whom beauty and the ordered world of nature still have a meaning that is deep and imperative.
>
> (Carson, 2000: 121)

The agrichemical industry was therefore astute in hating Carson. She had politicised nature more than anyone before her and would inspire the emergence of the green movement (Lytle, 2007: 205–27). Marwick (1999: 88) calls her the 'spiritual grandmother' to those who would follow. In Britain her influence was often spread through the campaigns of the Royal Society for the Protection of Birds (Jameson, 2012).[9]

And who was Carson the grandmother to? Despite the continued efforts of conservationists in the 1960s, environmentalism had not yet cohered into the political movement it would soon become (Marwick, 1999: 449). Instead, it usually resided in vague, barely articulated reactions on the part (largely) of the young against what many delighted in calling 'the system' or 'the establishment' (Rome, 2003: 541–52). It dwelt in searches for Eastern mysticism and ancient wisdom, for the back-to-nature simplicities of native peoples, for communal living, for non-organised, DIY spiritualism, assisted by drugs and music wherever possible. It was opposed to the 9-to-5 materialism of bourgeois society.

Was it *anti*-consumerist? To some extent. Keeping up with the Joneses was something your parents did. Yet most young people also found consumption as liberating and intoxicating as their parents had done. If you didn't want to steal *Sgt. Pepper* then you had to buy it, didn't you? For every person who denounced the Society of the Spectacle[10] there were thousands more who revelled in it.

And in the intellectual radicalism of the time there was also a reaction *against* nature. For the most part this was a challenge to conservative notions of nature as a fixed determinant of social roles and relations. There is no law of nature that takes us from 'women have wombs' to 'women must be the primary caregivers'. The meanings assigned to nature are always social constructions and there is no part of nature that is untouched by human activity (Giddens & Pierson, 1998: 207–8). All very exciting and innovative, though for too many social scientists and philosophers the long-term consequences were to render nature and the natural world invisible (Urry, 2011: 7–8).

Population fears

While Carson had balanced the positive and the negative, offering images of a better world that could be created through activism, a second book was more alarmist, offering images of a nightmare world created through persisting with business-as-usual.

By the mid-1960s if the term 'environmental crisis' was being recognised at all it was increasingly associated with a crisis of overpopulation. Such anxieties often emerged through images of famine and squalor in what was still being called the 'third world'. Dread about the future intermingled with post-colonial fears of what the peoples of the third world might do – and where they could migrate to – as food, safe drinking water and other resources ran out. How far from the surface of a humanitarian concern for mass hunger, etc. did some distinctly non-humanitarian instincts actually lurk (Huang, 2009: 355–6)? The question is important because the association of 'environmental crisis' with 'overpopulation crisis' led some on the Left to suspect that, yet again, the global poor were being blamed for the crimes of the affluent. The emergence of a red-green politics would be neither easy nor automatic (Irvine & Ponton, 1991).

If any one person popularised the notion that an overpopulated world would overwhelm social systems and the natural environment it was Paul Ehrlich in his 1968 publication, *The Population Bomb*.[11] Ehrlich does not ignore the capacity of science, technology and agricultural techniques to feed more people. Nor is the over-consuming, meat-eating 'first world' absolved of blame. Yet his basic point is simple: there are only so many demands that can be made of a finite world. So unless you are going to suppose the development of some 'miracle science' then the basic arithmetic means that, sooner or later, something's got to give:

> Too many cars, too many factories, too much detergent, too much pesticide, multiplying contrails, inadequate sewage treatment plants, too little water, too much carbon dioxide – all can be traced easily to too many people.
>
> (Ehrlich, 1975: 44)

Armed with this equation he ranges widely across both the physical and social sciences. In the social policy field, existing policies on birth control and family planning are condemned as inadequate and he recommends that the larger the family the higher its tax liability should be. He also advocates abortion rights, better sex education, taxes on luxuries and offers a criticism of an economic system which values destructive activities in its measurements of growth and productivity (Ehrlich, 1975: 131–5, 140–2).

But then follow proposals that threw Ehrlich (1975: 147, 152) headlong into controversy. He recommends a triage system in which countries that cannot be saved should be abandoned since it is better to treat 'the cancer' at source than to waste resources on symptoms alone.

This kind of Malthusian survivalism helped to popularise environmentalism in the 1970s when predicting the collapse of society became the newest horror-film-spectator-sport (Hay, 2002: 174–8). The Earth of Apollo 8 was now less a jewel of oceanic splendour and verdant beauty and more a punctured lifeboat on the verge of sinking. Hardin (1998: 33) contributed to this tone in a 1968 essay. In addition to his influential model of the Earth as a 'global commons' he also advocated a combination of private property and coercion, including abolition of the freedom to breed.

If such alarmist warnings helped to broadcast environmentalism via TV and newspapers, it also painted such ideas in apocalyptic colours that were unhelpful. If the world is doomed anyway then we might as well enjoy ourselves in the meantime, no? It would also take environmentalism some time to emerge from the shadows of survivalism. Two responses stood out.

First, some rejected the apocalyptic portents of these 'new Malthusians' (Commoner, 1972: 118–19, 239–42). Simon and Kahn (1998: 48) argued that the world is getting *less* crowded. As people become increasingly prosperous and mobile then more of the Earth's surface is accessible and habitable.

Second, there were those – especially on the Left – who emphasised distribution (Barry, 1999: 107–11). Malthusians exaggerate the importance of *quantity*. Numbers of people matter but they are not the only things that matter. If we share resources out more fairly we can accommodate more people and as nations become more prosperous population levels tend to plateau out anyway. This emphasis on distributive justice would grow over time and help to marginalise Malthusian alarmism. Those who advocate population restrictions – like the Optimum Population Trust – remain sensitive to accusations of illiberalism and tend to treat Malthus as a warning, not a manifesto (Mazur & Saperstein, 2009: 394–6).

Wilson's nature

All of which seems a world away from the legislative emphasis of the Wilson government (Rydin, 2003: 28–31).

A new Clean Air Act was introduced. An attempt was made to reintroduce a betterment levy on development land. It would not survive the next Conservative government (Cullingworth & Nadin, 2006: 28), though the Capital Gains Tax introduced in 1967 would last. The 1968 Town and Country Planning Act made development plans more flexible and subject to continuous review, made greater room for social and economic factors in decisions about land use and allowed for greater public participation. Countryside protection and access were extended (as was coastal planning), in part as a response to the greater demands on the countryside being made by those with the money and mobility to spend their leisure time there. And the 1968 Transport Act strengthened the public transport role of local government, allowing vehicles to be prohibited from certain areas at certain times. Plans were also laid for new road networks, however, with fears about population pressures leading to a significant growth in 'new towns' during the 1960s (Sandbrook, 2006: 185–91). Some of this expansion was curtailed when population projections were revised downwards, though the growth in households and car ownership pointed towards future pressures (Cullingworth & Nadin, 2006: 26).

It was, though, the response to the *Torrey Canyon* disaster that led to a new, potentially significant change in governance. Several inferences can be made from Sheail's (2007) overview of the event.

First, ministers had little idea of how to proceed and were making it up as best they could. There was no precedent for pollution on this scale or of this nature and no system of disaster management available.[12]

Second, the government's response was highly politicised. Experts disagreed with one another and, in any event, politicians must always negotiate between competing interests with one eye on the bigger picture. But for the government it was also an opportunity to show decisiveness, invoke WW2 memories of British pluck and demonstrate that the tourist and fishing industries were being protected. Wilson wanted to be seen taking charge on television and in newspaper pictures, especially once the decision was made to bomb the tanker and set fire to the oil to prevent things getting worse. Though 40,000 tons of oil were destroyed, embarrassingly one-third of the bombs failed even to explode.

Third, as with the smog and flood of 1952–53, the spillage highlighted the general helplessness of governing authorities in the face of a disaster that existed at the cusp of the natural and the human. As with the Aberfan disaster six months earlier – which killed 144 people, many of them children – the spillage served to illustrate the scale and complex interactions of socionatural processes. Too much detergent (used to disperse the slick) could be more damaging to marine life than the oil itself. And the contamination would have been much worse except for some favourable wind directions. So, how do you deploy science and technology to cope with the effects of science and technology?

But the disaster at least prompted one important assumption and one important question. The assumption: something like this will happen again. The question: how do we make ourselves better prepared?

The problem was that the next disaster might be something different. Is it therefore possible to devise a system that learns from the past while being flexible and nimble enough to cope with uncertainties? An analysis at the time found that a smorgasbord of 10 government departments were responsible for pollution control, with some responsibilities delegated to river authorities, local authorities, and others. It was clear that some kind of centralisation, rationalisation and strategic direction was required.

Alert to what he called "other problems…moving to the centre of the political stage" Wilson the TV star and party manager knew how to respond. In his address to the 1969 Labour Party conference, Wilson identified the environment as one of those other problems:

> There is a two-fold task: to remove the scars of 19th century capitalism – the derelict mills, the spoil heaps, the back-to-back houses that still disfigure so large a part of our land. At the same time we have to make sure that the second industrial revolution through which we are now passing does not bequeath a similar legacy to future generations. We must deal with the problems of pollution – of the air, of the sea, of our rivers and beaches. We must also deal with the uniquely 20th century problems of noise and congestion which will increasingly disturb, unless checked, our urban life.[13]

One month later a new minister for Local Government and Regional Planning was appointed, with a Royal Commission on Environmental Pollution acting as watchdog, and a White Paper was forthcoming in May 1970, promising a new government department with appropriate powers and responsibilities. The next election was due in June, with most commentators expecting Labour to be re-elected.

It wasn't.

Key questions

What relationships between the environmental and social policy agendas have emerged? To what extent have social policies and the politics of welfare reform deliberately informed and been informed by the principles and values of environmental ethics and politics?

Until the *Torrey Canyon* disaster there is little evidence of any development so far as integrating the environmental and social policy domains was concerned. Wilson's speech was potentially significant, therefore. The institutions and practices constructed to deal with problems generated by first industrial revolution were still needed, he said, but they had to evolve. Not only was a second industrial revolution underway, but the problems associated with it were, in part, created by those earlier institutions and practices. Growth was a solution to poverty but its products (like pollution) threatened not only to create new problems but to exacerbate the old ones too. We should not read too much into a few sentences, yet the speech arguably contains the seeds of an intellectual understanding at the highest level of government unlike anything to be found after the events of 1952–53.

And the background to such understanding came from broader social and cultural movements, articulating new needs and demands. Though it did not always initiate developments, Wilson's government itself oversaw an era of social liberalisation (re gender politics especially). Outside the parliamentary party, and given their opposition to nuclear weapons, the Left had long felt they connected to a peace movement which interpreted peace not only as the absence of war but as requiring attention to the social conditions which would make war less likely. As the 1960s advanced, with the palpable influence of those like Carson, to this social critique would be joined a critique of society's natural preconditions.

Yet although the P.M. had a populist, finger-on-the-pulse touch his act would wear thin as the economy sailed into ever-choppier waters: stop-go lurches and the 1967 devaluation. And comprehensive schools aside, there would be no new welfare state transformation: earning-related benefits were expanded, but so was means testing; legislation on equal pay would come too late in the day to be enacted.

And for all Wilson's recognition of the problems of pollution, the government's actual response to *Torrey Canyon* was inadequate and sometimes farcical. So, the questions by 1969 were these. Could government develop the mechanisms to make that recognition real and meaningful? Could a new era of social policies, suited to this second industrial revolution, be constructed? Developments in the final months of Wilson's administration suggested that something was stirring.

That momentum would be inherited by the Tories, but not the nascent vision that may have inspired them. Perhaps a post-1970 Labour administration would have done more with the new department (see Chapter 5), but speculation is pointless. After all, Wilson's environmental policies to date had been fairly modest. Measures to socialise land value had failed (again), though there would be a tightening of regulation re land use and countryside protection. So far as the ecosocial record of 1964–70 goes, therefore, the conclusion reached at the end of Chapter 3 can still stand.

Would the future now fulfil the promise residing in Wilson's speech?

Notes

1 Though these included make-life-bearable necessities like meat, chocolate, sugar, cheese.
2 To suit a planned visit of George VI to the Commonwealth.
3 Bevan's rejection of unilateral nuclear disarmament in 1957 (Campbell, 1987: 334–40) had already left the Bevanites looking like followers whose God had told them he was quitting the religion (Morgan, 2007: 174–5).
4 Or perhaps *back* to the Right, since in his earlier days he had been attracted to the Liberals.
5 He may even have seen planning as more important than Keynesian demand management.
6 In fact, days lost to strike action had been fairly stable, and on a level with other countries, until 1968 (Marwick, 2003: 130–1, 219–20). Was the government responding to industrial unrest or did it, unwittingly, stoke the resentments which inspired the unrest of the next decade?
7 And as some observe, in the 30 years after 1979 growth averaged 2%, with a flexible, low wage economy of market insecurities doing little for British productivity. See practically any article by Will Hutton (also Mathews *et al.*, 1982: 25) who puts the 1959–79 growth rate at 2.75% per annum; see www.theguardian.com/commentis-free/2013/apr/14/thatcher-economy-talk-based-fraud [accessed 7 July 2014]
8 Such as the association of race and ethnicity with being of a 'different colour'.
9 www.rspb.org.uk/about/history/milestones.aspx [accessed 3 July 2014]
10 A term popularised by Situationists denoting how the consumption of commodified images had replaced objects and goods as the means by which capitalism operates. In such a society people identify freedom with the opportunity to work laboriously for wages, which they then use to purchase their identities through consumerism.
11 Though I will make use of a later edition. Note that his spouse, Anne Ehrlich, made significant contributions to this publication.
12 There was provision for an Emergencies Committee of 15 ministers, but strictly speaking its remit did not cover the spillage (Sheail, 2007: 500).
13 www.britishpoliticalspeech.org/speech-archive.htm?speech=167 [accessed 8 July 2014]

5 Crises of power
1970–74

On 22 April 1970, 18-year-old Richard Grayson attended a rally in New York's Prospect Park. A group called the Smubbs sang, Governor Rockefeller was heckled and Richard's dad "was booed by the crowd as he drove through the streets near Union Square and people banged on his Cadillac".[1]

It was Earth Day. Congress was closed as hundreds of thousands participated in consciousness-raising events designed to celebrate the natural world and protest against its increasing despoilation. Still ongoing, almost half a century later Earth Day is said by its organisers to be marked by a billion people across almost 200 countries.[2] And, though several individuals claim to have founded it, as one of originators wrote:

> That was the remarkable thing about Earth Day. It organised itself.
>
> (Nelson, 2002: 9)

Earth Day seemed like a continuation of the 1960s but also the beginning of something new. The feeling of optimism and activism was still visible, as was the sense that this was part of the youth movement, a cry uttered by those who would have to live their lives in a world being ruined all around them. What was different, however, was not just the ideas granted a new title – environmentalism – but a feeling of decline, of time running out and an anxiety that it might already be too late.

With pollution seeping everywhere into the pores of the natural world, it seemed harder to generate a vision of a shinier, happier future than with other aspects of 1960s radicalism. Indeed, the apocalyptic, millenarian tone to environmentalism we noted in the last chapter was part of what distinguished it from feminist, civil rights, gay/lesbian and the other seminal movements of the time. To the usual disagreements and conflicts there was thus added a pervading sense of urgency and doom should the wrong decisions be made or the right decisions be made too slowly. The birth pangs of environmental politics were sometimes deeply traumatic.

To this must be added the fact that the queue of political priorities was already a very long one. In the early 1970s western nations were bombarded by a series of emergencies that avalanched onto one another with a frequency and ferocity that often seemed overwhelming. The tie-dyed optimism of the 1960s was giving way to a sense of a world hurtling to collapse at a speed too complex to control. Pollution, overpopulation and the like were no doubt regrettable, but to governments feeling increasingly overloaded and to publics feeling increasingly exhausted, they were just more links in a series of crises.

Breaking down

After a pre-WW2 shift towards protectionism it was widely agreed that post-war economies would have to be international and outward looking. Overseen by a new International Monetary Fund, the Bretton Woods system pegged currencies to the gold value of the dollar and stabilised exchange rates. The resulting post-war growth, full employment in particular, would fund welfare states. Yet the dependency was mutual. Welfare states were the domestic, social equivalent to Bretton Woods: designed to effect stability, assist productivity, equalise power between labour and capital and so make capitalism work better. GDP growth was therefore an imperative of moral justice, economic prosperity and domestic security.

Yet Bretton Woods expired in 1971 (Eichengreen, 2008: 242–5). The status of the US dollar as the de facto global currency meant that while currencies could change in relation to it, the dollar itself was fixed in value. With Nixon worried about America's competitiveness (exacerbated by the costs of the Vietnam War) and increased financial speculation, leaving the dollar more vulnerable than it had been in the previous 25 years, the dollar was taken off the gold standard. Currencies therefore began to 'float' against one another and, just as wolves will separate the weakest antelope from the pack, now the increasing power of international finance meant that if nation-states raised taxes, lowered interest rates or ran budget deficits they risked straying from the pack and being attacked by the wolves of Wall Street.

If that wasn't enough OPEC was sharpening its teeth too (Kesicki, 2010: 1597). The Organization of Petroleum Exporting Countries had been founded in 1960 to defend the interests of those nations who lost out when oil prices were low. With the Israeli-Arab War as either cause or convenient smoke-screen, in 1973 OPEC cut back on oil production and raised the price of a barrel of oil. With the west having become so dependent on cheap oil from the Middle East, newly installed and newly confident governments saw an opportunity to use that dependency as a weapon, especially against those nations hostile to the Arab cause (Childs, 2001: 173–4). By the end of 1974 prices were treble what they had been just 12 months earlier. Countries complained, motorists groaned and world economies buckled. What would eventually be called the 'first oil shock' therefore hit economies already reeling from currency instabilities.

Though western economies faced similar problems of declining productivity, the economic effects of this double whammy differed across nations (Eichengreen, 2008: ch. 9). Those already experiencing severe structural weaknesses were more vulnerable than those who were not. Unfortunately, the former group included the UK (Eichengreen, 2008: 229–38). With a balance of payments deficit, with unemployment and inflation rising, and with a pervading sense of Britain's best days being behind it due to industrial decline and social decay, the ground needed to make a prices and incomes policy work was becoming ever more contaminated and sterile (Marquand, 2009: 249–55).

For instance, if trade union leaders were often more than willing to work with the government the same could not always be said of rank-and-file members (Lindsay & Harrington, 1979: ch. 18; Sandbrook, 2011: ch. 3). And they had a point. A Conservative government was even less likely than Labour to add to its pay policy some kind of 'profits policy'. Without that sense of burden sharing, government struggled to form a consensus, and quickly found that the actions needed to douse one fire could easily start others. This was partly a matter of workers protecting their 'differentials' and partly because the UK government would pick fights it didn't need to and not pick them when it did.

But it was also because one-nation Conservatives like the new Prime Minister, Edward Heath, were genuinely conflicted (Gilmour & Garnett, 1997: 249–52; for Heath's relationship to the one-nation group see Walsha, 2003: 72, 85, 90, 101–3). They saw a need to reform and modernise the economy, combined with a recognition that underpaid workers deserved a greater slice of the economic pie (Marquand, 2009: 245–9). For Heath one attraction of the Common Market was that it was also the *social* market of French and German conservatism.[3] If the shattered Germany of 1945 could become an economic powerhouse in just two decades, without class conflict, then surely Britain could follow suit. By joining, Britain would have to become more competitive but without the shock therapy some on the Right seemed to think was necessary (Marquand, 2009: 241–5).[4]

Scepticism about the direction of the post-war economy – Keynesian, corporatist and statist, planned and regulatory – had already re-energised free market enthusiasts by the late 1950s; but while favouring various pro-market reforms no great break with that settlement had ever been envisaged by Macmillan for three reasons. First, due to one-nation convictions. Second, from a recognition of what was and was not possible when trade unions' political muscle was so strong (in an economy of full employment which was seen as sacrosanct). Third, from a hope that modernisation required the very economic stability that an incomes policies, a dominant position in the Commonwealth or membership of the Common Market, or all three, could deliver (Dorey, 2011: 94–5). As Leader of the Opposition, Heath had shown little willingness to break with Macmillan's approach.

But the circumstances of 1970 were very different to those of the late 1950s (Green, 2002: 228–9). Inflation and unemployment were both trending upwards ('stagflation'), industrial unrest was growing, Britain's competitiveness and position in world markets was shrinking and key industries were stumbling. At the Selsdon Park Hotel (in Surrey), Heath's shadow cabinet formulated an approach that, echoed later in the party's manifesto, promised something new: lower taxes, less state interference and a new entrepreneurialism (Cairncross, 1996; Page, 2015: 66–8). Heath's reputation on the Right was permanently soured when having described the Promised Land he failed to march them there.

Heath

What are we to make of Ted Heath, then? Was he ever Selsdon Man (Sandbrook, 2011: 58–62; Dorey, 2011: 92–3)? Neither Heath nor his cabinet had sought a full return to *laissez faire* doctrines, but then neither did they repudiate them either (Green, 2002: 231–3). Not for the first 12 months in office, anyway.

This shift fed a Leftist narrative in which Conservatives had only ever pretended to an accommodation with the post-war settlement, and now their true colours were showing. For such critics, Heath was the free market dogmatist trying to recreate the nineteenth century and betray the legacy of post-war reform. He would have to be taught a lesson. Trade unionists like Arthur Scargill saw an enemy they could not just defeat but humiliate – as duly happened in the miners' disputes of 1972 and 1974.

In years to come, the Thatcherite Right would gleefully adapt the basics of this account (Morgan, 2001: 318). Heath was the wet, one-nation collaborator trying to bury Britain beneath layers of bureaucracy (welfare state, European superstate) and betray our national traditions. Not a true blue Conservative. Not really one of us. Weak, 'wet' Tories had been bamboozled by socialism (Green, 2002: 324–5). For Keith Joseph in 1974 this would resemble a Great Awakening: a realisation that while he'd thought himself a Conservative he had been unwittingly implementing quasi-socialist policies for years (Denham & Garnett, 2001a: 247). Free marketeers could thus infer two lessons from the rise and fall of the Selsdon agenda: the country was not yet ready for it and one-nation Conservatives were too compromised to push Britain in the necessary direction (Page, 2015: 77–86).

What both narratives ignore is an economic course that Britain never took. If Selsdon Man meant 'Thatcherism before Thatcher' then Heath was never that man. For Heath, capitalism had an 'unacceptable face' and at the time it was still axiomatic that any government which abandoned full employment would be crucified at the polls.[5] But if Selsdon signalled a more continental-style, social market conservatism, which reconciled state and market, short-term interests with long-term ones, economic imperatives with social needs, then that was more Heath's politics. Heath's version of Seldson Man was Konrad Adenauer with a British accent.[6]

Yet the early 1970s was one of the least propitious times to attempt reform. With turbulent international waters, and its passengers endlessly fighting one another, the ship often seemed to be tilting out of control. Britain needed both wage deflation (so that excessive wage claims did not create the inflation which would erode their value) and reflation (to stimulate growth). These were very difficult objectives to reconcile. Not that the captain and his crew made things any easier (Sandbrook, 2011: 72–9).

Heath wanted continuity, conciliation, voluntary agreement and consensus. Unfortunately, it was laudable values such as these that would be blamed for the mess that resulted. Thus, rather than a statutory prices and incomes policy, Heath combined strong rhetoric with weak action, leaving the government looking as if it was being blown around by events and leaving Britain's industrial relations with an international reputation for chaos (Grieve Smith, 1997: 78–83; Morgan, 2001: 331–2).[7]

Thatcherites would later depict themselves as the saviours of a Britain, which, in the 1970s, had teetered on the edge of a cliff. That was never the case. But widespread power cuts and ailing, state-subsidised industries did symbolise a feeling that something was wrong and the free market Right slowly began to nurture that feeling, giving it a beguiling political and economic voice (Plant, 2004: 23–30; Hickson, 2004b: 35–41).

And that sense of losing control, of incompetent management, was also due to the nation's management being frequently incompetent! In two years Heath went from Selsdon Man to Keynesian Stimulus Man and Industrial Interventionist Man (Fleming, 1980: 143–4; Morgan, 2001: 321–4; Bale, 2012: 161–2, 176–80). The clenched, iron fist of 1970 had by 1972 unclenched, reached into the Treasury's pockets, brought out wads of cash and strewn them across the population. This was the Barber Boom, in short (Westaway, 1980: 17–19).

Designed to reduce unemployment and secure electoral popularity, in one of the greatest budget giveaways ever the Chancellor slashed tax, offered tax breaks to industry and increased social security payments. Inflation would not be a problem, Barber intoned, because productivity would rise and workers would be showered with cash they need no longer demand through excessive wage claims. A dash for growth would work, the reasoning went, because the last Labour Chancellor, Roy Jenkins, had not offered the electorate a pre-election bribe. Because Labour had 'saved, saved, saved' the Tories could now 'spend, spend, spend'.

But this happened at a time when not only oil but other commodities, like copper and zinc, were skyrocketing in price. The domestic boom sucked expensive imports into a UK-shaped sinkhole, stoking inflation and a new balance of payments crisis (Cairncross, 1996: 108–9). The stimulus worked to reduce unemployment but inflation climbed as alarmist voices warned of Weimer-style hyperinflation. By the spring of 1973 Barber had reversed direction abruptly, slashing public expenditure and raising interest rates. By the end of the year a dispute with the miners tipped the country into a 'Three Day Week'. It was boom followed by bust.[8]

The free market Right thus found leverage for their grandiose critiques in one area that even the most innumerate shopper appreciated. With prices that seemed to be continually on the rise shoppers had to run ever quicker to keep up. This is, sooner rather than later, both exhausting and deeply worrying to those on fixed incomes. And if the radical Right were correct about inflation, the suspicion would grow, perhaps they were accurate about much else too.

Thus, as the British economy staggered around, by the mid-1970s a new form of political discourse was slowly gaining traction: weren't our economic problems simply due to too much spending by a state that had been imprisoned by 'special interests', i.e. trade unions?

Social reforms

Under Heath's government there were significant increases in spending on health, housing, social security and education (Lowe, 1996; also Raison, 1990: 73–89; Glennerster, 1995: 124; Page, 2015: 69–72). Overall public expenditure rose by 5.5% between 1970 and 1974, compared to 4.1% under Wilson's tenure.[9]

For instance, though the reform had been passed by the previous government, the Conservatives oversaw the introduction of social services departments within local authorities, originally viewed as supports for *all* families, poor and non-poor alike. And the 1971 Conservative conference applauded (literally) the introduction of the disability benefits that had also been designed by Labour (Dean, 2013: 75). Ironically, it was the two stalwarts of what was to come later, Keith Joseph and Margaret Thatcher, ministers in the Departments of Health and Social Security (DHSS) and Education respectively, who were the high spenders.

There would be controversies. Family Income Supplement (a means-tested benefit) was introduced as a means of bolstering in-work income. This would be disliked massively by the Left and even free marketeers like Enoch Powell denounced it (Denham & Garnett, 2001a: 201–6). The take-up of Family Income Supplement was low while its impact on the families receiving it was as much to trap them in poverty as it was to help them (Timmins, 1996: 284).

Stung by the experience, it would be another 15 years before the Conservatives dared attempt to extend means-testing significantly. Otherwise, little changed in social security policy (Lowe, 1996: 199–205).

But not only this, in 1973 Joseph looked the Tory Party Conference in its sometimes rabid eye and stated bluntly that contrary to what Right-wing activists believed – and what he had stated himself while in opposition – the numbers of 'shirkers and scroungers' was less considerable than Conservative demonology liked to imagine (Denham & Garnett, 2001a: 219).

Joseph also introduced the first significant reform to the NHS since 1948 (Denham & Garnett, 2001a: 211–16). In an attempt to unify, rationalise and systematise the relationship between local authority services, GPs and hospitals, new regional and area health authorities were created (Webster, 2002: 100–9).

In education, Thatcher the loyal minister (who battled to save the Open University) co-existed with Thatcher the nemesis of the educational elite. Expansionism – extra nursery school provision and school building repairs, for instance – sat alongside distaste for comprehensive schools (Campbell, 2000: 212–15; Lowe, 2005: 219–21). The fact that Conservative-controlled councils usually welcomed comprehensives, and that her own civil servants were often aghast at her Black Paper instincts, was frustrating to Thatcher the reformer (Campbell, 2000: 222–8).

In housing, a shift occurred in subsidies from buildings to people, the long-term consequences of which have been pernicious.[10] Rather than using resources to keep rents down the emphasis was now upon allowing rents to find their 'market level' and directing rent rebates to those who could not afford them (Lowe, 2005: 267–9). Wanting to increase the proportion of private housing stock the Tories began to allow the sale of council houses to their tenants but, with only modest sales, became frustrated when even many Tory councils refused to do so. But that's all this remained for the present: frustration.

In key respects, then, not only was the post-war settlement still intact but the Tories seemed to be doing what they had done from 1951–64. Complain that the state was crowding out the private sector and introduce some pro-market reforms, but actually raise overall spending in the process.

Noises off

But as with economic policy things were no longer quite the same with social policy as they had been previously. Anti-welfare state voices were gathering in volume, especially as the economy faltered. Cracks in the cross-party edifice also started to appear (Abel-Smith, 1980). Those who argued that a modern, humane capitalism required state welfare were still dominant, but they no longer had the stage to themselves.

So, for every compassionate speech about 'Cinderella services' there was a Keith Joseph who tore red meat off the poor to feed it to the Tory faithful.[11] Joseph's long-term influence occurred precisely because his phrasemaking was Janus-faced (Denham & Garnett, 2001a: 219–24).

If the 'cycle of deprivation' traps the poor, he said, simply blaming them for their circumstances and walking away was not an option. But if the welfare state was to blame for the trap (all those disincentives against working and bettering yourself) then it stood to reason that once the trap was dismantled any remaining poverty was the fault not of the ladder (markets), nor of those who designed it (Conservatives), but of those too lazy, stupid or criminal to climb. Blaming the poor in 1970 was thus inhumane. Poverty was the fault of the socialists. Every right-thinking patriot knew that. But by 1985 blaming the poor was virtually compulsory. A lot of the Thatcherite mood music was composed and conducted by Joseph (Marquand, 2009: 258–60).

By the mid-1970s, then, the welfare state increasingly resembled an atavistic, compromise solution to a problem about whose causes fewer and fewer people agreed. Social service departments would represent almost the last stage in the expansionist state. As the economic weather became tumultuous the ship of the post-1945 settlement was starting to wobble. A reckoning was coming.

So, if the Conservatives were sometimes more pro-welfare than Labour, when they did cut and means test its significance was amplified beyond any of the cuts and reforms introduced *by* Labour. You end free school milk in secondary schools (as Labour had) and it was a regrettable adjustment in spending priorities; you end free school milk for 8–11 year olds (as Thatcher did) and it's the return of Gradgrind (Campbell, 2000: 231–3).

Symbolism mattered and the totemic quality of the welfare state was no longer what it had been for the previous 30 years. Left-wingers (interpreting every cut as the beginning of the end) and Right-wingers (hoping it was) sometimes constituted a bizarre echo chamber for one another. In the 1940s the welfare state had epitomised the future, but to many that optimism now seemed old fashioned. *Social spending on state welfare and cultural attitudes towards state welfare were beginning to diverge.*

And so the charge was increasingly made that since Keynes had underestimated the importance of inflation it is no wonder that Keynesian governments would find themselves infected by it (Wapshott, 2012: 249).[12] After all, for Keynesians a certain amount of inflation *was* regarded as desirable, a sign that growth and high employment rates were being maintained (Wapshott, 2012: 111).

The irony is this. Just as the Barber Boom risked crashing the economy and led to an austere period of retrenchment that presaged Thatcherism, so the Tories splurged on social policies at the very time when the regulatory capacities of the post-war state were beginning to falter. The Tories thus resembled parents who first overindulge their child to the point of obesity and then impose a crash diet. Yet in Conservative mythology ever after, it is the system that failed rather than their own management of it.

Environmental policies

Did the crises of the era help or hinder environmentalism?

There were opportunities to be sure. To concerns about the outcome of energy use in the form of pollution were now added anxieties about the very *production* of energy. If oil dependency was crippling countries and consumers alike then wouldn't the obvious solution – less reliance on fossil fuels – also be good for the environment, by reducing pollution and encouraging the development of clean energy? Popular consciousness about the possibility of solar and wind energy dates to the 1970s.

But of course that very dependency also made transition to a greener society impossible for many to contemplate. Environmental economics was still undeveloped. There were no credible models of a green society to inspire the millions of people struggling with bills and everyday dilemmas. Furthermore, while in its infancy stage there was an inevitable lack of coherence in the environmentalist message. If it was no longer simply about conservation, countryside and animal welfare, what was it? It simply wasn't clear what the infant would resemble as an adult. To the extent that it had name recognition, environmentalism was still closely associated with pacifism and unilateral nuclear disarmament, which most of the British people rejected.

Nor are crises necessarily conducive to progressive social change anyway. Green messages arose at a time when egalitarianism was tumbling out of fashion. Threats to living standards can make people deaf to the message that radical alterations to their lifestyle are needed.

Environmentalists therefore did spot an opportunity, but not one that could be easily articulated in the vocabularies of the time or translated into politics and policies with which most people could connect.

Yet the intellectual case for change *was* gathering credibility. Environmentalists were, for instance, quick to observe that what journalists and politicians enjoyed calling the 'energy crisis' went much deeper. Barbara Ward, who had earlier devised the phrase 'Spaceship Earth', was clear that although the planet both received and emitted huge amounts of energy the balance between "incoming and outgoing radiation" was in fact highly fragile. With remarkable prescience she wondered whether,

> ... the sum of all likely fossil fuel demands in the early decades of the next century might not greatly increase the emission of CO_2 into the atmosphere and by doing so bring up average surface temperature uncomfortably close to that 2 °C rise of which might set in motion the long-term warming-up of the planet.
>
> (Ward, 1972: 267–8)

Ward (1972: 183–6, 196) also observed that although energy reserves were still plentiful – particularly coal – the environmental costs of relying indefinitely on fossil fuels was too high. But with clean technologies like wind and solar still in their infancies she argued that the gap between one era and the next could only be bridged by nuclear power.

Similarly, for Commoner (1976: 2–4) a rational society would make (1) the economic system conform to (2) the 'production system' (the network of processes converting resources into goods and services), which would in turn conform to (3) the ecosystem of ecological cycles and natural resources. Yet what we have actually done, he observed, is subordinate the ecosystem to production and production to the economy. What were often thought of as separate crises, therefore, were manifestations of a "singe basic defect" in the design of modern society. Solutions – like new technological remedies or new taxes – which ignored the knotted, entwined nature of the problem could not succeed. The existing relationships between the above needed to be inverted. For Commoner (1976: 262), this would require some form of democratic socialism.

Of course, the difficulty was in translating such critiques into practical reality. The higher the hill you ask people to climb the greater their excuse to stay where they are. Whether and to what extent a substantive and worldwide shift in priorities could occur would depend on the movement's success in organising itself and mobilising opinion.

Green movements

The green movement was, in truth, a series of *movements* (Wall, 1999; Connelly *et al.*, 2012: ch. 3). The 'old environmentalism' (dedicated to conservation and countryside protection) was respectable and conservative, using familiar methods to lobby for change within existing institutions. Drawing upon its antecedents in peace and anti-nuclear campaigns, the 'new environmentalism' was more activist and obstreperous.

In some respects, conservationism would accommodate itself to this new, more highly politicised environmentalism. Inspired by Paul Ehrlich, for example, The Conservation Society adopted and helped to popularise an environmental message, effecting an uneasy alliance between traditionalists and radicals (Herring, 2001). Most of the older conservation groups persisted.

Nonetheless, by appealing to the young, much of the energy seemed to lie with the new environmentalism, with the new superseding the old.[13] Concerned with both the human and the non-human, it promoted an awareness of humanity's role in the biosphere allied to a sense of alarm at the former's effects on the latter (McCormick, 1995: 56–7). Social campaigns and political action on a worldwide scale was therefore required, necessitating an ideological engagement and coalitions with other movements and forms of activism (McCormick, 1995: 74–8).[14]

It therefore faced the same dilemmas as others within the 'new social movements': how do you mobilise action towards common goals and shared interests across multiple nations, communities and groups with their diversity of principles, methods and cultural traditions? How do you articulate shared universals *and* the particularity of local needs and customs?

Since there are so many ways of answering such questions it is no surprise that some familiar divisions appeared:

- Between pragmatists (who wanted to compromise and build alliances with existing political parties and the business community) and radicals (who wanted new social institutions and practices, fearing compromise would allow 'the system' to co-opt and dilute the movement's idealism).
- Between materialists (who focused upon the management and distribution of resources) and culturalists (for whom environmentalism implied a recasting of human identity, meanings and moral priorities).

Such divisions would manifest themselves in the vocabulary environmentalists would use to describe themselves: light green versus dark green, 'realos' versus 'fundis' (Doherty, 1992; cf. Barry, 1994). Ironically, many greens would identify themselves as 'beyond Left and Right' while demonstrating so many of the same sectarian tensions and factional bickering.

For the time being, though, a new energy seemed to have entered the political theatre (Klein, 2014: 201–3). By 1990 the environmental movement broadly defined would have 4.5m members in Britain alone (McCormick, 1995: 163–4).

Friends of the Earth (FoE) was founded by David Brower, ex-executive director of the Sierra Club, one of the US's most successful conservation groups. His determination to campaign on public issues had seen the Club's membership increase tenfold. But with his politicking losing the Club its tax-exempt status, with mounting debts and an alleged dereliction of administrative duties, Brower was forced out in 1969 and immediately founded FoE. Activist, international and publicity-minded, FoE would become one of the most prominent green organisations of the next 50 years, addressing a host of social, political, legal and technological issues (McCormick, 1995: 171–2).

Greenpeace grew out of direct action against nuclear testing in the early 1970s, with aggressive reactions by the French government giving those actions an international profile. As its campaigns spread beyond nuclear testing so Greenpeace's global membership exploded, reaching 4m by the 1990s (McCormick, 1995: 172–3).

The British political party originally entitled People, in 1973, would not have the success of sister parties in Germany and Switzerland (McCormick, 1995: 208–9). However, after being renamed the Ecology Party and eventually the Green Party, by 1987 it would be winning more votes than the Scottish Nationalist Party and the Welsh Nationalists. But in the absence of proportional representation, with its vote dispersed around the country, with many radicals still regarding the Labour Party as the best vehicle for social change and with local authorities often resisting controversial projects, the party would fail to make a similar breakthrough into national politics, not winning its first MP until 2010.

Yet it would be misleading to characterise the burgeoning green movement as a collection of I'd-like-to-teach-the-world-to-sing hippies. Various conservatives were prominent within the movement whether for positive reasons (nature conservation) or negative ones (attraction to a discourse of catastrophe and social collapse).

Many factions across the Right have long been drawn to – and influenced – environmentalism.[15] Wall (2010: 81) mentions several guild socialists and environmentalists who in the early years of the twentieth century migrated ideologically, eventually attaching themselves to the far Right with its emphasis on soil and sentiment, blood and belonging. In seeking to harness the forces of modernity *against* modernity, the Nazis typified a strain of anti-industrial romanticism and nature worship that environmentalists cannot erase from history (Uekötter, 2007).

This blend of moral conservatism, apocalyptic pessimism and back-to-nature traditionalism was in the early 1970s most conspicuous in the pages of *The Ecologist* (Sandbrook, 2011: 215–18). For several years this magazine was *the* public face of green ideas, one whose combination of social conscience, prescience and eccentric crankiness reflected the birth throes of the wider movement. These qualities were personified in the publication's editor-in-chief, Edward Goldsmith. It was Goldsmith's belief that the modern world was a pretty bad idea. One consequence was that for every proposal in the magazine which was ahead of its time, e.g. Goldsmith's support for organic farming, there were others which spoke to the apocalypse-spotting habits that so many at the political and religious extremes seem to savour. The welfare state, it may not need saying, was identified as one of the horsemen.

For instance, in the editorial for October 1976 Goldsmith links the cost of state welfare to its perceived ineffectiveness: the more that is spent the more needs are created, so ratcheting up demands for more spending.[16] A new class of the poor are trapped at the social periphery by inflation, low wages and morality-sapping benefits, serviced by a welfare industry of social workers and other self-interested professionals. All of which anticipates Charles Murray (1984) by a decade. But for Goldsmith, since social policy is an offshoot of industrialism, consumerism and modern technology, cutting welfare without addressing under-lying causes would be to abandon the periphery to its fate. The solution is to reinvent those social supports still found in tribal and peasant societies: extended families and strong communities.

Global politics

The green movement, then, was diverse and dynamic, passionate and, every so often, utterly bonkers. It was a movement that quickly took its place beside the women's, civil rights and gay rights movements because it seemed to tap not only into the zeitgeist, but into the thinking of many policymakers.

Two years after the first Earth Day, in June 1972, Stockholm hosted the United Nations Conference on the Human Environment (McCormick, 1995: ch. 5). This looked at the interrelationships between the social, economic, political and natural spheres, with a global focus that included issues of poverty and development. These were seen as issues not only for the UN and national governments but for inter-governmental organisations, NGOs and citizens' groups too.

It was here that a perennial dilemma was first crystallised: the world needed to act with greater environmental responsibility but the poorest countries needed growth (Macekura, 2011: 504–8). How to reconcile the two? This was a profound question, though both before and during the conference the contribu-tions of Britain certainly seemed more concerned with national self-interest than anything else (McCormick, 1995: 112, 115).[17]

Nonetheless, the Stockholm event was significant practically and symboli-cally. No longer was it possible to think of nature simply in terms of animals, raw materials and countryside; the human and the non-human were interde-pendent. And if the moral community extended farther out across space than orthodox thinking realised, so it extended farther across time.

The year 1972 also saw the publication of the *Limits to Growth*, commis-sioned by a think tank called the Club of Rome (McCormick, 1995: 90–6, 98–103). Researchers working out of the Massachusetts Institute of Technology built a computer model to track the world's economy and environment. Called World3, this computer model was cutting edge and its task ambitious. The team tracked industrialisation, population, food, use of resources and pollution. They modelled data up to 1970, then developed a range of scenarios for the next 130 years. If serious action on environmental and resource issues didn't happen, the model predicted 'overshoot and collapse' – in the economy, environment and population – before 2070. This was called the 'business-as-usual' scenario.

The book's central point, much criticised later (Mudd, 2013), is that 'the earth is finite' and the quest for unlimited growth in population, material goods etc. would eventually lead to a crash. In 2014 research at Melbourne University suggested that in terms of resource depletion, industrial production (including food) and pollution the 1972 report had got it more or less right (Turner & Alexander, 2014).

These two events – the Stockholm Conference and *Limits to Growth* – seemed to herald some kind of sea-change. Even if it was not always clear what needed to be done, the need itself was being well publicised:

> Appropriate national institutions must be entrusted with the task of planning, managing or controlling the environmental resources of States with the view to enhancing environmental quality.[18]

And if Brits had been a bit shame-faced in Stockholm, there was surely already enough evidence that the UK was ready to lead the world in cleaning up the environment. As we saw at the end of Chapter 4, in 1970 Britain became the first country to set up a department dedicated to such matters (Ziegler, 2010: 347, 408). The Department of the Environment (DoE) would surely achieve what Wilson had only been able to promise: bring social and ecological issues together.

World's first

In reality, of all the responsibilities expected to fit under the DoE's wide administrative hat, the environment would receive the least attention.[19] The 'lived environment' was largely taken to mean the 'built human environment'. And who would set the tone for this initiative? A successful city financier and ruthless asset-stripper. Yet, too much of a capitalist to worship capitalism uncritically, Peter Walker actually belonged to the one-nation tradition (Sandbrook, 2011: 519–21): "a Disraelian in a world of monetarists" (Thorpe, 2010).

Walker's time at the DoE was concerned much more with local government (Childs, 2001: 166–7) and inner city problems than with the natural environment – the second of Wilson's 'two-fold task'. This, plus the fact that Walker was moved on in only two years, indicated that having created a 'super-ministry' Heath did not quite know what to do with it. This was unsurprising because, for the PM, *the* environment often meant *his* environment. Irritated by roadworks that delayed his drive to Chequers, he asked whether they could be rushed. Heath was scathing about the reply, that greater haste would cost more: "It is sheer nonsense to say that it takes six months to flatten a roundabout. Any serious group of people could do it in a weekend" (Ziegler, 2010: 326).

On the face of it, then, established to oversee 'a whole range of functions which affect people's living environment', the DoE embodied the vision that Wilson had expressed in his 1969 speech of marrying the social and the natural.

Yet the cognitive and administrative dichotomy between the two, which had been a feature of British policymaking since the 1940s (see Chapter 1), was not so easily overcome. Therefore, though creating the DoE looked like a bold move it was largely a restructuring and rebadging of existing departmental responsibilities (especially housing, local government and transport) with no powers or resources additional to those that had existed already, and less actual influence over the environment than the Department for Agriculture (McCormick, 1995: 156, 159–61) – leading to conflict between the two (Sheail, 2002: 155–7). In his history of the DoE, McQuail (1994: 17) even claims that "the environment was not a determining factor in its creation"! By 1980 only 3.2% of its staff actually performed environmental functions.

And while Britain's centralised government machinery seemed conducive to policy efficiency and accountability, its actual policymaking traditions veered away from transparency, public consultation and democratic deliberation. British political governance was paternalistic and top-down, operating with the assumption that people would passively and gratefully accept what the scientific and managerial experts decided on their behalf behind closed doors. The DoE thus failed to combine a rounded, holistic vision with the administrative clarity, strength, focus and democratic openness that was required.

The DoE also established an unwelcome precedent: create a 'superdepartment', watch it underperform for a few years and then start to strip it down. Transport responsibilities were taken away from the DoE in 1976 and heritage responsibilities in 1992. Successive governments followed a similar pattern. The Department of the Environment, Transport and the Regions (DETR) was established in 1997 but this only lasted four years until transport and local government was sent off in one administrative direction with the Department for the Environment, Food and Rural Affairs (DEFRA) going off in another (Rydin, 2003: 92–3).[20]

All of that said, Walker established the DoE as an interventionist agency; a legacy that Thatcher tried to reverse, though with only partial success due to the increasing Europeanisation of environmental policy by the late 1980s (Jordan, 2002: 34–9) – see Chapters 8 and 9.

It was with the 1973 Water Act and the 1974 Control of Pollution Act that the DoE began to establish its ecological credentials (DEFRA, 2006: 12–21). The former took the function of supplying water and sewage away from local authorities and created 10 new water authorities (overseen by a National Water Board) who would integrate water and sewerage services, one aim of which was to reduce pollution in rivers and estuaries on a 'polluter pays' principle. The 1974 Act went further by treating pollution and waste together, covering waste on land, the pollution of water, noise and pollution of the atmosphere.

Ultimately, then, the DoE was a technocratic venture, which leant more towards the social rather than offering a comprehensive vision in which it and the ecological could be rebalanced and integrated.

Nor, as Heath's popularity plummeted in 1973, was another Labour government likely to change things much. The person Wilson had made Minister for Local Government and Regional Planning at the tail end of 1969 was Tony Crosland. But Crosland despised environmentalists and believed that ecological issues diverted attention away from economic growth and social justice (Jeffreys, 2000: 150). At the DoE (1974–6) he would recommend disinvestment in the rail network on the grounds that 'workers take buses' (Jeffreys, 2000: 186). His view of environmentalism as a middle-class indulgence blinkered his vision of the future (see next chapter).

Where next?

The early-to-mid 1970s, then, was a time of roller coaster excitement for some and anxiety for others. People were ready to listen to those with something new to say. In this context, environmentalism was well placed to raise its voice. With Stockholm, the Club of Rome, initiatives like the DoE and energetic groups like FoE it rapidly assumed a conspicuous public profile.

Yet by implying that the state should take on more responsibilities at a time when states looked increasingly powerless and ineffective, environmentalism also risked looking old fashioned already: a youthful decrepitude. The same systems-breakdown (in post-war affluence, planning and the regulation of capital) that opened up a space within which environmentalism could grow also slammed the breaks on the social conditions and expectations (mutuality, social equality, security about the future) that many greens supported. Particularly in its messages of doom, environmentalism therefore came across as symptomatic of a social malaise; more a sign of a general deterioration than a prognosis for renewal. The same newspapers, which might revel in visions of smog-shrouded, polluted, overpopulated future, would run a mile from the recommendations that greens were starting to formulate.

Morgan (2001: 352–7) notes how the civic culture, which had sustained Britain for three decades, was disintegrating, replaced by sectionalism and the polarisation of norms and values. Welfare state capitalism was finding it harder to reconcile its component parts (economic growth, fair distribution, social harmony). The resulting fractures seemed to run into the heart of the nation itself. One-nation Conservatives had thrived when it felt like there was just one nation. But now that Britain was rupturing into multiple, intransigent visions of what Britishness meant, they seemed powerless to stich those nations back together.

Representing themselves as architects of a national revival, *laissez faire* advocates were gaining a voice, and an audience, that they had not possessed for half a century. It wasn't just a matter of a new economic policy here or new social policy there. The cultural shift meant that economic and social battles were often surrogate clashes about national identity. Fighting inflation, cutting spending and enfeebling unions would eventually be seen as patriotic duties, opposed only by those who were the 'enemy within'.

The market liberal, corporate-driven governance, which would eventually emerge, would so often prove even less receptive to green arguments than the political circumstances of the 1970s had been (as we see in later chapters).

Key questions

What relationships between the environmental and social policy agendas have emerged? To what extent have social policies and the politics of welfare reform deliberately informed and been informed by the principles and values of environmental ethics and politics?

Did the DoE initiate something new? In terms of governmental organisation, yes. There had been nothing like it in the world before. In terms of government commitment to environmental policy, no. As indicated above, with one or two exceptions (such as the reorganisation of the water sector), the state rolled on as before. There was still to be little crossover between the social and environmental policy agendas, therefore.

As such, the DoE could be taken as evidence that the 1945 settlement was still in place: faith that government should and would take primary responsibility for collective wellbeing was reaffirmed; planning and intervention remained paramount; social problems were still understood in exclusively social and economic terms; policymaking was a matter for experts, party political machines and Whitehall insiders. True, 'the environment' now had a departmental home. But this, if anything, may have reaffirmed the notion that such issues were not a matter for cross-departmental and cross-sectoral incorporation.

So. rather than the familiar 'between the cracks' approach (see the end of Chapter 1) being overturned, if anything the new department was expected to catch the drips which seeped through those cracks. The DoE constituted a wastebasket into which all that 'nature stuff' could be politically, intellectually and administratively deposited. The cracks themselves remained unsealed and, tragically of course, even the natural environment itself was low down on the DoE's to-do list.

Some of those cracks continued to be found in social policy, as had been the case from 1945–70. Though Thatcher and Joseph were more likely to lament what they saw as the scars inflicted *on* capitalism rather than (as Wilson had implied) the scars inflicted *by* it, the welfare state continued to sail merrily on – for the time being. Reforms still coloured within the pre-existing lines. There were increasing noises about scroungers and the like, but mainstream Tories were still eager to demonstrate their commitment to state welfare and all it had represented for 25 years.

Yet this business-as-usual self-satisfaction collided with an increasingly loud discourse panicking about the overload, breakdown, fragility and impotence of political and social systems. Beset by economic eruptions threatening the very foundations of that post-war order, the government's emergency management wasn't very good at management and, if anything, worsened the sense of emergency. Slowly, the older, more optimistic solidarities were becoming less tenable.

In an alternative reality it's possible to envisage this inspiring a reconfiguration of politics around environmental activism and concerns about pollution, overpopulation and energy crises. But there was no agency to make it real. The Common Market, even in the early 1970s, was taking an interest in environmental issues but it was only much later that this would possess any real power or legislative force (see Chapter 9). Transboundary issues and agreements were just beginning, i.e. Stockholm 1972, yet these were only in their infancy and not yet as important as they would become in the 1990s.

Might the Labour Party offer a receptacle for the new environmentalism and therefore a new politics?

Notes

1 http://thoughtcatalog.com/richard-grayson/2013/02/an-18-year-olds-diary-entries-from-april-1970/ [accessed 10 September 2014]
2 www.earthday.org/earth-day-history-movement [accessed 10 September 2014]
3 The European Community was mainly concerned with economic integration. This provided the context for its first action plan on environmental issues as they related to trade as early as 1972 (Chasek *et al.*, 2010: 88). The first four action plans, for instance, included over 200 pieces of legislation relating to pollution and waste management. However, EU environment policy would not move centre stage until the Maastricht Treaty in 1992 and so we delay discussing it until later chapters.
4 Nationally, enthusiasm for entry was limited and what support there was was often negative: focused on the dire consequences of remaining outside the Common Market, given Britain's systemic economic weaknesses (Morgan, 2001: 340–2).
5 It's possible that Heath had originally intended to refer to the 'unacceptable facet of capitalism' but misread his speech because he was too vain to wear glasses (McManus, 2016: 132–3). So claimed journalist Simon Hoggart. Thanks to Robert Page for drawing my attention to this. Nonetheless, Heath liked 'unacceptable face' and would use it on several occasions (Ziegler, 2010: 409–10).
6 Adenauer was an influential Chancellor in post-war West Germany.
7 A statutory policy would not come until the very end of 1972.
8 For those on the far Right, visions of a country becoming ungovernable caused an upsurge in quasi-fascism and racism.
9 Though some of that was to pay for rising unemployment, of course.
10 Four decades later the size of the housing benefit bill is frequently cited as an archetype of reckless spending by those who wish to slash welfare.
11 Especially in his infamous Birmingham speech of October 1974 where, warning about the threat to the 'human stock' represented by the immoral poor, he torpedoed any chance of being Tory leader (Denham & Garnett, 2001a: 265–71).
12 Some would allege that had Keynes survived he would have seen the error of his ways and embraced the monetarism for which he had actually paved the way (Wapshott, 2012: 286–7). For an overview of monetarism see the next two chapters.
13 Indeed, The Conservation Society went into decline after 1973.
14 Such as 'environmental justice', an amalgamation of anti-poverty, anti-racist, civil rights and ecological concerns.
15 Ernst Haekel, who coined the word 'ecology', was a proto-fascist.

16 http://exacteditions.theecologist.org/read/resurgence/vol-6-no-8-october-1976-6373/5/2?dps=on [accessed 1 October 2014]
17 The defensiveness of the UK was not difficult to explain. The Swedes had been so enthusiastic to host the conference in order to publicise the acid rain which, created by sulphur dioxide from UK industry in particular, was destroying Scandinavian lakes and forests (Sheail, 2002: 251–2). Faced with the evangelical, head-shaking outrage of the Swedish, the Brits – no small lovers of dogs, gardening and nature rambles – squirmed a bit. See next chapter.
18 Principle 17, Declaration of the United Nations Conference on the Human Environment, Stockholm, 5–16 June 1972.
19 For a history of the DoE, 1970–2000, see Jordan (2002: 28–42).
20 The long-established Ministry for Agriculture, Fisheries and Food (accused of being too close to producer interests) was absorbed into DEFRA.

6 The party is over
1974–79

In April 1980 Tony Benn rose to speak in the House of Commons. He was primed to ignore the heckling he regularly received, though it arose on this occasion because Benn addressed Britain's first female Prime Minister as the Right Honourable Gentleman. Benn (1990: 590) claimed not to have noticed and apologised to Margaret Thatcher the following evening: "it wasn't a cheap smear on you". Yet it is difficult to picture Benn without a twinkle in his eye on both occasions.

Like many implacable adversaries Benn and Thatcher had a wary admiration for one another politically (Campbell, 2000: 309). Each bolstered their ego by viewing the other as the personification of something much larger: a warrior from an opposing force against whom war must be waged on the battlefield of history. Benn and Thatcher were both self-dramatists. That's what helped attract so many supporters and so many enemies to them.

Benn's verbal mistake seemed a fitting *faux pas* for the topsy-turvy decade just gone.

The lower middle-class daughter of a Grantham grocer occupied the summit of the western world's most successful political party. This unknown, initially underestimated woman had become a hectoring matron to the entire nation. Her enemies' hatred for her (plus a secret envy for her ideological willpower) growing the more she outmanoeuvred them year after year.

The 1980s could have belonged to Benn (Dell, 2000: 395–400). The son of a Viscount had renounced his peerage, changed his image (he was formally known as Antony Wedgewood Benn) and embraced socialism as the self-appointed spokesman of the working class (Panitch & Leys, 1997: 40–9; Adams, 2011).[1] Yet in his own way he was as traditionalist as any Conservative. Benn may have discovered Marx late in life but he retained a very un-Marxist faith in national and parliamentary sovereignty. Britain was so important, he believed, that, while they would not like it, the financial markets could not afford to bring a socialist Britain to its knees. Democracy was a counterweight to capitalism; the power of a vote counteracting the power of money and privilege. The democratic revolution would soon resume its forward march. The 1980s would be the decade the 1970s should have been.

Both believed that the welfare state capitalism of the previous 35 years was no longer sustainable. For Thatcher, the country would have to relearn how to live within its means. As she would observe years later, the Good Samaritan could not do good unless he was first prosperous. For Benn, egalitarian systems could not be founded on an economy that allowed a few powerful individuals and corporations to control it. And in 1980 both must have known that the real battles were yet to come. Many expected that by 1983–84 Benn would be Labour leader, forcing the country to choose which future, which version of itself, it preferred.

For Benn, nothing demonstrated the necessity of this choice more than the failures of the preceding six years.

Steady as she goes

The Labour Party of 1974 offered traditional conservative virtues: calm, prag-matism and quiet reliability (Dell, 2000: ch. 15). The somnambulance of its election campaigns was partly in order to hold internal divisions together but also an embodiment of what it believed the country preferred (Beckett, 2009: 157). Who wanted a repeat of 1973's turmoil? Socialism barely rated a mention because it didn't need one. Everyone knew what the party stood for: a mature, working partnership with the unions and an incomes policy based upon social fairness. People quietly forgot 1969's *In Place of Strife*. As such, inflation could be controlled, economic prosperity could be re-established and Britain could be reunited.

Fewer Cabinets in the twentieth century have been packed with as much experience and talent as the Labour Cabinet of 1974. And if Harold Wilson was now older and less energetic, he was also a less paranoid and divisive figure. His Chancellor, Denis Healey, offered a restrained, inflation-sensitive Keynesian-ism: bearing down on inflation without suppressing growth, while offering enough redistribution to keep the voters on side. Looming schisms over the Common Market were dealt with through the promise (first suggested by Benn) of a referendum, which duly followed in 1975. With two-thirds voting to retain membership of the EEC that, surely, was that.

The government's politics of pragmatism was understandable. Britain seemed an ever more fractious and fragile place. What the country needed in 1974 was a cup of tea and a good lie down. Yet this approach also made it more difficult for the new government to deal with the deep-rooted, systemic problems of the economy (Tomlinson, 2004): endemic inflation, reduced productivity, dwin-dling competitiveness. As a new Right-wing gang assembled down the street – they called themselves The Monetarists or sometimes the New Right (Sandbrook, 2013: 225–8) – pragmatic, corporatist agreements between govern-ment, employers and unions felt like the only way of defending socialist territory.

Some *did* concede that monetarists had a point (Denham & Garnett, 2001b: 104–5). The Barber Boom was more than an example of Conservative misman-agement; it was a sign that, because splurging now had inflationary con-sequences, which the first two decades of post-war reconstruction had avoided, tight controls on spending and wage rises were required. The much-cited speech of the new P.M. James Callaghan[2] to the 1976 party conference made the point well (Sandbrook, 2013: 477–80):

> We used to think you could spend your way out of a recession … by cutting taxes and boosting government spending. I tell you in all candour that that option no longer exists, and that insofar as it ever did exist, it only worked on each occasion … by injecting a bigger dose of inflation into the economy, followed by a higher unemployment …
>
> (Harrington, 1993: 123)

Productivity needed to go back up, labour costs to go down and public expenditure had to be restricted. Callaghan's son-in-law was Peter Jay: economist, Labour loyalist to his bones and a monetarist. The thinking was simple: by setting certain monetary targets pragmatically, the country could be saved from the full panoply of monetarist ideology.

Callaghan's speech was anathema to many across the labour movement (Pugh, 2010: 356–7). Stagflation notwithstanding, the Phillips Curve suggested that as inflation went down unemployment went up. Prioritising inflation would mean raising interest rates (so making investment more expensive), reducing the social wage, demoting the principle of full employment and suppressing earnings. It therefore meant abandoning the goals that had underpinned post-war social democracy and funded the welfare state. It meant inequality!

So what was the party to do? For some, a reckoning with the unions was overdue (Dell, 2000: 472–3). If you wanted social expenditure then a new economic discipline was required. There was no room for Keynesianism and social justice on the one side and reckless wages claims and petulant strikes on the other (Morgan, 2007: 362–4). Others hoped that the obsession of Callaghan and Treasury officials with inflation was a limited one (see Castle, 1993: 497–8, 507).[3] And farther on the Left there were those who shared elements of the Right's critique (Medhurst, 2014: ch. 10). The era of regulated, mixed economy capitalism had indeed run its course. Workers were desperate for higher wages because they had no access to the proceeds of capital, which still flowed largely into private hands. The solution was to spread ownership more widely. To socialise capital.

For a time at least, the 'social contract' seemed to placate all sides (Grieve Smith, 1997: 83–91).

This was an agreement whereby the unions would exercise voluntary restraint re pay claims in return for a guarantee that a Labour government would deliver prosperity and not interfere with collective bargaining (Taylor, 2004; also Morgan, 2001: 376–81). Yet what union leaders promised and what they could deliver struggled to coincide (Bogdanor, 2004: 10–11; Taylor, 2004: 98–103). In the wake of the oil crisis, and with food prices rising too, wage claims helped swell inflation to almost 27% by August 1975. The government's cap on wage increases received consent from across the spectrum, from Right-leaning stalwarts like Healey and

Roy Jenkins to those on the Left like Michael Foot (Morgan, 2007: 314–19, 341–2). It worked. By July 1976 inflation had fallen to 13%.

And this was both the strength and weakness of Labour's economic policy. It depended upon personal authority, negativity (fears about a future Tory government) and appeals to solidarity in a climate where neither government nor unions entirely trusted one another. So when circumstances change, when personal authority recedes and when you have a family to feed voluntary restraint begins to feel self-immolating. By June 1977 inflation was back up to 18%.

Thus, Labour's *raison d'etre* – its optimism and solidarity – was eroding (Beckett, 2009: 434–40, 464–9, 489–97). If even Labour could not reconcile workers' interests with Britain's needs then what was the point of it? Inflation would fall again and after January 1978 remain below 10% for the rest of Callaghan's time in office. A decent record to end on, in the context of the era, and in other respects the UK economy had performed well compared to Germany, France and Italy (Tomlinson, 2004: 63–5). But the damage to public perceptions had been done nonetheless.

Public support for unions was in sharp decline by 1975 anyway (Bogdanor, 2004: 12), even before they became widely blamed for causing high inflation – rather than simply responding to it (Tomlinson, 2014: 761–4). Slowly, and much more cautiously than her later reputation suggests, Thatcher began to believe that confrontation rather than conciliation was the way to win an election (Young, 1990: 114–17; Campbell, 2000: 390–5, 424–9). The 1978–79 Winter of Discontent was highly symbolic to a country which had had enough. The oil shock was forgotten as a 'Labour = inflation = unions = strikes' equation became solidified within public consciousness. His party's buoyant poll ratings notwithstanding, Callaghan's warning that a 'sea change' had occurred in the ideological tides was as prescient as it was self-serving.

Then there was the IMF (Panitch & Leys, 1997: 124–8; Hickson, 2004b: 41–5, 2005b; Morgan, 2007: 344–7; Beckett, 2009: 330–5, 339–45; Sandbrook, 2013: 480–503). The pound's slide – designed to improve exports – became a heart-in-mouth plunge on the foreign exchanges as investors sold sterling and the Bank of England had to use its reserves to buy those pounds back. This required the government to borrow money from other nations' central banks. Disaster was averted but by September 1976 the pound was in freefall again. Aided by a salivating media and bad timing – Healey's dramatic return from Heathrow Airport and subsequent barracking at the annual party conference – an economic emergency was transformed into a very public and very international embarrassment. With earlier loans due to be recalled, the government asked the IMF for £2.3 billion, the biggest sum ever requested by anyone. The IMF agreed the loan, in return for stinging cuts to public expenditure, particularly employment, housing and food subsidies:

> In fact, virtually everything cuttable – that is, excepting social security and local authority expenditure – was cut.
>
> (Burk & Cairncross, 1992: 105)

None of which played well down the pubs. That the loan was only one in a series (including loans made to Tory governments), that only part of it was used and that it would be repaid ahead of schedule was immaterial in the face of what your gut told you was a national humiliation. Labour's reputation for economic competence would not recover for almost 20 years.

That there was no real need for the loan, it being due to a monumental Treasury miscalculation, has become part of Labour's folklore. But was the miscalculation cock-up or conspiracy? Healey (1989: 432–3) never stopped claiming that the innate precaution of officials led them to get their sums disastrously wrong. But others spot conspiracy (Hickson, 2005: 90–1; Beckett, 2009: 355–7). Those wanting cuts, and perhaps a change of government, had found a way to engineer it. Britain had experienced a capitalist coup.

So why did Labour's popularity in the polls recover enough to tempt Callaghan to delay the next election until 1979? There was an economic recovery in 1977–78, but part of the reason lay hundreds of miles offshore and several miles down.

Beneath the waves

A gas field had been discovered in the North Sea in the mid-1960s, with extensive oil deposits following a few years later (Sandbrook, 2013: 514–15). By the late 1970s British production of both was still low but promised to deliver an absolute goldmine by the mid-1980s – as it duly did. Whichever government was in power would surely reap the rewards. This windfall to end all windfalls seemed *the* answer to Britain's prayers.

For Labour, expected to clean up the mess left by Heath, but having presided over continued turmoil in 1974–76, such oil and gas reserves offered a revenue flow that could fill some of the cracks in the British economy, particularly its imbalance of payments and rising unemployment bills (Hann, 1986: 57–63; Andersen, 1993: 88–94; Clapp, 1994: 157–8). It rapidly became addicted to the miracles the North Sea promised (Arnold, 1978: 314):

> … the North and Celtic sea reserves are so valuable as to make all the gold in Fort Knox look like a few savings certificates …
>
> (Benn, 1974: 238)

As well as the expected economic bonanza, British enthusiasm for the North Sea fields came from a hope that the nation could thereby avoid the 'energy crises' – symbolised by the oil price rises and fears that oil reserves would soon 'peak' – that characterised 1970s angst. Energy crises were themselves one manifestation of a generalised fear about ecological degradation.

Labour's Left and Right both wanted greater public control of what was seen as a national resource.[4] But what kind of control? Because much of the British part of the continental shelf had practically been given away on liberal terms, only so much could be renegotiated at the speed which an ailing economy required.[5] The message from all sides of the government was the same: National Recovery, as a 1978 White Paper put it. But what did this entail? A 1974 White Paper had promised that the state would take a 51% stake in the North Sea reserves, which the Left saw as support for nationalisa- tion. For the Right, though, it was more of a bargaining chip designed to secure supplies and obtain the best deal from the only companies capable of extracting oil and gas, but upon which a hungry economy could then feast through taxation (Hann, 1986: 9–18, 72).[6] Nationalisation was too expensive and unnecessary, they thought.

The main spokesman for the Left was Tony Benn who championed industrial reconstruction, public services and debt repayment (Panitch & Leys, 1997: ch. 3). Benn warned against regarding the oil and gas windfall as *the* answer to Britain's problems. He wanted it to reverse the process of deindustrialisation, by investing resources in manufacturing industry (Arnold, 1978: 316–18), and protect Britain's oil against an EEC he disliked. But Benn lost the argument. His proposals – to part nationalise North Sea deposits and funnel tax receipts into an investment fund – were rejected by Callaghan's Cabinet. It was estim- ated that 30 years later, by the 2000s, this fund would have been worth £450 billion (Beckett, 2009: 200–1), yielding anywhere from £24–66 billion per year, depending on the rate of return (Lodge, 2013). Instead, the Cabinet agreed that oil exports could help hold the exchange rate down and so make Britain more competitive and attractive to international investors.

Labour therefore fudged the choice between short-term consumption and long-term investment. It wanted both but there was no solid strategy for marry- ing the needs of the present to those of the future. Nor would it have the chance to develop one in office. The 1979 manifesto mentioned oil only briefly and in vague generalisations.

The Cabinet's position was at least more far-sighted than the Tory inclina- tion to use revenues to effect the liberalisation of the economy (Arnold, 1978: 318–25; for a defence of this approach see Robinson, 1981: 117–22). The Conservative expectation was that oil-funded tax cuts would boost incomes in the short term, thus helping to get the state off the backs of British companies and so clearing a space onto which the entrepreneurial sorcerers of the private sector could sprinkle their magic over the economy. But the 'economic miracle' of the 1980s would prove little more than a conjuring trick for which the oil and gas bonanza helped provide the smoke and mirrors:

> In the years between 1980–81 and 1989–90, the Thatcher governments received a staggering windfall of £166 billion.
>
> (Lodge, 2013)

So far from curing the economic weaknesses the Tories inherited, the bonanza merely enhanced Britain's addiction to short-term returns rather than long- term, strategic investment. North Sea oil and gas stands as one of the biggest wasted opportunities in British history.

And such short-sightedness continues to have consequences other than purely economic ones.

Take Norway (Andersen, 1993: 94–104). Somewhat unexpectedly, Norway pursued a radically statist approach to its North Sea reserves in the 1970s, in part because liberals and conservatives supported active government participation. National patriotism and political consensus thus formed themselves into a distinctive approach, which was left to the post-1971 Labour government to implement. A state oil company, Statoil, was created and small, private oil companies were coordinated into a single new company, Saga. Statoil was given a mandate to reduce foreign companies' influence on Norwegian fields, in part by building expertise and doing an effective job. The first oil crisis confirmed that national self-sufficiency was a worthwhile goal, as was the avoidance of deindustrialisation – the plan being to increase production slowly to avoid increased wealth sucking in exports and undermining local manufacturing.

Norway is today regarded as one of the world's environmental pioneers.[7] This was not necessarily the aim in the early 1970s but it was a happy consequence of a response to circumstances that was geared to long-term investment, which attracted cross-party support and which continued to see the state playing a central role.[8]

Social reforms

But all of this was to come. In the late 1970s the expectation remained that by helping to heal Britain's economic woes the North Sea bonanza would also repair the 'fiscal crisis of the welfare state'.

It was during the events of 1973–76 that the welfare state was perceived by many to be in crisis (Lowe, 2005: 317–21). Designed to fit an economy of full employment, state welfare now experienced increasing demands upon it at a time of shrinking fiscal supply, both of which were due to rising inflation and rising unemployment.

This view is distinct from, yet can sometimes be confused with, a more ideological insistence that the economy had stumbled in large part *because* the welfare state drained revenues and talents away from an embattled private sector (Kus, 2006: 504–6). The public sector was said to be bloated and leaving Britain with 'too few producers' (Bacon & Eltis, 1976). This alarmist scenario served a clear political purpose in which the state was accused of engendering:

- an organisational crisis (too much state bureaucracy, too few markets and commercial providers), and
- a cultural crisis (something-for-nothing entitlements versus discipline, morality and family values).

An important point should be made. The welfare state is as much for the winter as for the summer months by, for instance, stimulating spending and so helping to avoid the onset of a full-blown economic depression. It does this by keeping large parts of the labour force healthier, wealthier and better educated than would otherwise be the case (Iversen & Stephens, 2008). The economy is as dependent on state welfare as the latter is on the former.

Yet the language of 'draining' and 'burdening' sees the relationship simply as one-way. That there were limits on public spending and the de facto abandonment of full employment under the 1974–79 administration does not mean a process was initiated and that it was left to Thatcher to complete. The former did not embrace cuts with the ideological zeal of the latter.[9] Had Labour won the 1979 election a different path for Britain could surely have been taken (but see Judt, 2005: ch. 17).

In short, a crisis and the prevailing response to that crisis are highly politicised constructions. The equation of 1970s with 'welfare state crisis' would unfortunately become established.

But was the 1974–79 government in actual crisis mode? To some extent, there was definitely a sense of the 'party being over', that the upward curve of state welfare had peaked (Hobsbawn, 1994: 408–11).

From 1960–80 public expenditure increased by 103%, two-thirds of which was due to the welfare state; welfare expenditure itself increased by 170% over that period (Judge, 2004: 167–9). It now seemed unlikely that the next 20 years would replicate this record. From 1974–79 public expenditure fell as a percentage of GDP from a 1975 high of 49.3% to 44% in 1978–79, with cuts in 1976–77 being particularly brutal. Within these figures, welfare expenditure over the same period declined from 25.4% to 22.9% (Toynbee & Walker, 2004: 109–10). This, in the context of Callaghan's 1976 speech, suggests that spending had hit a ceiling the country could not afford it to exceed.

But if this was a retrenchment it was so only in terms of a state-society relationship that was completely unlike that of the pre-war years. The rate of growth declined (and the public sector as a whole now grew more slowly than total economic output) but real increases continued nonetheless. For instance, health spending increased by 5% per annum on average, compared to 5.5% under Heath and 4.5% during Wilson's 1960s government (Toynbee & Walker, 2004: 112). Furthermore, whether this slowing down was a crisis or a readjustment depends on *how* the deceleration was managed (Toynbee & Walker, 2004: 110–14). It is thus important to ask whether cuts were implemented indiscriminately or with a view to maintaining long-cherished principles of fairness and justice.

Plateaus

The 1975 Pensions Act introduced a state-earnings-related pension (SERPS) and earnings-related contributions. It had been clear for some time that the basic state pension was inadequate at providing a decent retirement income. SERPS was therefore a mechanism to supplement the basic pension, allow retirement incomes to keep pace with wages and ensure that retirees did not suffer a sudden drop in income. It began operation in 1978.

Labour also introduced a one-parent benefit, followed in 1978 by a Child Benefit, which, unlike the 'family allowances' it replaced, was provided for all children and typically paid to the mother. With some in the labour movement sceptical of this redistribution 'from wallet to purse' reformers had to perform some dainty, diplomatic footwork. Though paid at a modest level it represented a belated fulfilment of the 1945 Family Allowances Act.

Along with the Equal Pay Act (passed in 1970 but not enacted until 1975), the Sex Discrimination Act was also geared to improving gender inequalities, establishing an Equal Opportunities Commission and giving a right of redress to discrimination via employment tribunals.

Unlike social security, housing did not escape the IMF cuts. The 1977 Housing (Homeless Persons) Act provided the first statutory definition of homelessness (Crowson, 2012). This was controversial on the Right, which felt that this was a charter for queue-jumpers and rent-dodgers. Indeed, the Act sought to reassure the public by distinguishing between

> ... those who could not help their situation and were deserving (families and very vulnerable singles) and those who could 'help themselves' (the single, childless couples, and those without serious ill health).
>
> (Crowson, 2012: 446)

The notion that the Act actually encouraged homelessness took hold and 1980s reforms would make great play with the category of the 'intentionally homeless' from whom the state could therefore withdraw support with a clear conscience.

Health spending was already feeling the financial squeeze even pre-IMF (Timmins, 1996: 131–41). Though they were responsible for just 0.5% of the patients the NHS treated every year, the government now embarked on a two-year battle to eliminate pay beds.[10] The issue became entangled with that of renegotiating consultants' contracts and the ensuing storm then drew in junior doctors who, feeling short-changed, joined the consultants in 'working to contract'. The turf upon which this war was conducted was trudged over many months into a quagmire out of which both sides eventually plodded. The number of pay beds was slowly reduced over the next four years.

The dispute had two effects. First, it coincided with (and arguably inspired) the "spectacular growth" in private medical insurance from the mid-1970s to 1990 (King's Fund, 2014: 2). Second, the BMA acquired a reputation for dig-your-heels-in confrontation.

But it was the tremors felt in the field of education that were arguably the greatest signals of future earthquakes (Lowe, 2004). A tripartite partnership between central government, local government and individual schools and colleges had remained more or less intact since the 1940s. This involved a system of checks and balances designed to ensure a reasonable and effective distribution of power. But when in 1977 the government asked LEAs for information about their curriculum policies the answer, to paraphrase, was often 'Curriculum policies? What curriculum policies?' This indication of *non*-partnership did not sit well with two innovations.

First, Callaghan's famous 1976 speech at Ruskin College (Sandbrook, 2013: 684–8). While denying that the education system was in decline ("Black Paper prejudices"), Callaghan called for a new emphasis on raising standards and accountability (Chitty, 2002: 266; 2009: 34–45; also Callaghan, 2006: 410–12):

> I fear that those whose only answer to these problems is to call for more money will be disappointed … the proper way of monitoring the use of resources in order to maintain a proper national standard of performance.[11]

The nation's recent economic difficulties were conspicuous in the PM's call for a new emphasis on skills, qualifications, discipline, productivity and the needs of industry; much of which was couched in the language of working-class needs. Second, though the partnership system predated the introduction of comprehensives, controversy about one easily spilled over into the controversy about the other. Fearful of being seen to neglect the interests of parents and children, Labour – perhaps more in rhetoric than action – cleared a path for much of what followed in the 1980s.

Overall, then, the social policies of 1974–79 hardly amounted to crisis management. Overall spending plateaued, cuts were implemented and modernisation was called for. Yet long-cherished principles of fairness and justice were not being abandoned. Though Britain was experiencing a 'welfare peak' in the 1970s, there were some aspects (e.g. SERPS, Child Benefit, the Sex Discrimination Act) in which Labour was still eager to build additional, innovative structures on top of that plateau.

New ideas?

No, the real crisis on the Left at this time was more one of intellectual confidence. History no longer seemed to be flowing in its direction. Could there be a realistic alternative to the free market economics to which the Conservatives were speeding? And was the new environmentalism anywhere in the mix?

By the mid-1970s Tony Crosland was tired (Jeffreys, 2000: 171–86). As minister and shadow minister for the past decade Crosland no longer had time for the panoramic analysis that characterised *The Future of Socialism* 20 years earlier. His 1974 book *Socialism Now* was more of a manifesto, which argued for greater clarity and purpose in government. This was very much an account concerned with party management, one which took the existing labour movement for granted and contained little recognition of the need to build new alliances and establish dialogues with other progressive movements.

Four chapters are dedicated to 'the environment' but the tone is one where, properly managed, the benefits of growth (including reduced poverty) will exceed and so eventually cure the problems increasingly associated with it (increased population and pollution).[12] Crosland's ire is directed at the apocalyptic school of environmentalism, ignoring those like Barry Commoner who were striving for a green socialism that had its feet more firmly on the ground.

Crosland certainly deserves praise for coming closer than anyone else on the British Left at that time to outlining a 'green social democracy'.[13] The following observation has yet to be properly incorporated into British policymaking 40 years later:

> It is the less well-off who work and live in the worst environment; the rich can purchase a good environment for themselves.
>
> (Crosland, 1974: 155)

But by building so much around a 'growth versus no-growth' contrast, he falls lazily back onto a business-almost-as-usual approach. Most of those four chapters are actually about the social rather than the natural environment, and so, as with the DoE he ran from 1974–76, an opportunity for a comprehensive, cross-sectoral convergence is missed.

Which is not to claim that the Labour government made no progress (Rydin, 2003: 36–42). Several Acts dealt with water pollution, air pollution and waste disposal. Ministers could not have been unaware that membership of conservation groups multiplied greatly in the 1970s (McCormick, 1995: 163). And it was becoming clear that UK policy would have to take the European-level environmental policy increasingly into account.

However, Labour also gave new impetus to roadbuilding; the new towns programme was wound up; and though the issue of land value and betterment returned to the political agenda, the government's two Acts were failures, channelling profits to developers rather than communities due to cumbersome procedures and substantial exceptions (Cullingworth *et al.*, 2015: 31–2). An attempt to socialise the betterment of land had failed yet again and has now lain dormant within mainstream British politics for four decades.

What of those further to the Left (Panitch & Leys, 1997: ch. 4; Callaghan, 2000: 56–62; Plant, 2004b: 30–3; Wickham-Jones, 2004: 36–40)?

Largely forgotten now, Stuart Holland's *The Socialist Challenge* was a key point of reference in its day (Holland, 2004a: 178–80). Capitalism, said Holland, was increasingly dominated by private monopolies. The old macro/micro distinction in which the state inhabited the commanding heights, which corporations were too small to occupy, was being superseded by a meso-economy in which the biggest companies and super-firms dominate whole sectors of production (Holland, 1975: 48–58). Keynesian control of aggregate demand was no longer sufficient; for socialism to survive something more direct was required: public ownership, planning and workers' democracy. However, Holland (1975: ch. 14) has even less to say than Crosland about capitalism's ecological implications.

Holland's brand of socialism was given its most public expression by Tony Benn – though they disagreed vehemently about Europe (Holland, 2004b:

297–9). The British economy, Benn warned, was becoming a 'branch economy' of multinationals, facilitated by the financial power of 'The City' (Benn *et al.*, 1974: 4). Concerned to revitalise manufacturing industry, Benn's recommended Alternative Economic Strategy included:

- a doubling of investment in manufacturing (funded by taxation and through pension and insurance funds);
- state-centred planning, plus corporatism and financial support for firms;
- a return to full employment and resistance against the shift to low paid service jobs.

Like Crosland, he dismisses those 'eco-survivalists' who see only disasters in the making; technology can be a force for good, he declares. He also proposes that 'zero growth' would be a regressive option, inimical to the needs of the working-class as revealed during the economy's recent brush with economic freefall during the oil crisis (Benn, 1974: 236).

However, Benn sketches a quality-of-life agenda, which suggested an awareness of at least some aspects of environmental politics. First, attention to social consequences must be integrated into decision-making processes, he says, which implies input by a wider range of participants than shareholders and management boards (Benn, 1974: 52–61). Second, for reasons of economic and national self-interest Benn calls for an 'integrated fuel policy' that he regards oil companies, market forces and the EEC as incapable of delivering. Integration meant a commitment to coal and nuclear energy that most greens rejected. However, Benn (1974: 238–40) also supported energy conservation – building insulation, district heating, public transport, railway electrification – which chimed, and continues to chime, with environmentalist demands.

Crosland and Benn thus recognised important elements of the new environmentalism and discerned their connections to key aspects of socialism. Equally, they clearly think the latter provides almost all of the intellectual resources that are needed, with a continued emphasis on growth and heavy industry.[14] Working-class interests are to be protected by being funnelled through the workplace, and upwards towards national and international political arenas, via trade unions and Leftist parliamentary parties (Benn, 1974: 186). The green movement is given lip-service but not much else. The language of equality, solidarity, class and labour was not yet ready for a politics that stresses hybridity, cross-movement alliances, diversity and intersectionality.[15]

Some on the Left, then, were groping towards a new politics but this was far from being a thoroughgoing ecosocialism or socialist environmentalism (cf. Thompson, 1976). The time was not propitious and was rapidly running out anyway. Faced with economic crises and a resurgent Right there was no real opportunity to formulate a new political economy. And though high-profile issues around pollution, resource use, overpopulation and general ecological degradation had given environmentalism a public profile, its political impact was still marginal and so represented no fundamental challenge to the dominance of established parties and priorities.

Dirty old town

This marginalisation manifested itself not just at the level of principles and ideas but in government action too. For this was the period when Britain earned its label as the 'dirty man of Europe' due to its general refusal to accept European policies relating to air pollution and acid rain[16] (McCormick, 1989: ch. 6; Rose, 1991; Sheail, 2002: 251–5).

The UK had proved that it could clean up a mess after the fact on a local scale, with its response to the smog of 1952. But by the 1970s this '*ex post* localism' no longer looked adequate. Of increasing importance were 'transboundary issues',[17] which a political culture chuckling at TV's *Dad's Army* would struggle to accommodate. The 1972 Stockholm conference had declared the need for nations to ensure that activities within their jurisdiction of control do not cause damage to the environment of other states or to the global commons (Principle 21). But signing up to that and doing anything real about it were two separate actions. And in the case of Britain's ailing economy, of course, anything that smacked of raising costs and undermining taxable revenue would always be on the back foot.

The tragic irony was that an *ex post* localism created the harms that made a preventative, globally-oriented alternative so necessary.

In the wake of the Clean Air Act, UK smokestacks and industrial chimneys had been built ever higher to allow pollutants to disperse. This reduced local pollution but meant that areas farther away were more adversely affected. In effect, the 1956 Act internationalised air pollution in the form of acid rain (Thorsheim, 2006: 200). For those living downwind of the UK (and West Germany) this was clearly a social and ecological problem. Between 1956 and 1965 the acidity of the rain in parts of Sweden doubled, affecting forest growth and crop production and leading to decreased fish populations (McCormick, 1989: 73). The cost was estimated at 87 million Kroner per year. Swedish complaints thus led to Stockholm and to Principle 21.

For a long time the UK was recalcitrant.[18] For Wynne and Simmons (2001: 94–9; cf. McCormick, 1989: 107–12) the explanation for this resides ultimately in an institutional culture which has always been paradoxical. The UK's unwritten constitution, centralisation and dominance by the executive, means that policymakers can be slow to act and adapt *because they so often lack accountability*. Yet the more the doors are shut the more policymakers have sought to reassure those on the other side of them. Consensus and legitimacy is sought from a public to whom the corridors of power are closed. Secrecy thus enjoins caution and conservatism; discretion and flexibility accompany paternalism; commitment to pragmatism and empiricism leads to self-satisfied assumptions that the way things are already done must be the best way to do them.

This is reflected in the connections between public policy and science, according to Wynne and Simmons. The relationship in the 1970s resembled a club: intimate, informal but also exclusive. The laser-like focus of UK science meant that independent and dissenting voices were habitually ignored. The very emphasis the new environmental groups gave to the interdependencies of science and society (and therefore politics), often calling for radical changes, made it easier to depict them as 'anti-science'. Non-establishment views were casually depicted as maverick ones, from which a higher burden of proof concerning environmental harms could then be demanded. The precautionary principle – which is about weighing probabilities – seemed less rigorous to policymakers than a language of statistical absolutes. (A bias which industrial polluters clearly had an interest in supporting too.) All of which militates against a preventative approach.

In terms of acid rain, then, such institutional cultures joined with national economic self-interest to deafen British opinion against Scandinavian complaints until well into the 1980s (Wynne & Simmons, 2001: 97–9). On the Left, deafness may have also derived from a wish to defend a state-owned monopoly, the Central Electricity Generating Board (CEGB), in its commitments to coal and nuclear power. Following Stockholm, both the CEGB and DoE increased research funding into acid rain and its possible international effects. (And a 1977 OECD report confirmed Norwegian and Swedish allegations re acidification.) But their focus on SO_2 emissions led to other relevant pollutants being ignored, as were EEC attempts to introduce emission-control standards. Such resistance was a strategic delay. The UK was placing long-term faith in nuclear energy, i.e. that once nuclear power became more established, many of these air pollution and acid rain problems would resolve themselves.

So although the UK would sign the 1979 Convention on Long-Range Transboundary Air Pollution, two caveats are needed. First, it (along with West Germany) led the charge against any legally binding controls, even those that would merely halt increases in SO_2 emissions. Second, things only developed in this respect because, compared to energy and transport, air pollution was seen as the least politically charged issue on the pan-European stage (McCormick, 1989: 75–9). The Convention only committed nations in general terms to limit air pollution through the 'best available technology' and whatever was 'economically feasible'. In short, this was the kind of rhetoric that can permit a great deal of latitude.

Though toothless – until the mid-1980s anyway – the Convention was at least the first environmental agreement to which all parts of Europe were signatories, along with North America. With environmental issues rising up the political agenda the convention's relative success in reducing emissions of SO_2 and other pollutants could be held up as something of an inspiration once other issues came along: ozone layer depletion and climate change (see Chapter 8).

The end

By the end of the decade, the Conservative administration of 1970–74 and the Labour administration of 1974–79 felt like one long government. The consensus, which had previously been trumpeted as a virtue, was increasingly looking like a way of avoiding the strong medicine the country needed to treat its ailments (Callaghan, 2000: ch. 2). The radical Right and the radical Left both agreed on that much. The economic and social institutions constructed in 1945 were more or less intact but seemed to offer less resilience and fewer certainties than previously. The welfare state had weathered the economic storm, though it had been shaken.

For those wanting to build upon that legacy, rather than dismantle it, it was not difficult to find new energies. Feminism was continuing to grow (Judt, 2005: 487–90) and the peace and anti-nuclear movements would revive by the early 1980s. A distinct green movement had also emerged, with aspects of its message (primarily those concerned with pollution) beginning to exert influence on governments throughout the 1970s (Callaghan, 2000: 84–96; Judt, 2005: 490–4). The Left was slowly, if not systematically, becoming receptive to such ideas.

Yet the momentum the free market Right had been building for years was about to accelerate.

Key questions

What relationships between the environmental and social policy agendas have emerged? To what extent have social policies and the politics of welfare reform deliberately informed and been informed by the principles and values of environmental ethics and politics?

The Clean Air Act had been the most obvious piece of ecosocial legislation to date. Now, by the mid-1970s, it was clear that the Act had merely transformed pollution (creating acid rain), which, as well as falling on Britain, was exported to other nations downwind. Any confidence that the pollution from smokestacks would simply 'dilute and disperse', absorbed into the vastness of Earth's troposphere, was revealed as wishful. For all of its progressiveness, the Act had embodied a homespun old saying: out of sight, out of mind.

The response of the Labour government was to hunker down. Faith was being placed in nuclear energy as a means of reducing pollutants, though how this could be squared with the expectation of Britain soon becoming a major oil exporter was not a puzzle at the forefront of government thinking. Oil was going to solve a lot of the country's economic difficulties: unemployment, inflation, industrial unrest, exports and the fiscal crisis of the welfare state. Other matters would have to wait.

This is not to pretend that Labour was dismissive of the environmental case. As its 1979 manifesto said:

> We have initiated and will continue a major programme of alternative
> energy, energy saving, through insulation grants, advice to industry, the
> 'Save-It' campaign, and an energy-saving approach to transport.[19]

Yet the course upon which Heath's administration set the DoE (concerned
largely with local government and inner city problems) had remained
unchanged – indeed, responsibility for transport was taken away from it in 1976.
When intellectual heavyweights like Crosland were searching for new ideas,
which would resurrect the socialist momentum of 1945, they weren't peering
towards environmental science.

After six chapters we can now map environmental problems across four
categories.

First, the London smog had been an example of a *temporary, domestic*
problem: potentially devastating but relatively small in scale and brief in duration. The solution – the Clean Air Act – was an example of *ex post* localism, i.e.
something that is reparative and limited in geographical scale rather than being
forward-thinking and concerned with long-range, international consequences.
Note that this is not to condemn policymakers in 1956, though the foot-
dragging instincts of governments in the 1970s and 1980s should not be
excused.

Second, the 1953 flood had been a *shared, multi-national* problem, i.e. a disaster large enough to hit several countries simultaneously. Oil slicks, like *Torrey
Canyon*, might fall under either of these two categories.

Third, acid rain was proving to be a *unidirectional, transboundary* problem,
with Scandinavia bearing the brunt of emissions from Britain and West
Germany. Whereas a 'multi-national' problem takes existing national boundaries as given, the 'transboundary' denotes a reconfiguration of social space
where globalising risks start to blur borders and frontiers, such that negotiations
over national responsibilities and accountabilities become ever more fraught
and difficult.

The excessive consumption and consequent depletion of natural resources
might also fit under this heading. For who else than what was still called the
'third world' was going to bear the consequences of the affluent west's habits
and appetites? That many in the west inverted the problem into one of overpopulation emanating from underdeveloped nations was a convenient way of
inverting responsibility for resource depletion and ecological degradation.

Finally, before long it would become clear that some dilemmas constituted
multidirectional, transboundary problems, i.e. problems created everywhere,
experienced everywhere and for which only truly global responses could therefore be appropriate. We will encounter two examples in Chapter 8.

The strategy of the UK government had a fighting-the-last-war quality to it,
therefore. The 1956 Act had addressed a 'temporary domestic' problem by shifting it to the 'unidirectional transboundary' category. The attempt to cure the
former had helped create the latter. A much more creative, forward-thinking
and preventative approach was going to be necessary, then, especially with the

advent of 'multinational, transboundary' issues. Yet nothing of the sort was yet visible in environmental policy, let alone in what we are calling the ecosocial. The passage from Wilson's 1969 speech, quoted in Chapter 4, never set the tone for anything real, after all.

Notes

1 Dennis Healey loved Wilson's view that Benn 'immatures with age'.
2 Wilson had resigned and been replaced by Callaghan in April.
3 In his memoirs Callaghan claims his point about not raising expenditure or reducing taxes was referring only to the circumstances of 1976; however, the wording is so highly generalised no wonder the Conservatives treated it as a kick against social democracy – something Callaghan (2006: 425–7) complains about. Callaghan (2006: 477) represents the party as tiptoeing around the edges of monetarism. Panitch and Leys (1997: 107, 111, passim) propose that Labour inaugurated monetarism without necessarily embracing it as a credo (cf. (Sandbrook, 2013: 503–4, 690–1).
4 In Scotland, North Sea deposits were a shot in the arm for the Scottish National Party, then much more Right wing than they would later become.
5 During the oil crisis Heath informed the chairmen of BP and Shell that he expected Britain to receive preferential treatment; only to be told that the companies' contracts made such treatment impossible (Andersen, 1993: 90). There was no guarantee that British oil could be available for British consumers during a crisis!
6 Which is what occurred, since the UK was much more sheltered from the second oil crisis of 1979 then it had been during the first.
7 Controversially in Norway's case. Norway's environmental credentials coexist with it being one of the world's biggest oil and gas exporters. Thus, do the resulting fossil fuel emissions belong to Norway or to the nations that imported its oil? Investing North Sea returns in a sovereign wealth fund – which in 2013 was contributing $1 billion per week to the government and was expected to be worth $1 trillion in total by 2020 – has given Norway the means to finance social and ecological programmes. However, in 2014 a decision was made not to disinvest in fossil fuels, much to the anger of environmentalists.
8 Britain's closest equivalent to Statoil, the British National Oil Corporation (BNOC), was privatised in 1982 (Hann, 1986: 98–100). For BNOC's critics because the UK, unlike Norway, already had expertise in the form of BP and Shell it did not "have the same need to 'break into' the industry" (MacKay & MacKay, 1975: 42). But of course those like Benn argued that there was such a need, one relating to national sovereignty and the wider economy.
9 Though welfare spending did not shrink by anything like the amount the New Right spent much of the period anticipating. In 1978–79, social expenditure was 23% of GDP. In 1989–90 it was just under 22% and was about to rise steeply under John Major.
10 Bevan's concession to allow private, fee-paying patients to be treated in NHS hospitals.
11 www.educationengland.org.uk/documents/speeches/1976ruskin.html [accessed 8 December 2014]
12 One of Crosland's closest advisors was long-time scourge of the green movement, Wilfred Beckerman (Fitzpatrick, 2003: 151–2).
13 And in calling for the nationalisation of development land Crosland was articulating a long-standing socialist ideal (see Chapter 1) at which many greens would now jump.
14 It was Benn, more than anyone else, who oversaw the ill-fated Concorde airplane.

15 Benn (1974: 185–95) at least acknowledges the challenges posed by the youth and women's movements, seeing them as a "terrific source of ideas and strength" for democratic socialism. Meanwhile, Crosland saw permissiveness not as liberation but as "bourgeois elitism" (Morgan, 2011: 236–7).
16 This results when sulphur dioxide (SO_2) and nitrogen oxides from factories and power stations react with water droplets to produce sulphuric and nitrous oxides.
17 See the end of the chapter for a discussion of these terms.
18 Though Britain was also poisoning itself. Ninety per cent of the acid rain falling on Britain originated in Britain.
19 In its manifesto the party also signalled a continued interest in the issue of land speculation and value in relation to public ownership. See www.labour-party.org.uk/manifestos/1979/1979-labour-manifesto.shtml [accessed 17 December 2014]

7   The soul of a marketplace
1979–87

To save the country they believed they would have to wage war against much of it. According to the New Right, for 35 years the Tory Party had built bridges for its enemies and then retreated as those enemies used them to advance still further. 'Consensus' had really been one long surrender after another (Green, 2002: 216–18). The New Right therefore regarded their attacks as merely as overdue *counter*attacks (Green, 2002: 235–9; Dorey, 2011: 126–37). The unions had declared war. Local councils had been building their mini-socialist empires. Hooligans had lost respect for authority. And behind it all was the weak welfare parent, indulging the horrid behaviour of its brawling infants. No more. The harmony that Thatcher invoked when misquoting St. Francis of Assisi was to come by defeating your enemies, not by buying them off as Heath had done. In setting out to refight the battles of the 1970s Thatcherism would thus be a curious, inverted reflection of the fears and hatreds it projected out onto the world.

Yet relatively little of what came to be called Thatcherism was present in the 1979 manifesto, with its familiar emphasis on low inflation, union reform and some tweaking of state-owned industries (Heffernan, 2000: 29–64). What *was* new was the lack of respect for what had come before (Clarke, 1998). Thatcher was anti-socialist, naturally. But what really gave some a tremble of excitement was her stance as an anti-conservative Conservative. She was reaching back to the free market liberalism that had dominated thinking in the nineteenth century. This misdirected many and so gave her time to develop a game plan that opponents struggled at first to understand (Bosanquet, 1983). Tactical withdrawals and bold, opportunistic charges were part of the same campaign. Thatcher was an ideologue who knew when and when not to pick a fight.

Yet although Thatcher was canny she was also lucky with her enemies.

There would, first of all, be the exhaustion of her opponents' ideas, energies and focus. In the late 1970s there was no equivalent to Macmillan's *The Middle Way*. One-nation conservatism was fading in inspiration and influence and too many 'Tory wets' underestimated their new leader (Young, 1990: 201–2; Campbell, 2003: 105–6, 118). Fifteen years after publishing *Inside Right* – a mauling of Thatcher's economic instincts – Ian Gilmour's (1992) *Dancing with Dogma* would be an impassioned, sober warning of what had happened to the country during the interim. But neither publication heralded a counter-movement.

What about the Left? If an election had been called and won in 1978 perhaps some version of Callaghanism or Healeyism could have continued with business as normal (Marwick, 2003: 440–1). Yet the social contract had been insecure, incomes policies had not produced inflation low or stable enough for many, and there was growing public impatience with the unions. Would a 1980s Labour government have developed an alternative? A diluted form of monetarism and a new attempt at union reform, perhaps? Yet who – really – was enthused by that?

Not the Labour Party itself, if the newest civil war breaking out within it was any indication. Benn had his Alternative Economic Strategy, something which horrified the Right (Marquand, 1988). With the party apparently turning against the European Common Market, those such as Roy Jenkins, David Owen and Shirley Williams began to look elsewhere. Warfare in 1980–82 thus erupted on a scale that made the Bevan/Gaitskill arguments of 30 years earlier look like a playground spat and the Social Democratic Party (SDP) was duly formed. Though some Tories worried about the SDP capturing a centre-ground that Thatcher disdained, the severest wounds were inflicted on Labour – though Thatcher herself denied they were fatal ones (Young, 1990: 294–5; Campbell, 2003: 113).

There was also the Falklands Islands' conflict and the jingoism it energised. That Argentina's invasion was practically greenlighted by a Tory decision to weaken Britain's naval forces in the South Atlantic didn't matter (McSmith, 2011: 112–14). Not when you could see off the ships, wave a tearful goodbye to 'our boys' and feel good about your country again.

And then, finally, there was the miners' strike.

A new philosophy

The new government's economic philosophy claimed the status of scientific truths (Hutton, 1995: 58–72). Monetarists insisted that the volume of money was causally related to inflation, where prices rise the more the supply of money exceeds output: $MV \equiv PT$. Trying to increase output by borrowing for investment was anathema to monetarists (Grieve Smith, 1997: 105–9). Reducing the money supply therefore meant either raising taxes or reducing expenditure. Taxation was already too high, the Right contended, because it reduced incentives. All that was left was to cut government spending.

To its critics this was all about politics, not economics (Gilmour, 1992: 12–29, 50–5); a distribution of resources and wealth that would hurt the weakest.

No, the New Right replied, this would be the restoration of sound finance and the rescuing of the economy *from* politics – the special interests that had been placing upward pressures on public spending for decades. Reconfiguring the economy would be painful but everyone would gain eventually. To this end, the Right offered a set of axioms (Kymlicka, 2002: ch. 4; also Bosanquet, 1983):

- Individuals act rationally in their own self-interest.
- Liberty equals negative liberty, i.e. freedom from interference. The poorest are therefore as free as the rich.
- Property equals private property.
- Unregulated markets are self-correcting.
- Competition and incentives are the spur to innovation and excellence. The desire to prosper has driven social evolution (greed is good).
- Whereas markets facilitate independence, the state encourages dependency.
- The state is habitually inefficient, incompetent, nannying and 'overloaded'.
- The public sector 'crowds out' the wealth-creating, entrepreneurial private sector (there are 'too few producers'). The private sector should always be the preferred provider.
- Publicly-provided goods should be limited to those few things individuals cannot provide for themselves, e.g. a police force, a justice system, armies.

So when Thatcherites waged war against you it was for your own benefit. The best medicines are the foulest tasting. In the messianic tone Thatcher sometimes adopted: economics was only the method, the object was to change the nation's soul (Campbell, 2003: 498).

All of this, in short, sounded paradoxical. It was not enough to roll the state back. Markets had to be 'rolled forward' – forcibly if necessary – into the space left by government. The right kind of paternalism would thereby liberate people from the wrong kind of paternalism. The state had to do less so that its core functions could be performed with *greater* force and impact. Free markets require smaller but stronger states. To deregulate markets you had to reregulate people, institutions and social relations by changing expectations, motivations and incentives. Communists had been correct about one thing: people had to be forced to be free.

The objections of critics had already been absorbed into the Thatcherite view of the world, therefore. One central criticism (e.g. Scruton, 2006: xiii–ix; Sandel, 2012) is that unrestrained self-interest and unregulated markets are as destructive of those things that conservatives typically love (e.g. civic neighbourhoods, customs, traditional institutions) as they are of those things they often dislike (e.g. unions, benefit claimants, tax-funded public services). By switching the capitalist tap full on the Conservative Party risked washing the non-market aspects of life away too.

But for the New Right there was no contradiction, no trade-off between market freedoms and social order. The former had to be enforced as much as the latter; freedoms were always 'ordered freedoms'. The New Right were pick-and-mix libertarians, at best. So, to the above axioms could be added a series of deeply conservative principles:

- Marriage, traditional families and strong communities are the bedrock of a stable, decent society.

• Patriotism, respect for tradition, authority and the rule of law provide the moral orientation and civic values that people require.

Thatcher's reinterpretation – indeed distortion (Evans, 1997: 121–4) – of Victorian values as a moralistic iron rod was not just an emotional affectation. It was logic.

Criticisms therefore ricocheted off the government like hailstones pinging off a rock. Aided by a Right-dominated press and a small army of think tanks, the Tories could now get away with things that would have sunk Heath, Wilson or Callaghan.

Refashioning state and economy

The 'second oil shock' of 1979, plus some reckless government decisions, would help send inflation back up to 21% and it would not come down to below 10% until well into 1982 (Britton, 1993: 50–1). But by then a Thatcherite discourse – the unions are too powerful, the socialists bankrupted Britain – had taken hold. Labour's bad luck in 1974–76 now looked like the culmination of something old; Conservative travails in 1979–82 could be sold as a necessary period of pain before national healing began (Morgan, 2001: 445–8). No countervailing narrative could gain traction.

The fact that monetarists found it difficult even to define the money supply could be safely ignored. In fact, monetarism would be all but abandoned after 1985 (Campbell, 2003: 226–8), much to the chagrin of its supporters (Congdon, 1989).[1] Yet the British public either didn't notice or didn't care that much. What mattered was the big picture and its three principal elements (Grieve Smith, 1997: 92–100; Gilmour & Garnett, 1997: 306–16).

First, tax rates were lowered and allowances and thresholds raised (Evans, 1997: 19; Dorey, 2011: 147–9). The basic rate was cut from 33% to 30% (eventually falling to 25%) and the highest rate from 83% to 60% (eventually falling to 40%). Partly to offset this Value Added Tax (VAT) was increased from 8% to 15%.[2] Ironically, this meant that,

> … the overall tax burden was almost 4% higher in the penultimate year of Thatcher's premiership than it had been when she entered 10 Downing Street in 1979.
>
> (Dorey, 2011: 162)

Second, though it was not even mentioned in the 1979 manifesto 'privatisation' became definitive of the Thatcherite project (Young, 1990: 537; Gilmour, 1992: 95–104; Evans, 1997: 34–7; Campbell, 2003: 236–43).[3] Soon it had the force of a religious conversion, one designed to create 'popular capitalism' (Campbell, 2003: 244–5; McSmith, 2011: 203). Capitalism need no longer be viewed as it had been in the past: the preserve of boring pinstripe-types, wearing their bowler hats on the 7.37am from Horsham or wherever. The new capitalism meant taking control. A little flutter on the stockmarket here, a little ducking and diving there. It was Young Turks in red braces who knew how to decipher all those numbers on all those computer screens and of whom even Thatcher – though a puritan about money personally – seemed enamoured (Young, 1990: 536; Campbell, 2003: 248–9). Capitalism was fun! Why not buy a few shares? It was your money, wasn't it? The floodgates of privatisation duly opened: British Leyland (1981–87), British Telecom (1984), British Gas (1986), British Airways (1987), the electricity industry (1989–90), the water industry (1989).

The third element was industrial relations. Thatcher loathed trade unions, interpreting any restriction on business as socialism (Beynon, 2014: 225–6). That monetarism, strictly speaking, did not attribute inflation to wage claims per se was a technicality that need not be advertised.[4] Didn't everyone know that trade unions had helped make Britain ungovernable in the 1970s? Besides, if the economy was to be deregulated those who disrupted market forces with their restrictive practices had to be controlled (Letwin, 1993: 146–9; Crafts, 2013: 268–9).

Unemployment was helping to reduce union membership, but more was needed. The 'closed shop' was eroded and then abolished, collective bargaining was gradually dismantled, wages councils would be scrapped (in 1993), pre-strike ballots were required, secondary picketing was restricted and unions made financially liable for illegal stoppages (Dorey, 2011: 151–7).

But this was about more than industrial relations. It was an attempt to remould the entire British economy as an 'entrepreneurial culture' (Leys, 1985: 24–5). The days of heavy, smokestack industries were over, it was thought (Healey, 1993: 254–5). Manufacturing processes were changing, new technologies were appearing and competition now meant being responsive, flexible and efficient in international markets that – because of fax machines and those new cordless phones – were more interconnected than ever before. If you could not deliver what your consumers wanted when they wanted it you could find yourself losing contracts, profits and jobs in a heartbeat. Rigid, producer-dominated practices were becoming a thing of the past and the sooner workers changed their ways the better. The manufacturing sector would not only have to reduce its scope it would have to become 'lighter'. The era of the post-industrial, service economy had arrived.

In 1970 manufacturing industry accounted for about 30% of the total economy compared to 14% in 1997. In 1980–82 there was a particularly severe contraction in British manufacturing (Evans, 1997: 32–3). In 1990 the percentage of world trade of manufactures held by British companies was just one-third of its share in 1950. There were 8.5m manufacturing jobs in 1966, 5.6m in 1982, 4.3m in 1992 and 2.6m by 2014 (or just 7.8% of the workforce) (Rhodes, 2014). Services, meanwhile, have grown in importance from 54% of GDP in 1960 to 62% in 1990 and 80% by 2013 (accounting for 81% of jobs). Other countries were following a similar pattern (Nickell *et al.*, 2008).

This was partly due to economic evolution, then (Turner, 1995a: 9–17, 1995b; Nickell *et al.*, 2008: 1155; ONS, 2013). As automation develops so machines can take over much of the work of labourers – and perform it more efficiently. But it was also about politics (Gilmour, 1992: 55–9). From the New Right's point of view, British deindustrialisation had been underway for decades already, yet due to market rigidities and an overgrown public sector the country had failed to adapt and take advantage of the new opportunities. The real choice lay between a deindustrialisation that harmed international competiveness (hitting jobs and the balance of payments) and one that restored it. The latter option meant reducing wage costs, attacking what the Right saw as inflexible working practices and encouraging the growth of business and financial services.

And in pursuit of this goal, they suspected, a scalp was needed. Kill the biggest beast and the rest of the tribe will fall into line. And who was bigger than the beast that had defeated the Tories in 1972 and 1974?

On strike

A new skirmish was coming and both sides knew it. The coal industry had been contracting since the war and only the first oil crisis had given a brief respite. But the North Sea fields were now flowing and the government prepared to expand the nuclear industry (Rose, 1990: 315–19). Energy Secretary, Nigel Lawson, claimed that it was not for government to,

> ... plan the future shape of energy production and consumption.... Our task rather is to set a framework which will ensure that the market operates in the energy sector with a minimum of distortions.
>
> (Lawson, 1989: 23; also Helm, 2004: 58–63)

Planning implied a 'dirigiste mentality', often accompanying "alarmist projections of energy gaps as fossil fuels become exhausted" (Lawson, 1992: 163–4). The market was the best tool for allocating supplies.

And who stood in the way of competitive energy markets? Thatcher had backed away from confrontation with the National Union of Mineworkers (NUM) in 1981 when she anticipated that the government would lose (Helm, 2004: 53–4). The miners counted that as another victory: 3–0. But Thatcher believed the NUM had misunderstood the rules (Young, 1990: 366; Campbell, 2003: 101–3; Beynon, 2014: 217). She didn't have to score more goals. She had to change the game itself.

Helm (2004: 81–2) records the main causes of the 1984–85 strike as: too many uneconomic pits, i.e. the supply of coal outstripping demand; coal imports becoming cheaper; there being more energy alternatives to coal than before. But personalities also mattered. In the NUM – and in its leader, Arthur Scargill – Thatcher could combine her loathing of unions with her dislike of the coal industry (Campbell, 2003: 359). Both symbolised a socialism that she yearned to vanquish (Parker, 2000: 203–5). For his part, Scargill agreed that there was no room for negotiations and compromises. In many respects, Thatcher and Scargill were mirror images of one another. Neither believed in managing the contraction of the industry responsibly. Neither believed in a middle-ground and so, acting like First World War 'chateau generals', they proceeded to obliterate that middle-ground and all who depended upon it (Young, 1990: 375).[5]

The defeated miners returned to work with their heads held high but, a shell of its former self, the industry was privatised in 1994. By 2013 it was unrecognisable. There would be four deep mines compared to 219 in 1980 and less than 6000 miners compared to over 700,000 in the 1940s. Less than half of the jobs lost in coalfield districts had been replaced and 65% of the coal Britain burned came from Columbia, Russia and the USA (Beynon, 2014: 222, 225).

Though the Trades Union Congress had urged compromise the defeat of the NUM would rebound on it too. Added to mass unemployment and deindustrialisation, the strike broke the spine of the labour movement. Membership stood at 13.2 million in 1979 and declined by 5.5 million in the next two decades (Metcalf, 2005: 3). The movement would continue to march but with less confidence in its stride. The Labour Party would soon start to keep unions at greater arms-length than before – politically if not financially. Hopes would soon be placed in creating a 'social Europe', in re-socialising markets through EU law and political union with a Europe that offered other, less destructive forms of capitalism than Thatcher.

Post-industrial lightness?

That social Europe would come to regard itself as a *green* Europe, too, and in this respect the UK saw itself as a leader (see Chapters 9 and 11, especially). Conservatives would later cite the UK's sometimes-favourable record on climate change as a beneficial (if unintended) consequence of its shift away from manufacturing in general and coal in particular (Gummer & Moreland, 2000: 22–6; see Rose, 1990: 134–5; also Helm, 2004: 347–8). After all, air pollution in the North – mining areas especially – had not decreased by the levels it had in London and the South, in part because miners received 'concessionary coal' as a wage supplement and had been reluctant to shift to smokeless fuel (Thorsheim, 2006: 186–9).

In fact, there is no firm evidence that a service economy is necessarily greener than one based on heavy industry (Cleveland & Ruth, 1999; BSR, 2013). Carbon emissions from manufacturing were already falling in the two decades to 1990 due to higher fuel prices, technological innovations and energy efficiency programmes (Unander *et al.*, 1999).

In terms of coal the picture is also unclear. Coal is the dirtiest of the fossil fuels, though its defenders would point to research conducted into 'clean coal' by the Coal Research Establishment (Beckett & Hencke, 2009: 239; Durucan *et al.*, 2010: 12).[6] Whatever the merits of clean coal, critics observe that this fragmentation of the industry and of the energy sector more generally makes concerted effort to address climate change that much more difficult (Drake, 2009).[7]

It is worth quoting what Pearson and Watson (2012: 33) say about the 1979–97 period:

> ... the government and industry regulators' tight focus on economic efficiency as the destination and private ownership and competition as the means of getting there, did not properly embrace key features of the energy system. These features included unpriced 'externalities' such as greenhouse gas emissions. They also included the provision of 'public goods' such as investments in energy system security and energy research, which are underprovided by the market because the private actor often cannot 'capture' and be rewarded for benefits that accrue to wider society. These issues were not fully addressed in the privatisation process, partly from misplaced optimism about the market's ability to adjust automatically, in some cases from scepticism about their importance, and in others from the view that, even if they were serious, government and bureaucratic failure would make the cure worse than the disease.

Social reforms

Such claims and counter-claims were for the future. So far as this rapid and often sadistic deindustrialisation went, it was the employment and social policy ramifications that were more immediate (Burrows & Loader, 1994).

In addition to persistently high unemployment, the new labour market would be characterised by greater polarisation, casualisation, insecurity, subcontracting, flexibility and marginalisation than its Keynesian-era predecessor (Hall, 2007; Lansley & Mack, 2015: 99–110). For many, it meant low wages, poor working conditions, awful prospects, zero-hours 'jobs', involuntary self-employment and 'permatemping'.

Too often, the reduced costs attributed by some to new, competitive efficiencies have actually been due to reduced wages and working conditions. Deindustrialisation accompanied continued under-investment as investors, often with little commitment to that in which they were investing, sought greater short-term returns (Hutton, 1995: 154–68). If you can make easy money by cutting jobs and wages, in an under-unionised, insecure economy, why bother innovating or training your workforce? British productivity suffered as a result (Clark, 2014: 73–5, 89–90). The welfare state then has to supplement those low wages, while being simultaneously blamed for over-spending.

It was the industrial north that would experience greater unemployment and underemployment than a London-dominated south, closer to Europe and well placed to expand its financial sector (Hudson, 2013). Parts of the north would survive only because of the welfare state and, as the mantra of 'public = bad, private = better' took hold, the north could then be blamed for its decline rather than the politically engineered deindustrialisation which had been foisted upon it. The 'north-south divide' became part of the political vocabulary.

This new labour market was also more feminised (Turner, 1995a: 10). Women had been re-entering employment for several decades anyway (Smith Wilson, 2005: 251–2) but now, in the wake of deindustrialisation and the polarisation of employment in the 1980s, women were even more likely than before to be shunted into peripheral service sector jobs (Webb, 2009: 102–4). An interacting series of factors – including low wages, poor working conditions, reduced rights, shrinking trade unions, few benefit entitlements, limited childcare – would ensure that women were more exposed to the flexible economy and the retrenched welfare state.

Whither the welfare state?

Ironically, for the first five or six years social policy was far down the government's to-do list (Raison, 1990: ch. 8; Addison, 2010: 295–306; Page: 91–3).[8] From 1979–83 in particular, Thatcher was not interested in welfare reform (the wounds she'd received as Education Secretary still stung), there was little legislative time for it and she was hesitant of invading what she saw as Labour's natural territory (Campbell, 2003: 169–76). Get the economy right, the thinking went, and much else will follow. In social policy terms, by 1983 New Right radicals were disappointed in their New Right government (Raison, 1990: 120–2, 125–6).

The irony lay in the fact that by 1983 the most significant welfare reform of the whole Thatcher period had already been implemented (Lowe, 2011: 122–6). Conservatives had long been frustrated that even Tory councils were reluctant to sell council houses to their tenants. Such councils worried about the effect of sales on the remaining housing stock (Forrest & Murie, 2011: 52–3). During the highpoint of one-nation conservatism social housing was the norm: 55% of British people born in 1946, and 48% of those born in 1958, spent at least some of their childhood in social housing.

But by the late 1970s such qualms were fading (Murie, 2014: 150–4, 160–1). In 1980 the 'right to buy' at a minimum 30% discount on a property's market value (the discount rose to 70% by the end of the decade) was introduced. Who could resist those temptations? By 1992, 1.75 million council tenants had bought their home and 67% of the country's housing stock was owner-occupied (compared to about half in the mid-1970s). This was the most visible form of Thatcherite popular capitalism. Despite the discounts, the revenue stream to government from this one policy would be worth more than all other privatisations added together (Disney, 2015: 2–3)!

Thus the norm was shifting. Social housing and the role of local government were to be substantially reduced and the private-rented market was given a significant boost (Campbell, 2003: 507). The criticisms of these changes are well known (Jones & Murie, 2006: 210–22). The legacy would be one of increased personal debt, inequality (with those without the resources to become owner-occupiers left behind in sink estates or at the mercy of rising rents), greater homelessness, an explosion in the housing benefit bill and housing bubbles giving a false sense of national prosperity.

But for the New Right little of this mattered, then or later. Thatcher was very unsympathetic even towards the homeless – regarding homelessness as a result of personal failure that imposed few obligations on others (Gilmour, 1992: 145–9; Campbell, 2003: 247–8, 545–6). That focus upon individual agency was the most obvious feature of the government's thinking. No more sociological nonsense about it all being 'society's fault'. Either stand on your own two feet, or else don't expect the taxes I pay will bail you out (Campbell, 2003: 173).

Such principles underpinned other reforms of the 1979–83 period.[9] The state pension was indexed to inflation rather than wages, so its value began to drop, and SERPS was cut back. The ground was being laid for an expansion in the private pensions industry. By the mid-1980s there was a concerted effort to encourage people out of final-salary company schemes and into buying private pensions. This led to a massive mis-selling scandal where, between 1988–94, upwards of 2m people were wrongly advised to opt-out by advisors and firms who stood to make a profit if they did so (Waine, 1995).

So, although the social policy aspects of the first administration were relatively modest – council house sales apart – they did have long-term ramifications and the entire moral tenor of welfare state governance was altering. The totems around which the Macmillan and Heath governments had danced (full employment, more welfare schemes, higher spending, social rights and social needs) were collapsing.

Within a few years the Secretary of State for Health and Social Security, Norman Fowler, was being urged to tear the Beveridge system up by its quasi-socialist roots (Raison, 1990: 133–40). Earnings-related supplements to short-term benefits had already been curtailed and Child Benefit frozen (from 1981–88). Now, the 1986 Fowler Review encouraged an expansion in means-testing through creation of Family Credit and Housing Benefit. Supplementary Benefit (the heir to National Assistance) became Income Support and the cash-limited, discretionary Social Fund replaced the previous system of grants with loans.

Whatever hyperbole accompanied it at the time, though, the Fowler Review was not The Anti-Beveridge Report that some on the Right hoped it would be. But if the Conservative Party could somehow pull off a third election victory, who knew (Campbell, 2003: 499)?

Inequality

These economic and welfare reforms created inequalities (Addison, 2010: ch. 10; Lansley & Mack, 2015: 179–204). What is more, they were designed to do so.

Egalitarianism had not worked, the Right insisted.[10] Poverty had not been defeated by a public sector bloated by producers – teachers, doctors, social workers, civil servants, etc. – demanding ever more funding and holding governments to electoral ransom. Rolling back these special interests would leave more space for commercial providers and the voluntary sector. Welfare was to be freed from its Keynesian and Beveridgean shackles to encourage market flex-ibility and competition, through fewer entitlements, more benefit conditions, greater means-testing and through public services aspiring to the efficiencies and dynamism of the private sector (Dorey, 2011: 157–61). In a competitive race, inequality and insecurity would spur the laggards to run faster.

It was partly a matter of economics. If winners could not keep their winnings then how were innovation and effort to be incentivised? If losers were cush-ioned from the results of their failure then didn't that just encourage them to doze on the cushions? The Right often invoked the Laffer Curve (Kalman, 2010: 227–32), which maintained that high rates of taxation reduce incentives and increase non-compliance with the tax authorities. Thus, reducing tax rates will actually increase total tax revenue! As wealth increases at the top of the income ladder, improved incentives and rising consumption will generate greater economic activity and therefore jobs. In short, they imagined, wealth will 'trickle down' to everyone else, including the poorest (Richards, 1993: 229–38; Campbell, 2003: 247–8; Dorey, 2011: 145–6).

It was also a matter of moral and political philosophy. In *Equality*, Keith Joseph and Jonathan Sumption (1979; Denham & Garnett, 2001a: 330–4) argued that the redistribution of wealth was not a proper function of the state. Arguments about poverty had become confused with those about inequality. If by increasing the relative gap between rich and poor you also improved the *absolute* position of the poorest, then who could reasonably object? Markets and market inequalities respect and enhance individual liberties more effectively than state bureaucracies and social engineering, they insisted (Joseph & Sump-tion, 1979: 76–82, 122).

For Thatcherites, inequality was therefore morally just (a reflection of unequal merit), socially beneficial (the deserving poor will eventually benefit too, while the undeserving poor can legitimately be abandoned and/or discip-lined) and economically sensible (the wealth creators would no longer be held back) (Dorey, 2011: 137–47).

Dorling (2014: 250–3) confirms that inequalities rose dramatically during the 1980s and by the 2010s had returned to levels not seen since the 1930s. The incomes of the poorest may even have been lower in real terms by 1994–95 than in 1979 as the rise in UK inequality outpaced most other countries over the same period (Atkinson, 2000: 365, 368–70) and child poverty soared (Hills, 2005: 1–4). And 30 years later evidence poured in that rising inequality led to a stagnation in overall social mobility (e.g. Wilkinson & Pickett, 2009: 157–69; Judt, 2010: 12–21; Clark, 2014: 156–60; Social Mobility and Child Poverty Commission, 2014).[11]

All of which made Britain an outlier rather than just another exemplar of an inevitable, international trend. What mattered was domestic politics rather than unavoidable global economic developments.

The suspicion that this would prove to be the case was already discernible in the 1980s, in attempts to discredit relative poverty as 'mere inequality' (Joseph & Sumption, 1979: 27–8; cf. Gilmour, 1992: 107–37; Hutton, 1995: ch. 7;

Dorey, 2011: 143–4; Walker, 2014: 285–8). If you secretly suspect that greater inequality conflicts with your goal of meritocracy then 'poverty' – systemic deprivation and disadvantage – has to be conjured away and its characteristics attributed to individual failings. This means denying the existence of those things over which individuals have no or little control, e.g. Thatcherites rejected any link between social and health inequalities (Spencer & Dowler, 2007: 3–4).

Yet the concept of relative poverty continued to have widespread appeal (Lansley & Mack, 2015: 16–31). The government's hysterical reaction to the Church of England's *Faith in the City* report in 1985 was revealing. The report was a Galbraithian warning that pro-capitalist excess was leading to public squalor, to abandoned ghost-towns of aimless youths, boarded-up shopfronts, urban wastelands and general hopelessness. Denouncement of the report as communist thus revealed more about the denouncers than it did about the report (McSmith, 2011: 262). The welfare state remained stubbornly popular in opinion polls (Jenkins, 2006: 149).

Time would also reveal the downsides of popular capitalism. For a third of the population, owner-occupation would be an unrealistic dream.[12] And though by 1990 the number of private shareholders had increased from three million to 11 million, most individuals held very few shares for short periods only in order to seek a quick windfall (Evans, 1997: 36). By 2013 only 12% of shares in British companies were held by individuals, compared to 40% in the 1970s (Meek, 2014: 15).[13]

If this was a 'property-owning democracy', then, the implication was that democracy was being handed over to those who owned the most property and capital. Economic power and privilege are wiped from the picture and the realities of corporate capitalism are rendered invisible.

Democracy has always been the blind-spot of New Right, free market liberals.[14] They typically contrast states on the one side and individuals on the other, positing mainly hostile relations between them. The idea that democratic governments can – and sometimes *do* – reflect the participative sovereignty of peoples is pushed to one side. Markets are rarely viewed in terms of their most power actors as sources of domination, centralisation or oppression. Hayek (1982: ch. 15), for instance, was complacent about private sector monopolies while wanting to clamp down on trade unions and anything he saw as a socialist restriction.

Thatcherism therefore involved an assault on those 'intermediate institutions' (lying between state and civil society), which were seen as inhibiting both profit-making and a business-friendly government: the BBC, unions, local government, universities, public sector professionals (Morgan, 2001: 475–82; Marquand, 2004: 63–115; 2013: 107–18).[15] The New Right were as dismissive as civil society as Stalinists had been: where the latter had interpreted it as an adjunct of the state, the former saw it largely in terms of market exchange. So, many worried that civil society's democratic capacities had thinned, i.e. the enmeshed cultures, attachments and alliances that can form a windbreak against excessive interference by states *and* markets. The countervailing spaces to the marketplace began to contract in scope, reach, frequency and influence (Jessop *et al.*, 1990: 93–5).

Free market liberalism has therefore had two projects (Harvey, 2005: 66–7, 77–86): an *economic* project of freeing individuals from states and an authoritarian, moralistic *political* project of reinterning them within the bars of social immobilities, inequalities and corporate dominance (Linklater, 2014: 378–82). Markets would be freer for some than for others.

But if these critiques are reasonable, why has social egalitarianism remained marginalised in British politics (Lansley, 2012: 32–40, 140–2)? Why has the case made by Joseph and Sumption and others persisted like an ideological stain on the national carpet?

In part, it's because of the 'who' question. Redistribution to who? After 1979 the 'skilled working-class' would advance[16] while the political power of organised labour would fade. So there was less sense that greater equality would benefit one identifiable side of a social divide against another. The association of 'poverty' with 'the working-class' would crumble, despite the fact that most poor households have at least one person in work (Clark, 2014: 204–13). Many of the poor would be increasingly identified (including by some on the Left) as a distinct, underserving underclass (Field, 1989). The demise of an alternative egalitarian narrative, acceptance of Thatcher's 'there is no alternative' refrain,[17] and a compliant media created a vacuum of understanding into which all sorts of demons and scapegoats could tumble.

There is also the 'how' question. Having unleashed the globalised, corporate capitalist genie from the bottle, governments appeared powerless to get the evil genius back in there – even if they wanted to. The fact that markets are not the answer does not make the state the entire answer either, not in a globalised world of flat, horizontal networks where relationships all too easily bypass national governments. Thus, the above critiques of inequality have not overturned post-1979 orthodoxies because few of the people making them advocate a simple return to the political economy of the pre-1979 period.

New parties

Furthermore, if the ruling ideology was now one of private affluence and public squalor it did not always feel that way at the time. Many of the characteristics of the 1960s and 1970s initially remained intact. Unions were still prominent. Public spending was going up, not down (albeit driven by higher unemployment). The Royals were still royal and the Rolling Stones were still rolling. No government can sweep away the past overnight. And with support for state welfare remaining strong, public values had surely not shifted *that* much. If anything, it felt more like private affluence *plus public affluence* too. The 1950s all over again. Only this time with shoulder pads and legwarmers.

Grim-faced Cassandras remained vocal but, as good times returned in the mid-1980s, largely ignored. The new Labour leader, Neil Kinnock, could warn people under a Thatcher government not to get old, not to get sick, and so on. But the former still had their pensions and the latter their NHS. Why worry, therefore (McSmith, 2011: 335)? Wasn't the Left relying on its traditional, po-faced, killjoy, anti-consumerist puritanism?

With the New Right appropriating the 'have fun and discover yourself' ethos of the 1960s, and with old forms of civic cohesion fading, the Left struggled to respond (Bogdanor, 2004: 14–15; Judt, 2010: 85–106).[18] How do you recognise the appeal of hedonist individualism without losing communal solidarities? How can self-assertion and self-image be reconciled with the class loyalties upon which the labour movement had always relied? An inability to answer such questions (and sometimes an unwillingness even to pose them) left a moral and cultural space for Thatcherism to thrive (Mort, 1989).

Consumerism was no longer a reward for six years of war or a post-ration book splurge, it was now presented both as a social obligation and an expression of personal identity. By going shopping you got capitalism moving again. You did not just own your property; your property *was* you. The new individualism was not just hedonistic, it was heroic.

In time, the public squalor argument would gain more of a hearing. Consumerism would force the tensions in New Right thinking out into the open. A 'me, first' selfishness could not be confined. What happened when markets spread out into those aspects of the public realm that Conservatives considered sacred? When the wheeler-dealers in the City switched off their computers who imagined them going off to bed early after a devout prayer?[19]

Squalid Britain

One aspect of public squalor that forced its way to the front of the political stage was environmental squalor. As government left itself with less to do one obvious consequence lay in Britain's foetid beaches and trash-heaped landscapes.

Thatcher's warning about ecological degradation (see Chapter 8) would be remarkable in part because it had been preceded by so very little – and indeed would be succeeded by little more even after her intervention (Rose, 1990: 312–13). 'The environment' was another brake on business and enterprise and so something else to be scorned and marginalised. In her first two terms,

> Most of what was done to clean up water supplies, rivers and beaches was driven by Brussels, not London – fortuitously helped by the decline of dirty manufacturing industry – while the prevailing climate of cost-cutting and deregulation led to a steady lowering of standards.
>
> (Campbell, 2003: 648)

In addition to Europe, the little that was done re the conservation of species and habitats tended to derive from fears either of adverse media coverage or of alienating rural voters (Rydin, 2003: 56–8).

Inaction about pollution was longstanding – as previous chapters have made clear. But with ecological issues pushing their way more and more onto the social agenda, the Thatcher government had even less excuse for its general neglect than previous administrations. Rose (1990) extensively documents a depressing range of failures that confirm the above quote. For instance, the 1974 Control of Pollution Act was effectively neutered because it was seen as bad for business; and annual investment in sewage management was by 1982 half what it had been 10 years earlier:

> Government financial priorities and environmental quality had collided, and the environment lost. It was a deliberate programme of allowing more pollution in order to save money, unprecedented in modern times.
>
> (Rose, 1990: 48)

Government's assumption, one of 'dilute and disperse', was that the oceans and atmosphere will absorb and break pollution down, minimising its impact.

Rose summarises Britain in the 1980s as: a significantly bad polluter (and exporter of pollution), a procrastinator, a treater of symptoms rather than causes, an evader of Directives[20] and an abuser of science more interested in news management and public perception. Rose confirms the view expressed by Wynne and Simmons (see Chapter 6), such that governments demand,

> ... cause-and-effect pollution evidence that can be furnished only once damage (often irreversible) is done, and systematically accumulating volumes of small doubts while ignoring larger and more robust indications of ecological change ...
>
> (Rose, 1990: 296–7)

So:

- There was no national inspectorate of pollution until 1987 (Rydin, 2003: 57).
- The government opposed a European Community (EC)[21] directive requiring planning procedures to include an environmental assessment (but was eventually forced to comply).
- Using a cost-benefit analysis to justify its stance, it refused to join the '30% club' of nations committed to reducing acid rain emissions between 1983–93; despite Britain being the fourth biggest emitter of SO_2 in the world – and the fifth biggest emitter of nitrogen oxides (NO_x) (McCormick, 1989: 80, 85, 93, 100–12). Again, it was eventually driven to comply (albeit on terms more lenient than those applying to other countries) but only after its intransigence had delayed the EC Directive itself by five years (Rose, 1990: 131–5; McCormick, 1989: 87, 91–3; 1995: 242–3).
- Recycling, energy conservation and renewable energy had all been neglected (Campbell, 2003: 649).

Thatcher's scientific background would give her an advantage over other leaders, but her political priorities meant that the sound of birdsong was likely to be drowned out by the noise of car engines and cash registers.

It is therefore no surprise that notions of 'community benefit' were now rejected (Rydin, 2003: 50–3, 63–4). Labour's Development Land Act (designed to ensure that land was used in the public interest) was repealed and the accompanying Development Land Tax abolished in 1985, as was the New Towns Commission. A presumption in favour of planning permission was introduced – including 'special zones' in which no permission was needed at all – and so planning constraints on businesses reduced, with local authorities having less control and oversight than before. Statutory requirements for public participation in the preparation of plans were reduced. Planning was thought legitimate if and only if it demonstrably facilitated enterprise (Cullingworth *et al.*, 2015: 32). Encouraging the growth in private housing meant that more land must be freed from restrictions and markets in land allowed to flourish. In transport policy the emphasis was on roads, cars, deregulation and privatisation; while buses and trains had their funding cut (Rose, 1990: ch. 6; Cullingworth *et al.*, 2015: 487–90).

Here too, then, the government was creating a free market + strong state combination (Marquand, 2013: 108–9; also Charmley, 2008: 226): a centralisation engineered by anti-state libertarians, in which intermediate institutions lying between the state and the individual were scythed away. Government was to do less by devolving decisions and responsibilities to lower-tier agencies (both public and private). But those agencies had to work within a strict framework set by the centre whose powers to monitor and control were if anything enhanced. 'Compulsive competitive tendering', for instance, meant that certain local government services had to be sub-contracted (Gilmour, 1992: 212–20). No argument.

I do not propose to return to the book's key questions at this stage. This lamentable record on environmental policy notwithstanding, we cannot yet give a proper appraisal of the Thatcher's government approach to ecosocial issues. For 1988 was going to be a very important year.

Notes

1 Nigel Lawson rejected the accusation that monetarism had been abandoned by claiming that it meant no more than using monetary policy to reduce inflation (Lawson, 1992: 480–2).

2 The fact that indirect taxes are regressive was not a problem. Inequalities were seen by the New Right as desirable and inevitable (see below). It was Heath who had introduced VAT in the first place.

3 The manifesto spoke only of taking "the recently nationalised aerospace and shipbuilding concerns" into private ownership and selling shares in the National Freight Corporation. Within a few years, Harold Macmillan would be warning of the long-term dangers from selling off the 'family silver' (Thorpe, 2011: 603–4).

4 Monetarism saw wage inflation as itself a symptom of an excessive money supply.

5 For an account of the strike itself see Campbell (2003: 355–70), Helm (2004: 85–8),

Beckett and Hencke (2009: chs 3–9). For an anti-Scargill view see Beckett and Hencke (2009: 230–2, 245–52); for a more sympathetic view see Milne (2014: 17) and Helm (2004: 80–1).

6 Abolished when John Major privatised the industry.

7 More recently, the benefits of Carbon Capture and Storage (CCS) have been emphasised by coal's defenders. But though it has many fervent supporters CCS, at the time of writing, remains in its technological infancy. CCS can provide 20% of the carbon cuts needed by 2050, according to the International Energy Agency, requiring 3000 CCS plants around the world (see www.iea.org/topics/ccs/ [accessed 15 January 2015]). But successes to date have depended on increasing oil production (where CO_2 is used to push oil out of oil fields); the widespread development of CCS plants is not yet cost-effective (existing plants are heavily dependent on state funding and it is more expensive than renewables); public acceptability of the technology (especially of those living near burial sites) is still low. CCS may be part of the solution, but there is a question mark over how quickly technology can be disseminated and applied around the world (Stephens *et al.*, 2011).

8 Though in 2016 newly released Treasury documents indicated that she supported a paper that proposed to charge for state schooling, introduce compulsory private health insurance and a system of private medical facilities that would have meant the end of the NHS. The paper led to a serious revolt in Cabinet and Thatcher claimed at the time she had never seriously considered it. Over three decades later it was revealed that she had lied. See: www.theguardian.com/politics/2016/nov/25/margaret-thatcher-pushed-for-breakup-of-welfare-state-despite-nhs-pledge [accessed 25 November 2016].

9 We look at the NHS and education reform in Chapter 8.

10 With some justification. On key indicators, health and educational inequalities in the mid-1960s were wider than in the latter part of the 1940s (Kynaston, 2015: 536–7, 546–7; also Le Grand, 1982: 46–8, 75–7). The middle-class had benefited the most from welfare reforms, even while being more likely to complain that it was the poor and the working-class who were being favoured.

11 For an overview of literature on social mobility in the earlier 1950–75 period see Heath and Payne (2000: 270–5) who conclude that relative mobility was more evident than it would become after 1975.

12 The figure for householders who were owner-occupiers in the early 1990s (67%) would climb, but only to a peak of 69% ten years later, after which it would fall. http://webarchive.nationalarchives.gov.uk/20160105160709/www.ons.gov.uk/ons/rel/census/2011-census-analysis/a-century-of-home-ownership-and-renting-in-england-and-wales/short-story-on-housing.html [accessed 17 May 2015]

13 Childs (2001: 245) shows that in 1963 the equity owned by individual shareholders amounted to 54% of the total. By 1993 this had fallen to 18%.

14 This blind spot is traced by Linklater (2014: 352–8) to the Austrian School of economists: Menger, von Mises, Hayek. Since democracy in the Austro-Hungarian Empire of the nineteenth century was weak (echoing Werner Sombart, politics took second place to business) they had an aristocratic disdain for it, allied to a view of markets that portrayed them as liberatory while knowing they actually maintained the privileges of the already powerful. The families of Menger and von Mises derived from the nobility; Hayek's mother's family were wealthy landowners.

15 Though a government minister's 1983 attack on the Citizen's Advice Bureau backfired badly. See: http://hansard.millbanksystems.com/commons/1983/apr/12/citizens-advice-bureaux#S6CV0040P0_19830412_HOC_270 [accessed 10 April 2015]

16 The 'loadsamoney' C2s who would welcome Thatcherism as an upward-escalator for their aspirations.

17 There has always been a gap between the percentage of people who think that inequalities between rich and poor are too wide and the percentage who think that

government should redistribute from the former to the latter. However, the gap noticeably widened from the late 1980s onwards, from 30% to around 40% (Park *et al.*, 2013: 40). To three-quarters of the population, inequality resembles fate or an economic necessity or is something for which those on low incomes are responsible (by not working hard enough, presumably) (Orton & Rowlingson, 2007: ch. 4). Many people are clueless about the extent of inequality and where they are themselves located in the distribution of income and wealth.

18　Now the politics of the self and self-fulfilment was to be found not in communes and flower power but in the marketplace. Richard Branson, Bill Gates and Steve Jobs would epitomise this. In *The Buddha of Suburbia* Hanif Kureishi shows how easily hippy individualists could morph into anti-state capitalists. And as the self became privatised so the cooperative, participative habits upon which healthy democracies depend began to wither (Judt, 2010: 106–35). The capitalist revolution bred, and to some extent relied upon, a democratic deficit. Salvation was now to be found in consumerism.

19　McSmith (2011: 207–10) describes the antics of the Bullingdon Club whose members in the 1980s included future Prime Minister, David Cameron.

20　It would have a poor, though not the poorest, record in the league table of legal proceedings against EC member states.

21　For a note on terminology see Chapter 9, footnote 7.

8 Venus in capitalist furs
1987–90

It was sweltering. Rivers were drying up. Crops were being destroyed. Forest fires were breaking out all over the nation.

Crowded with onlookers and reporters, the Senate committee room offered little respite from the heat. In the Washington streets it was 101°F. Jackets were on the backs of chairs, ties were loosened and shirtsleeves rolled up. But heat was not the cause of the stillness in the room as the latest speaker made his case. His calm authority was mesmeric. Everyone leaned in to hear. Soon, the entire world would be listening too. It was 23 June 1988.

NASA scientist James Hansen was an expert on Venus who, during the previous decade, had turned his attention to another planet, having noticed some striking and disturbing similarities between the two. On first hearing, this seemed ridiculous. The mean surface temperature of Venus is 464°C. But Hansen knew that billions of years ago Venus probably resembled the Earth, perhaps even possessing oceans. Then water vapour trapped heat and gradually baked its surface, releasing carbon dioxide, which trapped more heat and so on. The description of such self-amplifying, 'positive feedback' was known as the 'runaway greenhouse effect'. To get the point you just needed to know that certain conditions – like a packed committee room! – could make a hot day even hotter. Its water vapour having evaporated long ago, 97% of the Venusian atmosphere is now carbon dioxide. Carbon dioxide? Yes, Hansen replied. The very stuff we have been pouring into Earth's atmosphere with reckless abandon for the past two centuries.

Hansen's message was as clear as it was incendiary:

> The Earth is warmer in 1988 than at any time in the history of instrumental measurements.... There is only a 1 percent chance of an accidental warming of this magnitude.... The greenhouse effect has been detected, and it is changing our climate now.[1]

The subsequent newspaper and TV coverage was electric – and international. The *New York Times* ran with the headline 'Global Warming has Begun' (Shabecoff, 1988). Public awareness skyrocketed and by the end of the year 32 climate-related bills had been introduced in Congress.

The scientific evidence had been mounting for years (Rose, 1990: 273–5). Though scientists acknowledged various uncertainties, e.g. about the rate of warming, Hansen merely stated on a public stage what most other experts had come to believe: the Earth is warming and we are to blame.

In retrospect, the association of Hansen's words with the heat of that particular Washington day left a dubious legacy. The simple association of climate change with droughts and heatwaves does not capture its complexity and variability. 'Global warming can't be happening,' the deniers were practically invited to say, 'because it's snowing!' Years later Hansen (2009: xv) admitted that he should have stressed that warming also leads to more rain, floods, thunderstorms and tornadoes.

Still, the next few years were instrumental in pushing the issue further onto the political stage. In 1988 the Intergovernmental Panel on Climate Change (IPCC) was established and charged with the task of periodically assessing the scientific evidence on human-induced global warming. Involving thousands of scientists, as time passed the work of the IPCC would also encompass warming's social and economic aspects too. And by 1993 the USA would have a Vice-President who not only took global warming seriously but who had published on the subject (Gore, 1992).

Disasters in the making

What made the timing of Hansen's testimony so potent was that it coincided with the public prominence of three additional events.

First, there was the 1986 disaster at the Chernobyl nuclear reactor, spreading radioactive contamination throughout Europe and highlighting the extent to which national boundaries mattered less and less.

Second, in 1983 the UN's Secretary General established a World Commission on Environment and Development – otherwise known as the Brundtland Commission. Following the 1972 Stockholm Conference (see Chapter 5) the United Nations Environment Programme (UNEP) oversaw a number of conventions and protocols relating to marine conservation, waste, endangered species and pollution (McCormick, 1995: 251–3; Connelly *et al.*, 2012: 266–7; Cullingworth *et al.*, 2015: 259). Yet for all the good intentions such measures felt piecemeal and technocratic.

Now, the 1987 Brundtland Report would help to crystallise and focus many of the relevant issues around the concept of 'sustainable development' (World Commission on Environment and Development, 1987). *Our Common Future* attracted massive international attention largely because its definition of sustainable development was pithy, intellectually respectable and yet broad enough to attract support from almost everyone. Ssustainable development was *that which met the needs of the present without compromising the ability of future generations to meet their own needs.*

This enabled people from across ideological, religious and geographical divides to infer what they wanted to infer. The Commission thus offered a fulcrum around which a series of issues could turn and a host of actors could gather (Connelly *et al.*, 2012: 268–9, cf. 333–4). For instance, economic growth was implicitly treated as good *so long as* it addressed poverty, environmental degradation and other social development problems. This potentially gave growth a new moral direction. But the report was not so radical that it could be seen as seriously contradicting the new enthusiasm for free markets or the consumption habits of the global North (Christoff & Eckersley, 2013: 55–7).

One year earlier, Brundtland had proposed that the environment and the economy were inseparable. Now Hansen was emphasising that they either prospered together or they collapsed together. Yet wasn't the scale of the challenge just too daunting?

This is where a third event becomes relevant. As we have seen, action to combat acid rain had proceeded at a pace that would put a foot-dragging, school-bound teenager to shame. But by the 1980s an even greater dilemma had appeared that seemed truly global and urgent. There was a hole in the ozone layer (Rose, 1990: 267–72; Benedick, 1998; McKie, 2015).

For years, there had been speculation about the effects of spray cans and airplanes on the upper atmosphere. Then, in April 1985, three members of the British Antarctic Survey found that every spring a hole appeared above the Antarctic, one that was getting bigger with every year that passed, due to atmospheric ozone reacting with chlorofluorocarbons, which were largely used in refrigeration devices. What sent shock waves around the world was not just this breach in Earth's defences against solar radiation, but the fact that the hole had developed so rapidly. International action followed swiftly. Established in 1987, and coming into force in 1989, the Montreal Protocol was an agreement to phase out and eventually ban the production of chlorofluorocarbons (McCormick, 1995: 243–6).

Three lessons were drawn from the ozone layer scare. First, human activities had created serious, albeit unintended, damage to the planet. Second, when it really mattered nations could cooperate quickly and efficiently to change the behaviour of manufacturers and consumers. Finally, healing the damage did not require any kind of economic or political revolution. With the USSR about to dismantle itself and China 10 years into its market reforms, Montreal was taken as proof that *capitalism could be reformed in an environmentally ethical direction.*

For all the alarmism, then, Hansen's testimony, following so soon behind the Brundtland and Montreal precedents, was inserted into this narrative of optimistic, post-communist realism. Yes, damage had been done but the damage could and would be reversed. Humans possessed technological ingenuity and capitalist democracies possessed all the capabilities they required without the need for further ideological distractions (Fukuyama, 1992). The Manichean despair of (most) environmentalists was misplaced. Berlin walls were coming down everywhere.

Thus, the first era of globalisation viewed itself as a can-do political effort to identify and tackle global problems.[2] Foot-dragging about environmental issues like pollution could become a thing of the past. Climate change looked worrying, true. Yet wasn't it just the latest in a series of battles that had been won already – against fascism, against socialism, against the social and economic crises of the 1970s?

The newest crusade

On 27 September 1988, at the Fishmongers' Hall in London, Margaret Thatcher rose to address the Royal Society. Most of the speech was mundane but the PM was preparing a surprise. "Protecting [the] balance of nature," she proclaimed, "is ... one of the great challenges of the late twentieth century."[3]

Thatcher outlined key problems: the increase in GHGs, the depletion in the ozone layer and acidification of soils, lakes and trees. Addressing such matters, she opined, would require an extensive research programme, government action and coordinated international agreement, citing the Montreal Protocol as a template for the future. All of which, in turn, implied funding:

> Even though this kind of action may cost a lot, I believe it to be money well and necessarily spent because the health of the economy and the health of our environment are totally dependent upon each other.

In one sense, Thatcher's speech was *not* surprising. She had always been good at reading the signs of where things were going. Did she anticipate that what would soon be renamed the European Union (EU) would be taking environmental issues increasingly seriously (see Chapter 9) and that it would therefore be better for Britain (and for free market liberalism) to take the initiative? Furthermore, after nine years in office, some senior Conservatives sought a more positive message. Not a return to one-nation Toryism but a civic-minded citizenship (Davies, 2012: 6–8); perhaps an embryo of what, a decade later, would be called 'compassionate conservatism'. With Hansen's testimony coming just three months earlier Thatcher was very quick to propose that protecting the natural environment could be one aspect of this (see also Thatcher, 1990).

Thatcher's intervention would be significant in three ways. First, she helped to raise the profile of environmental issues to an extent that no national leader ever had before (Campbell, 2003: 642–3, 648).[4] Second, coming from a Conservative who was a trained scientist, her speech could be cited as resistance to the upsurge of climate change denial, which came largely from the political Right (Oreskes & Conway, 2010). Third, her speech sought a rapprochement between what had so often been regarded as adversaries: free markets and environmentalism.[5] That the Tory record on the environment had been lamentable and would continue to be (Rose, 1990: 5–6, 282–95), that the rhetoric diverted attention away from a 'dirty man of Europe' reality, was not something that the Tory Party or the Tory Press felt the need to dwell upon.

Fourteen months later, in a speech to the UN General Assembly, she would make this rapprochement explicit. In attributing climate change to human activity Thatcher emphasised *population increase* rather than western affluence. Indeed: "It is no good squabbling over who is responsible or who should pay".

For Thatcher there was, to take one example, no contradiction between expressing a concern for global warming and wanting to develop a 'great car economy'. For if markets were the solution to environmental problems, and since railways were collectivist, then a car-based economy was essential (Campbell, 2003: 649–51). Car journeys rose by 50% from 1980–90, as did the number of households with two cars (Root, 2000: 448–9).

In short, Thatcher was not just promoting the importance of climate change she was giving it the Right-wing inflection that would heavily influence the next two decades of international negotiations. This is not to pretend that had Thatcher lost the 1987 election things would have been very different. Recognition of the threat posed by global environmental problems came at a time when the USSR was expiring, China was initiating a market economy, Reagan's America was dismantling the 'Great Society' and, in Europe, Keynesian economics, statist social policy and the egalitarian ethos of the post-war settlement were in retreat. Yet Thatcher articulated this shift and, in doing so, helped give legitimacy to the new political economy of global, corporate capitalism. Her New Right instincts were being greened so that environmentalism could be absorbed into the New Right's ideology (Campbell, 2003: 644).

Take these assertions in her UN speech:

> ... we need to get the economics right. That means first we must have continued economic growth in order to generate the wealth required to pay for the protection of the environment.... And second, we must resist the simplistic tendency to blame modern multinational industry for the damage which is being done to the environment. Far from being the villains, it is on them that we rely to do the research and find the solutions.
>
> As people's consciousness of environmental needs rises, they are turning increasingly to ozone-friendly and other environmentally safe products. The market itself acts as a corrective [as] the new products sell and those which caused environmental damage are disappearing from the shelves.[6]

International agreements should not, then, be seen as restrictions on markets but simply as agreeing a new set of rules for existing institutions and practices: "Otherwise those nations which accept and abide by environmental agreements, thus adding to their industrial costs, will lose out competitively to those who do not". Environmentalism was not about markets doing less. If anything, it would be a continuation of the forward march of market forces. States had a role to play, but as umpires and not as one of the players.

The speeches are therefore as notable for what they choose to ignore. First, the simple point that innovations in industry and infrastructures have typically been underpinned and often driven by research in a public sector so frequently assumed by the Right to be citadels of inefficiency and stagnation (Hutton 2010: 234–45) – not to mention the entire assembly of publicly-funded education.

Thatcher's worldview was one where miracle technologies and products spring unaided from the minds of entrepreneurial wealth-creators.

Second, and similarly, it assumes that consumer preferences can be taken as given, such that the green agenda will be driven inevitably forward by the inter-action of supply and demand, i.e. we can be confident that new products will replace old products on the shelves. There is no hint here of any need for tax reform or regulation, or any recognition of the existence of negative externali-ties (see the Introduction, plus my additional comments on market preferences below.)

Finally, the references to context[7] are all about the *natural* environment. What Thatcher occludes is the wellbeing – the health – of society. Otherwise, she would have to explain why the massive social inequalities created over the previous 9–10 years were *either needed* to solve environmental problems *or at least irrelevant* to their resolution. By highlighting the economy-environment relation she implicitly tries to draw attention away from relations of economy-environment-society.

Entering the mainstream

The developments sketched above offered environmentalists an opportunity to influence policymaking as never before. But there were risks, too.

Concerns about pollution and depleting resources had given rise in the 1970s to new branches of economics. 'Environmental economics' deals with the things economic activity adds *to* the environment, e.g. pollution. 'Resource economics' deals with extractions *from* the environment, e.g. it has facilitated debates about peak oil. Both recognise the centrality of human-nature interactions to eco-nomic wellbeing. Yet there is no reference to Mishan, Ilich, Schumacher or Commoner in Common and Stagl (2005) or Hanley *et al.* (2007), and relatively little discussion of growth.

The first risk, therefore, resembled a Faustian bargain: in becoming part of the mainstream environmentalism might be captured by a discipline whose fundamental assumptions remained unchallenged. As post-Keynesianism took hold this could arguably solidify the grip of *laissez faire* doctrines on environ-mental issues, overlooking the conflicts between them.

For instance, in responding to critics of his earlier *Blueprint for a Green Economy* Pearce (1991: 4) states that economists do not value (or devalue) the environment in itself, they merely *cost people's value* of the environment: their preferences "*for* (or against) the flow of services from the environment".[8] Yet such a defence – with its distinction between 'value in' and 'value of' – only confirms the critics' charge that nature is being kept at arms-length (Scott Cato, 2009: 6–9). Without a central political and moral critique, market-specific pref-erences are always allowed to do the valuing while escaping *being evaluated* (Beder, 1996). If people were to prefer plastic trees as much as real trees would Pearce claim this is irrelevant to what economists do and how they do it? Free market economists have always been happy both to pretend that preferences emerge in a social vacuum, unshaped by social structures and inequalities, while simultaneously helping to refashion desires, motivations, expectations and social relations so that they obey market forces.[9]

The second risk, therefore, is that nature's intrinsic value is either marginalised or ignored entirely by environmental/resource economics (Fitzpatrick, 2014a: 41–4). In the same volume as Pearce, Taylor (1991: 221) argues that 'biocentrists' have no cause to worry because, with modifications, an economic paradigm will preserve the things they hold dear anyway.

Risks aside, however, environmental economics has undoubtedly had beneficial impacts too.[10] When in 2006 Nicholas Stern called climate change the "biggest market failure in history" (see Chapter 12) he was dramatising the pernicious effects that unregulated markets in particular have had both in exacerbating the problem and in hindering those solutions that require interference with markets. For if markets are indeed a means to an end – as Thatcher observed (see footnote 7) – and if climate change is a market failure then the end presumably allows us to reshape markets to an extent that free market liberals have denied (Snowdon, 2015: 90–6). In time, it would become as naïve to avoid mention *free market failures* as it would be to avoid mention of government failings (Ostrom, 2012).

Social reforms

So, Thatcher regarded her pro-environmentalist interventions as consistent with the reforms she had initiated since 1979. If anything, the market revolution was accelerating. For it was during this same period (1987–90) that social policy was coming more firmly into her sights (Barry, 1987; Taylor-Gooby, 1996; Page, 2015: 100–5). With a third election victory behind them, the time had finally arrived (Campbell, 2003: 499, 542–57).

What the Right condemned as identikit comprehensive schools were an obvious target (Gilmour, 1992: 167–74; also Raison, 1990: 159–62). Too long a haven of trendy teaching methods, low standards, ill-discipline and Bolshevik teachers, the suggested remedy was a dose of *both* centralisation and control *plus* quasi-market incentives (Denham & Garnett, 2001a: 397–8).[11]

Education reforms in 1988 (Timmins, 2001: 418–32, 438–46) introduced a National Curriculum (where the Department for Education prescribed what was to be taught across 10 subjects), established standards and tests for children at ages 7, 11, 14 and 16 and, based upon test results, initiated a system of league tables. These tables were intended to empower parents to judge the quality of a school, namely others and so demand, as consumers, the highest possible standards and services. Bad practices and bad teachers could thereby be identified and eliminated. Instead of taking what they were given by LEAs, parental choice could dominate. The money would follow the child, instead of the other way around.

The balance of power would theoretically be shifted towards parents – and so away from teachers, unions and local government – overseen by a Secretary of

State. The 1988 reforms thus allowed state schools to opt out of local authority control and become 'grant-maintained' (funded directly by central government), controlling their own budgets and competing for pupils. The rationale was to increase diversity, spur competitive innovations and increase choice for parents.

Critics alleged that these reforms would increase bureaucracy rather than reduce it (Dorey, 2014: 111–16, 125–31). A National Curriculum involved form-filling conformity to a set syllabus, undermining trust in, and the professional autonomy of, those expert in actually teaching children.[12] And if a school butted heads with a LEA why was this less preferable than being accountable to revolving-door Ministers, civil servants and unelected QUANGOs hundreds of miles away in Whitehall? There were also fears that league-tables would distort priorities.

First, if being at or towards the bottom of a table risked fewer pupils and so job losses then exam results would overwhelm other priorities. Yet rather than this inspiring higher standards, the need to keep paying the mortgage meant that teachers would 'teach to the test' rather than taking the time to enthuse pupils or doing any of the creative, risk-taking activities that real education involves. Decades later, some of the evidence suggested that many schools had indeed become 'assessment factories' producing students skilled at passing tests but less adept at independent thought (Seldon, 2010: 55–7).

Second, tables repositioned schools as business competitors rather than as partners with a joint responsibility to meet local needs. The danger of Leftie teachers ignoring their new status as 'delivers of an educational service' is partly why Whitehall centralisation was thought necessary. Sheep have to be corralled. Local cooperation was therefore out and the notion that what happens in one school remains heavily influenced by what happens elsewhere could be ignored.

In fact, third, it *had* to be ignored. An ideology of individual choice has to downplay and preferably erase schools' social context. For marketisation to be justified markets had to be seen to empower everyone, including those on low incomes. Inequality in parental or household resources was no longer a factor. If your school was performing badly then that had nothing to do with social class and everything to do with choice. Exercise some voice and demand a better service! Or, take your business elsewhere. The primary responsibility lies with you, the parent-consumer, not with us, the government (for a critique of the 'choice agenda' see Clarke, 2010: 75–88).

As such, the fact that such reforms empowered the already empowered (middle-class parents with cultural capital, sharp elbows, access to resources and networks) could be written out of the script. School selection via estate agent became even more prevalent than before. And in a competitive environment inequalities easily become self-perpetuating. The best pupils flock to the best schools who then can attract more of the best teachers to whom more of the best pupils will flock … and so on. A self-reinforcing process that exacerbates existing inequalities.[13]

Out of 24,000 schools in the UK just 1100 had become grant maintained by 1997. But a post-comprehensive system had been initiated nonetheless (see Chapters 10–12).

NHS on the agenda

The reform of the NHS involved a similar introduction of market values and practices (Gilmour, 1992: 155–61; Timmins, 2001: 405–17, 453–72; Lowe, 2005: 354–6). Sensitive to traditional accusations that it intuitively disliked the NHS, health expenditure was one feature of public spending that the Tories had protected (Hills, 1998: 2). Nonetheless, a funding crisis had been mounting for years, fueling Right-wing disquiet about the 'black hole' nature of the system (Seldon, 1968): that the NHS could never satisfy the demands made upon it which, added to assumptions about the inherent wastefulness of public services, meant that the revenues committed to it would swallow up ever larger chunks of government finance. The more radical suggestions – such as implementing user-charges or privatisation – would have constituted electoral suicide.

The preferred alternative involved the creation of an internal market where purchasers (primarily GPs and health authorities) would buy services from providers (public and private hospitals). GPs practices could apply to become 'fundholders', controlling their own budgets. And public hospitals would be encouraged to apply for 'independent trust' status, i.e. with their own managerial and budget autonomy. Purchasers would thus have to shop around for the best deal and observe harder budget constraints than before. In short, NHS practitioners could no longer spend other people's money with abandon and then, when the cash ran out, dig out the begging bowl and demand more. By 1989 the government was ready to move.

The subsequent 1990 Act was vehemently opposed by many. Critics warned that, if anything, an internal market would increase costs, e.g. more managers would be required to negotiate and monitor contracts between purchasers and providers (Pollock, 2004: 19–25).

There were also worries about introducing commercial values and disciplines into healthcare. Excessive managerialism and business models might come to dominate, eroding the professionalism of front-line staff. Surely doctors should make decisions based upon medical needs. If practitioners, like fundholding GPs, were required to have one eye on the accounts sheet then wouldn't they be motivated by a desire to save money rather than ensure patient care?

As with schools, there was an anxiety over fragmenting a cooperative system into independent units and setting them against one another as competitors seeking the best financial deal. And what happened if, say, a hospital did overspend? In a market, inefficient and/or unpopular businesses would have to downsize and perhaps even shut down. Was the government saying that fundholding GPs and hospitals were now businesses? Would the least successful be required to close?

A final worry concerned equality of treatment. If the internal market exacerbated inequalities between the most successful GPs/hospitals and the rest then patients lucky enough to access the former could benefit to the detriment of others. This could easily generate a sense of unfairness, eroding the system's universalism. It might even be that some fundholding GPs could queue jump their patients ahead of others less savvy at navigating market forces.

Were such criticisms justified? Lowe's (2005: 356–9) defence of the reforms has an *ergo propter hoc* quality to it: any healthcare improvements made *after* the reforms must have been due *to* the reforms. In truth, the problem, as with any evaluation, is in discerning cause and effect. Ten years on, West (1998) struggled to find evidence that the reforms had achieved any objectives that could not have been realised without such a radical upheaval. Baggott (1997: 285–7) concurs that the reform's impact on efficiency was unclear but that it had raised administrative and managerial costs:

> Between 1989–94, the number of managers increased fourfold and other administrative staff by over 10%. Over the same period the number of nurses and midwives fell by 12.4%.
>
> (Baggott, 1997: 287)

The more softly-softly approach of Major's government would help to win some critics over to at least some aspects of the reforms, suggesting that a consensual method would have been more persuasive (Baggott, 1997: 300–1). Thatcher's ideologues seem to have allowed the example of American healthcare to set the agenda (Greener, 2002: 167–9).

Private is best

In the long term, what these education and health reforms did was to promote the notion that the public sector is inherently inefficient, resistant to innovation and so requires the importation of private sector dynamics. What started out as a New Right prejudice would, in time, become a 'common sense' part of the political landscape. They therefore accelerated a process already begun in the 1970s, when social expenditure on, and cultural attitudes towards, state welfare began to flow in opposing directions (see Chapter 5).

Administratively and financially speaking, Tory politicians knew that many people – including their own supporters – benefitted from state welfare (Farrall & Hay, 2014: 335–8). The NHS in particular was still widely seen to embody a sense of solidarity and fairness. From 1980–90, the middle-class elements of the welfare state remained largely untouched (Campbell, 2003: 555), therefore. Indeed Lowe (2005: 373) ponders whether Thatcher *saved* the welfare state by keeping middle-income earners locked into what substantially remained a state-centred system. (Services for the poorest were much more vulnerable, however.)

So, at the end of the decade the welfare state still cost as much as it had at the beginning – about 25% of GDP – though unemployment benefit accounted for much more of this than it had in 1980.

Ideologically and ethically, though, state welfare *was* under assault as never before (Mishra, 1990: ch. 2). Beneath the statistical headlines, divisions between 'deserving' and 'undeserving' had reopened. Admittedly, the universalist, egalitarian rhetoric of the 'golden age' had probably papered over the crack rather than sealing it. But now, the New Right saw it as something that could animate policymaking and bear electoral dividends. As noted in Chapter 7, poverty was now seen as due to a lack of the correct values, habits and attitudes. The rhetoric of undeserving 'scroungers and skivers' was popular because it reactivated so many of the prejudices, fears and resentments towards others, which have motivated welfare reforms for centuries.

And although the voluntary sector could be lauded if and when it assisted the anti-state drift, at other times it could be condemned as a remnant of socialist nannying, e.g. the *Faith in the City* report (see Chapter 7). How many one-nation Conservatives increasingly worried that, rather than restoring Victorian civicness, a market society encourages a 'me, now' selfishness that erodes the invisible strands of the social fabric upon which we all depend?

Overall, then, the Thatcher decade represented:

- An end to the 1940s–1970s era of welfare state collectivism and public sector expansion;
- An emphasis on individual choice, market disciplines and the private sector that would subsequently dominate social policy debates;
- A shift in the economic environment from full employment to low inflation, from manufacturing to services, from a mixed, regulated economy to a privatised, marketised deregulated economy in which management and shareholders wield power.

What she left behind was a hybrid. The mixed economy was gone. So was Keynesianism. But with the welfare state itself proving to be more robust and resilient than Right-wing critics had assumed, many institutional structures from the 1945–79 period remained, though now contextualised by economic and moral principles that were circling back to the nineteenth century. The next two decades would involve a tug-of-war between the key elements of this 'welfare hybridity'.

Public sector in retreat

The 1980s therefore represented a Rightwards shift in ends and in means. In many respects, the scope of public goods had shrunk. Yet if her 1988–89 speeches are taken at face value, Thatcher now wished to make a healthy environment the object of government concern it had failed to become during the previous two decades. And if public goods were now supposed to be delivered through markets and quasi-markets, it was no surprise that two resources were seen as ripe for privatisation: water and electricity.

Water

For most of the twentieth century the big municipalities controlled water supply and sewage was mainly the responsibility of local authorities. The DoE integrated these functions (plus river management) within the Regional Water Authorities in the 1970s, coordinated by a National Water Council. At that time, the amount a household paid for its water did not vary according to how much water it actually used. The 1989 reforms effectively turned those authorities into private firms and created several other bodies: the Office of Water Services (Ofwat) and a Drinking Water Inspectorate.[14] Ofwat's role was to regulate the supply, delivery and disposal of water services, and to ensure efficiency, competition and customer protection (including price monitoring).

The justification was simple (Meek, 2014: 105–16). Spurred by competition and the profit motive, private firms were assumed to be more efficient and accountable to users than a publicly managed industry, especially where a natural monopoly like water is concerned. A separation of production and regulation was therefore called for. The government was also worried at the demands on the Treasury that years of underinvestment could impose – as much as £24bn was needed according to some estimates (Graham, 2006: 437), with higher EU-mandated environmental standards on the way. Better to have capital investment funded via household bills than through income tax, it was thought.

Unlike some earlier privatisations, though, this one was not popular. First, there was no solid evidence regarding efficiencies. Prior to 1989, 23% of water was already supplied by private companies, though subject to strong regulatory control, and subsequent analyses suggested that *public* provision was more efficient (Lynk, 1993).

Second, the reforms failed a 'common sense' test. If you weren't satisfied with your local London firm could you, instead, hire a Scottish firm to lay pipe to your house from Inverness or somewhere? And how can privatisation raise environmental standards if consumers cannot choose a non-polluting supplier versus a polluting one (Rose, 1990: 306)?

The government could and did cite 'charging structures' and 'customer representation requirements' but these were obscure, technocratic terms to most people and probably only fed suspicions that while turning on a tap delivered water to you it just as surely started a second flow: your money to obscure shareholders and managers (especially as metering became more common). Under privatisation, water bills would become a de facto tax.

Much hinged on the powers of Ofwat to challenge the water companies. The increase in water charges was initially steep (almost 40% from 1989–1995), effectively giving companies a license to exploit customers, particularly those on the lowest incomes. Ofwat ordered a lowering of prices in 1994 to compensate, though its Director General at the time subsequently admitted that this review was inadequate (Byatt, 2013: 7, n31). And disconnections for non-payment of water bills almost trebled in the first few years after privatisation (Graham, 2006: 440–1).

The initial period (1989–97) of regulatory oversight was dominated by economic imperatives, in other words. As environmental sustainability became more important, in the 1990s, it would therefore have to be grafted onto a mode of regulation already dominated by a business model (Cashman & Lewis, 2007; also Rose, 1990: 63–5), leading to a complex entanglement of environmental and economic goals that future governments would have to unpick (Schaefer, 2009). According to some (Dore *et al.*, 2004) huge environmental improvements did follow water privatisation, e.g. in the quality of drinking water. However, they also found that this was largely due to compliance with new EU standards and that privatisation mainly served to raise the profits of the new companies.

Electricity

Electricity privatisation followed a similar pattern (Graham, 2006, Meek, 2014: ch. 4; also Parker, 2000: 83–92).[15] The miners' defeat had fired the starter pistol and now the 'dash for gas' was on (Parker, 2000: 95–100). This meant that, in the electricity generating process, coal-based steam turbines now gave way to gas turbines – the latter also made it easier to meet EU targets on acid rain emissions (Winskel, 2002: 572–9). Lower prices were expected to follow as sunshine follows rain. This was in accord with the 1989 Electricity Act. The Act mentioned environmental impacts but the overwhelming concern was to see people primarily as,

> … consumers of electricity provided by the market, interested in its price and availability, rather than in the overall cost to them of energy services such as lighting or the use of appliances, or in their externalities.
>
> (Shaw *et al.*, 2010: 5928)

Yet, somehow, the sunshine did not burst through. The energy generators dominated and there was very little competition initially. Prices *rose* as a result and the regulator (Offer) was virtually toothless (Green, 2006: 78–80). O'Mahony and Vecchi (2001) found no evidence that privatisation led to increases in productivity, either.[16]

The end

Thatcher hit the canvas three times before retiring from the ring (Charmley, 2008: 231–7).

First, there was the 1988 spending boom engineered by Nigel Lawson (Gilmour, 1992: 59–75). Unlike the Barber Boom of 16 years earlier there wasn't even the vaguest reason why the government should now stoke consumer spending through massive tax cuts, other than hubris. They believed that the economy had been transformed, such that growth could be restored without it overheating. They were wrong. With house prices accelerating and interest rates very low, inflation doubled in two years, reaching almost 10% by 1990. Slamming on the brakes would tip the country into its second recession in a decade. Tory claims to have engineered an economic miracle turned to ashes (Wells, 1993).

Second, the Poll Tax was another example of hubris (Campbell, 2003: 555–63; cf. Raison, 1990: 147–59). Having engineered an explosion in home ownership, and wanting to take yet more power away from local authorities, this was an attempt to shift the funding of local services from buildings to individuals. Almost everyone would pay exactly the same flat tax, both Duke and dustman. The expectation was that people would be incentivised to vote for low taxing and low spending Conservative councils. 'No representation', the motto seemed to be, 'without taxation'. That the tax was introduced by the Secretary of State for the Environment (1986–89), Nicholas Ridley, a devout libertarian, tells you a lot about the government's attitude to the DoE.

The result was predictable to all but the bombastic fantasies of ministers. Many individuals left the voter registration rolls in order to disappear; many refused to pay what was a very regressive measure; protests and even riots broke out. And with the Poll Tax introduced in Scotland one year earlier than the rest of the country, Scottish nationalism revived after lying moribund for a decade.

Finally, and most importantly, the Tory Party was beginning to split over Europe (Weight, 2003: 630–43; see next chapter). The Single European Act (SEA) agreed to create a single market across the EU by 1992. But now the European Commission was advancing a plan for a single currency. For the Commission's President, Jacques Delors, this was the inevitable next step: markets worked best in a cooperative, *social* context; and most European conservatives seemed to agree. But this was anathema to Thatcherites and many, including the lady herself, regretted her signing the SEA.

The initial split come over the Exchange Rate Mechanism (ERM), designed to reduce volatility in exchange rates and prepare the ground for a single currency. This offended the free market preference for floating currencies. Thatcher wanted nothing to do with it. However, her Chancellor, Nigel Lawson, wanted Sterling to 'shadow' the Deutschmark. The split widened and the PM was forced to give way – Britain joined the ERM in October 1990. Thatcher's continued obstreperousness caused the resignation of the pro-European Geoffrey Howe, whose resignation speech in the Commons triggered a leadership battle that Thatcher could never win. She resigned on 22 November.

And behind all this was a sense that Thatcherism had lost momentum. The events above never allowed a more civic-minded conservatism to emerge and by 1989–90 much of the country was fed up with the hectoring, patronising style of Thatcher herself. For the Tories, her legacy would be double-edged. She had remoulded British society, but left Conservatives with a dilemma – not dissimilar to that which Labour had faced 40 years earlier. Should they drive forward with more anti-state, pro-market reforms: Thatcherism without Thatcher?

Or, should they try to consolidate what had been achieved? And who could possibly replace her as leader and PM?

After 1990 Thatcher was a sad figure. By the late 1990s she had even embraced global warming denial (Campbell, 2003: 652). Thatcherism was partly a victim of its own triumph. The more successful it became the more arrogant and yet insecure it grew. Any and every restriction or regulation came to appear a hindrance to achieving a market utopia, and so was hysterically magnified in scale accordingly. The more markets were rolled forward the more everything outside the marketplace came by definition to appear socialistic, harbouring the potential for resistance (Beynon, 2014: 215).[17] The same force which congratulated itself for toppling the USSR still looked at Labour leader and ex-socialist Neil Kinnock, saw a 'crypto-communist' and felt itself to be embattled.

Perhaps with some cause. Thatcher would regard New Labour as her greatest success and, indeed, by the 1990s Keynesians and Marxists were alike in hiding. Yet, somehow, the welfare state legacy of the Webbs, of social liberals, of Attlee and Bevan, of Beveridge and the one-nation Conservatives was still standing, even if some of the foundations had subsided. Thatcherism changed the country, yet her revolution was also constrained in turn by the revolutions that had preceded it.

Key questions

What relationships between the environmental and social policy agendas have emerged? To what extent have social policies and the politics of welfare reform deliberately informed and been informed by the principles and values of environmental ethics and politics?

Something had changed even before 1988.

Until 1979 what mattered primarily in the field of the environmental and the ecosocial was the organisation of government. If the state was meant to be at the forefront of running the economy, administering welfare services and overseeing the environment then the effectiveness (or otherwise) of departmental organisation was paramount. It was this that kept the relationship between the environmental and social policy agendas weak. The environmental branch of government was always residual compared to the economic and social welfare institutions of state.

Only in the Clean Air Act had Britain adopted a truly preventative, future-oriented form of legislation – or at least so it seemed until acid rain became a political issue in the 1970s. Otherwise, governance would be characterised by a curative, *ex post* approach, which operated through a between-the-cracks, departmental fragmentation; a schema that the DoE had not altered radically. All of this persisted into the 1980s, with an even greater neglect of the environment and with Ridley running the DoE after 1986 – a lamentable record that was hidden from view because most initiatives emanated from the EEC.

Yet by Thatcher's second term the actual divisions of ministerial responsibility and departmental organisation mattered less than the ideology which was meant to envelope, unify and smother each and every aspect of governance: self-interested individualism, market deregulation, the privatisation of public goods and services, constraints on the public sector, competitiveness and entrepreneurialism, a shift away from universal, egalitarian welfare provision designed to ameliorate socioeconomic inequalities. Thatcher was an obsessive micromanager, but you didn't need her to be. So long as you were 'one of us' and understood what Thatcherism meant, then it was enough for you to 'think and work towards' the leader. Sub-commanders like Ridley didn't have Thatcher leaning over their shoulders because they didn't need her there. The ends were now so well defined that the organisational division of labour mattered less than it had prior to 1979.

Perhaps curiously, then, a distinct ecosocial politics was emerging by the mid-1980s. Though they may appear on the surface to be disparate, the government's policies vis the economy, welfare services, natural resources (coal, water and electricity) and the natural environment more broadly were united by the ideology just outlined. This amounts to an alignment of economic policy, social policy, public policy and environmental policy. Yes, organisationally there was still a great deal of diversity, e.g. education and healthcare experienced quasi-markets rather than full-blown privatisation. But this diversity and unevenness now mattered less than it once had, in an era when the state was meant to be doing much of the work. What mattered increasingly more after 1979 – especially as market reforms took hold across social policy and energy policy from the mid-1980s onwards – was the overall philosophy animating these policy domains, the fact that they existed within the same constellation of ideas.

One effect was this. Those on low incomes were being hit through higher indirect taxes, falling wages, labour market insecurities, lower benefits and narrower benefit entitlements. Now, following privatisations of key resources, they also faced increased utility prices because of mismanaged privatisation, driven largely by ideology rather than evidence.

And this was occurring at a time when the EEC was pushing for higher environmental standards, at least some of the cost for which would presumably have to be added to household bills. EEC-wide environmental policies were appearing just as the UK's public and social policies were increasingly regressive, with a significant risk that the costs of the former would augment that regressiveness. The need for robust, long-term strategies was occurring when the UK was adopting a market-based, light-touch regulatory regime designed to favour short-term profit making.

So, as important as Thatcher's 1988 speech seemed at the time, it actually sought to extend into the 'multidirectional transboundary' sphere the kind of approach that the government had already been applying and would continue to apply. Global warming was taken by Thatcherites as a confirmation of what they had been saying all along: since the state was too blunt an instrument for the nature and the scale of the challenges we face, only market instruments will suffice. The insertion of climate change into public discourse and inter-governmental relations thus coincided with the globalisation and hegemoni-sation of what many would call 'neoliberal economics' in which markets expand, states shrink, the public sector is liberalised, regulation weakens and notions such as planning and social ownership are off the agenda. The ascend-ancy of *laissez faire* capitalism in 1980s would therefore set the agenda for eco-nomic, social and environmental policies for decades to come (Christoff & Eckersley, 2013: 55).

The eruption of climate change into politics also altered the parameters of debate. It is not as if earlier issues – like rural-urban relations, pollution and waste, resource depletion, acid rain and so forth – disappeared. If anything, global warming began to tie them, their causes and their implications, together. Nonetheless, this was a Kraken Awakes moment in which the concerns of earlier periods found themselves swallowed and forced to peer out at the world from inside the belly of this new behemoth. Consequently, the issue of climate change will similarly dominate the chapters to come.

Notes

1 This was testimony to the Senate Committee on Energy and Natural Resources. See 'A look back at James Hansen's seminal testimony on climate, part two', Ben Block, http://grist.org/article/a-climate-hero-the-testimony/ [accessed 1 March 2015]

2 There were early warnings that any optimism was misplaced. None of the 32 climate-related bills mentioned above passed.

3 Quotes from this and the following UN speech are taken from transcripts available at: www.margaretthatcher.org/ [accessed 3 March 2015]

4 In November 1988 the United Nations General Assembly passed Resolution 43/53, identifying climate change as "a common concern of mankind". In the 1989 elec-tions to the European Parliament the UK Green Party received 15% of the popular vote.

5 For example, the 1974 Cocoyoc Declaration had spoken of basic needs, the destruc-tive effects of social inequalities and the importance of changing consumption habits (Bernstein, 2001: 54-6).

6 Margaret Thatcher, speech to the UN General Assembly, 8 November, 1989. www.margaretthatcher.org/document/107817 [accessed 3 March 2015]

7 For instance:

> We should always remember that free markets are a means to an end. They would defeat their object if by their output they did more damage to the quality of life through pollution than the well-being they achieve by the production of goods and services.

8 The point would be reiterated constantly, e.g. in Pearce and Barbier (2000: 7–16) where any moral argument that goes beyond costing preferences is denounced as 'elitism'.

9 See the chapters in Anderson and Leal (2015) as an example of this practice. The habitual contrast is between states on the one side and individuals and groups on the other. 'Environmental entrepreneurs' are seen as emerging from and thus serving the latter. Anderson and Leal have long championed the Hayekian view that because our knowledge of both nature and the economy is always limited and local, market decentralisation is superior to state centralisation. The centralisations created by

markets are thereby disregarded; and our capacity to create democratic, 'small-scale collectivisms' are never explored.

10 More recently, an 'ecological economics' has gained traction. Costanza *et al.* (2015: 58) characterise this as being more sensitive to the downside of growth, to longer timescales and as incorporating a more holistic analysis, including nonmarket goods (cf. Scott Cato, 2009: 9).

11 Anthony Seldon (2010) argues that the 1988 reforms were a "curious mixture" of free market principles and centrism. As indicated in Chapter 7 and again below, I am proposing that this 'curious mixture' was and is central to free market liberalism.

12 The Curriculum would be scaled back in the early 1990s to make it less onerous.

13 For research on how and why income inequalities lead to education inequalities see Blanden and Gregg (2004). For an overview of pre-1997 educational inequalities see Smith (2000: 216–18).

14 The Environment Agency would follow in 1996.

15 British Gas had been privatised a few years earlier.

16 Outside the UK there was a similar trend towards greater liberalisation in energy sectors though nowhere near the extent found in, say, telecommunications due to the greater likelihood of the former being dominated by relatively few providers (Bartle, 2002). But such liberalisation was rarely taken to the privatisation extremes pursued by the UK's Conservative government (Dagdeviren, 2009: 642–4).

17 She once remarked that "socialism is never defeated" (quoted in Marquand, 2009: 282).

9 The long shadows
1990–97

In the TV comedy *Spitting Image* John Major was depicted as drab, boring and grey-skinned, his dinnertime conversations with his wife limited to comments about the peas. While the audience laughed the real PM was one of the most quietly radical leaders the country had had in a long time.

Whether or not he was more Thatcherite than Thatcher (Dorey, 2011: 166–70), Major was not the one-nation Conservative he sometimes portrayed himself as being (Dorey, 1999a: 226–40; cf. Seldon, 1997: 126, 133–4; Taylor, 2006: ch. 2; Marquand, 2009: 317–25). Where Ted Heath's grating personality had concealed many economic and social orthodoxies, Major's unassuming style hid a determination to finish what Thatcher could never have finished herself. If Tory Left and Right both shouted 'betrayal!' it was because Major was a mercurial politician who seemed to be in many places on the political spectrum at the same time (Gilmour & Garnett, 1997: 350–3).

The very fact that he rose to high office remarkably quickly – from Chief Secretary to the Treasury to PM in barely more than three years – should have been a clue (Taylor, 2006: 13–21). If the man was grey it was a greyness that could shade, chameleon-like, into different tones depending on his surroundings. The son of a former music-hall performer and trapeze artist, Major retained an image of the lower-middle-class-boy-made-good even while heading a party funded by the uber-wealthy. The blurriness of Major's demeanor was partly a result of hesitation and dithering. But it was also because he saw his project as carving out a post-Thatcherite politics: to consolidate the 1980s while moving on. In this respect he deserves association as much with his successor as with his predecessor.

That Major oversaw a considerable amount of chaos – centred upon Europe – need not qualify the above appraisal (Bale, 2010: ch. 2). It is difficult to imagine any other senior Conservative steering the lifeboat successfully away from the wreckage of HMS Thatcher. Not given how things stood with the Tory Party in 1990. Major, like Wilson 27 years earlier, seemed the least worst option to the largest number of people.

But chaos there was. This was principally due to sterling crashing spectacularly – and humiliatingly – out of the ERM (Bonefeld *et al.*, 1995: 86–100; Seldon, 1997: ch. 21; Wincott *et al.*, 1999). It was Chancellor Major who had taken sterling into the ERM when the currency was overvalued, threatening British exports at a time when the country was trying to recover from recession (Bonefeld *et al.*, 1995: 79–83; Seldon, 1997: 110–15). The parity was defended for two years but by September 1992 sterling was under attack from speculators. The government went into crisis management, scrambling to raise interest rates in a single day to preserve the parity. It wasn't enough. The value of sterling continued to fall. Panic set in. There was only one option: leave the ERM. In a matter of days the Tory's reputation for economic competence exploded.

Anti-Europeans harrumphed and flexed their political muscles. And though Major had pulled off a surprise victory in the 1992 election it wasn't enough to endear him to the faithful. He might still be dedicated to privatisation and other 1980s totems but he didn't *sound* like a Thatcherite. He didn't thump the table and tell you who to hate today. The free market Right felt they'd been duped and never forgave him for it. Warfare broke out (Gilmour & Garnett, 1997: 370–3). Europe was frequently the spark but it was more the trauma of a party, which, having lost its nanny, enjoyed throwing its toys around the room as compensation.

Even so, there was that electoral victory and the mandate it brought. And if you were trying to sketch a new, post-Thatcherite map there were plenty of ideas lying around. To take one example, a 1990 white paper, *This Common Inheritance*, echoed the EU's emphasis upon integrating environmental standards into economic practices. It even talked about the 'precautionary principle' (O'Riordan & Cameron, 1994: 238–40). Had Thatcher been right in 1988? Could a new civic Conservatism possibly be a *green Conservatism*?

Environmentalism in the 1990s

Indeed, Carter (2006: 753–7) reveals that electoral interest in the environment peaked in 1992, as all three major parties gave the issue considerable prominence in their manifestoes. The from-nowhere surge of the Greens in the 1989 European elections had spooked them. The Liberal Democrats dedicated 12% of their manifesto to the subject. Conservative and Labour were not far behind – about 6% each. But that's about it. It was lip-service. Environmental matters were barely mentioned during the actual campaign and the 1997 and 2001 manifestoes would see them pushed back to the margins. In short, for Tories and Labour at least, this was an issue that had to be absorbed into business-as-usual politics, and thereby neutered. There was a price to be paid *from being seen* to neglect the environment, less so from *actually* neglecting it in your social and economic reforms.

Still, for a time at least, environmentalism looked like the Next Big Idea. One event symbolised this more than any other.

Politics of the globe

There had been Stockholm 1972 and annual Earth Days for the last 20 years, but nothing like Rio de Janeiro. The 1992 Earth Summit, including an independent Global Forum, involved the participation of over 170 governments, including 105 national leaders, 30,000 activists and 8000 NGOs (Rogers, 1993; McCormick, 1995: 253–7; Connelly *et al.*, 2012: 269–74).

Was there a danger of the summit turning into a talking-shop for the Great and the Good? Pointing out the dangers of complacency fell initially to a 12-year-old girl. Severn Suzuki addressed delegates for 6½ minutes, telling them she and they all belonged to a family 30 million species strong, a fact that national borders and governments could not change (Rogers, 1993: 105–7). But once you'd been charmed by Severn, how can you actually frame universal principles in the context of diverse cultures and beliefs?

The Rio Declaration on Environment and Development outlined 27 principles that tried (Rogers, 1993: ch. 10). Principle 5 states:

> All States and all people shall cooperate in the essential task of eradicating poverty as an indispensable requirement for sustainable development ...

And Principle 12:

> States should cooperate to promote a supportive and open international economic system that would lead to economic growth and sustainable development in all countries ...

Governments found it easy to nod their heads at this kind of thing and, ultimately, Rio's outcomes were all about aspirations and good intentions (Christoff & Eckersley, 2013: 100–2). Even at its best there was a tightrope being walked here between business-as-usual (does an 'open system' imply the free movement of capital?) and something more ambitious (eradicating poverty). Transnational Corporations are barely mentioned. Indeed, many NGOs felt that, if anything, it was *they* who were being marginalised (Rogers, 1993: 235–6, ch. 11; Connelly *et al.*, 2012: 273). With the fall of the USSR, global capitalism was now presented as the solution to *all* problems.

The Rio summit had four additional outcomes:

- Convention on Biological Diversity – dealing with genetic resources;
- Forest Principles – recommendations for sustainable forestry;
- The United Nations Framework Convention on Climate Change – commitments and principles that could be used in time to shape international law and relations, including the Kyoto Protocol (see Chapter 11);
- Agenda 21.

The purpose of Agenda 21[1] can best be described by quoting its opening paragraph:

> Humanity stands at a defining moment in history. We are confronted with a perpetuation of disparities between and within nations, a worsening of

poverty, hunger, ill health and illiteracy, and the continuing deterioration of the ecosystems on which we depend for our well-being. However, integration of environment and development concerns and greater attention to them will lead to the fulfilment of basic needs, improved living standards for all, better protected and managed ecosystems and a safer, more prosperous future. No nation can achieve this on its own; but together we can – in a global partnership for sustainable development.

This association of sustainability with poverty, hunger, health and illiteracy denoted a new agenda for social policy – and paragraph 3.1 also mentions the importance of "greater equity in income distribution". Post-Rio, for example, the World Health Organisation (1997) published a series of documents as part of its Healthy Cities project, meant to offer a framework for municipal action through Local Agenda 21 (LA21). In seeing the need to reconfigure nineteenth and twentieth century structures of governance, including the welfare state, so that they can address twenty-first century problems (e.g. sustainability, equity, energy, food) it was inching towards a vision of green social policy. For its part, the EU felt it was well placed to translate such initiatives into practice (Leontitsis, 2011: 458), as we see shortly.

Globalisation

The Earth Summit was one manifestation of what was by now being called 'globalisation': the increasing significance of global events, networks, interconnections, processes and flows of information, people, finance, spaces and products, and thus greater interdependencies as regions, nations, cultures, communities and localities are reconfigured, sometimes dramatically (cf. Ritzer, 2010: 2; also Christoff & Eckersley, 2013: 29–31).

Describing Rio as a 'summit' was instructive, therefore. Globalisation implies multiple summits – all of which are constantly shifting and in dynamic interchange with one another – but also multiple plains and valleys upon which equally significant activities may be occurring. There was globalisation 'from above' and 'from below' in other words. Yet the above/below categories only fleetingly captured a landscape that was perpetually evolving and so immensely difficult to snapshot.

Globalisation from above no longer quite meant what it once had (Bernstein, 2001: 71–83). The Montreal Protocol on chlorofluorocarbons harkened back to the 1972 Stockholm era where the emphasis was on public, statist and regulatory solutions. It was largely a 'command and control' measure in which market forces are subject to collective action: drafting legislation, monitoring compliance and penalising non-compliers through the law. The US government went along with Montreal, somewhat reluctantly (Gareau & DuPuis, 2009: 2307–11).

At Rio just a few years later, with the US now the only superpower in town and corporate capitalism entrenching itself almost everywhere, the rules had changed and the rule-makers were more enamored of market-based solutions than ever (Klein, 2014: 18–24).

If anything, the piling up of environmental crises *may have helped to spread market liberalisations*. Dealing with almost 200 nations[2] and thousands of inter-governmental organisations required a series of interlocking, horizontal networks. Global agreements could set the targets and governments might have to do some navigating and steering, but otherwise Hayekian assumptions seemed to dominate (Weale, 1992: 87–8). The thinking was: since nature is too complex for a single agency to understand and control we need markets to coordinate the information and actions that are necessarily dispersed. There was no place for the Leviathan state.

Globalisation from below was also changing, especially with the emergence of worldwide social movements of which, by the early 1990s, the green movement was one of the most visible (Hamel *et al.*, 2001). These movements were often immense, pluralistic and fluid. Protest groups could appear, disappear and reappear. They might be single-issue groups or those concerned with social identity.

Diversity notwithstanding, most within the green movement rejected the new Hayekian logic. Not being able to plan and control *everything* does not mean that you cannot control and plan *somethings*. Wasn't 'democracy' more essential than 'markets' and couldn't democracy become more participatory and horizontal? But activists and supporters faced a problem of knowing how to proceed. What should addressing climate change, pollution, resource depletion and the like involve? Should you put on a suit and stand for parliament? Should you drop-out, smoke weed and chain yourself to a tree? Should the movement embrace all of those things ('one no, many yeses') or not?

In response to such questions, by the 1990s the green movement had attenuated (Rootes, 2003a: 4–7; Connelly *et al.*, 2012: 116–18). Its growth and the increased public awareness of ecological problems had, perhaps inevitably, meant a loss of the momentum and focused direction of the 1970s and 1980s (McCormick, 1995: 258–9).[3] In being consulted by governments Greenpeace and FoE had become respectable. Was there a price to be paid for this? Respectability risked exacerbating a division, which the oppositional stance of earlier decades had obscured, between those who were flexible about working with and within existing institutions and structures, and those who thought such compromises betrayed the deeper, more systemic changes that were needed. As it moved away from the margins the green movement faced an age-old 'radical's dilemma': how do you work within and use a system *to effect change* when that system is itself *in need of change*?

Greens on the move

In Britain such dilemmas were perhaps less acute. The Green Party never repeated its 1989 surge, though non-parliamentary activism was large and getting larger.

From 1981–91, membership of FoE rose by 533%, of Greenpeace by 1260% (to almost half a million) and of the RSPB by 93% (to 850,000) (Della Porta & Diani, 1999: 24). By 1998, 20% of Britons claimed to belong to at least one environmental organisation (Rootes, 2003b: 20). From 1988–92 first Thatcher and then Major raised expectations about a breakthrough into politics and government policymaking that were not fulfilled (Carter & Lowe, 2000). The early-mid 1990s therefore become an era of protest and direct action, as a lot of pent-up frustration had to go somewhere (Rootes, 2003b: 49).

Take a group like Reclaim the Streets. This was a response to the 'shopping mall' phenomenon, where public spaces are increasingly commercialised, privatised, homogenised, regulated and surveilled so that anything that does not fit the dominant norm, i.e. spending money and not looking out of place, attracts attention, suspicion and eventually security guards (Fitzpatrick, 2005: 172–7). Reclaiming public space for the public therefore becomes a political act. Street parties began to spring up as a Situationist, Rabelaisian celebration of the city in the name of diversity and spontaneity. Beginning in London in 1991 Reclaim the Streets originated within the anti-roads movement, before disbanding, reforming a few years later, reaching its peak in 1996–97 and seeing its example spread around the world. Anti-roads protests continued throughout these years (Rootes, 2003b: 30–1), especially against a motorway bypasses across Twyford Down, near Winchester and Newbury (Sheail, 2002: 189–90).

And in 1995 the country witnessed a series of protests against the unethical transportation of livestock for export, protests that flared up and drew in many middle-class demonstrators, often female and elderly, who had never gone anywhere near activism before (Harris, 1995). The government's Criminal Justice and Public Order Act of 1994 had been introduced to clamp down on anti-social behaviour. A populist response when it's a bunch of Crusties being arrested. Not so much when the person being handcuffed looks like your gran.

Such groups were the precursors to the anti-globalisation movement that we explore in Chapter 11.[4]

Did such protests have any effect? Not much. The road-building strategy was downsized in the mid-1990s but not necessarily due to environmental concerns (Root, 2000: 454; Rydin, 2003: 61–2), nor even necessarily to a recognition that building roads *exacerbates* congestion (Robinson, 2005: 190–1). If anything, Tory hostility to public transport had intensified (Cullingworth *et al.*, 2015: 487–90).

Anyone over 26 still using a bus was a failure, Thatcher was reported as saying.[5] Bus deregulation (with the exception of London) began in the mid-1980s. Society is an association of individuals, Tory thinking went. Going wherever you want to go is a fundamental freedom. Therefore, anything that inhibits such freedom is wrong and should be reformed. The privatisation of mobility and of social space is thus a counterpart to the privatisation of state-owned companies and utilities. So if you couldn't get rid of buses and trains you could at least make them behave a bit more like private vehicles.

Privatisation of the railways duly followed in 1996. This was a hasty, disorganised process that fractured the industry into 100 organisations, linked through labyrinthine contracts and penalties, with the main divisions lying between the owners of the tracks (Railtrack), the train companies and those responsible for renewal and maintenance (Wolmar, 2007: 301–11). The tactic was slash-and-burn. Get the system into the private sector and any post-1997 Labour government would probably not spend time, energy and political capital on renationalising it. Another public good had been diminished (Judt, 2010: 207–16).

Anyone expecting that this Byzantine system would compel latter day John Betjemans (see Chapter 3) to wander nostalgically down platforms whispering 'marvelous, marvelous', while old maids cycled to communion through the morning mist,[6] were to be cruelly disillusioned. This wasn't even a reinvention of nineteenth century entrepreneurialism. It was a simple cash machine for private operators, with taxpayers and 'customers' expected to keep feeding the ATM. Railtrack and the train companies began their incessant game of blaming each other for delays. High-profile crashes led to a sense that safety had been compromised in the pursuit of profit. And despite the anticipated wonders of private sector efficiency, fares and subsidies now proceeded to rise. Travelling across the south from one Tory shire to another could be particularly difficult.

No matter. British Rail had been under-resourced for years, giving apologists for the private sector a familiar defence: no matter how bad the service the public sector equivalent must always, by definition, be worse.

Europe united

By the 1990s, then, environmental issues and politics were unavoidable in one form or another. And though in the UK neither the green party nor protest groups had much sway in Whitehall, there was one influence that even the most recalcitrant Tory could not ignore.

The EU was searching for a role and an identity.[7] At their most optimistic EU architects like Delors felt that the EU was well placed to navigate the tensions between globalisation from below (increasing demands for participation and partnership) and globalisation from above, which implied:

- the increased power, influence and velocity of financial markets;
- the greater openness of markets;
- competition from Asia's 'tiger economies' (where labour was cheap yet well trained and high-tech);
- accelerating technological development and communicative capacity.

The EU would in time present its approach to environmental problems as exemplifying a successful navigational strategy.

The 15 years prior to 1987 were dominated by three Environmental Action Programmes (EAPs), mainly designed to reduce pollution, conserve an 'ecological equilibrium' and encourage the rational use of natural resources (Hey, 2005: 18–20; Knill & Liefferink, 2007: 2–12; Leontitsis, 2011: 449–50; Connelly *et al.*, 2012: 294–8; Morphet, 2013: 144–6). But, resembling injunctions to act within the existing competencies of the common market, no legal powers of enforcement were attached to these programmes.

It was the SEA that established the environment as a distinct policy domain having the force of law (Knill & Liefferink, 2007: 12–20; Leontitsis, 2011: 450–2). This created a benchmark of environmental protection that all member states would have to observe and reduce the ability of governments to block legislation in the name of national self-interest. Environmental policy was thus a key point of tension between national states – though some more than others – and the EU. In conjunction with the European Environment Agency, established in 1994, the EU Commission would be at the forefront of environmental policymaking (Knill & Liefferink, 2007: 57–61): formulating policy, monitoring the compliance or otherwise of member states (whose role it was to implement said policy) and, if necessary, taking cases of non-compliance or underperformance to the European Court of Justice.

The fourth EAP (1987–92) was very much about preparation for the creation of the single market in 1992, i.e. a stress upon the economic benefits to be derived from harmonising environmental standards in the exchange of capital, goods, services and labour (Connelly *et al.*, 2012: 299–306). It was consciously modelled on the principle of sustainable development and a win–win strategy in which environmental sustainability and economic prosperity were assumed to be mutually reinforcing. It signaled a role for 'market instruments' like green taxes, subsidies and tradable permits (Hey, 2005: 20–2).

The fifth EAP (1992–99) was in many respects continuous with its predecessors (Leontitsis, 2011: 452). There was now, though, an emphasis on 'ecological structural change'. This meant, first, integration across sectors and policies (like public transport, energy efficiency and waste prevention); and, second, a role for NGOs in the political process (Hey, 2005: 23). In tandem with the shift away from command and control at the global level, the fifth EAP also made greater room than its predecessors for market-based policy instruments, eco-labelling and voluntary agreements (Jordan *et al.*, 2003a: 562–70). The focus was now very much upon principles of cost effectiveness and competition.[8] It is in this context that the fifth EAP's targets (relating to air and water quality, energy and waste, agriculture and biodiversity, and urban environments) should be understood.

However, it was now that conflict between the Commission and member states sharpened. Part of the problem was that the fifth EAP had been launched before Rio and seemed to be inflexible. Responding to Rio became a responsibility of member states, therefore. Furthermore, Germany and Britain, in particular, preferred to emphasise *the economic costs and burdens* of EU proposals, such as that for an energy tax. In short, impetus swung away from the Commission and back towards member states and the fifth EAP was ultimately perceived as something of an irrelevance (Hey, 2005: 23–4).

So the emphasis in the 1990s would be less upon new legislation and more upon forcing members to implement laws already adopted: a period of consolidation (Jordan, 2006a: 6). According to Knill and Liefferink (2007: 25), "EU environmental policy lost momentum on the European agenda ..." To some extent this paralleled a general move away from vertical, hierarchical governance towards flatter, more horizontal modes. But the growing influence of the UK and its free market agenda was also instrumental. In the EU the German-driven regulatory approach of the 1980s was now being superseded by a UK-inspired 'cost-benefit' one (Sbragia, 2000).

Reluctant Britain

For, by the early 1990s the UK had evolved a kind of *adaptive compliance* in the face of EU developments (Morphet, 2013: 149–50).

Governments in the 1970s had been self-satisfied about Britain's environmental record, even as they were resisting measures to combat acid rain (see Chapter 6). Because Britain had created the DoE, the world's first government department dedicated to the environment, surely the EU should be learning from us, it was thought (Jordan, 2006b: 206)! Such views had been bolstered by the decimation of the coal industry and the subsequent dash for gas (see Chapter 7; Jordan, 2006a: 13), both of which reduced UK GHG emissions.

Yet Thatcher had underestimated the significance of the SEA, even as she was signing it. In effect, Britain had locked itself into a reactive, defensive complacency.

Under Major the UK approach became less defensive and more concerned to negotiate and form alliances rather than to lecture others (Seldon, 1997: 163–8, 242–52; Taylor, 2006: 44–50). His government was not exactly pressing its foot onto the accelerator, but nor was it riding the brake anymore (Jordan, 2002: 83–93; Jordan *et al.*, 2003b). The DoE now became one of the most Europeanised departments (Jordan, 2006c: 239) and by the end of the decade over four-fifths of UK environmental policy originated in the EU. The UK went from being a laggard to a more proactive player – perhaps even supplanting Germany's former dominance (Leontitsis, 2011: 461).

In short, Major was a chameleon here too, except now it was the chameleon who was colouring his surroundings.

Major himself was fairly indifferent to environmental issues. It was not one of his 'core instincts' (Seldon, 1997: 133, 183). He attended only the last two days of the Rio Summit, managing to visit a British Petroleum installation at the same time. But Major spotted the political angle sure enough (Weale, 1992: 156–67). Talking green would help the Tories cure their image as a party which always wanted to slash, cut and dismantle. John Gummer, appointed as Environment Secretary in 1993, was the one senior Conservative with a genuine passion for ecological issues.[9] Major also recognised that ceding some national sovereignty on these matters was inevitable and desirable. At Rio, two conventions were signed: one to cut emissions of GHGs to 1990 levels by 2000; the other to protect biodiversity (Seldon, 1997: 301–2). The former in particular would become an important point of reference.

Yet once you had made the correct noises in public, was much else needed? For instance, in its lack of detail and targets, of a sense of urgency and of a strategy concerning institutional reform, *This Common Inheritance* set the tone for what was to follow under Major (Voisey & O'Riordan, 1998: 158–66). This Janus quality was consistent with a PM who was a Thatcherite about objectives, if not about the means of achieving them. Four key elements of Major's environmental record should be noted (also Jordan, 2002: 40–2).

First, the environment continued to be thought of in terms of its actual or potential costs to the economy. Any integration of the two elements was fairly modest because conceived in zero sum terms: the more you have of one the less you have of another.[10] The government was eager to be seen as taking a positive stance on the environment because this helped offset its negative stance on other EU issues (Lowe & Ward, 1998: 286–7). The former was therefore something of a bargaining chip that could be sacrificed if and when necessary.

Second, the environment could be sold as a way of making local authorities more efficient and accountable to the needs of their communities and businesses than hitherto (Morphet, 2013: 153–4). 'If the EU needs improvements in waste management,' the narrative went, 'what better way than to have private refuse companies do what inefficient local councils cannot?' The environment could therefore be seen as an opportunity for the commercial sector to take activities away from local governance and democracy. The EU could be framed as a means of facilitating what a Tory government had long wanted to do anyway.

Third, the principle of subsidiarity was also promoted as a way of resisting any hint of federalism. Environmental standards meant a 'baseline minimum' that member states could improve upon if they desired. The evisceration of local government in the 1980s ensured that in the UK 'subsidiarity' would not reach much lower than central government itself. This was fully in keeping with a British tradition of governance that centralises power on Westminster and Whitehall (aided by an unwritten constitution), is short-termist, characterised by interdepartmental divisions and a lack of strategic coordination between regulatory agencies (Morphet, 2013: 151–3). This tradition constituted the wall into which LA21 would ultimately smash (see below).

Finally, the UK was also at the forefront of promoting voluntary agreements between regulators and industry. In one sense, such 'soft policy' tools are arguably more suited to generating consensus than what can often be the heavy hand of command and control. Voluntary agreements enable all sides to listen to one another and share knowledge. The habitual problem with voluntary agreements is that they are *voluntary*. They leave resistors and non-compliers with a greater degree of power to set agendas and room to wiggle out of even when agendas have been agreed. Voluntary agreements are not just means to an end but ways of determining ends. 'Soft' can also mean 'weak'.

These four elements allowed pro-EU Conservatives to portray EU environmental policymaking as consistent with its free market ethics (Voisey &

O'Riordan, 1998: 166–9). One legacy of trying to square this circle was to instill in the public a scepticism towards green taxes.

Despite the low tax rhetoric, free market economies will always need to raise some taxes somewhere, on someone.[11] What better way to avoid accusations of hypocrisy than to blame others? So, the 1993 introduction of VAT on fuel was sold as a post-Rio necessity but was really about improving public finances in the wake of recession (Seldon, 1997: 367–8). Nobody was fooled. A proposal to double the fuel VAT a year later was defeated in the Commons (Seldon, 1997: 513–15). The suspicion that green taxes were really just another raid by the Treasury on your wallets and purses was thus inculcated. A key instrument of environmental policy thus became tainted from the outset.

In sum, the Major years were ones in which the UK first played 'catch-up' with the EU before, in its promotion of alternatives to command and control instruments, experiencing convergence between the UK and EU agendas (Lowe & Ward, 1998: 288). Environmental policy illustrated that though the UK must comply with EU mandates, local cultures, systems and traditions of governance continued to dominate.[12] Hence what I called 'adaptive compliance'. Far from being a victim of a federalist EU, Britain actually helped to reshape EU governance in this field in the 1990s.

Climate change issues therefore emerged onto the global agenda at a time when the emphasis in the EU was increasingly upon (1) integrating common environmental standards into the economy to aid competitiveness, (2) financial incentives (taxes, subsidies, permits), (3) subsidiarity, such that member states had the whip hand, and (4) voluntary agreements. As we see in the next three chapters this left the EU (like the UK itself) occupying an ambivalent role vis climate change. It was frequently more radical than other regional blocs (especially the USA), yet it would also illustrate the deficiencies of an approach so dominated by the principles of a market society.

Local agendas

Yet if Major was lukewarm about environmental issues was this the case across the rest of British government?

The DoE's response to Rio was full of good intentions, including recognition of "the importance of tackling poverty, one of the root causes of environmental degradation" (Department of the Environment, 1992: 3). A sustainable development strategy followed in 1993–94, but many NGOs complained that this was another lip-service exercise, bereft of genuine participation (Dalal-Clayton, 1994: 30). In any event, one result was the 1995 Environment Act, which committed the government to national strategies on air quality and waste, and set up the Environment Agency. The latter assumed the responsibilities of the National Rivers Authority, the Inspectorate of Pollution and took waste regulation away from local authorities.

But perhaps the most striking reform concerned the implementation of LA21 (Cullingworth & Nadin, 2006: 256–61; Connelly *et al.*, 2012: 364–9). By the mid-1990s local authorities were eager to reclaim back some of the powers that had been filtering away for a decade. Did LA21 represent a rapprochement between a Conservative central government and local councils where Labour was often dominant?

When the Rio summit spoke of poverty it was largely of poverty in developing countries. But it also acknowledged that poverty manifested itself in different ways in different places and so required diverse solutions. LA21 required cities to devise and implement an appropriate local plan for sustainable development (Evans & Theobold, 2003). By the turn of the millennium, 4000 European cities were doing so (Garcia-Sanchez & Prado-Lorenzo, 2008), with early evidence of real achievements (Selman, 1998).

Inevitably, some cities were more focused and committed than others, in terms of organisation, budgeting, public participation and involvement of the private sector. Some plans were properly integrated into the rest of the municipal agenda, but some were not. What also mattered was the degree of leadership and assistance (both locally and from the national state). Early research suggested that (along with Sweden, Norway and the Netherlands) Britain was engaging with LA21 more enthusiastically than most other European nations (Tuxworth, 1996).

It was, however, better at 'social sustainability' (dog crap, litter and traffic) than a genuine 'ecosocial sustainability', which systematically integrated the economic, social and environmental dimensions.[13] In fact, Bond et al. (1998) found that UK authorities tended to see the natural environment as an add-on (something to be managed by environmental departments), so avoiding a proper integration strategy. Real integration seemed to require the fostering of a culture that embraces change, more effective participation structures and new forms of coordination:

> Without all the complementary actions of international organizations, national governments, businesses and other major groups, the progress made by local communities and individuals will remain part of an incomplete picture.
>
> (Tuxworth, 1996: 296)

Without proper integration, the risks were that LA21 might fail to engage local people and encourage them to see environmentalism as unrelated to daily bread-and-butter problems.

So, there was an opportunity here to incorporate social and environmental policies but it was exploited only weakly and intermittently. The Aalborg Charter[14] referred to 'Social Equity for Urban Sustainability', which acknowledged that basic social needs (e.g. access to water, food, housing, healthcare, education and employment) were essential for social and urban sustainability. This implied a quality of life emphasis and, in social policy terms, reference to education, social inclusion, community development, deprivation, transport, health (re air quality and pollution), energy use, housing and land use.

Yet even a leading centre of LA21 excellence like Leicester found it very difficult to engage people on low incomes (Roberts, 2000: 18). And across the country, Evans and Theobold (2003: 788) found that the social equity dimension of sustainable development was interpreted in terms of traditional social welfare rather than notions of environmental justice. Sustainability was not being applied to education and social services, for instance.

In LA21, then, we have real hints of an agenda capable of bringing social and environmental policies together in practical and progressive terms. For the most part, though, progress was slow, uneven and departmentally fragmented. One of the main barriers lay in the control that now resided in Whitehall over local authority expenditure and revenue-raising (Voisey, 1998). For all of the warm words emanating from Gummer's DoE, effective political leadership and the required social distribution of resources were missing. There was only so much that even pioneering cities like Leicester could do on their own.

Assessing the long-term 'ecosocial' impact of LA21 is therefore difficult. Tony Blair would voice his enthusiasm but actual funding was still lacking. And governments eager to make an impact want to start with a blank sheet of paper, which frequently means erasing what already exists rather than building upon it. New Labour's 'National Strategy for Neighbourhood Renewal' would *not* be promoted as LA21 in action (Rowe, 2000: 88; Power, 2009). In 1997 Blair asked local authorities to 'complete' their LA21 strategies by 2000 (Cullingworth & Nadin, 2006: 262).

By the early years of the new millennium, European cities were already dropping the rhetoric of LA21. For those who had taken it seriously this was because environmental policy had become an accepted part of local governance. For others, LA21 had never really mattered anyway. Though many UK local authorities had embraced the language of LA21 the erosion of local powers and the failings of national government meant that its potential was under-exploited.

Social reforms

That local action on social and environmental policies was heavily constrained is no surprise. A business-as-usual approach also characterised Major's wider approach to social policy (Marwick, 2003: 359–72; Page, 2015: 106–14).[15] The early-mid 1990s was mainly about consolidation and continuation of what had come before, in other words (Bonefeld *et al.*, 1995: 137–54).[16] As noted in the last chapter, Major's consensus-seeking approach enabled healthcare reforms to bed down and there was a consolidation of Thatcher's education reforms too (Dorey, 1999b).

There were three policy innovations during Major's tenure.

First, the Child Support Agency (CSA) was designed to reduce state assistance for single mothers by chasing absent fathers and enforcing a financial contribution to their children and former partner (Hill, 1999: 172–3). This ticked the usual Conservative boxes: lower government spending and clamping down on 'the irresponsible' (deadbeat dads and queue-jumping single mums).

Those warning of the disaster to come were safely ignored. One problem was that, for often very good reasons, some mums did not want the dad anywhere near them or their children. Was the government going to insist on reattaching them to someone who might be abusive, for instance? Nor did mothers have an incentive to cooperate since their state support would shrink in line with increased maintenance payments from the absent father. In any event, the CSA had a lamentable record of chasing absent parents; a huge backlog of cases quickly built up. And where the CSA did intervene it was often accused of interfering with existing arrangements with which both ex-partners were perfectly happy (especially when the wellbeing of second families was at stake). The CSA was a catastrophic policy failure (King & Crewe, 2013: ch. 6).

Second, the 1995 Disability Discrimination Act was a welcome extension of such legislation to a long-neglected group. However, it did allow many exemptions for employers on grounds of cost. Disability rights campaigners were heavily critical of such exemptions and of other reforms too. Claimants for Invalidity Benefit had had to show that they were unfit *for work that was available*. In 1995 this was replaced with Incapacity Benefit, where claimants had to show they were unfit for *any* work (Hill, 1999: 171). The new premise was that your employability was separate from the actual availability of jobs and the suitability of those jobs. The emphasis was shifting away from demand and towards supply, i.e. your motivations, your behaviour, your values.

And that shift affected everyone else, too. The third and single most important of Major's reforms came the same year (Howard *et al.*, 2001: 55–60). Jobseekers Allowance (JSA) consolidated unemployment benefit and income support into the same scheme, with a contributory element[17] and a less generous means-tested element.

The change of language was significant. Was 'jobseeker' meant to be empowering – an active noun compared to a passive one (unemployment)? Or, was it a way in which government divested itself of responsibility, implying that unemployment and unemployment levels are due to the efforts, or otherwise, of individuals and nothing to do with the state of the economy, the government's management of that economy, employers' activities (like providing childcare and skills training), institutional discrimination, bias in the education system, international circumstances, or indeed anything that affects the condition of the labour market and over which individuals have little or no control?

Quietly, then, a key ambition of the 1945 system had been overturned. The fact that an insurance element and a means-tested element were now fitted under the JSA umbrella signaled the collapse of the moral and administrative gap that Beveridge had urged between the 'earned benefits' of social insurance and 'unearned benefits'. Therefore, Major's reform arguably represented a further erosion of the insurance principle in the name of targeting and an encouragement of the view that all claimants are dependent skivers living off the independent, hard-working taxpayer.

This emphasis on making policy by remaking the *language* of policy reappeared in less effective guises elsewhere. In 1993 Major called for a 'Back to

Basics' remoralisation of society (Gilmour & Garnett, 1997: 363–5; Seldon, 1997: 404–8, 431–7): self-discipline, respect for law, commitment to family. This, too, continued with the theme of Thatcherite individualisation in which the poor are poor because they lack morals and the affluent are affluent not because of class, parents and social background or simple good luck but because they took risks, worked hard and 'got on'.

It was therefore to the subsequent amusement of everyone that the Back to Basics rhetoric was demolished when various Tory MPs were exposed as having extra-marital affairs – including, it turned out, John Major himself! A further blow was delivered due to cash-for-access scandals that hit the government in the mid-1990s. The insistence that virtuous behaviour and good character were *the* cures for poverty was exposed as hypocrisy and cant.

Opting out

Social policy under Major was also defined by what it did *not* do: it did not sign the EU's Social Charter (Seldon, 1997: 248). A social dimension had been discussed since the early 1960s, but it was the SEA that gave impetus to a distinct Social Charter of employment rights and principles (Hantrais, 1995: 2–15; Ross, 1995: 368–84). The UK was the only member state to refuse to adopt it and subsequently vetoed its inclusion as a 'Social Chapter' within the Maastricht Treaty. This gave it nothing more than the status of a protocol, designed to complement national legislation, rather than anything with greater power.

Tory hostility to the Chapter was undoubtedly a subset of its fears about the EU. Thatcher had signed the SEA on the basis of a calculation that any loss of sovereignty would be worth it due to the economic benefits of membership. It was her last act of loyalty to Heath. But anxieties about sovereignty quickly took over – signified by Thatcher's Bruges speech of September 1988 – as the Delors agenda became clear. Why defeat socialism at home only to see it being snuck in through the EU backdoor?

Two versions of Thatcherism now raced for poll-position. Major believed that the best way to revive the pre-Delors vision of Europe as a trading block was through engagement with the EU. His critics, though, thought that small-state capitalism required detachment from a project, which, they now delighted in observing, called itself European *union* (Forster, 2002: 301, 304–5; Baker *et al.*, 2002: 415–18). Major's 'back me or sack me' threat to rebellious backbenchers worked but the party had now entered a self-harming phase that no amount of therapy could cure (McAllister & Studlar, 2000: 361–2; Lynch & Whitaker, 2013). Pro-EU opinion became less and less vocal.

Some hostility must also have been motivated by regret over Britain's status in the world compared to what it had been 50 years earlier. With the demise of the USSR, Brussels became the new Moscow. A lot of anti-EU feeling would therefore have been generated by the EU's perceived threat to an alliance that had served one of the most successful political parties in the world well: that between national identity and centralised parliamentary control.

And some Euroscepticism was actually about globalisation (Baker *et al.*, 2002: 400–1, 408–10). In a Thatcherite worldview, the *laissez faire* revolution was meant to respect national borders; hardly realistic without the kind of statism that the Tory Party had long since rejected. Beware of unintended consequences when it comes to genies and bottles. All of which built to an uncomfortable realisation the party found it easier to sublimate. Thus when the EU implemented the free movement of labour rather than seeing this as a fulfilment of *laissez faire* doctrines many nationalistic Tories preferred to see it as an anti-British act – becoming hysterical about the additional, fairly modest attempts by the EU to underpin markets with common social standards. 'It's not free markets eroding British sovereignty', went the thinking, 'it's the socialistic EU'. Having unleashed the forces and logic of unregulated capitalism it was Thatcherites who would make the most ardent Eurosceptics.

Were Eurosceptic fears grounded in reality? Not so far as EU social policy was concerned. Anxieties about the adverse impacts of the Social Chapter on business were not borne out by actual research into actual business attitudes (Sapsford *et al.*, 1997). But politics is about perception and perceptions are always local.

So, in addition to its veto of the Social Chapter, the UK was the only member state to utilise a provision, in the 1993 Working Time Directive, allowing an individual to opt out of the 48-hour upper limit on weekly employment. The justification was that the directive would otherwise interfere with the needs of private and public sector organisations. It also derived from a peculiarly British assumption that productivity comes from working longer hours.

Social Europe

Yet such one-eyed vision misread what was actually the dominant influence on EU social policymaking: economic imperatives. EU social policy was almost entirely synonymous with employment policy, particularly vis equal opportunities, vocational training, freedom of movement, health and safety. Healthcare, education and so forth remained within the purview of national legislatures. EU social policy was, therefore, never about the creation of some pan-European welfare state.

This influence was unsurprising.

From the Treaty of Rome onwards, social policies had occupied a subservient position to economic policies (Geyer, 2000: 246–50). Developments from the late 1980s onwards added a stronger social dimension, to the point where some began talking about a 'Social Europe' (see Leibfried & Pierson, 1995), but in truth this dimension was minimalist and designed to support the internal market, rather than any politics of decommodification (Streeck, 1995: 412–13; Bonoli *et al.*, 2000: 158–9). The Working Time Directive, for instance, was driven more by the goal of job creation than considerations of workers' well-being (Barnard *et al.*, 2003: 462). The emphasis in EU social policy tended to be upon voluntarism. Legally binding measures were few and far between.

This gave EU social policy a curiously old-fashioned demeanour. The emphasis on labour market participation meant that whenever 'European citizenship' was mentioned it seemed to exclude those whose lives and activities lay outside the wage-earning domain. And the policymaking process itself was highly technocratic, bureaucratised, legalistic and undemocratic. It resembled, if anything, a man-from-the-ministry approach circa 1945.

This is not to slate it, necessarily. Workers' rights can become an important platform for broader reforms. After all, what made Thatcherites brake out in cold sweats was the EU's talk of parental leave, anti-discrimination, the European Social Fund, social exclusion and the general language of social rights.

On balance, Geyer (2000: 256, 259; Deacon, 2001: 69–76) is surely correct to propose that EU social policy was neither a threat to, nor a saviour of, national welfare states. After more than 10 years of Thatcherism, it is understandable that the British Left latched onto the EU social agenda as a counterweight to Tory-dominated, Whitehall centralisation. But member states would continue to forge their own welfare paths. For social democratic states, the EU's emphasis on employment might reinforce their resilience in the face of financial globalisation. But for those sliding down the free market chute, like Britain, there was little sign that the EU – with its emphasis on minimal standards – would implement a counter-revolution.

To some extent, then, the EU was acting as a *conduit* for globalisation where welfare states were expected to become 'leaner and meaner' in order to service greater market liberalisation (Ginsburg, 2001). This implied:

- Enabling economic competitiveness.
- Stressing employability and labour market flexibility.
- Making greater room for private providers and commercialised values.
- Effecting social cohesion in the context of greater socioeconomic inequalities.
- Increasing penalties for the unproductive who do not seek employment.

Was it possible to combine both agendas, i.e. to preserve the legacy of 1945–79, while also modernising and adapting to the demands of global markets? New Labour certainly thought so, as we begin to see in Chapter 10.

Key questions

What relationships between the environmental and social policy agendas have emerged? To what extent have social policies and the politics of welfare reform deliberately informed and been informed by the principles and values of environmental ethics and politics?

Although with domestic economic and social policies it was very much business-as-usual, the increasing Europeanisation of British politics was significant.

On the face of it, there was not much scope within the EU for anything resembling an ecosocial agenda. The principal activities concerned preparation for a single market (1992) and then a single currency (1999). Yet if this was another economy-first approach it was more the 'social economy' ideal that attracted consensus across the continent, from Christian Democrats, social democrats and greens. The idea that the legitimacy and effective functioning of markets depends upon markets' moral contexts and social consequences was commonplace everywhere – with the UK an obvious exception.

Thatcherites had painted themselves into an intellectual corner, imagining that markets require an *absence* of social props and supports. No wonder it was usually they who depicted Delors as desiring a socialist, federalist superstate. Major set about trying to remould Europe in more of a free market image. By opting out of the Social Chapter there would be a misalignment between the economic component of EU integration and its social component. The attempt to create cross-national social economies was thereby undermined.

What the architects of the new Europe really stood for was a relative conjunction, a crystallisation of what would remain politically and culturally diverse nations. The relative harmonisation of economic and social policies was to *enable* the free movement of goods, investment and workers within a broad 'social market capitalism'.

As such, the EU's environmental policies were relatively modest and concerned to develop market instruments (taxes, subsidies, permits). It was about creating a level playing field, a solid platform that would not allow nations or firms to gain an unfair advantage on others by compromising on environmental standards. That said, once this platform was in place then presumably those standards could be raised as required – just as the portability of welfare entitlements or the robustness of income safety nets could be improved over time. There were already signs of this in the shift from the fourth to the fifth EAP.

Therefore, what you had in Europe by the early-mid 1990s was not the immediate integration of the environmental and social policy domains, but arguably a marshalling of elements, which could slowly mingle and coalesce, converging on this ideal of social capitalism. It was therefore possible to envisage the ecosocial as one element of this long-term aspiration for EU-wide social markets.

Inspired by Rio, LA21 was an embryonic form of this. If the EU was that which could enable the local, the national and the cross-national to be interwoven, then LA21 represented a means of bringing that intersection together with another: encompassing economic, social and environmental policies. In the mid-1990s it felt like an era of new possibilities was opening. Yet much of that promise would remain unfulfilled.

In the UK, the radical aspects of LA21 were limited and any hope that the municipal would become a new laboratory of civic experimentation was dashed. The centralising, market ideology of Thatcherism had sought to neuter any possible counterweights to its power on the part of intermediate institutions. The highly marketised form of ecosocial politics described at the end of the last chapter was not going to free up space within itself for alternatives to be nurtured. If socialism through the backdoor (Europe) was going to be resisted then so was any hint of the ecosocial popping its head up through the internal cellar door of local government.

Notes

1 See https://sustainabledevelopment.un.org/content/documents/Agenda21.pdf [accessed 6 June 2015]
2 In 1991–92 alone, 20 new independent states were created as a result of the dissolution of the USSR and Yugoslavia.
3 Note that by the 1990s the peace and anti-nuclear elements of the earlier green movement were – for now at least – less prominent than before.
4 The Brent Spar incident anticipated this (Yearley & Forrester, 2000: 138–44). Shell proposed to dispose of this oil-storage platform by sinking it off the western coast of Scotland. A successful campaign spearheaded by Greenpeace – including a consumer boycott of Shell – led the company to abandon the proposal.
5 www.parliament.the-stationery-office.co.uk/pa/cm200203/cmhansrd/vo030702/debtext/30702-10.htm [accessed 30 June 2015]
6 This is to satirise Major's clumsy attempt in 1993 to appropriate Orwell in defining Britishness.
7 Time for a terminology check. Prior to the early 1990s European integration was made via the EEC (itself a successor to the European Coal and Steel Community). This would sometimes be called the 'common market' though by the 1980s it was more usual to refer to the EC. The title European Union (EU) began in the early 1990s.
8 The UK had actually been something of a dawdler when it came to market instruments in the field of environmental policy. This would change only moderately at first, with green taxes used as revenue raisers rather than ecological protectors. Such instruments would only become really significant under New Labour (Jordan *et al.*, 2003b).
9 It was under Gummer that sustainability indicators were introduced into British policymaking: 1230 of them across 21 areas, though these were dominated by economic values such as the assumed benefits of GDP (Voisey & O'Riordan, 1998: 169). They were the precursors to John Prescott's initiatives later (see next chapter).
10 This meant that it was slow to incorporate the principles of ecological modernisation, leaving New Labour to present itself as if it had originated the idea. See next chapter.
11 It was Heath who had introduced VAT and, as noted in Chapter 7, Thatcher had lowered direct taxation but doubled VAT.
12 Those whom in a candid moment Major described as 'bastards' were entirely unconvinced, of course. Arguments about the Maastricht Treaty in 1992–93 were the first manifestation of a split that would continue to dominate Tory politics beyond 1997 (Seldon, 1997: 292–6, 338–42, 389–91; Childs, 2001: 285–7; Morgan, 2001: 516–18, 521–2).
13 In this respect, LA21 was frequently replicating the template established by the DoE in the 1970s.
14 A 1994 conference in Aalborg, Denmark, kick-started LA21 in Europe.
15 There was one innovation we consider in the next chapter, since it was key to New Labour's reforms: the Private Finance Initiative.

16 For instance, although the Poll Tax was scrapped its replacement – Council Tax – was heavily regressive. The valuation of properties in 1991 concentrated tax bands at the lower end of the property scale. With two-thirds of households valued within the lowest three bands this effectively meant that the majority were paying to reduce the tax liability of the wealthiest.

17 Which only lasted six months, after which claimants were transferred onto the means-tested element. Previously, Unemployment Benefit had been payable for 12 months.

10 New dawn, new politics, new Britain

1997–2001

What was there, before the desert smoke and sands obscured everything?

If his critics are right and Blair was always a shallow opportunist at heart (Pugh, 2010: 387–92) it was remarkably foolish of him to join a party, which, by the early 1980s, had not been this socialist for half a century. Blair himself does not always make the best defence witness:

> I didn't really think a Labour victory [in 1983] was the best thing for the country, and I was a Labour candidate!
>
> (Blair, 2010: 13)

Yet Blair's commitment to Labour *was* serious and occurred in the mid-1970s before he met his future, more Left-leaning wife (Seldon, 2004: 49–54, 73–6, 82).[1] Additionally, we should not forget the fact that after 1983 he rode the same wave, towards the Right, that the rest of the party and movement were riding (Heffernan, 2000: ch. 5; Callaghan, 2000: 118–22).

For no one wanted a repeat of the early 1980s, surely (Dell, 2000: chs 16–17; Morgan, 2007: ch. 11; Pugh, 2010: 381–74). The party's split and the subsequent 1983 election trouncing ended any realistic hopes for a socialist economy. Leftist parties everywhere faced the same dilemma. How to mobilise a shrinking working-class beguiled by foreign holidays, home ownership and personal consumption? How to socialise capital when it now surged too quickly to *be* socialised within any one country?

Neil Kinnock was able to reshape the party because he was guiding it away from a space that he, as a young firebrand, had himself occupied just a few years before. The Militant Tendency was shouted off the stage, the red flag became a red rose and spin-doctors like Peter Mandelson began to hover at the edges of TV screens. And if the 1987 election defeat was only slightly less disastrous than 1983 then didn't that reemphasise the depth of the healing required? With the Poll Tax and a second Tory recession in the works, Labour soon soared in the polls.

The 1992 election defeat was therefore an unexpected blow. Major looked reassuring and the recession had made people *more* nervous of political change. But soon Labour had its own safe pair of hands. John Smith may have resembled a portly bank-manager from the 1950s but he regularly slapped the Tories around in parliament. Plus, there was an exciting new generation around him: Robin Cook, Gordon Brown, David Blunkett, Mo Mowlam and Tony Blair. With just one more push, the prize would be theirs. The premature death of Smith in 1994 was a shock not just to the party but to a nation whose heart Labour had by now reoccupied. Blair was elected leader because he spoke to that heart, but his victory was entirely continuous with a process that had been ongoing for 10 years.

The old Left/Right divisions seemed to have abated, therefore. With everyone so desperate for victory who cared if Blair knelt in homage to the Tory tabloids? Power and purpose appeared reunited. If anything, still unsure of itself after 18 years of Tory rule, the leadership tried to dampen expectations with only modest electoral promises. Expectations were high, nonetheless.

To understand why you only had to open your eyes. Britain in the mid-1990s was a curious jumble of abundance and scarcity, wealth and poverty, private affluence and public squalor, hope and fear (Morgan, 2001: 522–31). Since 1979 the income of the richest tenth had risen by 60% in real terms while that of the poorest tenth had fallen by 13% (after housing costs) (Sefton *et al.*, 2009: 21). Inequality, insecurity and relative poverty had returned to levels not seen in decades. The effects on social mobility, health and opportunities were as the critics of Thatcherism had long warned. Those with wealth, shares and property were guaranteed more of the same; those without could simply be blamed for being lazy. The country felt harsher, meaner and ill at ease with itself.

Even before 1997 it seemed that Blair's 'New Labour' had internalised that muddle of prosperity and social unease. Whether via Britpop or the 1996 UEFA Championship the party reinserted itself into the nation's sense of self: a forward stride that plagiarised the self-confidence of the past. Oasis versus Beatles, 1996 versus 1966. 'Labour is coming home'. 'Things can only get better'. There was a nervous earnestness to it all.

There was, then, an uncertainty within the party that echoed that of the country. The Social Justice Commission, reporting in 1994 and setting the tone for much of what followed, bemoaned the effects of inequality while denouncing egalitarians as 'levellers'. Will Hutton's (1995: ch. 12) bestselling *The State We're In* provided a new buzzword: stakeholding. But it was the terminology alone that was appropriated. Hutton's desire to give British capitalism a new architecture – where suppliers, customers, employees and relevant communities would have a say in what organisations do – sounded dangerously interventionist. In the years to come, 'stakeholding' would mean little more than having a job and a mortgage (cf. Prabhakar, 2003: ch. 6).

Yet such attempts to dampen expectations didn't work. If power and principle now walked in tandem then surely another 1945 was in the offing! The same 18 years of wandering in the wilderness, which motivated some to be over-cautious, drove others to be feverish. To someone dying of thirst a single drop of water resembles an ocean. Labour therefore suffered from a weight of both low *and* high expectations (Blair, 2010: 11–12).

For a time, doubts were buried by the 1997 landslide that had entombed the Tories. Every breath now felt like a lungful of fresh air. Blairites could talk about the need to be pro-business, about the wealth-creating wonders of The City, and it didn't matter too much. Not so long as they introduced a minimum wage, Sure Start and the like. In truth, old divisions were always just below the surface. The pledge to maintain Tory-spending limits for two years[2] worried many. It was meant to demonstrate 'fiscal responsibility' and 'prudence', but once the two years were over the government tried to make up for lost time. Blair was panicked into announcing a sharp rise in healthcare expenditure and the image of a spending splurge would, by 2010, return to haunt Labour.

That something-for-everyone atmosphere lasted approximately five years. Few leaders have seen their political capital fall so far and so rapidly as a result of one decision. For its critics, the invasion of Iraq typified the New Labour project. Arrogant, elitist and submissive to the Right. For its defenders, this was Labour's coming of age: the real world might not always bend to your will but better that than the inward-looking, utopian visions of Leftist self-righteousness.

Re-emerging divisions congealed around the personal animosity between Blair and Brown. The latter may have been one of the architects of New Labour, yet critics of the former could see Brown as a keeper of the traditional flame. So as the New Labour coalition crumbled commentators began, retrospectively, to project what they wanted to see onto the years preceding 2002.

Who was correct? The critics or the defenders? What existed in the years before the smoke and the sands?

New Labour and globalisation

The ditching in 1994 of Labour's totemic commitment to state ownership was symbolic, but few powerful voices were raised in opposition (Robinson, 2015: 6–8; Blair, 2010: 75–87). The real question was this: how constrained are nation-states in the context of a corporate-friendly, free market globalisation (Driver & Martell, 2002: ch. 5; Evans & Cerny, 2003: 28–32)?

One perspective favoured a strategy of accommodation. International capital is now so mobile and powerful, it was thought, that states must attract financial and industrial investment to their shores through supply-side measures: ensuring a compliant, low cost, but educated workforce; low inflation; minimal regulations; low taxes (L'Hôte, 2010). 'Neoliberalism', as many would call it, is the only game in town and the best social democracy can do is to ensure fairer distributions and progressive ends.

For its critics, this was a damaging *self*-constraint (Hay, 1999: 67). Labour risked limiting its own freedom of movement by underestimating the extent to which diverse political economies were consistent with economic globalisation (McGrew, 2004). What capital says it wants (higher profits now) may be against capital's own long-term interests. A proper strategy for improved investment and productivity was one of economic *re-shaping*, e.g. through a national investment bank (Hay, 1999: 170–1).

New Labour's was largely a strategy of accommodation (Hutton, 1995: ch. 9; Callaghan, 2000: 156–65). As Blair claimed:

> I hear people say we have to stop and debate globalisation. You might as well debate whether autumn should follow summer.... In the era of rapid globalisation, there is no mystery about what works: an open, liberal economy, prepared constantly to change to remain competitive.... Because the dam holding back the global economy burst years ago.[3]

Not that his government saw itself as having *no* freedom of movement (Driver & Martell, 2002: 26–36), yet freedom was defined largely in terms of supply; hence the emphasis on employability and 'education, education, education'. Regional Development Agencies were established to promote regeneration, employment and competitiveness, but they were not there to socialise anything. Government was therefore seen more as an assistant to the free market magician: look pretty and distract the audience. Independence for the Bank of England implied a separation between economics and politics that would surely have made even Hugh Gaitskell choke (Keegan, 2003: ch. 7).

Trade unions were no longer the 'enemy within', though nor were they regular visitors to Downing Street. The EU's Social Chapter was duly signed in 1997 and so employment rights, e.g. to paid maternity leave, were back on the political agenda for the first time in 18 years. The 1999 Employment Relations Act allowed unions to apply for statutory recognition. All of which was encouraging but, by 2004, several major unions felt let down. The subsequent 'Warwick Agreement' – promising greater fairness, protection at work and representation – was negotiated as a peace-keeping treaty between unions and party.

The government also stepped carefully when introducing Britain's first ever minimum wage legislation, despite the fact that wages had long been falling as a proportion of national wealth (Lansley & Reed, 2013: 5–6).[4] The Confederation of British Industry and the Institute of Directors chewed the carpet at the prospect. The legislation was duly sold as a productivity measure: higher earnings equalled happier, more productive workers. The minimum wage was set at a level lower than trade unions wanted (and lower still for the under-25s), but when its introduction did not lead to economic apocalypse a consensus on an important and overdue reform had been reached.

And with Keynesianism off the agenda it was no surprise that New Labour seized on the Private Finance Initiative (PFI) as a Godsend (Keegan, 2003: 268–86). Devised by Major's government this was basically a form of hire purchase. High spending and high borrowing were not things governments were meant to do anymore. So why not get the private sector to build your hospitals, schools and infrastructure projects? The state then rented the hospital, or whatever, back over 30, 40, 50 years before assuming full control. The genius of it was that government could spend while keeping that spending out of today's accounts.

Critics warned that channelling finance through the private sector, at interest rates higher than those available to the state, actually *raised* public sector borrowing over the long term (Connolly *et al.*, 2008: 955–8, 963–6). Furthermore, faced with wily operators, civil servants, advisors and ministers ended up with PFI schemes where the public sector retained the risk and the private sector walked away with the profits.

Yet such critics were swimming against a tide of success. From 1997–2001 the economy was thriving and jobs were booming. National debt fell even as public expenditure was set to rise after 1999. When Gordon Brown intoned 'No more boom and bust' he was crafting a synergy between Labour's dominance domestically and a flourishing global economy of low inflation and dotcom innovation. So long as sterling remained competitive vis the Euro[5] was much else required? The decline of the manufacturing industry seemed unproblematic when service jobs were blossoming.

So reforms to ensure greater regulation of the financial and banking sector were never contemplated; London being heralded as one of the world's centres for financial trading. What went on in boardrooms (directors' remunerations) and trading rooms (bonuses) could remain behind closed doors. After a 'windfall tax' in 1997, raids on corporate profits were only occasionally and quietly made, so that few beyond the readers of the FT would know or care (Toynbee & Walker, 2001: 107–9).

Third Ways

Did all of this add up to a new philosophy of government capable of replacing Thatcherism (Heffernan, 2000: ch. 2, ch. 9; Seldon, 2004: 31–3)?

'Blairism' would initially denote a centrist communitarianism (Driver & Martell, 2002: ch. 3). Originating as an alternative to the liberal emphasis on individualism, communitarians stressed the importance of community, the common good, moral character and shared, public values. In Etzioni's (1995) work, Clinton and Blair found a means of remoulding Conservatives' emphasis on patriotism, neighbourliness, civic membership and family values. This would be a philosophy of synthesis rather than conflict. Responsibilities were important not by *shrinking* the space of individual rights and choice but by *rebalancing* them. States and markets could be seen not as adversaries but as partners. Charities were not a replacement for public services but a philanthropic (and even entrepreneurial) addition to them.

The 'old Left' and the 'New Right' therefore stood equally condemned. The former for its obsession with collectivism, state ownership, egalitarianism and paternalism; the latter for allowing inequalities and market forces to shred the public realm and social justice.

In the 'Third Way' New Labour found both a handy slogan and a kind of intellectual route-map to the future (Powell, 1999: 13–23). Step forward Tony Giddens (1998, 2000, 2002). As perhaps the world's most famous sociologist Giddens was an articulate heavyweight who could kick *laissez faire* sand back in the faces of Friedman, Hayek and the minions who clustered around them.

Though socialism is dead, Giddens proclaimed, capitalism was far more flexible than many of its critics *and supporters* realised. Forging a capitalism that was both fair and dynamic meant prioritising the sphere – civil society – where people encounter one another as people and not as either the bearers of class identity or as competitors seeking positional advantage. The job of states and markets was to support this active civil society as a place of democratic values and social innovation.

Modernisation thus implied a perpetual rebooting of social institutions in order to maintain cherished principles (Finlayson, 2003: ch. 3). Rather than rejecting markets or regarding them, defensively, as necessary evils, social democrats should call capitalism's bluff by demanding that markets serve the cause of social justice. If anything, this made New Labour louder proselytisers for markets than the Tories had been.

At its most ambitious his formulation was too broad (Fairclough, 2000). Giddens (2001) presented almost every social democratic political party around the world as a convert to the Third Way. Insisting that 'Left' and 'Right' were no longer relevant terms of reference, Giddens (1994) neglected the continued Left/Right distinctions among those seeking progressive, even radical, alternatives to the hegemony of free market liberalism. It wasn't difficult to detect that the Third Way's inclusiveness was actually a subtle form of *exclusion*.

However, such shortcomings were immaterial to the political objective. The commentariat was buzzing again via broadsheets, periodicals and Radio 4. 'Thatcherism' had taken years to enter the lexicon. 'Blairism' and the 'Third Way' had done it in a matter of months. The political ground was shifting Leftwards.

Yet how far to the Left? That was what made some uneasy. In the mid-1980s *Marxism Today* had encouraged a pluralistic, consumer-oriented but Leftist response to Thatcherism. Now it returned in a one-off special to warn that, though Labour's post-1983 journey had been necessary, Blairism had not been the only destination (Hall, 1998; Finlayson, 2003: ch. 4; cf. Callinicos, 2001). If anything, Blair treated Thatcher's legacy as an immovable bedrock.

Nor were those on the 'old Labour Right' necessarily happy either. Were they being denounced too? Anti-Bevanites like Gaitskell, Crosland, Healey and so forth? Roy Hattersley (e.g. 2001) worried about New Labour mimicking the teenage impulse to denounce anything that predated it as boring! The leadership seemed addicted to a thrill that comes from disparaging your own natural supporters so that the *Daily Mail* bully will pat you on the head.

Thus for all its self-avowed communitarianism, New Labour valorised market individualism and, like its predecessor, assumed the private sector to be more efficient and just plain exciting than the public sector (Finlayson, 2003: 89–95). And for all of its language of synthesis (e.g. 'tackling crime and the causes of crime') New Labour was at risk of attributing social problems to the usual,

Conservative-friendly suspects: lack of morals, of aspiration, of the habits of hard work (Levitas, 2005; see below). There was a continued appreciation that social background constrained people's opportunities, but this was now disassociated from the concept of class, e.g. Giddens (2000: 41–4) viewed class primarily through the lens of social identity. New Labour deplored Thatcherism's neglect of poverty and health inequalities but by accepting key components of the Tory case it had become semi-detached from a 'structural' understanding of systemic disadvantage. In racing away from socialism it ditched too much of 'the social' too.

Social reforms

This gave its approach to social policy a flavour of 'tough love' (Johnson, 2001; Toynbee & Walker, 2001: ch. 2; Driver & Martell, 2002: 36–53, ch. 8).[6]

Giddens (1998: 65–6, 114–22; Blair, 2010: 210–16) talked about the need for the state to invest in human capital through 'positive welfare'. For New Labour this translated into 'education, education, education', giving the most help to those who helped themselves and ending the 'something for nothing' culture. Other New Labour mantras included:

- 'rights imply responsibilities'
- 'hand-ups not handouts'
- 'from welfare to work' such that 'wages are the best form of welfare' (Department of Social Security, 1998: 23)
- 'work for those who can, security for those who cannot'.

In one sense this *was* different from what had come before. The concept of human capital implied that rather than seeing the welfare state as a drain on resources it was, if properly reformed, a means of ensuring economic prosperity. Health and education could aid economic productivity. New Labour therefore saw the state as having an active role to play by helping people adapt to new risks, social changes and the uncertainties brought by ever-accelerating innovation and global competition. In Beveridge's system your entitlements signalled an orientation to the past (having paid sufficient insurance contributions); in the new century, it was thought, security came from a perpetual re-orientation towards the future.

In another sense, New Labour also sought continuities with the Conservative approach.

Those who would not play ball would have to be shown the error of their ways. If social justice had once implied decommodification (freedom from market forces and the cash nexus) it would now have to imply a widespread recommodification. Those who couldn't or wouldn't integrate themselves into market society would be targeted through a behavioural resocialisation (Finlayson, 2003: 149–66). New Labour would dangle carrots but you could not choose *not* to eat them.

Additionally, for Blairites the actual size of the state no longer mattered. As the era of mass unemployment fell behind, Labour could even lower spending as a percentage of GDP below what it had been under Major (Toynbee & Walker, 2001: 102). The state had to be lean and, if necessary, mean. It was the ends that were important. So long as a patient was treated, did it matter whether the provider was profit making or not? Would the patient care? 'What matters is what works', the government intoned (Blair, 2010: 212).[7]

Take its approach to income maintenance and poverty (Oppenheim, 2001: 77–85; Hewitt, 2002; Connell, 2011).

Sticks and carrots

The main carrot was 'making work pay' through the minimum wage. But, because it was also necessary to keep British businesses competitive, wages could not do all the heavy lifting.

The notion of in-work supplements dated back to the 1960s (see Chapter 4) and now the Chancellor borrowed from the USA an idea that had been around almost as long: a partial integration of the tax and benefit systems in the form of tax credits (Lowe, 2005: 404–6). The Working Families Tax Credit was designed to improve the financial incentives to work and reduce in-work poverty. A tax credit therefore denoted 'active welfare' (a reward for labour market participation) rather than the 'passive welfare' of benefits (compensation for losing a job) (Lowe, 2005: 402–4).[8]

The potential advantage of tax credits was that they provided a more secure minimum income floor than that offered by benefits, smoothing the transition of people into work and up the income ladder, and being less stigmatising than means-tested benefits. But tax credits did not eliminate the poverty trap, nor facilitate an effective work-life balance (Kelly, 2001: 176–80). Since tax credit eligibility fluctuates with earnings, changes in the latter may create underpayment or overpayment in the former. Finally, employers may be tempted to offer low wages in the knowledge that these will be topped up by the state. Did tax credits offer security or give unscrupulous employers an excuse to pay the lowest possible wages?

New Labour also wielded various sticks. No one above the age of 16 would be allowed to 'do nothing'. Unless you were incapacitated through illness, accident or disability you would have to be in education, training or an environmental taskforce. Such compulsion was initially applied only to those aged 24 or less but was gradually extended to others, with lone parents and disabled people increasingly required to attend interviews with benefit officers.

New Labour rarely used the term 'underclass' but the inference was similar: income distribution alone was insufficient because those with irresponsible attitudes and habits would simply waste the money on alcohol, drugs, cigarettes, shell-suits, Rottweilers and fatty food. If means testing was a way of targeting resources on the needy, conditionality was a way of targeting those genuinely deprived through no fault of their own while isolating those condemned as bringing misfortunes on themselves. 'Active welfare' frequently meant *workfare*.

'Social exclusion' was therefore a useful concept in this respect (MacGregor, 2003). Originating in Europe it denoted not just a snapshot of income distribution but a longitudinal analysis of what kept some people at the edges of society. It was a film rather than a photo. Social exclusion was not just a lack of income but the marginalisation that comes from a host of intersecting deprivations across time: low skills and education, poor job opportunities, ill-health, housing squalor, plus the self-harming habits of many of the excluded themselves.

The concept thus allowed Labour to address a social process while also targeting a group, however ill-defined, for intervention: 'the socially excluded' (Fairclough, 2000: 58, 63–4; Levitas, 2006: 124–7; Todd, 2014: 338–42). Workfare could be presented as humane and progressive rather than punitive ('blaming the victim'). Socialist Sweden had workfare schemes, after all (cf. King & Wickham-Jones, 1999: 275).

Labour's justification was this. You couldn't condemn 18 years of Toryism and pretend that the poverties and inequalities thereby created had not filtered down into the cultures and psyches of those affected. If people internalised their social environments then clearly those who had experienced deprivation for years would adapt their beliefs, values and habits to those circumstances, coming to regard as normal that which was actually dysfunctional: low-level criminality, gang culture, multiple pregnancies by different fathers, family instability, lack of respect for authority. If 'anti-social behaviour' derived from unjust conditions then tolerating it would only perpetuate them.

Critics worried about Labour's politics of welfare (Lister, 1998).

First, it was arguably constructed on spurious foundations. The active/passive distinction conjured an image of a state that used to hand out money unconditionally. New Labour was distorting the party's own past as a way of earning brownie points with the media and with voters. The risk was that by validating popular prejudices and misconceptions regarding the deserving and undeserving it only pulled the rug out from beneath the feet of social justice. Stoking 'them versus us' divisions on the basis of desert makes it harder to defend principles of care, needs and solidarity.[9]

Second, where was this tough love meant to lead? To a lifetime in a call-centre or stacking supermarket shelves? Traipsing from low-paid job to low-paid job, from crappy training scheme to crappy training scheme? *Full* and *fulfilling* employment was barely mentioned by New Labour. If all this talk of desert and obligation implied years of insecure, service industry misery, then what was the point?

Finally, it meant that the government was torn between an ethos of community on the one hand and possessive individualism on the other. It was scared of proclaiming its commitment to social justice too loudly, of scaring away voters in marginal constituencies. The government *was* redistributive (see Chapter 12) but it was often redistribution by stealth (Sefton *et al.*, 2009).

Publicly, the line was, as Peter Mandelson declared, that the government was "intensely relaxed about people getting filthy rich" (Toynbee & Walker, 2009: 17). The height of the social floor was to be raised but a Labour government was no longer concerned with that of the social ceiling. Mandelson's qualification ("as long as they pay their taxes") bypasses the objection that the wellbeing of those on or towards the floor and those on or towards the ceiling are interconnected. This cannot just be about paying taxes. It has to involve a social-moral recognition and respect also. Yet Labour had no strategy to 'remoralise the rich' – by addressing social exclusion at the top – and its absence raised the suspicion that it bought into the Thatcherite narrative, in which the poorest 'lacked values' and made the wrong 'lifestyle choices' (Dean, 1999: 221–6). The affluent were judged to already possess the correct values *as long as they paid their taxes.*

New Labour thus played the 'benefit fraud game': exaggerating its extent, condemning it as simple criminality (when much of it derives from desperation) and launching numerous anti-fraud initiatives (Sainsbury, 2003).

Yet in the midst of all this came a surprising and deeply ambitious announcement in 1999: the government would commit itself to abolishing child poverty in 20 years (Lowe, 2005: 406–9; Lloyd, 2006: 317–20; Stewart, 2009a: 48–9; Dean, 2013: 248–53; also Waldfogel, 2010: 34–6). It was awful politics, with the government now binding its own hands with targets it was, in truth, never likely to meet: reducing child poverty by a quarter by 2005 and one half by 2010.[10] Yet it was also exhilarating and allowed defenders and critics of New Labour some rapprochement (Stewart, 2009b: 288–90).

Unfortunately, knowledge of the announcement among the British public was always weak (Kelly, 2008). This was not surprising given the mixed messages being sent out. The child poverty pledge invoked an earlier age of egalitarianism and universalism in which, by recognising their shared needs and vulnerabilities, people across the strata of income and wealth regard each other as members of the same social endeavour. But New Labour also sought to make political capital by gleefully ringing the death knell of that era. The child poverty reductions would thus come from a technocratic programme, understood only by policy wonks, rather than from a moral and social crusade.

Finally, social security policy was also dominated by pensions reform (Taylor-Gooby 2005; Evandrou & Falkingham, 2009: 165–76). To address the 'demographic timebomb' should a government increase the retirement age, raise more revenue through higher taxes and contributions or lower the generosity of pensions? Labour was simply unsure and so manufactured a patchwork of reforms:

- a Minimum Income Guarantee,
- a Pensions Credit,
- privately managed stakeholder pensions for those on just-below average incomes,
- a second state pension for those on the lowest incomes.

In short, New Labour's social security policy was a mixture of the socially progressive (minimum wage, tax credits, child poverty pledge), the morally punitive (benefit fraud and workfare measures) and the just plain confused (pension reform).

Health and education

With health and education reforms some of the same tendencies were in evidence (Toynbee & Walker, 2001: ch. 4; Glendinning, 2003; Lowe, 2005: 415–31).[11]

After two years of financial purdah, steep rises in healthcare spending were announced. This, plus an objective of reducing health inequalities and waiting times, made Labour's commitment to the NHS appear solid.[12] In other respects, however, Labour traditionalists were uneasy. The purchaser-provider split was maintained though now with a greater emphasis upon cooperation and inclusion (Paton, 2002). And with an expansionist set of policies in place the government felt able to invite commercial providers into the NHS on a scale not witnessed before, accompanying unprecedented levels of fragmentation and marketisation (Pollock, 2004: 49–80).

In short, New Labour's healthcare reforms were not only more social democratic *and* more market-oriented, they were more market-oriented *because* they were more social democratic. The government's very commitment to the NHS gave it a license to go where the Tories could never have gone without being condemned as NHS-haters.

A similar strategy was visible within education (Muschamp *et al.*, 1999; Toynbee & Walker, 2001: ch. 3; Brehony & Deem, 2003; Lupton *et al.*, 2009): spending was increased, ambitious numeracy and literacy targets for primary schools were announced, extra nursery places and reductions in class sizes were introduced. Yet such measures were accompanied by a quantification of education, particularly in terms of university tuition fees, school league-tables and performance-related pay. On the one hand, for instance, most teachers received a pay rise, which flew below the radar of tabloid outrage. Yet was a typical teacher being praised for high performance or redefined as an output-maximiser whose effectiveness could be assessed somehow independently of the school, local community or policy context within which they worked? LEAs lost influence as schools were increasingly seen as independent units rather than as nodes in a local, democratic network.

As with healthcare, then, extra resources accompanied a cultural shift initiated under the Tories (Marquand, 2009: 353). Targets and auditing increased. School management was separated from wider questions of social environment (social conditions would no longer be a legitimate 'excuse' for failing standards, the government insisted). The 'bog-standard' comprehensive was condemned in contrast to a new era of diversity in which academies and specialist schools would import private sector expertise and funding. Those with the magic touch ('superheads') would be parachuted into 'failing schools' to get results. Ofsted saw itself as raising standards by raising expectations and criticising those who fell short, without much actual evidence that this was the case (Jones & Tymms, 2014: 321–8).

Was there anything else to New Labour's social policy? For instance, any hint of convergence between it and environmental policy (Jordan, 2000)? To some extent, yes (cf. Levett, 2001: 154–7).

Modernising the environment

For Giddens (1998: 45, 54–64; 2000: 137–42), environmentalism was one element of the Third Way smorgasbord. We are now in an era of risks, he claimed. Human-nature interactions are so complex and rapid that they denote a space of profound uncertainties: ecological risks. The security provided through the welfare state was still vital, but uncertainties meant that future security would have to come from the willingness and capacity to embrace risks. The concept of risks therefore constituted an intersection for welfare reform, economic policy, environmentalism, scientific and technological development and geopolitical change.

The new government's approach was, of course, less intellectualised than this (see below), yet the discursive tone was similar. In a world of rapid transformation neither chaotic markets nor top-down statism could work any longer. A hybrid approach was needed, one that pollinated ideas from diverse sources in a spirit of exploration and forward thinking. There was, then, a willingness here to splice social and environmental policies together in ways that 1970s Labour would not have recognised.

But there was complacency too. What if you didn't have the resources to embrace risks? For those to whom 'older' notions of security remained important, a language of globalisation, cosmopolitanism and risk could begin to look like an excuse for allowing Eastern European plumbers and builders to come and take your jobs and housing.

There was, then, a potential contradiction in New Labour's worldview. Its employment-centred approach to welfare reform stressed the securities of paid work. Yet it also thought that the national walls, which protected people from market forces and globalisation, were no longer secure or even desirable. The result was this: for many, having a wage was an ineffective means of distributing the resources needed to empower them to take risks, not when their job could be outsourced, automated, downsized or simply exported to a low-wage country thousands of miles away.

This is just one aspect of a larger story we don't have time for here. The point is this. In time, once the economic miracles of the 1990s and early 2000s had faded, Labour came to be associated with new forms of *insecurity*: financial (the 2008 crash), political (party elites leaving voters adrift) and cultural (poorly managed immigration). None of which was conducive to an environmental politics that also invoked a language of risk, danger, collapse and uncertainty.

Hesitations

Labour was both hesitant and bold in its environmental policies from the outset.

Its hesitancy was manifest within a few years of its landslide.

- The Countryside Alliance posed as a grassroots social movement when its *sotto voce* slogan was really 'whatever is good for agribusiness is good for the environment'. The government would tiptoe around proposals to ban fox hunting for years.
- When road hauliers staged a series of protests Labour took flight at these small businessmen on wheels. The 'fuel price escalator', designed since 1992 to increase fuel duties by 5% a year above inflation, was dropped.

Increasingly, Labour looked like the head prefect who attracted the girls but scarpered when the school bullies showed up.

Yet during the same period, Labour was instrumental in securing agreements around the Kyoto Protocol and, as we see in Chapter 11, this is where its boldness was most evident.

As with other features of its reform agenda, then, Labour sought out circles to square. Political credit could be gained by making the right noises about the environment, but political votes potentially lost if it looked you were going to do anything too radical. A language of 'ecological modernisation' seemed perfectly suited to its strategy. This implied adapting existing institutions and systems to make room for environmental needs and objectives (Jacobs, 1999; Barry, 2005: 303–6; Connelly *et al.*, 2012: 73–9).

But how much room, exactly? Was the economy to be 'greened' or were environmental issues to be squashed by prevailing assumptions about economic relations and expectations (Toynbee & Walker, 2001: ch. 9)? New Labour was eager to be seen as amenable to business and City interests. Regulation and intervention were to be light-touch unless there was a compelling case otherwise. And the party was wary of alienating both natural supporters and hard-won voters with demands that they change their lifestyles and consumption habits significantly. Would Blair's government represent a real advance beyond Major's, then?

Let's first catch up on a subject we have shelved for several chapters now.

In the 1980s policies on land use and urban-rural development had, unsurprisingly, been driven by the same imperatives as every other aspect of governance (Cullingworth & Nadin, 2006: 434). The premise was that controls should be reduced because planning was a burden, as should anything that stood in the way of the development by and for the private sector. This included local consultation and public participation. Planning procedures were therefore streamlined and shifted away from the sphere of democracy since this was seen as a drag on markets, enterprise and profit-making. Here, again, was the great paradox of Thatcherism: in order to achieve market-based decentralisation Whitehall would have to accumulate the statutory powers and centralise the organisational functions needed to override objections by local authorities, communities and other intermediate interests.

In reality, the government often found itself forced to pursue a more pragmatic path. The institutional structures and cultures, which had driven the planning system for decades, could not be swept away overnight. Furthermore, Tory voters in the shires objected to the suggestion that their voices could be discounted. After 1988, with 'sustainability' on the political agenda, thinking would evolve again to embrace community interests. Major saw pragmatism as a virtue rather than as a regrettable retreat from ideological ideals. So, the Environment Agency was designed to assist businesses with environmental regulation while dealing with EU negotiations (Cullingworth & Nadin, 2006: 263–4).

New Labour took this post-Thatcherite approach further by embracing the idea that government can proactively facilitate new partnerships and networks (Cullingworth & Nadin, 2006: 435–40). Furthermore, social exclusion and social needs were no longer to be seen as extraneous to development issues. This gave its agenda something of a schismatic quality. National plans and economic planning were associated with the old Labour era. Overarching *targets* were therefore preferred. So that these targets could be achieved, government saw its job as assembling a multitude of public, voluntary and private actors and facilitating inter-agency partnerships. So while the planning of the 1940s–1960s was seen as inimical to diversification and flexibility,[13] there could be (and there was) a proliferation of development plans, community plans, action plans, and so forth, at local and regional levels (Cullingworth *et al.*, 2015: 33–4).

What about other aspects of Labour's environmental policy?

The Climate Change Levy announced in 1999 was a tax on the energy consumption of businesses, the proceeds from which were designed to encourage job creation and energy efficiencies (Toynbee & Walker, 2001: 182–3). After years of Thatcherism even this modest, market-based policy was anathema to many businesses and the government wilted. Introduced in 2001 the surcharge would not be raised until 2007. Neither the business nor the green lobby was happy as a result. It was not an auspicious start.

One of the first things Blair did was to create the DETR, in effect the latest incarnation of the DoE. On the face of it this newest super-ministry gave the environment a prominent place within a government that would soon commit itself to achieving reductions in carbon emissions of 20% (below a 1990 baseline) by 2010. An Old Labour stalwart, Michael Meacher, was made Minister for the Environment, with John Prescott having overall control of the DETR. But although Prescott was Deputy Prime Minister he had nowhere near the influence of Gordon Brown at the Treasury and Meacher was not a member of the Cabinet. If anything this structure enabled other departments to compartmentalise 'the environment' as the responsibility of the DETR and, in practice, cross-departmental and cross-sectoral coordination would be minimal. The prospects for an organisational integration of the social and environmental policy domains did not look promising, therefore.

Programmes and plans

The DETR published an integrated transport plan in 1998 and a Climate Change Programme in 2000. We summarise these shortly.

But it was the 1999 strategy for sustainable development, *A Better Quality of Life*, which arguably represents its most systematic attempt to gather the social and environmental policy agendas under one roof. It begins:

> Our Strategy for sustainable development has four main aims. These are:
>
> - social progress, which recognises the needs of everyone;
> - effective protection of the environment;
> - prudent use of natural resources; and
> - maintenance of high and stable levels of economic growth and employment.[14]

The economy was thus central to national competitiveness, job creation and sustainable development.

This was an interventionist document that would have made Thatcher and Major recoil, but it was also in line with New Labour's approach: set measurable targets and define 'improvements' accordingly, encourage partnerships, monitor developments. It was intervention-at-a-distance in which government sets the goals and then oversees a culture in which those enjoined to actually achieve them are audited and appraised through data management systems (Clarke *et al.*, 2000).

The above aims were thus operationalised across 15 indicators.

Economy
- GDP
- Investment
- Employment

Social
- Poverty and Social Exclusion
- Education
- Health
- Housing
- Crime

Environmental
- Climate Change
- Air Quality
- Road Traffic
- River water quality
- Wildlife
- Land use
- Waste

Within the DETR itself a new Sustainable Development Commission was established to review trends against these indicators and make policy recommendations accordingly.

The 1999 strategy was welcome after the regressiveness of the 1980s and the inertia of the 1990s. But it came with a cost.

The strategy's approach satisfied the need of busy ministers and journalists for easy-to-digest summaries. Glossy reports with neat tables and a series of ticks and crosses could quickly tell you what was happening. One potential problem is that quantifications can stop reflecting reality and start *substituting* for it. There is a potentially thin line between data measurement and data manipulation when your job, your funding or your autonomy depends upon the numbers going in the right direction.

A related problem was that, on the one hand, the government was highlighting the complexities of social-environmental interactions; on the other, it was slicing through those same complexities in its search for statistical summaries which would demonstrate progress, preferably in line with the electoral cycle. The subsequent reports on the 15 indicators could contain a bewildering array of headings, lists and bullet-points. Evidence of successful impacts was often thin, with the existence of a strategy being itself taken as a sign of success (Cullingworth *et al.*, 2015: 264). The reports conveyed a feeling of forward momentum, but the language was technocratic rather than moral and engaging.

Those reports were sold as the government 'holding itself to account', of course. But was this brave governance or an opportunity for self-congratulation? By 2001 (DETR, 2001) it was giving itself the kind of score that governments regularly give themselves: 'we are doing better than our opponents ever could but there is still much to be done'. By 2004, eight of the 15 headline indicators were said to be showing improvements and only one of them (air quality) was revealed as slipping backwards (DEFRA, 2004).[15]

In one fell swoop, then, Labour had flagged up an ecosocial agenda under the heading of 'quality of life', and then devolved it into a series of quantities and discrete categories. Wanting to engineer a progressive consensus (and avoid risking electoral unpopularity) this unfortunately skipped across not just the complexities, but the conflicts at work and the need to identify, honestly and systematically, the kind of trade-offs that it is the responsibility of governments to make.

In the 1999 document there is no mention of green jobs, for instance. The depletion of natural resources is noted as a potential threat to employment, e.g. in the fishing industry, but there is no distinction between jobs which protect ecosystems and biodiversities and those which do not. There was no acknowledgement that a job, which improves output and reduces poverty, might also contribute to global warming. The need for pension fund investment to be socially and environmentally responsible is also mentioned but the massive economic consequences that come from 'disinvesting' in fossil fuels are not discussed. Labour was avoiding driving down particular roads by simply eliminating them from the map.

In other respects the document *is* more adept at identifying synergies. Action to combat fuel poverty would become one of the government's most progressive innovations, involving raising the incomes of poorer households *and* improved energy efficiencies (Hills, 2009: 337; Fitzpatrick, 2011a: 171–7). Health, too, was discussed in social and environmental terms, with air quality being prominent.

Labour's approach was dualistic, in other words. Where synergies clearly corresponded to its please-everybody politics of ecological modernisation they could be highlighted (Barry, 2005: 311–13). But where the development of potential synergies required honest reflection on conflicts and trade-offs – and the need to challenge vested interests (whether employers, workers or consumers) – then Labour averted its gaze. In this respect, its social indicators and lists tended to sit side by side with its environmental indicators and lists, having oil-and-water characteristics where each barely permeated the other. Challenging critiques were avoided and its approach to 'ecosocial policies' was correspondingly weak.

Transport

Unsurprisingly, then, the policy programme was strong on rhetoric and targets but less so in terms of the nation's long-term environmental needs (Page, 2003: 253–65). Anticipating the 1998 White Paper, *A New Deal for Transport*, Prescott said,

> I will have failed if, in five years' time, there are not many more people using public transport and far fewer journeys by car. It's a tall order, but I urge you to hold me to it.[16]

New money for public transport was promised, road building was to be minimised and disincentives for cars introduced through charges for congestion and workplace parking (Toynbee & Walker, 2001: 186–92). But wary of upsetting the motoring lobby and road hauliers (see above) government policy would be more equivocal (Cullingworth *et al.*, 2015: 491–3).

The 10-year plan (DETR, 2000a) launched in 2000 made £60 billion each available for rail and another £60 billion for local transport, yet years of underinvestment in the railways was difficult to reverse, especially when the separation of tracks and stock was retained and renationalisation off the agenda – though Railtrack was turned into a non-profit company in 2001. An emphasis on roads returned in the 2000 plan (it too was allocated £60 billion) and proposals for road pricing would later be shelved. Local councils may have been given new powers but without leadership from central government they were vulnerable to the power of the motoring lobby. Only in London was a congestion charge introduced, reducing congestion by 30% and increasing cycling and bus use.

In summation, the transport legacy of the previous 20 years was not being overturned. So, even when documents identify ecosocial synergies – between transport, health and social exclusion, carbon emissions and air quality – Labour was stronger on rhetoric and aspiration than on challenging interests, changing behaviour and reordering priorities.

Emissions

Climate Change: the UK Programme (DETR, 2000b) was also very good at identifying the problem and formulating laudable aspirations. For instance, by 2010 the government wanted 10% of the UK's electricity to be generated via renewables and to this end a Renewables Obligation was introduced requiring electricity suppliers to provide a specific proportion of their electricity from approved renewable sources each year (Carter & Ockwell, 2007: 78). The 2010 target would be missed, however.[17] The 2000 Programme was also enthusiastic about a UK emissions trading scheme designed to marry economy, energy policy and environment (Carter & Ockwell, 2007: 90; see next chapter). But, again, the language is win-win and systemic conflicts are smoothed over.

Overall, Carter and Ockwell (2007: 70–4) portray New Labour as complacent in its over-ambitions. The target of reducing emissions by 20% (below the 1990 baseline) by 2010 was made because emissions had been reducing in the 1990s as a result of the dash-for-gas. But this was not set to continue beyond 1997 due to economic growth, transport growth and higher-than-expected energy demands. Labour expected to ride the ecological wave, which the Tory assault on the coal industry had inadvertently initiated. Progress in reducing emissions thus stalled. And as the waters became choppier the government was left floundering at best and drowning at worst.

An ecosocial politics?

In 1997–2001 New Labour made environmental issues more central than they had been before and signalled the beginnings of a potential ecosocial agenda in terms of the quality of life. Yet knowing where you want to hit the ball is not the same as having the skill and confidence to do so. The flaws in the above documents and strategies were partly due to its own timidity and unwillingness to be honest with the country about the need to make sometimes difficult priorities. It was also partly because Labour had no foundations to build upon. The party of Attlee and Crosland seemed to offer few real signposts; and after 18 years of Thatcherite hostility to the idea that markets work best as servants, to a range of social and environmental ends, there were few institutional roadmaps. New Labour, in short, was having to work from scratch (Carter, 2006: 762–3). The DoE became the DETR but with most environmental policy originating in the EU (see Chapters 9 and 11) the precedent was one of adaptation rather than UK-specific innovation.

Still, this was only a start. Surely more – and better – was to come? This would not be the case and, until 2008's Climate Change Bill, 1997–2001 represented something of a high-water mark.

The GDP share of environmental taxes was lower in 2005 than in 1997, for instance (Carter & Ockwell, 2007: 16). And after a shelf-life of only four years the DETR was abolished and with the 2001 creation of DEFRA the 'environment' was effectively separated from development planning and transport. From being fairly central the environment was suddenly at the margins of government action again. DEFRA would have lots of objectives, perhaps too many to be truly focused and effective: lots of teeth without much bite (Cullingworth & Nadin, 2006: 46–8, 316–17).

Ultimately, New Labour's ecological modernisation was one in which, rather than a mutual adaptation, environmental policy would have to adapt to economic imperatives. It was weak modernisation at best (see Christoff, 1996).

But to continue this story we need to incorporate something so far neglected: the global stance of New Labour. How and why did it relate to the EU, global poverty and developments in and around the Kyoto Protocol?

Key questions

What relationships between the environmental and social policy agendas have emerged? To what extent have social policies and the politics of welfare reform deliberately informed and been informed by the principles and values of environmental ethics and politics?

It was a new era. Where free market liberals tended to reform through subtractions (cutting budgets, reducing entitlements, scything at the public sector), New Labour reformed through additions (extra spending, expanded employment and welfare rights, partnerships between public, independent and private sectors). It sought to rebuild the capacity and scope of the state.

To some extent it did so imaginatively, e.g. Scottish and Welsh devolution, but in other respects it was more conventional (Pugh, 2010: 405–6). Its centralizing tendencies often predominated: the Treasury became the locus of social policy, directing resources to low income households; there was to be no grand revolution in local government; and the audit culture was a form of governance-at-a-distance.

Labour therefore missed several steps. It was concerned with poverty but not inequality per se. And where it did speak a language of equality this tended to be highly economistic – associated with jobs, wages and tax credits, rather than non-employment forms of social participation. Its moralistic discourse (in which social exclusion was closely associated with the attitudes, habits and values of 'the socially excluded') fostered social divisions that conflicted with the more progressive, redistributive aspects of its politics.

The government understood the salience of environmentalism in its vision of a new politics and its connection to social wellbeing and welfare services. Where the typical mantras of Labour's social policies often felt like rhetorical reinventions of a very timeworn distinction between deserving/undeserving,

Prescott's quality of life agenda felt like a genuinely innovative form of modernisation.

New Labour prided itself on its joined-up thinking approach to policymaking. The quality of life agenda did not always connect the dots particularly well (as critiqued above) but the 15 indicators of wellbeing at least conveyed a sense that Prescott and others now had a greater understanding than previous generations of what the real dots were and how they interrelated. In addition to Labour's engagement with international developments (see next chapter) this seems more important in retrospect than it did at the time. True, the Third Way's 'everything is new' intonation wore thin quickly. But in seeking to conjoin economic, social and environmental policies, quality of life embraced the new and the old, as if a sculptor could find the statue that had been suspended already within the stone for decades.

If Thatcher's version of the ecosocial nestled inside her desire to marketise everything and everyone, New Labour's was more about a remobilisation of government resources so that the as-yet unknown risks of the future could be anticipated and prepared for.

That there was no follow-through on this is tragic. After 2001, environmentalism would not be a domestic priority again until 2007–8. The conjunction of policies was largely confined to the drawing board. The dots would remain isolated. It was the glad, confident morning of Labour's return to power. Unfortunately, the day was grinding on.

Notes

1 His desire for advancement was that of a typical politician, of course. In July 1982 he would write to the Labour leader, Michael Foot, denouncing the Tories for having succumbed to "petty bourgeois sentiments" (Morgan, 2007: 417, also 469–70). Yet Blair was also as much a product of his times as the rest of us.

2 Limits, which the previous Conservative Chancellor acknowledged as an election gimmick, to which a post-1997 Tory government would not have stuck.

3 Speech to the Labour Party conference, 27 September, 2005. http://news.bbc.co.uk/1/hi/uk_politics/4287370.stm [accessed 13 September 2015]

4 The wage share peaked at 65.5% of GDP in 1975 and by 1997 had fallen back to 51%.

5 Brown was largely the person responsible for Labour's refusal to join the new EU single currency.

6 One of the most significant changes in UK social policy post-1997 centred around greater devolution to the regions, particularly Scotland. The subject is too big to consider here (see Burchardt & Holder, 2009).

7 Yet this was mainly one-way traffic. The public sector was subject to the importation of management techniques (and jargon), consumer-driven expectations and market-style practices from the private sector (called 'New Public Management'). The private sector, though, was not assumed to need lessons enforcing 'public sector values'. Here, voluntary agreements were deemed to be sufficient.

8 And, happy coincidence, gave Gordon Brown's Treasury sway over huge areas of social policy (Keegan, 2003: 254–63).

9 Such divisions also obscured the existence of the 'fiscal welfare state' (e.g. generous tax allowances) from which the middle-classes largely benefit.

10 In fact, New Labour would reduce child poverty by one-quarter by 2010 (Stewart, 2012).

11 Relatively little change occurred within the housing sector (Ford, 2003).

12 Note that any healthcare system is only one factor in a complex of social and economic determinants of ill-health. After 1953 health inequalities widened because the health of the richest was improving faster than the rest of the population (Fitzpatrick & Chandola, 2000: 110–13, 120–4).

13 A knee-jerk prejudice experts condemn this as a misreading of what the post-war planning system had actually involved (Cullingworth & Nadin, 2006: 320).

14 http://collections.europarchive.org/tna/20080530153425/http:/www.sustainable-development.gov.uk/publications/uk-strategy99/index.htm [accessed 11 September 2015]

15 Though even here this was attributed to the extreme heatwave of 2003.

16 *Guardian*, 6 June 1997. In fact, from 1994–2009 road traffic increased by nearly 25% (Cahill, 2011: 237). A 'predict and provide' model encouraged the growth in aviation.

17 The figure achieved was 6.5%, see www.ref.org.uk/publications/229-renewables-output-in-2010 [accessed 20 October 2015]

11 Fixing the planet
1997–2005

For a time it felt like Europe was the capital of the world again. The Berlin Wall's demise crowned a new era of outward-facing, self-confident citizenship and global leadership. And in the late 1990s it was the Centre-Left making all the noise. Labour's victory was not an isolated one. By 1999 12 out of the 15 EU member states of the time were being run, either wholly or partly, by social democratic parties. Their ascendancy would last just a few years but, for a while, their politics (market-friendly, social justice, efficient management) was dominant. Thatcherism suddenly seemed like a very long time ago.

Not that it appeared so to all. The 'anti-globalisation' protesters were an inevitably varied bunch (Klein, 2000: Chs 12–17; Shepard & Hayduk, 2002; Wallerstein, 2004). Some were opposed to the contemporary operation of capitalism and some to its very existence. Some recommended specific programmes of reform, while others preferred a more inchoate sense of protest. Some forged alliances, others sought an ideological purity. If there was commonality it lay in a general disillusionment that the promises of 1989 had not been fulfilled due to capitalist fundamentalism, the subservience of governments to multinationals and the hegemony of the WTO, IMF and World Bank.[1]

The highpoint of the movement (1999–2002) thus coincided with the electoral victories of numerous Centre-Left parties in Europe. Many protesters and activists maintained that social democracy was no longer a worthwhile vehicle for change, having grafted itself onto the new order of corporate governance (Hardt & Negri, 2000; Bové, 2004: 147–9). To some extent, such critiques mirrored the black/white logic of free market pro-globalisers: the era of regulated capitalism is dead, democracy and markets are in opposition, the welfare state cannot be revived.

Few politicians were amused and after Carnivalesque chaos in Seattle (1999), Prague, Washington (both 2000) and Genoa (2001) the security apparatus clamped down and the protests subsided. For several more years the World Social Forum would help to focus an 'alter-globalisation' movement, until complaints that it had become too NGO-heavy. Then came the financial crash and politics mutated (see Chapter 12).

An alternative thinking within the movement was that the radical energies of social democracy *could* be recharged and blended with a new kind of politics based around grassroots and communal democracy, social (but not necessarily statist) forms of ownership, ecological sustainability, mutable networks of resistance and activism, non-monetary values and relationships, fair trade, land and taxation reform (George, 2004: 92–9, 178–85; Klein, 2004: 227–8). Monbiot (2003: 159–80) observed how Keynes had argued for a system that would have been radical in 1945, let alone five decades later. Could social democratic parties reimagine themselves, therefore?

What were such parties trying to do as the new millennium dawned? Did they deserve to be struck by the missiles some were lobbing at them? Did New Labour? We need to address these questions, since by the 1990s it was becoming difficult to debate social policy without reference to cross-national and global contexts. Let's try to understand why by reviewing three issues and tracing their interrelationship: the EU, the Millennium Developments Goals (MDGs) and the Kyoto Protocol.

New Labour in Europe

By the early 1990s, the Labour Party had come to regard the EU as a haven against Thatcherite storms (Fella, 2006: 623–5). The Social Chapter was about social rights, with EU laws and protocols offering protections that Britain's unwritten constitution often neglected. If most Eurosceptics (Major's 'bastards') were 'little free market Englanders' then surely a Social Europe offered a progressive alternative.

To this would be added a Blairite accent (Smith, 2005: 707–14; Fella, 2006: 625–34). The Chapter's social rights were primarily *employment* rights. This chimed well with the Third Way insistence that social participation centred on the obligation to earn – that any job is better than no job. To this way of thinking, in an age of mass unemployment the reinsertion of individuals into the labour market was more of a progressive goal than ever. The EU offered a social model of capitalism rather than anything socialist, and a model moreover that was increasingly receptive to the importance of flexibility, competitive openness and the free movement of capital and labour. It was also a means for New Labour to signal its modernity, its cosmopolitan, welcoming, business-friendly face (Driver & Martell, 2002: 128–32). So, when national self-interest prevailed – as in the decision to remain outside the Euro – this could be sold as pragmatism in contrast to the ideological dogma and federalist fears of the 'bastards'.

Labour was thus committed to working more constructively with the EU than at any time in its history and in 1997 it now did what the Tories had refused to do: sign the Social Chapter.[2] But note that the employment chapter in the Treaty of Amsterdam permitted a greater role for labour market flexibility than had formally been the case (Fella, 2006: 626).

In short, New Labour was pro-EU in so far as the EU shared its preference for lighter-touch regulation than previous Labour governments would surely have preferred. The Working Time Directive (see Chapter 9) became law in 1998, though individuals could 'choose' to work longer hours if they (presumably, without any pressure from employers) wished. Other aspects of the Directive – particularly the exemptions Labour negotiated – indicate a shift away from interventionism and corporatism (Blair *et al.*, 2001: 68–71).

The subsequent Lisbon Treaty in 2000 also coincided with important aspects of the Third Way, especially its emphasis on open markets and social investment. Indeed, in alliance with Spain and Italy's Conservative governments, Blair's influence was central to the Lisbon agenda (Smith, 2005: 710). There were, for instance, targets for employment creation but not for social inclusion (Vandenbroucke & Vleminckx, 2011: 452). Was the latter being seen as an automatic consequence of the former?

Years later, some defenders of Lisbon would concede its ineffectiveness at combatting poverty, in part because the social investment approach sought recommodification mainly through 'negative incentives', i.e. prodding people into labour markets by restricting benefit entitlements (Vandenbroucke & Vleminckx, 2011: 460–2; also Rhodes, 2007: 392–4; cf. Hopkin & Wincott, 2006). By uncoupling social investment from social protection, the Lisbon Treaty undermined its own redistributive aspects.

Therefore, rather than the victory of Centre-Left parties driving forward a new Social Europe, the turn of the millennium saw the marketisation of that social agenda: its 'capture' by a politics of liberalisation, competiveness, corporate dominance, privatisation and deregulation. This would not manifest itself in the same way everywhere. Where UK privatisations had emphasised shareholder profits, the Germans and French were less willing to lose sight of broader, stakeholder interests (Driver & Martell, 2002: 102–8). Nonetheless, critics worried that social democratic parties had conceded too much to free market, globalised liberalism.

What explains those concessions?

First, they were motivated partly by anxieties about globalisation; that investment and so jobs would be harmed if EU taxes and regulations were 'anti-business'. They were also, second, due to the institutional constraints of the EU itself, the extent to which its cultures and structures lock governments into established priorities and practices: economics before politics, private before public, growth before fairness (McGowan, 2001: 83–97). The EU appeared more successful at changing social democratic parties than the latter were at changing the EU. Finally, the electoral mandate of Blair also mattered. Labour seemed set for a longer, more stable period in government than the French Socialists or the German SPD. It was thus New Labour who helped consolidate the EU's drive towards market liberalisations, and away from the interventionism promoted by Delors just a few years earlier.[3]

If the EU experience was an illustrative test case, then, 'alter-globalisation' critics had good reason to feel sceptical about the direction in which established social democratic parties were travelling. Though it would be simplistic to spot no differences between *laissez faire* Conservatives and social democrats – especially in terms of employment rights and industrial policy – the latter seemed to have capitulated to the former on many essentials (Finlayson, 2007). Those who argued for an alternative approach (e.g. Lionel Jospin, Oskar Lafontaine) were too often outpaced by those enthusiastic for a globalising, liberalised version of capitalism (Clinton, Blair, Gerhard Schroeder).

Energy markets

So although the EU continued to be characterised by institutional diversity, it was a diversity within a *laissez faire* context. Take energy markets as one example.

It was the European Commission that lobbied for the deregulation of energy provision – as a corollary of the desire to create a single market – with the UK's post-1989 experience as a key inspiration (see Chapter 8; Veith, 2010: 51). Due to an EU Directive, by 2003 most member states had adopted market-based systems: privatised generators and suppliers, with only modest regulatory interventions. Public and semi-public monopolies remained in France, Belgium, Ireland and Greece alone (Veith, 2010: 52–6). Energy was no longer being conceived as a natural monopoly.

According to Rutledge (2007) New Labour in particular repeatedly overestimated the benefits of competition for energy supplies and prices. The period 1981–97 saw a large international growth of energy supplies and so of overproduction. Therefore, while liberalisation of the British system was a factor in reducing energy prices *it was only a secondary one*. Indeed, Rutledge argues it was regulation (including the 'partial' regulation of 1996–2002) that kept UK gas and electricity prices low, reductions that came to an end once full liberalisation began in 2002.

Why does this matter? As we see later, Kyoto laid the groundwork for carbon markets at the very time that the European shift in policy instruments was accelerating. The globalisation and liberalisation of energy markets thus coincided with and no doubt inspired the EU's Emissions Trading Scheme (ETS), the world's first cross-national scheme of its kind, covering two billion tonnes of annual emissions. We investigate this below.

In other words, as climate change raced up the political agenda it would be addressed to a large extent via market-based instruments and offsets rather than either the more top-down approach of the 1970s and 1980s or the communal, participatory, decommodified, socialised approach for which so many within the alter-globalisation movement were calling (Klein, 2014: 218–25). In Fitzpatrick (2014a: 115–18) I argue that the privatisation, marketisation and fragmentation of energy systems makes it harder to create a policy synthesis of social objectives (reducing fuel poverty) and ecological ones (greater energy efficiencies).

Does this imply that the EU's commitment to tackling climate change was a sham? Not at all. The sixth EAP (2002–12) had some ambitious themes, including 'environment and health' as well as climate change.[4] In fact, by the end of the last century and into the 2000s the EU was providing the environmental leadership which the USA had by then surrendered.

This is because the global order that the Labour government and the EU promoted was one characterised by a much stronger moral component than had been the case in previous decades. Look at the MDGs.

Development

In 1997 the new Foreign Secretary, Robin Cook, had promised to give British foreign policy an ethical dimension. Blair and Brown subsequently offered public support to relevant campaigns, including Make Poverty History and Jubilee 2000. From 1997–2005 international aid doubled (Margo *et al.*, 2007: 85) and the new Department for International Development was nominally separate from British commercial interests, with some clout at cabinet level (Porteous, 2005: 282).

This emphasis paralleled a shift in the strategies of global agencies, especially the World Bank. 'Structural adjustment' remained important but there was also a new recognition that poverty and debt were humanitarian challenges distinct from considerations of economic prosperity and military security. Indeed, it was this moral dimension that would drive UK intervention in Kosovo, Sierra Leone and elsewhere, giving Blair reason to believe that intervention in Iraq would be equally expeditious and effective (Seldon, 2007: 167).[5]

At the UN the obvious manifestation of this new humanitarianism was the MDGs. The main goals for 2000–15 were to:

- eradicate extreme poverty and hunger;
- achieve universal primary education;
- promote gender equality and empower women;
- reduce child mortality;
- improve maternal health;
- combat HIV/AIDS, malaria and other diseases;
- ensure environmental sustainability;
- develop a global partnership for development.

Were the MDGs successful? According to the United Nations (2015), over one billion fewer people were experiencing absolute poverty (living on less than $1.25 per day) in 2015 than 1990. The number of undernourished people almost halved over the same period, as did child mortality rates. The goal to halve the number of those without access to improved sources of water was achieved by 2010 – though 663 million were still without improved drinking water and 2.4 billion people in developing countries lacked access to improved sanitation facilities.

Bourguignon (2015: 25–38) similarly reports that from 1990–2008 inequalities between countries were declining, in part because growth rates in China and India surpassed those of developed nations, though African countries had largely been left behind. The proportion of the global poor had therefore diminished even as numbers rose overall (due to population increases). Over the same period, though, inequalities *within* countries were increasing. Many benefits of growth accrued to the already-haves and the price paid for growth was downward pressure on social protection services, due to a perceived need to 'improve competitiveness'.

And some of the MDGs targets were missed. For instance:

> Efforts to ensure global environmental sustainability have shown mixed results throughout the last 15 years.... Therefore, it is crucial to ensure that the development agenda for the future reflects the links between socio-economic and environmental sustainability ...
>
> (United Nations, 2015: 61)

Nonetheless, and despite some excessive backslapping, these were achievements that were only dreamed about in the 1980s and 1990s.

To and from Kyoto

In one respect, the agreement on the MDGs was no surprise. A few years earlier the Kyoto Protocol had already indicated the futility of treating international development separately from ecological issues (Burnell, 1998: 787–9). Kyoto was the perfect articulation of New Labour's view that considerations of justice and sustainable development converged upon those of economic prosperity. This is no coincidence. With some justification, the Labour government would give itself much of the credit for the Kyoto agreement.

Negotiated in 1997 – though not coming into operation until 2005 – the Protocol committed the nations ratifying it to average cuts in CO_2 emissions of 5.2% (below 1990 levels) by 2008–12 (Tickell, 2008: 33–51; Christoff & Eckersley, 2013: 103–4).[6] Some countries would have higher targets, some lower. The reason the Protocol took so long to gestate was that it needed those nations on board who accounted for at least 55% of emissions. Only when Russia ratified the Protocol in 2004 did this occur – with the USA and Australia not ratifying it until 2008. Therefore, Kyoto was practically redundant before it had begun, with post-Kyoto negotiations beginning in Bali in 2007.

According to the UK's Deputy Prime Minister, without British efforts (specifically, his own) Kyoto would never have happened. Since Britain was about to hold the presidency of the EU Council, John Prescott saw himself as de facto representative for the EU at the negotiations. According to Prescott (2009: 222–6), Japan was willing to accept an emissions reduction target only so long as it was lower than the USA's, and the USA was willing to accept a target only so long as it was lower than the EU's! He agreed to these stipulations because the EU, he says, was eager to occupy the moral high ground (Brown, 2005: 420–1). Prescott's account – of his staying awake for 48 hours to reach an agreement with minutes to spare – paints himself as the hero of the hour.

Self-dramatisations aside, Jonathon Porritt concurs that the UK was indeed key to the success of Kyoto (see Carter & Ockwell, 2007: 62) and he is not alone in believing so (Schreurs & Tiberghien, 2010: 50–1). This was partly because of enthusiasm from the new government and partly because the dash-for-gas had helped to stabilise UK emissions by the end of the 1990s anyway (Carter & Ockwell, 2007: 71–2). It was also a way for Labour to signal its pro-EU and pro-internationalist credentials. The UK and Germany together would eventually account for most of the emissions' reductions achieved by the EU (Harrison & Sundstrom, 2010: 267).

Even in its own terms, Kyoto was far from perfect (Tickell, 2008: 34–8):

- Shipping and aviation were omitted.
- It was characterised by weak compliance mechanisms, as binding agreements are difficult to establish at a transnational level (Giddens, 2009: 192) – though the EU was a partial exception to this.
- It gave little emphasis to long-term investment.
- Developing countries were not included in the Protocol at all – the sad irony being that their carbon emissions shot up after 1997 (primarily in China and India).

Kyoto thus became an issue around which the environmental conflicts of the new century would turn. The USA was fearful that the Protocol would give developing nations a competitive advantage. For their part, many developing nations were certain that environmentalism was a convenient mask for an affluent west determined to maintain its dominance. The inadequate sums devoted to 'adaptation' (i.e. adapting to and coping with the consequences of global warming) symbolised this disagreement. Only towards the end of the 2000s were various funds established with any substantial finance behind them.

While acknowledging the above criticisms, Stern (2007: 541) argued that Kyoto at least "established an aspiration to create a single carbon price and implement equitable approaches to sharing the burden of action on climate change". This is the 'important first step' defence in which it would be thought better to build upon Kyoto rather than trying to start again from scratch (Gao, 1997).

But for Kyoto's critics, building upon such shaky foundations could only provide a false sense of progress. It is not just that Kyoto's targets would come to seem so painfully inadequate as the climate science developed, it's also that a combination of inflexibility and vacuity seemed built into the system. Tickell (2008: 45) refers to Kyoto as a cap-and-trade system[7] without an overall cap! Among the many issues that would bedevil negotiations about a post-Kyoto system was the question of whether to have a binding cap, one that would (preferably) be subject to periodic review as the impacts and timescale of global warming became increasingly manifest.

Unities

In any event Kyoto was for many years the only game in town and by the mid-2000s New Labour was at the forefront of bringing it and the MDGs together (Seldon, 2007: 319–27, 364–72).

In 2005, Blair would make this connection between climate change and global poverty central to the UK's presidency of the G8 (Payne, 2006: 918, 920–1). The main outcome of that year's Gleneagles Summit was to,

- double aid to all developing countries (half going to Africa);
- develop innovative financing mechanisms;
- cancel all debts (over US$40 billion) owed by heavily indebted poor countries;
- boost investment in healthcare and education services in Africa.

A separate statement on climate change committed the G8 to 'act with resolve and urgency' by working together with emerging economies to achieve 'substantial reductions' in emissions.

Blair was thus attempting to establish climate change as a matter of global leadership in the face of continued resistance from the USA and Russia in particular (Blair, 2007: ch. 18; Walker & King, 2008: 235–6). Developed countries should take the lead on climate change, it was declared, freeing developing nations to concentrate on economic development and domestic poverty.

There is always room for scepticism. Payne (2006: 933–4), for instance, is highly critical of the Gleneagles Summit, seeing it as an example of spin and rhetoric, which preserved the very divisions (North/developed vs South/developing) that were debilitating. But his reaction is confined to matters of finance and trade. On climate change, he acknowledges, Gleneagles did move the environment closer to the centre of global politics than it had ever been before. This was in part because alliances were forming in order to counter the USA's obstructionism.

Many in the Green movement worried that getting the USA on board meant paying too high a price: an emphasis on technological fixes and market-based instruments (Hovi & Sprinz, 2010: 139–42). Yet it would be cynical self-indulgence not to recognise the good intentions demonstrated by Blair, not only by promoting the connections between international development and environmental issues but by bringing those who had been left out of Kyoto, i.e. developing countries, into the process (Payne, 2006: 932–4).

Europe and the world

Labour's efforts re Kyoto and the MDGs inevitably influenced, and enhanced the reputation of, the EU itself.

Kyoto may have embodied the US preference for market-based instruments and offsets, but the EU had been travelling in a similar direction for years. Its continued funding of fossil fuel industries, enthusiasm for road transport and export credits (all of which contribute to climate change) leads to a mixed conclusion: if it was not acting ethically, it was certainly acting less unethically (Harris, 2008: 133–4). Harris (2008: 122) therefore observes:

> … while Europe can be relatively proud of its actions compared to most countries, notably the U.S., it ought to do much more.

But even former critics acknowledge that the EU's effectiveness and global leadership re climate policy improved significantly in the 2000s (Oberthür, 2011: 669–76; see also Walker & King, 2008: 225–7; Giddens, 2009: 202). The EU (with Labour at the forefront) was largely responsible for saving Kyoto when it came close to being derailed.[8] What gave the EU authority was the fact that its own target – an 8% reduction on 1990 levels – looked like being exceeded. Oberthür (2011: 674) states that by 2009, GHG emissions from the EU had fallen by slightly more than 12% compared to 1990. Though according to the European Commission (2013) itself the actual reduction was 18%.[9]

The EU thus assumed the mantle of authority and leadership on climate change due to its relative unity on the issue, strong political and public pressure, its desire for world leadership and for energy security. Once its own Kyoto target looked like being met, by 2007–08, the EU recommended that developed countries should reduce emissions of GHGs by 30% by 2020 – committing itself to a 20% cut which it proposed raising to 30% if other nations signed up (Giddens, 2009: 193–7).

Labour's influence is palpable here too. The UK's Kyoto target was a 12.5% reduction on 1990 levels, but the government announced an additional, voluntarily imposed target of 20% reductions in CO_2. It achieved the former but the latter was widely ambitious, for the kind of reasons given at the end of this chapter. Still, this at least embodied a radicalism New Labour was so often accused of lacking.

As announced in 2002, utility compass would be required to generate 10% of their electricity from renewables by 2010, and 20% by 2020 (Walker & King, 2008: 232). The 2010 target was missed – 6.5% would come from renewables – but the objective was bold given that in 2004 the figure was just 3%. Then, in 2003, the Labour government announced its ambition of cutting CO_2 emissions by 60% by 2050 – though climate science quickly suggested that a cut closer to 80% was needed. Not to be outdone, the following year the French announced a target of −75% by 2050.

As such, a large part of the EU's success (both in reducing emissions and in influencing international politics) was due to Labour:

> … the UK has been one of the world's most proactive countries both in implementing national measures and in driving the international process.
> (Walker & King, 2008: 231; also Knill & Liefferink, 2007: 134–9)

For much of the 2000s, Labour was a hub that had the EU, the MDGs and Kyoto as its spokes.

Trading emissions

We therefore come back to the central characteristic of the period, the one that had many in the alter-globalisation and green movements worried: the use largely of market-based instruments and offsets to address climate change (Christoff & Eckersley, 2013: 104–7). As just noted, this would result in some successes. But were these results as considerable as those that could or should have been achieved? Let's explore some key developments.

In its opposition to tax harmonisation Labour, like Major before it, led the charge against an EU-wide carbon tax. Therefore, policymakers were forced to turn to emissions trading as the primary way of determining carbon prices (Convery, 2009: 392–3). The New Labour government itself pioneered a British ETS. Phase I of the EU ETS ran from 2005–07 and was seen very much as a learning curve. This was to be succeeded by the 'compliance period' of Phase II (2008–12) during which the scheme was to be fully up and running (Connelly *et al.*, 2012: 308–11).

Though the actual operation is extremely convoluted (Veith, 2010: 23–44), the basic idea is straightforward. The ETS is a cap-and-trade mechanism. First, specify the maximum level of emissions permitted (the cap) and issue 'allowances' to firms, which permit them to emit within the upper limit of that cap, trading with others so that they can fulfil their obligations cost-effectively. At the end of each year firms must hold enough allowances to cover the pollutants they have emitted. Once the scheme is established you can then reduce the cap year on year, thus effecting behaviour change by altering the structure of prices and incentives.

Though it included all member states, the bulk of the ETS would centre on Germany, Britain, Poland, Italy, Spain and France; and it was limited to oil refining, energy generation and metals processing. This covered about 40% of the EU's total CO_2 emissions.

Phase I was not an auspicious start, partly because of (1) problems specific to it, (2) flaws in the scheme more generally, and (3) inherent limits to the efficacy of carbon trading. Let's review these in turn.

First, Phase I covered no GHGs other than CO_2 and permits were allocated through 'grandfathering', i.e. on the basis of past emissions. Grandfathering is not a process conducive to the behaviour change that price signals are meant to engineer (Farnsworth, 2007), nor to social justice and fairness, since it gives to those who already have (Dirix *et al.*, 2015: 716–17). Individual nations were more or less allowed to set their own National Allocation Plans, to which relatively few changes were demanded by the European Commission, which meant that national self-interest prevailed with governments favouring their domestic companies. The result was that almost all nations distributed too many allowances, reducing the scope for the very incentives the ETS was meant to embody

– if permits are to have value there must be a *scarcity* of them to bid for. Enforcement of the scheme was therefore weak.[10]

Phase I was styled as a period for learning lessons (Dekkers & Oudenes, 2007: 189). Stern (2007: 371–5, 383–4) defends carbon trading as being more cost-effective than regulation while acknowledging the considerable problems with Phase I. The Commission therefore announced that Phase II would include a stricter cap, a harmonised system of allocations and tighter enforcement.[11]

A less generous interpretation, though, would suggest that failure was inevitable and symptomatic of the Commission's commitment to liberalisation. The same Commission that was pushing the privatisation of energy systems was now promising a stricter regime of regulation, intervention and oversight. The same Commission that celebrated the diversification of energy sources and delivery systems was now promising greater harmonisation and standardisation. There was certainly a lot of nervousness emanating from the Commission regarding expansion of the scheme's scope (to include aviation and shipping) after 2013 (Farnsworth, 2007).

Second, then, Dekkers and Oudenes (2007: 187) observed the extent to which commercial and financial objectives were as important to the overall scheme as environmental ones. Tickell (2008: 38) quotes Gordon Brown's observation that carbon policy was meant to serve the needs of carbon markets, rather than the other way around. Therefore, was the ETS a necessary means of greening the economy, or a means of marketising the environment and seeing it as just another business opportunity? Given the opportunity for making offsets (to be described shortly) critics alleged that environmental goals were being downgraded (Tickell, 2008: 49–51).

It may also be that EU unity is a very thin paper covering some very deep cracks (Parker & Karlsson, 2010: 934–6), ones running through the structure of EU decision-making and undermining its democratic legitimacy (see Knill & Liefferink, 2007: ch. 4). Burns *et al.* (2013: 952) note how often the Commission sides more with the Council of Ministers than with the EU Parliament, leading to the side-lining of the latter. For instance, like green NGOs, the Parliament wanted the ETS allowances to be restricted in number and allocated via auction, but the Commission sided with member states (Convery, 2009: 404).

As such, if what Phase II needed was more centralised and effective allocation, better mechanisms of enforcement and compliance, harmonisation, transparency and accountability, was this consistent with the long-established principle of subsidiarity?

It is ultimately difficult to say because Phase II coincided with the global financial crash and emissions fall anyway whenever economies falter. So trying to assess the efficacy of the ETS would become very complex (Vlachou, 2014: 134–5).

Finally, Gilbertson and Reyes (2009: 12–14) propose that carbon trading is inherently flawed for two key reasons:

1   Carbon prices are volatile because contingent upon numerous factors, such that any price is somewhat arbitrary and uncertain.

2　Trading schemes are limited to their own narrow parameters and so do not drive the innovations needed to shift societies away from their fossil fuel dependency.

To the objection that the ETS can always be revised they argue that there is no point in changing the rules when the game is wrong:

> Powerful economic and elite interests are at stake here, which are unlikely to be shifted by academic exercises in how to 'perfect' carbon markets, as though they existed in a power vacuum.
>
> (Gilbertson & Reyes, 2009: 89)

For instance, even guaranteeing a 'floor price' for carbon tends to be resisted by the business lobby (Macrory, 2011: 315).

Therefore, some critics observe that the context for the ETS is not just climate change but a capitalist economy that values profits before people. The ETS was a fall-back reform, given how successful the energy companies had been in lobbying against a carbon tax (Vlachou, 2014: 137). And as a market, the ETS carries the deficiencies of other markets: the devaluing of non-quantifiable goods, asymmetrical information, negative externalities and the entrenchment of existing inequalities. We might also note Dobson's (2003: 208) argument that the attitudinal and value changes we need to tackle environmental problems cannot be addressed sufficiently by the informational changes given through prices.

So, EU reductions in emissions were welcome, but from 2005–12 the ETS may have constituted a hindrance rather than a help.

Trading offsets

Another key aspect of Kyoto was the use of offsets. The Clean Development Mechanism (CDM) enabled industrial nations to move towards their emissions reduction targets by generating credits (Certified Emissions Reductions) through funding clean energy projects in developing countries. Stern (2007: 569–75) argues that the CDM built cooperation between developed and developing nations, strengthened understanding of development opportunities and stimulated private sector interest in climate issues.

However, he also acknowledges considerable problems:

- it is difficult to demonstrate that a project has reduced emissions below what would have occurred without it;
- the CDM did not allow for the higher risks associated with using new, renewable technologies;
- it did not counter familiar market failures, e.g. the fact that there is a high discount rate on long-term projects (the conservation of existing forests was not part of the CDM, for instance).

By allowing developed nations to relax their own reduction activities domestically, the CDM got the world's main polluters off the hook of making substantial changes to their economic infrastructures and business practices.

Hansen (2009: 182–3; Klein, 2014: 218–25) is a strong critic of offsets, arguing that only rarely do they compensate for the climate effects created by overshooting emissions reduction targets. In fact, it is possible the CDM was making things worse: by inviting corruption and accountancy tricks and by encouraging easy-to-establish projects whose significance to climate change was negligible (Giddens, 2009: 190). Thus, developing countries could be diverted away from energy efficiencies (since the more emissions they have the more offsets they can sell) and towards corruption (*creating* climate damage so that they can sell reductions as offsets to developed nations) (Tickell, 2008: 35–40).

Like the ETS, then, the CDM may have constituted more of a hindrance than a help.

To summarise. Both New Labour and the broader EU aspired to be world leaders in the fields of international development and climate change, with some EU countries achieving the highest emissions reductions in the world prior to 2010. However, it is doubtful that policymakers were understanding the limits of carbon markets and offsets sufficiently. If we compare the 1997–2010 period with the preceding decade then great strides *were* made. If we assess it against the strides, which climate scientists were indicating urgently needed to be made then the picture was less rosy.

Poverty and society

Within Labour's international agenda, then, we can spot the outlines of a more distinct ecosocial politics than existed at the domestic level. This politics is summarised at the end of the chapter.

Legge (2012) therefore observes a curious disjointedness in New Labour's approach. Domestically it remained content to ally its anti-poverty policies to a moralistic rhetoric, which stressed the responsibilities of the poor (its more progressive, redistributive achievements tended to be hidden). This played well with Right-wing tabloids. But in terms of global poverty a self-serving moralism was much less in evidence.

On one level this disjunction is unsurprising because it probably echoed public attitudes.[12] Yet looked at another way, it was strange. If you are willing to concede that people in developing countries are, to whatever extent, the victims of circumstances for which they are not responsible then why not extend the same logic to deprived people in the UK? Why not challenge the narrative of the Tory tabloids more forcefully (Levitas, 2005: ch. 8)?

The explanation lies in the context. New Labour's approach toward international development was where it could signal to the party membership its most radical departure from the 'see nothing, know nothing, do nothing' politics of the Thatcher and Major years without fearing the electoral consequences too much (Plachciak, 2013). How many voters noticed the government's progressiveness on the world stage?

But domestically, it needed to keep voters on side. To do so, New Labour had wedded itself to an economics, which was fundamentally continuous with the 1979–97 period (see Chapter 10; cf. Balls *et al.*, 2007). As such, and despite welcome anti-poverty initiatives, its discourse all too often echoed the marketised individualism of Thatcherism, where a person's social position is attributed primarily to their personal agency and moral character. Even when the government spoke in another vocabulary, e.g. about health inequalities, the emphasis was on geographical inequalities and postcode lotteries rather than on social class (Sassi, 2009).

Social reforms

Not that this is necessarily to condemn Labour's actual record on domestic poverty, not given the social conditions it inherited in 1997.

Researchers would later find that the high watermark of New Labour's assault on poverty occurred in its first six or so years in office (Sefton *et al.*, 2009: 28–34; see next chapter). After 2004 progress was slower and more modest. The lowest hanging fruit had been picked (improvements made to the incomes of many just below the poverty line) and more commitment would be needed to reach households in 'deep poverty'. But with resources now, finally, pouring into the NHS, Labour was reluctant to reacquire the reputation of 'tax and spend'.[13] Even the top rate of tax was thought untouchable.

By 2005–06 it was clear that its first target re child poverty (a 25% reduction) would be missed – though 600,000 children were brought out of poverty – and further reductions would be much harder to achieve (Lloyd, 2006: 316). The redistribution by stealth, which had occurred behind the backs of most voters and Tory newspapers prior to 2001, was becoming less and less effective. New Labour sat on a huge parliamentary majority, yet still feared that this was paper-thin and easily shredded if the more progressive aspects of its agenda became explicit.

Its second-term strategy was basically a continuation of the first-term, then (Stewart, 2009a: 50–1). The minimum wage rose at a rate higher than inflation but remained inadequate for most without supplements. To this end, in 2003 the Working Tax Credit and the Child Tax Credit replaced and consolidated the tax credit schemes introduced four years earlier. The former entitled 90% of families to claim against childcare costs. Childcare was thus a recurring theme, e.g. the introduction of Statutory Paternity Pay, though Labour's hope that the private sector would rush to provide childcare places was dashed.

At the other end of the lifecourse, a means-tested Pension Credit replaced Income Support for people over the age of 60. This, with increases in the basic state pension, plus the introduction of a second state pension and a savings credit, boosted the incomes of most pensioners while targeting the most on those with the least (Toynbee & Walker, 2005: 63–6). But it was less clear that the goal of establishing a secure income floor could be achieved through an ever more complex system of schemes. The Pension Credit would remain unclaimed by one third of those entitled to receive it, or 1–1.6 million potential claimants (Fitzpatrick, 2012: 228).

The more disciplinary, supply-side aspects of New Labour's approach also continued (Dwyer, 2008: 201–4), e.g. benefit claimants were required to attend interviews with 'personal advisors' (this now included disabled people and claimants over 50).

There were some second-term innovations. The Child Trust Fund was a scheme designed to encourage savings (which government would top up), educate the next generation about financial responsibility and build up the assets of the poor. The scheme was never heavily promoted, however. Its entrepreneurial, investment aspects struck many as too complex and it failed to capture public imagination.

The government's achievements were real, nonetheless (Toynbee & Walker, 2005: 55–8; Hills et al., 2009: 347–8). More redistribution was being directed towards children than by any previous Labour administration and by 2005 a family with two children had on average experienced an 11% increase in their tax credits compared to 2001. Fuel poverty was in decline, too (Fitzpatrick, 2011a: 172–3). Even so, though brakes were applied to the growth of income inequality, *wealth* inequality continued to accelerate (Margo et al., 2007: 62–5, Lister, 2007).

Labour's successes and failures were more than coincidental, then. It raised the social floor but, shying away from egalitarianism, underestimated the disadvantages stemming from the distances, which continued to separate the floor from the social ceiling (Dorling, 2010: 404–7).

The big three

From 2001–05, health, education and housing policies were also continuous with those of the first term.

After the 1997–99 spending freeze ended, New Labour poured a torrent of money into the NHS and by its second-term the dividends were being reaped (Chote et al., 2010: 8–10). With UK spending doubling from 1997–2005, ascending closer towards the EU average, waiting times were down to unprecedented levels. With its pro-NHS credentials intact, the government could present the continued role played by independent 'foundation hospitals', commercial firms, greater competition and quasi-markets as managerial efficacy rather than ideological dogma. 'What matters is what works'.

Increasingly, the government looked towards preventative measures as ways of transforming the NHS from an ill-health service towards a wellbeing service. Some of this was about education and information, e.g. encouraging healthier habits from a young age through Sure Start centres. Some of it was about prohibition, e.g. with fewer people smoking the time seemed ripe to discourage the practice – culminating in the 2007 ban on smoking in enclosed public spaces.

Prevention is the context within which discussions of a green healthcare system often occur too (Verrinder, 2011). The contribution of pollution to cancers, lung and cardiovascular diseases has been long known, with the poorest being particularly vulnerable (Fitzpatrick, 2014a: 188–9).

Yet here we encounter the limits of New Labour's approach. It was comfortable intervening at the level of personal behaviour, e.g. smoking habits, yet less so when it came to anything more systemic. You can get people to recycle more but capitalism depends upon consumer demand and therefore waste. You can encourage healthy eating but changing the infrastructure of food chains and the dominance of supermarket corporations smacks of socialistic interference in markets. And Britain was to remain not just a car- but a plane-dependent economy (see below and Chapter 12).

So, domestically, the social policy and ecological agendas largely remained apart. For instance, I have elsewhere commented on the fact that Labour's air quality strategy made little mention of poverty and deprivation (Fitzpatrick, 2014a: 191).

The characteristics of first-term education policy remained in place (Ball, 2008: 93–105; Drakeford, 2008: 168–70):

- targets and league-tables,
- less emphasis on local cooperation and more on parental choice and business models,
- the view that what mattered was pedagogic standards rather than social background,
- the continued bureaucratisation and micro-management of teaching,
- greater diversity among schools and specialisation in subjects taught via Foundation Schools and City Academies.

Left critics worried that all this was emptying education of its public values and purposes (Benn, 2011: 71–81). Critics on the Right began to mount a backlash against the year on year improvement in assessment results, suspecting that these were getting easier. From a green perspective, while the implementation of citizenship education provided a space for 'ecological citizenship' to emerge (Dobson, 2003: 194–5), the former would prove to be less than the Socratic revolution some had hoped for and the latter would be overwhelmed by the consumerist and productivist emphasis within New Labour's education reforms (Huckle, 2008).

But, for now, the critics were marginalised with the education budget rising three times faster than it had under the Tories, so that spending doubled in the decade following 1997 (Toynbee & Walker, 2005: 116–17; Lupton *et al.*, 2009).

The government continued to neglect housing reform, however. Though Labour required builders to include affordable housing in their development plans in order to receive planning permission, house building had slumped to levels not seen since the 1940s. The assumption that the power and responsibility for housing construction lay in the private sector remained unchallenged.

The housing market was overheating. Between 2001–11 average house prices rose 94% compared to a 29% increase in average wages. It would now take first-time buyers an average of eight years to save a deposit, compared with one year in 1995 (Fitzpatrick, 2014a: 143–7, 162). For the most part, local councils were given few new functions, resources or powers (Toynbee & Walker, 2005: 157–62). Housing poverty continued to be addressed through an ever-rising housing benefits bill, rather than through investment in bricks and mortar.

Ironically, the housing sector was perhaps the obvious area through which an ecosocial approach might have developed (Boardman, 2007: 10, 16). Indeed, in 2003 Prescott's super-department produced a Sustainable Communities plan as part of its neighbourhood renewal agenda. This would largely be oriented around growth in the south of England, however.

Budgeting the environment

So, despite the UK ETS, the Climate Change Levy and the Renewable Energy Obligation, in other respects Labour was actually quite complacent and *unambitious*. After the initial pro-green stance, relations between the government and green organisations turned frosty in the first five years of the new century, with Brown blaming the latter for not defending the Levy and for its lack of support during the fuel protests of 2000. The greens, for their part, were unenthusiastic about a government generally hostile to regulation and to taxing environmental bads (Carter, 2008: 199, 202).

Carter (2008: 201) compares the paucity of the environmental budget with those for health and education. To which we might add that there were few of the 'ecosocial synergies' that could allow welfare budgets to help develop an effective climate change programme. In Labour's second-term, the quality of life agenda that Prescott had championed evaporated.

Complacency characterised even the Gleneagles Summit. Agreement on improving energy efficiencies (including across different modes of transport) was a key outcome of the summit (Jollands *et al.*, 2010). Yet since New Labour's own transport strategy was poorly coordinated (see Chapter 10) was this a case of telling others to 'copy what we say, not what we do' (Carter & Ockwell, 2007: 103–14; Rayner *et al.*, 2008: 377–85; Cullingworth *et al.*, 2015: 493–5)?

From 1990–2006, transport CO_2 emissions actually rose for several reasons: a thriving economy, a lack of joined up government, the falling costs of car travel compared to rail, and a persistent bias against public transport (bus deregulation was not reversed, for instance, though councils were given extra powers vis bus operators). Labour was wary of being seen as opposed to small hauliers and the car owners in general. A 2004 transport plan attempted to play catch-up but the impetus that might have been gained between 1997–2001 was lost forever. In 2010 transport was responsible for 21–24% of the UK's carbon emissions, compared to 19% in 1999 (Fitzpatrick, 2014a: 165–71). Indeed, as we see in Chapter 12, New Labour supported the growth in air travel and airport expansion – including a third runway at Heathrow – as essential to Britain's global competitiveness.

And Britain's reliance on market instruments contrasted with the level of government assistance and coordination found in Germany and Denmark. Central government kept its distance from even the more radical use of economic instruments:

- As noted in the last chapter, the GDP share of environmental taxes was lower in 2005 than in 1997, the Climate Change Levy was frozen and the fuel price escalator was dropped.
- Investment in London Underground was to come through a complex public-private partnership – an obsession of Gordon Brown's – which bedevilled the government for years, rather than through a more cost effective bond scheme, which had been shown to work in New York.
- London's congestion charge was introduced by Ken Livingstone, who did not sing from the Third Way hymn sheet. Labour initially held its nose and kept its distance. After the charge was a success, central government became more favourable to road charging than previously, but primary responsibility for implementing this was left with local authorities.
- A resocialisation of energy companies was never contemplated and even reregulation was characterised by a consensual, softly-softly approach. Perhaps most significantly, voluntary 'social tariffs' where introduced to reduce fuel costs for vulnerable and low-income customers, but the effectiveness of this approach was less than the government assumed (Fitzpatrick, 2014a: 104–5).
- The government generally failed to promote the merits of renewable energy despite the opportunity for business growth here (Toynbee & Walker, 2005: 242–3, 244–6). This would begin to change after 2005, however.

As intimated above, then, that continued lack in a domestic convergence of the environmental and social policy agendas is not particularly surprising:

> The Labour government's climate change policy has been characterised by a curious disjunction between its actions on the international stage and in the domestic arena.
>
> (Carter, 2008: 194; also Margo *et al.*, 2007: 83–4)

While meeting its Kyoto obligation, the government fell short of the other, self-imposed targets mentioned earlier.[14] And even its success was largely due to pre-1995 reductions which resulted from the dash-for-gas (Carter, 2008: 194–6).

So, by and large, the second-term saw New Labour continuing to tread water vis environmental policy and an ecosocial politics. The un-synthesised, 'oil and water' characteristics of the glossy reports (mentioned in Chapter 10) persisted. The reports themselves would soon fade away. With Labour approaching its ninth year in office and its third election it began to feel as if the government was, if anything, moving backwards.

Key questions

What relationships between the environmental and social policy agendas have emerged? To what extent have social policies and the politics of welfare reform deliberately informed and been informed by the principles and values of environmental ethics and politics?

While at home Labour failed to connect the ecosocial policy dots convincingly, its record on the international stage was more impressive.

The government's vision of capitalism was in line with the social economy traditions the EU sought to embody. So, not only was Britain central to the EU ETS, New Labour had already test-driven the idea of carbon trading with its own UK scheme. Market instruments were therefore central, though these were regulated rather than out and out *laissez faire* markets. The ETS was not successful in its earliest phases, though. A generous reading regards this as teething troubles; a less generous one says that the EU's social market programmes were more committed to the 'markets' than they were to the 'social'.

All of which occurred at a time when the EU became a world leader for objectives from which the USA had withdrawn and for which China was not yet prepared. Rio had incorporated the concept of sustainable development and though Kyoto largely bypassed developing countries the overall itinerary was similar. By the early-mid 2000s various components were swirling around one another: global poverty via the MDGs and climate change via Kyoto. Labour deserves some credit for placing these into a stable orbit at a time when the 'war on terror' was sending so much else into a tailspin.

None of which is to ignore the problems identified above. Too much faith was still being placed in market instruments and in offsets. And by the end of the 2000s, with post-Kyoto negotiations beginning, developing countries were finding a collective voice, which articulated long-standing grievances. Given the centuries-old appropriation of resources upon which the west had built its wealth, global divisions were not going to be settled with a few trading schemes here or offsets there. Some profound questions of global, distributive justice were going to have to be confronted.

Nonetheless, by bringing climate change and poverty together, two of the most important aspects of environmental policy and social policy were now coupled more strongly than at any time in the past. And if the post-Kyoto process was going to be a tough one then at least, somewhat surprisingly, the biggest theatre – a worldwide stage – was offering a more effective arena than the domestic one for integrating the key social and environmental issues at play in the new century.

Labour's version of an ecosocial approach can therefore be summarised as follows:

*Developing countries needed to grow so that they could address their social prob-
lems, but this growth had to be sensitive to global warming, the effects of which
were already impacting most dramatically upon developing countries themselves.
To square this circle, developed countries should take a lead in reducing emissions
(Kyoto) and facilitating reductions in global poverty (MDGs).*

Notes

1 The argument here was that governments were emasculating themselves; i.e. using
their power to hand power over to the WTO, etc. and acting as policemen for global
corporations.
2 The UK then adopted the main legislation previously approved under the Agreement
on Social Policy: the 1994 Works Council Directive, which required workforce consultation in businesses, and the 1996 Parental Leave Directive.
3 No doubt a desire to protect London's status as a financial centre was a crucial
motivation given how much the UK economy was now dependent on financial
services.
4 That said, it underachieved due to a lack of targets, plus problems relating to financing and implementation (Morphet, 2013: 147).
5 So convinced were they of their moral grounding, Blairites saw no great contradiction between this new moral dimension and a continuation of business as usual. Britain's commercial interests (including arms sales) and enthusiasm for market reforms
(usually code for privatisation) would often conflict with its express commitment to
development (Porteous, 2005: 295–6) but that's not how the architects of New
Labour typically saw things.
6 The EU had initially lobbied for a 15% reduction for all signatories (Knill & Liefferink, 2007: 74–5).
7 For an explanation of what this implies see below.
8 The EU had done a deal to bring Russia into the Protocol in 2004, helping to isolate
the USA by the time of Gleneagles.
9 However, Parker and Karlsson (2010: 932–4) insist that the statistics for emissions'
reductions were not as rosy as EU likes to pretend. By 2008 only Germany, Greece,
Sweden and Britain were on course to meet their Kyoto obligations.
10 There was also a suspicion that (a) national governments had exaggerated their emissions prior to 2005 in order to make Phase 1 look efficacious and so conceal their
game-playing, and (b) power generating companies passed on to consumers the cost
of permits they had received for free (Giddens, 2009: 197–9)!
11 But even by Phase III (after 2013) it was still the case that 43% of allowances were
available through free allocation. For an overview of Phase III see de las Heras (2013:
588–91; Vlachou, 2014: 135–6).
12 'British people have enough opportunities to better themselves. If you are poor it's
because you are lazy. Real poverty is found in Africa. All those poor children with
swollen bellies and fly-encrusted eyes'.
13 A slight increase in National Insurance contributions by 1p in 2002 was a rare exception to the rule.
14 The 20% CO_2 reductions and generating 10% of electricity from renewables by 2010.

12 Crashing and burning
2005–10

On 1 November 1988 something electrified the Labour benches. John Smith had recently experienced a heart attack and so the person deputising as Shadow Chancellor had to give the Opposition's response to the Treasury's Autumn Statement (Keegan, 2003: 70). It was his first significant appearance at the Despatch Box in the House of Commons. Few really knew very much about this jowly, big-boned, sombre Scot and expectations were low. As it turned out, the Scot not only filleted and fried Nigel Lawson – successfully predicting that his boom would lead to bust[1] – but served him on a plate of ridicule. Here was something new! In Smith they already had a reassuring bank manager. Now, it seemed, Labour had acquired an attack dog. The Rottweiler who sniffed your crotch wondering what was for lunch.

More than that. Gordon Brown combined an intellectual brain with a socialist heart. In 1975 he had edited *The Red Paper on Scotland* and in 1989 published *Where There's Greed*, which blasted Thatcherism as economically illiterate and morally vacuous.

If you want to understand why, 15–20 years later, such hope and faith was invested in Brown then the answer lies there (Rawnsley, 2010: 434–6, 440–3). Kinnock was regularly mocked as a lightweight by those who worshipped the evil machinations of Milton Friedman. Now the dynamic duo, Smith and Brown, socked! biffed! and walloped! on the side of the good guys. Labour's future was looking bright again. A fourth successive election defeat was disappointing but, hopefully, only a stumble before one last push. By 1993 you looked at Gordon Brown and saw the man who would follow the next Labour Prime Minister, John Smith, into Downing Street.

Yet those hopes became entangled with a schism, the fissures of which would grow throughout the years (Richards, 2010: 65–80). With Smith's premature death, and through an arrangement reached in a dimly-lit Islington restaurant, it was agreed that the telegenic youngster who had shared office space with Brown, and had always been regarded as his junior, should take centre-stage. Elder brother had been usurped and, not liking this, elder brother wasn't going to bite his lip forever. A feud opened up that would dominate British politics for two decades, while enabling Labour to scale electoral heights that even the Tories had never attained. The feud was also a sign that these pioneering heroes were more fallible than they seemed. One loss of balance and the project could go tumbling down the slopes back into the depths. New Labour was always fearful of heights.

Once in government sides formed quickly, squabbling for Labour's soul and future direction (Rawnsley, 2000). Brownites saw themselves as torch-bearers for the realistic Left. Here is Brown, alchemist of the economic miracles for which that grinning ninny beside him takes credit. Isn't there a risk that the PM will leave the anatomy of Thatcher's Britain intact? No, let's allow Blair to seduce Middle England and then we can get down to the serious work of changing the country behind their backs. Who was reducing poverty rates if not Brown's Treasury?

That New Labour was Blair and Brown's joint progeny was easily ignored. The wistful memories of 1988 were strong. Brown was therefore loaded with expectations that few could have satisfied, let alone someone whose chief leadership skills, it turned out all too late, were indecision, chaos and occasional rages that could strip Downing Street wallpaper from across the room (Rawnsley, 2010: 520–7, 550–2; Seldon & Lodge, 2010: 70–6).[2]

All governments face the same problem, of course: how to renew yourself in office? When you are a minister working 14, 16, 18 hours a day almost every day, you are constantly in reactive mode to the backbencher who wants your job, the civil servant who wants 100 decisions by lunchtime, the reporter who wants a good quote, the opposition party who wants to expose your mistakes, the constituent who wants his wall mended, the party leadership who wants eye-catching headlines, the party membership that demands to know why you haven't created a social utopia since it last pestered you. Additionally, Blair, Brown and Mandelson had created a Third Way project which, by only needing to surf the good times of global capitalism, became complacent. Once fair weather turned foul it floundered in the storm, growing ever more fatigued (Rawnsley, 2010: 739–42).

After 2005, Labour increasingly resembled the Conservatives after 1987: still in the lead yet anxious at the lack of petrol in the tank. Yet this, too, fuelled expectations. Wouldn't Brown do what Major had done for the Tories? Why else had he been manoeuvring towards No. 10 for a decade if it wasn't because he had some marvellous, secret masterplan that would keep Labour in office (Rawnsley, 2010: 465–6)? Brown's time at No. 10 would be largely one of disappointment. Was it a case of wasted potential or had this potential, first demonstrated in the Commons that day in 1988, been frail all along?

Changing direction?

That Brown's government signalled no major evolution in welfare reform was unsurprising. He had effectively been the Prime Minister of Social Policy for 10 years already (Seldon & Lodge, 2010: 80, 424). Was there an opportunity for a change of direction? Perhaps. For although Brown was all in favour of private sector involvement in the delivery of public services, he was less willing to fetishise 'choice' (Richards, 2010: 259, 272).

The choice agenda symbolised Blairism. It was decentralising (public services should emulate the private sector and be subject to consumerist, market-like disciplines) *and* centralising (because the self-serving 'producers' of public services are usually obstacles to reform[3] national government must govern from a distance). The empowerment, as customers, of passengers, patients, parents and other welfare clients therefore involved the disempowerment, deprofessionalisation and bureaucratisation of public sector staff. The 'new public management' (see Chapter 10, note 7) was merely the beginning of a process whereby the public was reconstructed as consumers whose interests conflict with welfare 'producers', such that state and senior management must realign themselves with the former against the latter (Newman & Clarke, 2009). In the language of a senior policy advisor, service users must be transformed from passive pawns into sovereign queens and service producers from self-interested knaves (albeit ones who see themselves as altruistic knights) into pawns (Le Grand, 2003).[4] So, in addition to Whitehall directives and a new culture of auditing, inspection and hectoring, opening the public sector to competition was seen as a further way of disciplining professionals and practitioners. Improve your performance, or else your customers will take their business elsewhere.

Ironically, if you wanted evidence of both public *and* private sector inefficiency you need look no farther than New Labour itself. According to Craig (2006: 2–5) by 2005 Labour had wasted £70 billion on consultants and on IT projects that starry-eyed ministers barely understood. Amid a rash of failures those involving the NHS stood out, including a 'Choose and Book' system (Craig, 2006: 185, 215–20) and a patients' record system, which might have wasted £20 billion alone (King & Crewe, 2013: 195–200). Not to mention PFI (see Chapter 10). Government naivety also led to fraud. A system of Individual Learning Accounts – giving people discounts they could use for training from a range of providers – was an invitation to bogus trainers setting up bogus courses (King & Crewe, 2013: ch. 9).

But now, under Brown, there seemed to be an initial shift in emphasis away from choice per se. Personalisation and localism became more prominent themes. Earlier in the decade 'personal budgets' had been introduced within social care. These allowed users greater power to determine how the money available for their care is spent on their behalf (Duffy *et al.*, 2010). Personal budgets were rolled out nationally in 2007. Personalisation could therefore be interpreted as a new alignment, in which the dedication, expertise and local knowledge of professionals/practitioners conjoined with the needs of users in a mutual relationship of deliberation. User choice was important but as a means of enhancing, rather than supplanting, professionals' skills.

Along similar lines, in July 2007 most of the 110 Whitehall-imposed public service agreement targets were phased out:

> The implication was that it is professionals, rather than central government, who best know how to run these services.... This could be seen as a substantial break with the Blairite tradition.
>
> (Griffiths 2009: 57).

Yet if there was any light here it would prove a false dawn. Given Brown's own legacy, given that there were only two to three more years to a general election, given the efforts needed to deal with the financial crisis (see below), given a general sense of exhaustion after 10 years in office and given a revitalised Tory opposition, the above initiatives would ultimately signal no new direction. Brown was too attracted to an ethos of top-down targets, league-tables and inspections to change now (Griffiths 2009: 57–8, 62).

Within a year of entering No. 10, it seemed that personalisation meant consumerism after all. For instance, the implementation in 2009 of a NHS Constitution of patients' rights assumed that rights are best promoted via choice and competition. The questions that a brain as big as Brown's might have asked – e.g. how can people in need of specialised healthcare act as empowered consumers when they will be typically be vulnerable and afraid? – were neglected (Fotaki, 2014).

Brown would often stress that he was interested in the moral underpinnings of markets; that Adam Smith's *Theory of the Moral Sentiments* was as important as *The Wealth of Nations*. Frequently pegged as an Atlanticist, he was arguably as influenced by European thought to prefer a social model of capitalism (Gannon, 2015). In practical terms this meant that he did not believe in competition for its own sake and acknowledged a role for partnerships and co-production (Griffiths, 2009: 63). Yet Brown was also both dogmatic in his beliefs and weak as a leader when reality undermined those certainties. He could give a lecture expressing passion about his values yet the ability to translate those values into statecraft was painfully lacking.

Rudderless, then, Brown was as much a victim of New Labour as he was its architect. Somewhat akin to Major being more Thatcherite than Thatcher, some have characterised Brown as more Blairite than Blair (Driver, 2009: 75–6).

The 2007 Welfare Reform Act, a subsequent White Paper and a 2008 Green Paper tightened up on welfare entitlements and conditionality (Driver, 2009: 77). In 2009 benefit sanctions were introduced for non-attendance at Jobcentres, partners of claimants were required to search for jobs and disabled recipients of the new Employment and Support Allowance had to perform some work-related activity.

And Brown stumbled badly in 2008. Believing it justified by a reduction in the basic rate of Income Tax, from 22% to 20%, he abolished the 10% tax band, which helped poorer households, later being forced to acknowledge this as a mistake.

Brown also invited into the highest echelons of policymaking a former financier who, by his own admission, knew nothing about social policy but boned up on the subject over an Xmas break while his wife was ill[5]:

> At the heart of the Freud review was the view that the market is better able to judge the costs and benefits of getting individuals back in work; and that competition between providers will deliver more efficiently and effectively

welfare-to-work for the hardcore economically inactive than a single state provider.... Markets not the state will deliver a more personalised service.

(Driver, 2009: 79)

Some new ideas would be introduced under Brown, e.g. polyclinics. These were accessible, community-based health centres providing a diverse, integrated range of specialised services, which had traditionally been provided by GPs and hospitals separately. However, fearful that GPs' surgeries and hospitals would close, it failed to capture public imagination. The sector was ambivalent about the reform and there were key organisational questions that, left unresolved, hampered implementation.

Overall, then, there was no great reshaping of the social policy agenda.

Social reforms: 1997–2010

So, how can we sum up the Blair/Brown years vis welfare reforms? From 1997–2008[6] total public spending rose from 38.5% of GDP to 39.1%. This percentage increase was less than those achieved by Attlee and the first Wilson administration but much better than the years 1974–79 (Mullard & Swaray, 2010: 514). Social expenditure on three sectors (education, health and social security) increased more rapidly during the period of the Blair/Brown governments when compared to previous Conservative and Labour governments (Mullard & Swaray, 2010: 518).

Spending on education increased from 4.5% of GDP in 1997 to 5.6% in 2010, i.e. from £42 billion to £65 billion – an increase of 54% leaving it at the OECD average (Mullard & Swaray, 2010: 515). The sector had also acquired a culture of targets, auditing, testing, micro-management and policy fatigue as Minsters sought to reassure middle England its money was being spent efficiently. There was also both greater diversity in provision and inequality in outcomes. Academies could work well – unsurprisingly, since they typically had greater resources and could 'cream-skim' the best staff and pupils. However, they could also attract all sorts of charlatans, self-serving business practices and religious fanatics eager to wage war on Darwin. The statistics for qualifications improved but those at the bottom were more left behind than ever, excluded as schools chased top spots in the league tables. Ultimately, schools cannot compensate for socioeconomic inequalities, yet New Labour often gave the impression it thought otherwise (Toynbee & Walker, 2010: ch. 1, 350–6).

The NHS also had more money, increasing from 6.1% of GDP in 1997 to 7.9% in 2010 (Mullard & Swaray, 2010: 514), with waiting times falling dramatically. Yet health inequalities remained a problem with the government reluctant to intervene in 'the market', e.g. pubs offering happy hours or supermarkets pushing foods with high fat, salt and sugar content. The private sector shrank but this was because more competition and commercialisation among providers *within* the NHS meant that carework and healthcare began to resemble shopping and retail. New Labour's social democratic credentials depended upon an acknowledgement that 'markets cannot do everything' yet it opened the door to healthcare markets without systematically securing their limits. The assumption was that choice and constant reorganisation – where providers, like shops, must perpetually adapt to consumer demands – would improve quality (Toynbee & Walker, 2010: ch. 2).

Labour did little with the housing sector (Keegan, 2012: 18–20). Being resistant to state intervention, it regarded social housing as an old fashioned concern (Toynbee & Walker, 2010: 138–42). Both of the previous Labour governments had spent more on housing than Blair/Brown (Mullard & Swaray, 2010: 516). This may therefore count as New Labour's greatest social policy failure given the dismal supply of new homes for sale and of social housing, the dominance of private landlords and the consequent upward acceleration of rents.

The years 1997–2008 saw social protection expenditure increase by £60bn, reflecting increases in child benefit, housing benefit and family tax credit (Mullard & Swaray, 2010: 518). The expansion of in-work assistance via tax credit schemes was Labour's most significant reform, designed to 'make work pay'. Wages and non-wage supplements were still far from working smoothly together but this was the beginnings of the tax-benefit integration of which some had been dreaming for decades. The pension system remained a mess, however.

Labour also relied upon a number of myths: believing the old system to have been 'passive' demonstrated a self-imposed amnesia regarding full employment and Beveridgean social insurance. Nor was it shy about indulging in hysterical rhetoric about dependency, benefit fraud, underclass values and undeservingness which Conservatives would later repeat as if in evidence of the very narrative they had themselves revitalised in the 1970 and 1980s (Lister & Bennett, 2010).[7]

Inequality and poverty

What were the main effects of all this?

Joyce and Sibieta (2013) provide a comprehensive analysis of Labour's record on addressing inequality and poverty (also Lansley, 2012: 15–16). Measured via the Gini Coefficient, inequality rose from 0.33 to 0.36 between 1996–97 and 2009–10 (Joyce & Sibieta, 2013: 182–4).[8] However, much of this was due to trends at the very apex of the income ladder. If these are discounted inequality *declined*, though only slightly, in the middle part of the distribution (Joyce & Sibieta, 2013: 185). So although Labour's policies often favoured the poorest deciles, this did not offset the growth in earnings for those with high-skills and for those in the top 1% (Joyce & Sibieta, 2013: 188). Lansley (2012: 22–3, 40–1, 48–9) highlights how, by 2008, the share of income and wealth held by the lowest six deciles had been falling due to a 30-year squeeze on wages.

So far as relative poverty is concerned the overall rate fell from about 20% in 1997–98 to about 16% in 2010–11. Much of this had occurred by 2004. Over the next six years reductions were far more modest, with poverty actually rising from 2005–08 (Joyce & Sibieta, 2013: 191). Had the rate of decline achieved by 2004–05 been maintained then it is possible that the government could have met its target of halving child poverty by 2010. Relative pensioner poverty fell from 25% in 1997–98 to 17% in 2010–11 (Joyce & Sibieta, 2013: 192). By contrast, the relative poverty of low-income working-age adults without dependent children actually rose during its time in office.

According to Joyce and Sibieta (2013: 194–5) all this was largely a product of tax and benefit policies, with the introduction of tax credits (effectively, an expansion in welfare entitlements) being the single most important factor. Without them relative child poverty would have continued to increase. Increases in employment and the introduction of the minimum wage[9] were much less important, they find:

> Overall, reforms between 1997 and 2010 amounted to an £18 billion annual increase in spending on benefits for families with children and an £11 billion annual increase in spending on benefits for pensioners.... On an entitlements and liabilities basis, the poorest half of children were about £4390 (28%) better off in terms of annual net household income in 2010/11 than they would have been under an unreformed 1997/98 direct tax and benefit system; and the corresponding annual gain for the poorest half of pensioners was about £1970 (19%).
>
> (Joyce & Sibieta, 2013: 195)

Ironies abound, therefore. Despite the images of itself New Labour projected onto the electorate via the media ('no more tax and spend'), it used the tax and benefits systems to redistribute and so score some of its biggest successes (Richards, 2010: 329–32).

Was it as redistributive as it could have been? Probably not – though Left critics needed to be honest about the possible electoral costs of greater radicalism. New Labour always relied upon stealth. It tended to speak Right while acting more to the Left. And because Labour was often nervous of advertising its real achievements its critics could similarly marginalise them. Conservatives found it easy to make New Labour's statism seem unfair and unnecessary; the Left would describe its extra spending and redistribution as too modest. It was that disalignment between speaking and acting which enabled Labour to assemble the grand coalition, which, by keeping it politically dominate for a decade, resulted in its achievements. Yet that same disalignment meant that those achievements were destined to be underestimated by critics on both Right and Left.

From Brown to Green?

If Brown's social policies were largely a continuation of what he, at the Treasury, had been doing for a decade anyway, another area did offer an opportunity for a new start: environmental policy.

Brown's greatest contribution to *the* environmental issue of the day lay in commissioning a major report into the economics of climate change by Nicholas Stern. Though the report was almost 700 pages long the basics are easy to summarise (Stern, 2007: xv–xix):

- Without action, climate change will cost the world 5% of its GDP per year every year. On a broader scale of risks and impacts that figure could rise to 20%.
- By contrast, the costs of action to adapt to and mitigate global warming can be limited to about 1% of global GDP per year.
- The target should be to stabilise GHGs between 450–550 ppm CO_2 equivalent,[10] requiring an eventual cut in emissions of 80% below current levels.
- Sustainable growth is a realistic goal.
- Internationally coordinated, state action is required to finance and encourage the new research, technologies, sectors and markets, which are needed if capitalism is to be greened. "Climate change is the greatest market failure the world has ever seen ..." (Stern, 2007: xviii). The real price of carbon must therefore be 'internalised' into market exchanges.

The Stern Report had a massive, worldwide influence (e.g. Atteridge, 2013: 61). However, Stern (2009: 39) did later admit that 550 ppm was too high and that the upper limit should be 500 ppm with the longer-term ambition of reducing this to 400 ppm.

The 2008 Act

A new start therefore beckoned.

By 2006–07, with the new Conservative leader threatening to steal Labour's green clothing,[11] it was clear the lassitude of the second-term would have to be overcome. The new Environment Secretary, David Miliband, acknowledged that "New Labour has been good at driving the international environmental agenda, not good enough at reducing domestic carbon emissions" (quoted in Carter, 2008: 194). It was time for the domestic agenda to catch up with its international standing (Carter, 2008: 202).

The zenith of Labour's environmentalist aspirations came with the 2008 Climate Change Act (Cullingworth *et al.*, 2015: 281–3). This would show the influence not only of Stern, but of the 4th Report from the Intergovernmental Panel on Climate Change in 2007. The targets Labour was now setting were firmly rooted in the newest scientific evidence. A Department of Energy and Climate Change was founded which, taking some powers and responsibilities away from DEFRA, would oversee both energy security and climate change. The new department had real clout at Cabinet level and the 2008 Act did the following (Hayden, 2014: 549):

- Set a statutory foundation for CO_2 reduction targets of at least a 26% by 2020 and 80% by 2050, including reductions in overall GHGs of 34% by 2020 (based on 1990 levels).
- Instituted a system of five-yearly carbon budgets which would specify permitted annual emission levels across the short-term (the subsequent five years) and medium-term (the subsequent 10–15 years).
- Established a Committee on Climate Change, an independent body of experts, to make recommendations on carbon budgets, and other measures, needed to achieve the 2050 target and periodically evaluate the UK's progress – or otherwise – in doing so.

Unfortunately, the Act came at a time when the good will – and huge majorities – of 1997 and 2001 had evaporated. New Labour's re-election in 2005 had a definite better-the-devil-you-know feel to it. And as Labour rushed to make up for lost time, one consequence was to squeeze out any possibility of systematically connecting the Act to social policy.[12]

Labour had always shrunk away from making the case for green taxes, for example. The case being that their introduction – if effective at diminishing the environmental bads that have to be paid for eventually anyway (such as ill-health caused by pollution) – could fund reductions in other, non-green taxes. Similarly, a massive programme of building retrofits would be required to meet its 2020 targets (Toynbee & Walker, 2010: 221). Such a programme required insulating 10 million lofts, 2.3 million walls and installing 12 million new boilers. This would require massive public recognition of and support for the need for retrofitting, but New Labour's default setting was to de-radicalise issues and get things done through stealth.

So although its commitment to environmental policies was now ahead of the public's, e.g. when it came to investment in solar power, it failed to take a lead in politicising the problem of global warming (Toynbee & Walker, 2010: 239) and of joining the dots between environmental welfare and social welfare issues.

Some of this paralysis was due to its inheritance. Some was due to its own timidity and captivity by vested interests.

Too little, too late?

One example of a poisoned inheritance was the fragmentation and marketisation of the energy sector, e.g. through electricity privatisation (see Chapter 8), making its regulation and rationalisation that much harder.

This may explain why prior to 2006 the government had pursued an incremental approach only, one in which 'climate' and 'energy' were often perceived as opposites. But in its third-term Carter and Jacobs (2014: 125–6) highlight the extent to which it sought "an almost complete overhaul of energy policy", based upon stronger, statutory targets for emissions reduction. So, the Low Carbon Transition Plan of 2009 dovetailed with the targets set in the Climate Change Act – with targeted reductions in CO_2 equivalents, which were three to four times higher than those proposed in the Climate Change Programme just three years earlier:

> The Plan aimed to change the composition of the UK's energy system, including an increase in renewable supply by sevenfold to 15% (over 30% in electricity). In establishing a 'low carbon industrial strategy', it introduced a brand new field of activity …
>
> (Carter & Jacobs, 2014: 126)

Shaw *et al.* (2010) show how, also during Labour's third-term, regulation of the privatised energy industry slowly made room for sustainability issues. In particular, the 2008 Energy Act encouraged renewable electricity through feed-in tariffs, smart meters and renewable heat. This marked recognition of the need for stronger intervention to drive the industry in a direction and at a speed that could not be achieved via market instruments and competition alone. This shift was confirmed in the 2010 Energy Act, for which reductions in GHG emissions were a central concern.

Additionally:

- in 2006 the fuel duty escalator was restored and the government announced that after 2016 all new homes should be zero-carbon (Carter, 2008: 194);
- from 2007 stamp duty was not payable on homes (worth less than £500,000) with a zero-carbon rating (Toynbee & Walker, 2010: 233);
- the Warm Front Scheme would cut 40,000 tonnes of carbon in 2008–09 alone (Toynbee & Walker, 2010: 225);
- feed-in tariffs were announced in 2010, allowing people with solar panels or wind generators to sell electricity to the grid (Toynbee & Walker, 2010: 224).

These were laudable reforms yet it all came very late in the day and in the context of an energy system that, still in private hands and dominated by the imperatives of competition and profit, was difficult to coordinate and integrate. Furthermore, since homes are where much of the nation's energy is used, how could energy policies be made sustainable in the context of a housing sector that Labour had practically neglected (see above)?

So, the legacy of Thatcherism, plus New Labour's own hostility to re-socialisation, left the government looking like a harassed nursery teacher desperately trying to control a herd of squally infants. It was not a politics conducive to joined-up policymaking nor to a comprehensive, systematic, ecosocial approach to energy and housing reform (for a lengthier justification of this conclusion see Fitzpatrick, 2014a: chs 6 & 8). For instance, the Minister for Energy (and ex-Social Policy academic), Malcolm Wicks, said "we are not going to sacrifice fuel poverty on the altar of climate change" (*The Economist*, 2008). Yet by 2008 already, the two were inseparable (Boardman, 2010; Fitzpatrick, 2011a: 171–7).

A similar lack of coordination would be apparent in another area of energy use, one related closely to health and healthcare: transport (Fitzpatrick, 2014a: Chs 9–10). The cost of motoring fell by 13% during Labour's tenure while that of bus and coach fares rose 17% above inflation (Toynbee & Walker, 2010: 226, 232). Some of this was due to its inheritance too. As we saw in Chapters 8 and 9, the Tories privatised, deregulated and fragmented the nation's transport systems. But New Labour came to church with the naivety of a recent convert, if sometimes as reluctant one (its instincts were in favour of rail renationalisation, but it feared the message it would send).[13] Only in London was some planning and coordination of transport still possible.

We can see, then, that while a poisonous legacy is one thing, Labour was too often willing to drink the poison. And though it picked up the pace after 2006, this spurt of acceleration was belated to say the least. Other decisions conflicting with its environmentalist credentials were more firmly of Labour's own making (Sheail, 2002: 191–6). Such as its tailspin over Heathrow.

Air travel was conspicuously absent from the Kyoto Protocol but this could not, surely, continue indefinitely. Miliband promised to reverse domestic inertia on the issue but the authority he needed to put pressure on the aviation industry was undermined in 2007 by Blair commenting that people had a right to fly wherever they liked (Carter, 2008: 203). The government's subsequent approval of Heathrow expansion contradicted its environmental goals (Hayden, 2014: 546–7) given the ecological damage that is done by aviation. Even the business case was weak, with estimates of the third runway's benefits declining from £5.5 billion to less than £1 billion (Hayden, 2014: 548). No matter. The importance of defending London's position as a financial centre trumped all.

In effect what Labour had been doing with one hand, e.g. belated shifts in energy policy, it was undoing with the other. Even the Tory Party's Quality of Life Policy Group opined that the Labour government's "policy of actively encouraging aviation growth is at odds with the UK's commitment to tackle climate change" (quoted in Hayden, 2014: 540). If aviation was allowed to grow then it could only mean that non-aviation sectors like energy would have to achieve *even higher* reductions in emissions if the 2050 target was to be met! Aviation was being groomed as a free rider.

To conclude, some of the ingredients of an ecosocial meal were being compiled (due to the shift in energy policy) but the cook was still missing. How would domestic and even global politics have changed had the 2008 Climate Change Act been a 1998 Climate Change Act? That remains one of the tortuous 'what ifs' of the New Labour period.

The turning globe

And while it was reengaging with environmental policy domestically, things turned sour for Labour on the international stage it had previously dominated.

A world leader on climate change for much of the previous decade, the EU's role suffered an abrupt diminishment at the 2009 Copenhagen Summit – arranged to agree a post-Kyoto framework. Assuming that little had changed since Bali in 2007, the EU proposed that developed countries should reduce their emissions by 25–40% by 2020 and by 80–95% by 2050 (Oberthür, 2011: 670). It also recommended a 'one-track' approach whereby developing countries would be integrated into the same reductions plan as developed ones. Everyone objected and the EU found itself totally marginalised in the final stages of negotiation.

The resulting Copenhagen Accord was largely a waste of paper, anyway, consisting of vague aspirations that were not legally-binding. What had happened?

First, with the election of Obama in the US and the emergence of China and India as major players, the vacuum into which the EU had previously stepped forward to don the crown of leadership was now being filled by others. Obama was sympathetic to environmental issues but deemed the speed at which the EU wanted to move[14] as unrealistic. For their part, developing nations felt that one-track ignored the greater responsibilities, which the west had for stoking global warming historically. The EU failed to recognise and therefore adapt to this new multipolarity, trying to build alliances only at the eleventh hour. Ironically, its own success in reducing emissions meant that it now had less 'currency' to trade with compared to the USA and China.

Second, the EU itself was riven with growing divisions between those pushing for the 30% commitment and those (especially Poland and Italy) who resisted it as being detrimental to growth (Oberthür, 2011: 676). Non-EU countries were able to exploit these disagreements.

Where was the UK in all of this (Seldon & Lodge, 2010: 356–63)? Well, Britain was the main country arguing for a 30% target, with Germany, France and Sweden behind them in the 'undecided' camp (Skovgaard, 2014: 9–11). Should we therefore blame Brown for the EU's failure and the subsequent debacle that was Copenhagen? Or, should we laud the UK's ambitions?

The answer to both questions must be 'yes'. Brown's government wanted to parade its post-Stern credentials on climate change. And if in 2009 it was being idealistic about what could be achieved[15] those who reappraise it during the 2030s or 2040s may be kinder. After all, someone has to lead the pack and Britain was the first country to substantially incorporate climate science into its policymaking. If it ignored the grubby realities of global politics it at least lay down a marker that the world was eventually going to have to reach. For the time being, *realpolitik* would prevail with the EU proving more effective at alliance building at the 2011 Durban Summit (Bäckstrand & Elgström, 2013: 1379).

There was, of course, another possible reason why Copenhagen was a fiasco. The world was still reeling from its biggest economic crisis in decades.

The crash

It began as a 'credit crunch' and became the '2008 Financial Crash' (Gamble, 2009; Sorkin, 2009; Rawnsley, 2010: chs 28 & 34, 528–31). In Britain the sense of a world being upended started with the sight of huge crowds swarming around the doors of Northern Rock branches (Seldon & Lodge, 2010: 86–90). The first run on a British bank since 1866!

Events began in the US housing boom. For years prices had been rising along with the sense of increasing wealth. By the 2000s many houses were overvalued but lending to those with barely two beans to rub together continued nonetheless. The real estate bubble began to deflate in 2006–07, throwing millions of middle-class families into negative equity. What this also exposed was the vulnerability of the 'sub-prime' market where many low-income households found themselves unable to afford rising mortgage payments. Many households began to default, leading to foreclosures and, in a depressed market, to a large surplus of vacant homes that banks could not now sell.

The subsequent losses triggered a crisis in the wider banking system. One problem was that American banks had sold mortgage 'bundles' to other banks and financial institutions throughout the world. As the housing crisis unfolded it became clear that many of the debts that had been purchased were 'toxic', or valueless. Banks' assets tumbled and, with many American institutions owning large parts of non-American ones, and vice versa, the crisis went global. The result was the greatest run on the banks since the 1929 crash. The effects were especially pernicious in the 'shadow banks', those institutions that act like banks without being subject to the same regulations and guarantees (Krugman, 2008: 158–62). Lending to businesses, consumers and homeowners collapsed, as did stock markets.

The initial response by governments was tardy and inadequate. Conventional logic said that once interest rates fell, people would have incentives to borrow, invest and spend again. But this didn't happen. As Keynes predicted, risky times mean people stop taking risks – they understandably hoard and save at the very point where the economy needs them to splurge. Only the state has the muscles and the long-term guarantees that can provide the investment to get things moving.

This explains why the Left was originally so excited (see Choonara, 2009; Callinicos, 2010: ch. 1). Wasn't this proof that three decades of deregulation and the dominance of financial corporations was a glorious con trick? The share of wages as a proportion of national wealth had been falling since the 1980s. No wonder that people compensated through their credit cards. The collective security of the welfare state had been eroded. No wonder that people looked to individualised safety nets, e.g. the rising house prices and private pensions that would be needed to fund retirement incomes.

The real face of Thatcherism was thus revealed in 2008. Might a new economic model now emerge (Stiglitz, 2010)? Might this even be a green economy? Capitalism's fantasy casino-economy had become detached from the 'real economy', so what could be more real than the stock of natural resources?

But politics always matters (e.g. Schlipphak & Mause, 2015). Busy with actually trying to solve the crisis[16] (Richards, 2010: 373–90; Seldon & Lodge, 2010: 166–79; Keegan, 2012: 36–43), Labour now played the role of the gormless idiot in a film who, coming across a murdered body, picks up the blood-dripping knife at the very moment someone looks through the door, sees idiot with said knife, draws obvious conclusion and screams 'Murderer!'. Cut to sight of gormless idiot scampering desperately away from outraged, pitchfork-wielding villagers (Rawnsley, 2010: 607–16).

In other words, the Tory Party and Tory press smelled an electoral opportunity. In an ever-louder whisper, Conservatives began to insist that the problem all along was public debt, i.e. public *spending*, rather than private debt or a deregulated financial system. Before the crash the Tories had been promising to match Labour levels of public spending; now, excessive public spending could be blamed for the greatest crisis in capitalism for 80 years.[17] Before the crash Tories had been calling for even *lighter* regulation of the banking and financial sector. That could now be quietly forgotten too.

New Labour had, after all, pretty much left the golden goose of The City alone to lay its eggs in the expectation that the proceeds would help fund a growth in public expenditure. In 2007 the banking sector accounted for 14% of the UK's tax revenues (Fraser, 2014: 425–6). The fact that the goose was the real villain meant little to the outraged villagers. Labour had been the one in charge, hadn't it?

Complacency?

The accusation was not unreasonable. Brown's favourite mantra – 'No more Tory boom and bust' – was a mirage that concealed quicksand. According to Farlow (2013: 19), household debt rose from £570 billion in 1997 to £1500 billion 10 years later (or from 100% of net disposable income to 175%). From 1997–2007 bank lending trebled, but most of this was for real estate. Lending to manufacturing firms fell. By 2008, of the £6 trillion in the banking system only 3% involved lending to businesses. £1 trillion went on mortgages. The real economy was being neglected, in short (Farlow, 2013: 57).

Not long before the crash, in fact, Blair had worried about the fragility of the economy but had been reassured by the Treasury. After all, Brown was himself a master at keeping liabilities off the balance sheet: underfunded public pensions, student loans, PFI, and so forth (Farlow, 2013: 3, 24, 95). The ex-socialist had forgotten the nature of capitalism and there were few in New Labour capable of re-educating him.

The recapitalisation of the banks was presented as a triumph in October 2008, yet Brown had been procrastinating about it for months (Farlow, 2013: 119, 132–3). This hesitation was no doubt due to reluctance to admit an even bigger blunder (Seldon & Lodge, 2010: 144–8). In an attempt to avoid nationalisation of HBOS, Brown had persuaded Lloyds TSB to merge with HBOS and so absorb its debts – conveniently bypassing European competition laws. But far from good practices driving out bad ones, the contagion spread to Lloyds.

Things were even worse at RBS. RBS had assets worth twice as much as the UK's GDP due to its strategy of high risk lending and aggressive acquisitions.

This left it highly vulnerable, since only 2% of its capital was available as a buffer against losses (Fraser, 2014: 169–77). So in October and November 2008 £37 billion was poured into RBS and Lloyds Banking Group, with government ownership now amounting to 83% and 43.4% respectively – the state already owned 100% of Northern Rock and Bradford & Bingley. A second bailout package would follow in January (Seldon & Lodge, 2010: 179–80, 212–18). By 2010 the losses to the government equalled £38bn (Farlow, 2013: 110–11, 141).

Critics like Farlow go too far. No single government can turn back the tide of global capitalism. New Labour was trying to repair the public realm after years of neglect and the British reliance on rising house prices long predates Brown's rise to power. Farlow fails to pin the catastrophe's tail on the Thatcherite donkey.

By contrast, Keegan (2012: 61–71) defends Brown's efforts – from the autumn of 2008 through to the following spring – to engineer through shuttle diplomacy a recapitalisation of the banks across the USA and Europe. Brown feared that unless the pack of domestic economies huddled and travelled together they could be picked off, one by one, by the very financial wolves who had caused the global economy to collapse in the first place. Was the Brown of 1975 now somehow whispering in his ear 33 years later? Brown did what arch-Conservatives like Bush, Merkel and Sarkozy seemed ideologically unequipped to do. When he saw that the globe's driving seat was empty he sat down in it and started the engine.

But it would not be enough to save him from the electorate's disapproval.[18] The admirable work of a few months could not repair the neglect of a decade. As late as 2007 Brown was lauding bankers and reassuring them that regulation would remain light-touch (Hutton 2010: 148–50; Fraser, 2014: 181–3).

Brown (2011: 77–9) would later defend his record, trumpeting the Financial Services Authority (FSA) as a key achievement. Yet the FSA was being emasculated even before it began (in 2001) by being forced to work within the constraints of a restrictive orthodoxy: credit is good, risks can be managed, bankers/markets should be largely self-regulating (Fraser, 2014). Its remit – to protect the international competitiveness of the UK financial sector (by nurturing market confidence and stability) – was a recipe for turning a blind eye, especially given a fuzziness in the relevant responsibilities of the FSA, the Treasury and the Bank of England.

Brown's (2011: 11–13, 95–103) own account of the crisis condemns what he calls a 'passive model' of capitalism in which governments resemble absentee landlords. Governments and markets must have a shared commit to the public interest, he recommends (Brown, 2011: 109–12, 237–42). How true. Yet for Brown it is as if the world began in 2007, the previous decade being spirited away.

Alistair Darling's (2011: 20) retrospective is better.[19] "Now, in 2007, it was clear to me that the relationship between the Bank and the FSA was not good," admits the man whose responsibility it had been to establish the FSA in the first place. But, "It was felt that judgements were for the markets" (Darling, 2011:

21). There is even macabre comedy. Darling (2011: 317) reveals his horror at being told by a leading banker that his bank would no longer take on risks they didn't understand!

Because he gives some acknowledgement of Labour's naivety, Darling's attribution of overall responsibility to global financial markets is more convincing than Brown's. Furthermore, UK national debt in 1996–97 was 42.5% of GDP compared to 36% in 2007, says Darling (2011: 310; Keegan, 2012: 9). It is precisely because they were nervous of the market response that Labour were not the profligate wastrels of later, post-2010 stereotypes.

Third Way in retrospect

The crisis illustrated what many had long felt. New Labour was good at distributing the proceeds of capitalism but far less adept at reshaping its norms, institutions and practices. When the global economy fell ill, the government's naivety was left exposed.

Which is not to discount the positives of its distributive strategy. Despite exceptions like housing and pensions, Labour had gone some way to rebuilding the welfare state after years of comparative decline. Its greatest successes were in improving the NHS and reducing relative poverty (for most groups). Yet this renovation also amounted to a reconstruction with New Labour's social policies accepting and often accelerating key aspects of the 1979–97 revolution:

- an expanded role for markets,
- complacency about social and economic inequalities,
- a combination of centralisation on Whitehall (given a suspicion of local government and of welfare professionals) and decentralisation (greater diversity in delivery and an emphasis on choice),
- an instinct which said that the private sector was inherently more efficient and adaptive,
- the recasting of welfare citizens as service consumers,
- an eagerness to placate tabloid myths about low income households as 'others' always on the take.

For its defenders this was inevitable (Giddens, 2007). Taxpayers would no longer spend, spend, spend without seeing the benefits of doing so clearly. Expectations in an era of iphones, Facebook and point-and-click access were completely unlike those of the late 1940s, with its ration books and furniture-sized wireless sets that could receive just three stations. But for its critics and even some supporters (Giddens, 2007: 28–9), New Labour was frequently naïve about the motivations of business and its capacity to deliver services efficiently. Its claims to 'modernisation' had a curiously retrograde feel, as if the foundations of the capitalist model (circa 1983–87) were set irretrievably in stone.

And without this willingness to reshape capitalism the prospects for an ecosocial capitalism were never on the cards.

Key questions

What relationships between the environmental and social policy agendas have emerged? To what extent have social policies and the politics of welfare reform deliberately informed and been informed by the principles and values of environmental ethics and politics?

In their first term Labour devised a potentially interesting framework for an ecosocial politics under the heading 'quality of life'. Internationally, they had also engaged productively with a range of issues concerning poverty, development and global warming. Would Labour now be able to draw upon these archetypes in its third term? Could it possibly construct new foundations, renewing itself as Blair departed from political life? Giddens (2007: 143) had identified a,

> ... need to bring environmental measures directly within the framework of a reformed welfare system.

Was a new paradigm genuinely in the making?

The answer to all these questions is 'no'. Many of the reasons why would emerge before 2005.

Prescott did much to promote the basics of an ecosocial agenda. Yet this was never presented as central to the Third Way and would soon vanish, as would his super-ministry, the DETR. The general problem was that Labour's ecological modernisation was ultimately a case of slotting environmental issues into priorities that continued to be thought of in non-environmental terms. Labour would do much to save Kyoto, spur the EU to ambitious targets and corral the USA at Gleneagles, giving the outline of a global ecosocial politics (summarised at the end of Chapter 11). Yet these mid-2000s efforts would only highlight the disjunction between Labour's global commitment in this field and its domestic one (recall its lamentable record on green taxation, for instance).

Now, in its third term, social policy was allowed to coast on a pre-established path. And while environmental policy began picking up the pace it was having to play catch-up, yet again, and in the context of sectors that the government had neglected. So, housing reform was practically non-existent; reforms to the energy sector were belated and seemingly detached from the housing and transport sectors; public transport was given a boost but resocialisation of buses and trains was never on the cards and New Labour was fearful of the car and aviation lobbies (Cullingworth *et al.*, 2015: 496–8).

With its electoral support and intellectual energies flagging, Labour would have struggled to construct a new political apparatus around environmental and welfare reform. It needed to have done some real thinking and planning years earlier on how to allow environmental and social policies to converge so that cross-cutting synergies could develop. The quality of life agenda had fallen away, allowing its flaws to loom larger in the rear-view mirror than its good intentions. Brown had too much to defend to start his tenure with honest reflection. And the economic ground was about to open up. Labour still possessed enough energy and ingenuity to scramble the nation out of a hole, but not enough to avoid blame for having caused the subsidence in the first place.

So in terms of developing anything resembling an ecosocial politics and policymaking Labour's record after 13 years in power was both patchy and stuttering. Its politics left environmental, economic and social policies in the same archipelago as always: part of the same confluence but never really joining up. For instance, after what had occurred from 1979–97 Labour could celebrate much of its record on poverty but, with environmental issues having become ever more important to economics and politics, its inability to think through the social policy implications meant that the ecological dimensions of its anti-poverty reforms were threadbare. The analysis I present in *Climate Change and Poverty* begins at that point.

If this was modernisation it was weak modernisation at best.

Notes

1 The second recession in a decade was then 18 months away.
2 Brown was in No. 10 for just over 34 months, from June 2007 to May 2010.
3 Symbolised by Blair's complaint in 1999 that he had 'scars down his back' or his Press Secretary's later reference to 'bog-standard comprehensives'.
4 Note: Le Grand's own reform prescriptions were more sophisticated than this.
5 As confirmed by David Freud himself at a conference run by my department at Nottingham University in September 2007.
6 Before the crash decimated public finances.
7 Margaret Thatcher was reported as saying that New Labour was her greatest achievement. See http://conservativehome.blogs.com/centreright/2008/04/making-history.html [accessed 6 January 2016]
8 From the early-1960s to the early-1980s Britain hovered around the 0.26 range before taking off. Under New Labour it pretty much remained where it had been under Major, before inching upwards around 2005–06. Note that in April 2010 the government introduced a new marginal rate of tax of 50% on incomes above £150,000. Anticipating this, it is likely that many high-income individuals brought forward their income by a year (to avoid the 50% rate), which may have caused top incomes to artificially inflate in 2009–10, sending the Gini score upwards.
9 The minimum wage was of most help to those in the third and fourth deciles above the poverty line. However, Joyce and Sibieta (2013: 199) do acknowledge other factors, e.g. "the introduction of Sure Start and increased financial support for childcare may have allowed more mothers to return to work and could have longer-run pay-offs in terms of child development".
10 As indicated in the Introduction, don't worry about the terminology. If you are interested, ppm = parts per million; 'CO$_2$ equivalents' is what allows the other GHGs to be expressed in terms of CO$_2$ via their global warming potential.
11 The Tories has said practically nothing about the environment from 1997–2005 (Carter, 2009). But now the general weakness of New Labour's approach domestically created a political opportunity (Hayden, 2014: 546–7).
12 Miliband was interested in the idea of having personal carbon budgets, which, given that low income households emit fewer GHGs than wealthier ones, could have

redistributive impacts. In 1997 the proposal would have had time to gestate and become real. In 2007, time was running out.

13 For a more favourable reading see Cullingworth *et al.* (2015: 497–8).

14 A 20% cut, which it proposed, raising to 30% if other nations signed up (see Chapter 11).

15 Was hubris at work, following Brown's success in shuttle diplomacy (see below) during the financial crisis (Seldon & Lodge, 2010: 155–66)?

16 Quantitative easing: buying up banks' debts so that they could begin lending again, amounting to £375 billion in the UK alone. This turned out to be a pallid Keynesianism at best because (1) they didn't start lending again to anything like the extent required, and (2) it boosted the assets of the richest 10%, with 40% of those gains going to the richest 5% of households (Elliott, 2012).

17 To be fair, there was a precedent. Prior to sterling crashing out of the ERM in 1992 (see Chapter 9) Labour had promised to maintain its parity. That, too, was conveniently forgotten as the Tory reputation for competence nose-dived.

18 Not helped by a verbal stumble in the Commons in December 2008, when a claim to have "saved the world's banks" first came out as a claim to have "saved the world".

19 Darling was Chancellor of the Exchequer, 2007–10.

Conclusion

Many histories understand the significance to post-war Britain of trends and developments in social policy. The modern British state has in large part been a welfare state, not simply through public expenditure, legislation, departmental organisation, administration and public sector activity, but also in terms of the culture and purpose of government: the requirement to attend to the needs and wellbeing of the population through taxation, to distribute social resources equitably, to preserve public goods, to ensure the maintenance of safety nets, to enable the sharing of risks, to enhance the common good. The ideological shift from 1979–97 altered some of this, but by the end of that period Britain had *not* returned to the ethos of the nineteenth century.[1]

And as the century advanced so environmental problems became more important – recall the four categories described at the end of Chapter 6 – though governments were typically slow to understand how crucial and respond accordingly. Environmental issues have been vital not just for their own sake, then, but for their implications for and interactions with the economic and political realms. They have altered what the state does and how it does them – particularly in an era of globalisation.

Therefore, unless we imagine that social policy is detached from economic and political systems, the story of the environment must also be a story of welfare reform, and *vice versa*. The aim of this book has been to show how, why and the extent to which the environmental and social policy domains have converged upon and influenced one another. A conjunction I call the ecosocial. Figure 13.1 depicts how these dimensions reside side by side. Is there much evidence of strategic integration, though?

Although environmental policy would grow in prominence, the ecosocial has never occupied a central place within British economics, politics and welfare policy.[2] There have been few precedents, fewer templates, no founding fathers instructing us how to bring social and environmental policies together systematically. Together with the blinkers of national self-interest, an absence of party political consensus on the issues, a lack of participatory policymaking traditions, organisational cock-ups and general institutional inertia, this makes us less prepared for the challenges of the twenty-first century than we often like to imagine.

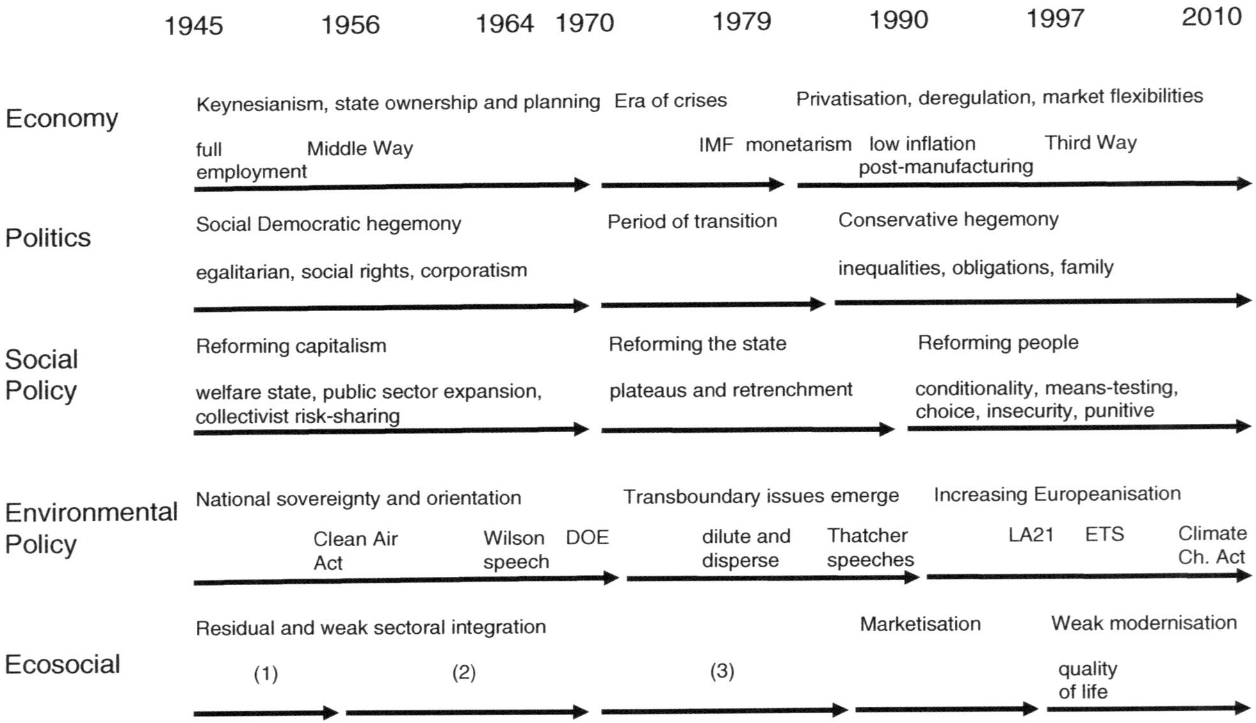

Timeline years: 1945 1956 1964 1970 1979 1990 1997 2010

Economy

Keynesianism, state ownership and planning   Era of crises   Privatisation, deregulation, market flexibilities

full employment   Middle Way   IMF monetarism   low inflation post-manufacturing   Third Way

Politics

Social Democratic hegemony   Period of transition   Conservative hegemony

egalitarian, social rights, corporatism   inequalities, obligations, family

Social Policy

Reforming capitalism   Reforming the state   Reforming people

welfare state, public sector expansion, collectivist risk-sharing   plateaus and retrenchment   conditionality, means-testing, choice, insecurity, punitive

Environmental Policy

National sovereignty and orientation   Transboundary issues emerge   Increasing Europeanisation

Clean Air Act   Wilson speech   DOE   dilute and disperse   Thatcher speeches   Marketisation   LA21   ETS   Climate Ch. Act   Weak modernisation

Ecosocial

Residual and weak sectoral integration   quality of life

(1)   (2)   (3)

Figure 13.1 Summary, 1945–2010.

It has certainly, however, hovered at the edges of our sightline to the extent that three distinct periods can be identified on the basis of the preceding chapters.

1945 to mid-1980s

Residual and weak sectoral integration

The economy and the environment were seen as separate spheres, with the former taking precedence: 'economy-first'. There was a between-the-cracks fragmentation of departmental responsibilities towards the environment, only partially addressed with the implementation of the DoE. There was a tendency to defer decisions, to treat symptoms (a curative rather than preventative approach) and to offload consequences on to the future or on to other nations. Unsustainable practices were allowed to proliferate, key issues ignored and a lack of connection discernible between government policymaking, representative welfare groups, environmental science and participation by relevant NGOs. Three sub-periods can be identified.

1945–56

In the form of town and country planning, environmental policy counts as one of the Labour government's greatest successes, despite the administrative separation between it and housing, yet it has rarely been heralded as such. See the end of Chapter 1 for a summary.

1956–70

The Clean Air Act was a preventative, ecosocial piece of legislation, recognising the mutual intersections of human health and the natural environment. See the end of Chapters 3 and 4 for summaries. However, by the early 1970s it was clear that it had displaced the problem of pollution from the 'temporary domestic' to the 'unidirectional transboundary'.

1970 to mid-1980s

Inspired by Wilson, the DoE was a welcome and truly original innovation but in reality it failed to integrate the social and environmental policy zones. See the end of Chapters 5 and 6 for summaries.

Mid-1980s to 1997

Marketisation

Most of the above features remained, especially economy-first. Thatcher's administration was particularly neglectful of the environment, seeing it as an economic burden and another excuse for the kind of statist, welfarist interventions that at its most dogmatic the New Right dreamed of ejecting from government responsibility in its reengineering of state-market relations. It was the EEC/EC driving many of the necessary ecological reforms. Thatcher's speeches on climate change may have signalled a compassionate Conservatism, but more likely represented a further attempt to associate the Conservative account of our responsibilities to nature with free market liberalism. In the 'multidirectional transboundary' era of climate change, Major furthered this agenda through an adaptive compliance with the EU, discouraging the goal of a 'social Europe' and encouraging the increasing use of market-based instruments. This was the rawest, neoliberal version of the ecosocial, if only because departmental fragmentation mattered less once everything within the scope of government was meant to advance the cause of free markets. In this context, an interventionist, ambitious innovation like LA21, creating a space for social and environmental policies to converge, foundered. See the end of Chapters 8 and 9 for summaries.

1997–2010

Weak modernisation

New Labour initially promoted a framework that integrated social and environmental welfare concerns under a 'quality of life' heading. Internationally, it engaged admirably with Kyoto, the EU and the MDGs, highlighting their interconnections. However, that former framework was never central to the Third Way and was allowed to fade with the demise of the DETR. This highlighted a disparity between Labour's rudimentary domestic approach to the ecosocial and the extent to which it had a more coherent set of priorities and strategies vis global politics. The third-term failed to bring these dimensions together, leaving social and environmental policies largely estranged. Labour sought to rebuild the capacities of the state within what would remain an overall framework of free market liberalism. The difficulties – perhaps impossibilities – of doing so, allied to organisational deficiencies, meant that two of most crucial areas of policymaking for the twenty-first century state, the social and the environmental, remained semi-detached at best. See the end of Chapters 10, 11 and 12 for summaries.

All of which concerns the past.

Yet you knew all along that this book is really about the future, didn't you? The Introduction posed two questions I stated could only be properly addressed at the very end. How effective or ineffective has the welfare state been at helping to deal with environmental problems in the past? On that basis, to what extent can it assist policymaking in the future?

In answer to the first question, the above summary suggests that any assessment must swing towards the 'ineffective' side of the ledger. It has not been all bad. Town and country planning, the Clean Air Act, LA21, 'quality of life', the

Climate Change Act – these well-intentioned reforms have been worth cheering. Yet any overlap between those two policy domains has largely been philosophically thin, unplanned, haphazard and unsustained.

So, what of policymaking in the future?

The most obvious harmonies between the welfare state and environmental politics can be heard when we attune our ears to the language of values.

As was most clear in the years 1945–70, the welfare state derived from a notion of *shared public spaces* in which those from different backgrounds rubbed shoulders on housing estates, GPs surgeries and classrooms. Social insurance was about *pooling risks*, not just across a person's lifetime, but across *the social community*. There was thus a greater, *egalitarian* sense of people rising and falling together, in which my fate is entwined with yours. The individual and the collective were therefore intimately connected. As Tawney (1952: 127, 164–73) understood, personal freedom and flourishing depends upon the freedoms and flourishings of others in a spirit of *cooperation*. No inherent conflict was seen between individuals' interest and *the common good*. At its best, the state was genuinely concerned with *social wellbeing*, with fair shares and with the economic conditions of social life. This meant having rights, opportunities and duties not simply re a job or a house, but regarding those things that lie outside the market place and the consumption of commodities. *Decommodification* indicated that a new form of socialised capitalism was required, one in which key industries and utilities were subject to *social ownership* and which thought that key elements of the future could be anticipated and made an object of *planning*.

Though they disagreed on many details, most of these principles offered a common point of reference across the political spectrum, from one-nation conservatives to democratic socialists. Those who disagreed were side lined for several decades until they and their ideals came raging back in the 1980s:

- the fetishisation of profit, competition, private property and the privatisation of public space and the public sector;
- an emphasis on cutting people loose from the social, reconstructed as 'responsibilised' consumers motivated largely by a possessive materialism;
- the desirability of inequalities, self-interest, an ethic of desert and the personalisation of risk-taking, spurred by an authoritarian moralism, which targeted fears, frustrations and hatreds on vulnerable 'others';
- a redistribution back towards the economically powerful in a 'free' market where structured systems of social power and privilege are vanished by the magical 'freedom to choose'.

This resurgence coincided with the era in which the ecological consequences of modernity caught up with us. So as the EU began to plan for its single market, it was clear that common rules on trade and investment would have to be agreed if the bad was not to drive out the good – with the ecological dimension being crucial. This may help to explain the (belated) enthusiasm of Thatcher's government for environmental problem solving.

But the naivety of EU vis market instruments also helps to explain the implementation problems of the ETS. In short, if you start with the premise that regulation is at best a necessary evil then is it any great surprise when the subsequent regulation is so ineffective? So while the ideology of free market liberalism implies that prices and profits should become the dominant, perhaps the only, drivers in a small-state capitalism, global warming operates on a wider and deeper stage than this. The prices of environmental bads need to be pushed up and the prices of environmental goods pushed down. We cannot wait for market forces to coalesce or market demand (including consumer preferences) to change. Only governments acting in unison can nudge, cajole and, where necessary, force and penalise. We have thus been repeatedly confronted with the limitations of free market liberalism, its refusal to face the difference between the ideals and the reality of markets and its consequent inability to repair the breach (Harvey, 2005: 172–5).

For the most part, then, with its anti-regulatory ethos, hostility to the notion of public goods and its fetish for profit, competition, consumerist materialism and 'business interests', free market liberalism constitutes an habitual roadblock (Marquand, 2013: 74–5). If it does not always ride the brake it rarely exerts pressure on the accelerator. Added to other pressures and developments – the dominance of a USA addicted to cheap fuels, the multipolar politics of globalisation, the growth rates of China, the need to address poverty in developing countries, cultural changes and technological advances that encourage a 'buy today, discard tomorrow' consumerism – the ascendancy of free market liberalism has appealed to and nurtured our darker angels.

No wonder that the vast majority of its defenders have been hostile to environmental politics, except in the very narrow limits permitted by *laissez faire* doctrines. They implicitly recognise how much environmentalism revitalises the welfarist principles and ideals sketched above. What is the 'political philosophy of the ecosocial'?

It would surely encompass the following. The need to expand the notion of shared public spaces and social risks so that they encompass the *environmental commons* and *ecological dangers*. The idea that 'being well' requires the social community to understand its place in a web of *socionatural interdependencies* that stretch farther across space and time than was once envisaged. The claim that a new egalitarian sense of the common good, rebalancing self-interest and cooperation, must include the equitable sharing of the Earth's inheritance, so that the poorest are not just protected but are able to participate in those institutions ensuring *global social justice* and a *ecocentric stewardship of natural resources*, which they, rather than unaccountable corporations or the faceless state, own. The imperative to redefine and reimpose the limits to markets so that our economies are reimagined as the servants, one of several sub-systems, of nature's *inherent value* and *reproductive capacity*. The recognition that long-term, strategic investment, regulation, rationing and inter-sectoral coordination are at the very heart of *sustainability*.

And, like the welfare state, these environmental principles and concepts are capable of attracting a wide consensus of politically diverse opinion.

There are similar lessons to be drawn from that earlier, post-war period vis human motivation and interaction.

Titmuss (e.g. 1970: 235–40) talked famously of the 'gift exchange'. Gifting is not some naive one-sided bequest but a form of symbolic social interaction. It is a non-monetary form of exchange, which acknowledges and maintains a web of mutuality but does not necessarily demand a contractualist return – one resembling a purchase in a shop. The reciprocity it implies is non-commodified and looser than this, realising that the value of something does not reside in its price tag. In so far as they nurtured the notion of service (not that of 'service delivery' but the idea of being of service to others) post-war reforms embodied a much broader, richer notion of social participation and relationships than that offered by many contemporary Conservatives and social democrats alike, in which 'obligation' implies devoting your life to the wage-earning grindstone. The 'welfare state' was always a constricting nickname for the *service society*.

Similarly, environmental politics seems to demand an other-regarding ethos in which others are not reduced to one of the three archetypes of *laissez faire* capitalism: the type who can help you to accumulate money (associates, compliant employees, gullible consumers), the type who may constitute an obstacle (competitors, savvy consumers, organised labour) and the type who is a burden to be discarded (the ill, the old, the damaged, the workshy). And since we all free-ride on nature, the divisions upon which contemporary capitalism depends – between winners and losers, haves and have-nots, deserving and undeserving – seem like the obsessions of children telling themselves comforting stories about who they are and what they are doing.

Instead, an environmental ethic sees others as mortal and fragile members of nature's frighteningly rapid cycles of birth and death. We are all equal in the graveyard, it has been said, and looked at through nature's eye we are all just flotsam blown around in earlier stages of decomposition, heading in the same direction. But far from this being a counsel of despair it means that life is ever more precious. The more we deny the ubiquity of nothingness the more we fail to hear the brief noises of existence. Gifts and services are not just about social exchange but are forms of existential recognition: points of light and warmth interconnecting amid an infinite coldness and darkness.

Despite such harmonics, the actual welfare state has been a child of the fossil fuel era, dependent upon GDP growth and often either oblivious to the damage being wrought or treating it as a necessary cost of modern progress. Something to be addressed later and through appropriate economic reforms, first and foremost. Where does this leave us as we look ahead?

The Introduction defined social policy as addressing social problems and enhancing wellbeing. The green welfare state must therefore be both reactive and proactive. It must enable us to cope with what *is* while reshaping social conditions towards what *could be*. It must adapt and mitigate, not only with respect to climate change but across the wider panoply of environmental problems identified in this book.

Recall the distinction on page 3 between (1), (2) and (3). The welfare state – particularly in its classic, pre-1979 form – can be defended in terms of (1) when it comes to coping, repairing and adaptation. Education systems can alert the next generation of citizens to the ecological challenges they face; healthcare systems can be reorganised to cope with weather extremes, pollution and a changing climate; housing policies can target energy and transport poverties; reformed social security systems can facilitate transitions to renewable industries. The adaptive aspects of a green welfare state, in short, could have a considerable role to play.

And what then?

There is no extant model of a green welfare state and, as this book has shown, precious little recognition on the part of policymakers of the need to design and implement one. In one sense this is not surprising. Since we cannot green the welfare state without also greening our economies, political institutions, social relations, cultural expectations and moral values, the task of building an ecosocial system is immense (see Figure 13.2). If it was just a case of scattering a bit of legislation here and there, we would surely have done it by now. And it is not just social democratic parties seduced by free market capitalism that have failed to introduce the measures needed for a green society. Klein (2014: 179–81) highlights the extent to which the self-proclaimed new socialists of the twenty-first century – including those in Latin America – not only refused to prioritise green reforms but, in many instances, obstructed them.

So because it has been a child of fossil fuel dependency, the preventative and mitigating aspects of a green welfare state (one which reduces environmental harms for us, for other species and for future generations) is more likely to direct our attention beyond existing institutions, to (2) and (3). Think of it in these terms.

Our unsustainable economies impose an 'ecological burden' on nature via GHGs, the depletion of natural resources, the pressures on remaining resources (especially food production amid a rising world population), pollution and waste disposal. This burden is represented by the column in Figure 13.3 – this is just for illustrative purposes. The dashed line represents the declining burden, which we need to place on nature by the end of the century. This implies decarbonisation of economic activity, a steadily increasing use of renewable energy and materials,[3] and societies that are in general living within the planet's means.[3] In Britain, in the first decade of the century, social policy expenditure accounted for approximately 30% of the national economy. If we treat this as a proxy[4] for the proportion of the overall burden for which the welfare state is responsible (but see the cautionary note, below) then this can be represented by the lower, shaded part of the column. Now, what should happen to that shaded box?

One possibility is given in Figure 13.4. The dashed line declines as before, but the ecological burden of state welfare remains constant (the horizontal dotted line). In short, the overall burden declines because of reductions in personal consumption only. The green welfare state would therefore be a 'free rider' on the rest of society and economy. This option, though, by separating the welfare state from its contexts, seems untenable.

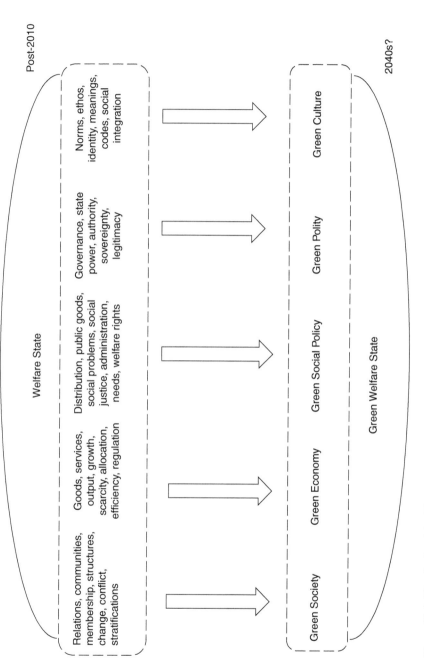

Post-2010

Welfare State

Relations, communities, membership, structures, change, conflict, stratifications

Goods, services, output, growth, scarcity, allocation, efficiency, regulation

Distribution, public goods, social problems, social justice, administration, needs, welfare rights

Governance, state power, authority, sovereignty, legitimacy

Norms, ethos, identity, meanings, codes, social integration

Green Society

Green Economy

Green Social Policy

Green Polity

Green Culture

Green Welfare State

2040s?

Figure 13.2 The Scale of the Transition.

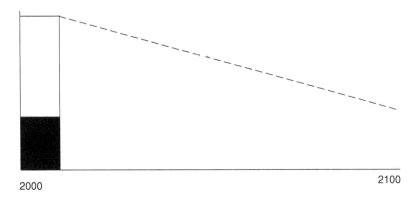

2000   2100

Figure 13.3 Declining ecological burden.

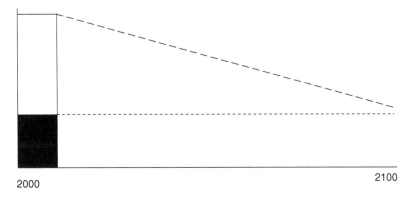

2000   2100

Figure 13.4 The free-riding welfare state.

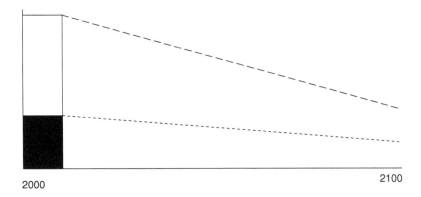

2000   2100

Figure 13.5 Options for a green welfare state.

Another possibility is offered in Figure 13.5. Now the dotted line declines too, maintaining its 30% parity with the dashed line. Is this the mitigating welfare state? If so, can we speculate what it might resemble (see Fitzpatrick, 2011a, 2011b, 2014a)?

- Using education to promote social values of ecological stewardship, green consumption and facilitate a participative democracy whose citizens regard themselves as members of communities that stretch beyond the human and beyond the present.
- A reinvigorated 'third sector' of co-productive associations, integrating social and environmental goals, which are no longer adjuncts either to the state or to markets.
- Green economies serving preventative healthcare addressing the 'socionatural' determinants of health and wellbeing;
- Shifting the tax burden onto 'bads' and encouraging green jobs.
- Creating sustainable energy and transport systems through reforms to housing, land, social infrastructures and urban design on a zero-carbon basis.

There could be many other important components and, obviously, none of this is to address debates about how to devise global solutions for global problems.

Yet even the above still leaves room for several possible scenarios, which could take these broad recommendations in any number of directions. For instance:

Diminution

Though expenditure remains the same in relative terms, a contracting burden means that the welfare state has to contract too. It has to do less, which might imply less emphasis on national schemes and services and more local organisation, perhaps on a bioregional basis. This is the *ascetic* ecowelfare system and its ethos is one of making do and mending via local production, exchange and consumption.

Hyper-productivity

The welfare state can continue pretty much in its present form, doing what it already does, but will have to do more with less (particularly as the population ages). This requires ever-increasing levels of productivity and efficiency across the public sector as a whole: increased output per unit of input. In part, this would mean emphasising the benefits of new technologies, particularly in relation to 'green jobs'. This is the *industrious* ecowelfare system.

Post-Productivism

This implies doing things differently since we cannot regenerate nature without regenerative forms of social activity too. This implies nurturing post-materialist sources of wellbeing and forms of exchange. For instance, reforming employment and social security policies to facilitate a 'part-time economy' in which work is no longer synonymous with 'waged labour', informal economies are more prevalent and time becomes a currency as important as income and wealth. This is the *restorative* ecowelfare system, which aims at a renaturing of the social (Fitzpatrick, 2014a: ch. 2).

Each of these no doubt has its merits and it would take too long to expand on those here. Much depends upon what the Introduction called the matrix of society, economy, environment and government and, in particular, the meaning and measurement of future economic growth. The cautionary note is therefore this: the declining column in the above figures should not be taken to suggest that nations like Britain have to start impoverishing themselves through drastic cuts to national wealth. I have suggested elsewhere that the burdens on affluent countries of addressing global poverty and financing worldwide mitigation and adaptation measures are less imposing than many fear (Fitzpatrick, 2011b: 85–7) – and surely less than the long-term costs of doing nothing.

In sum, the green welfare state will need to adapt and mitigate, cure and prevent. This implies that (1), (2) and (3) are all likely to be incorporated. We require all the resources we can muster. (1) As just noted, we need existing systems of intervention to intervene more strategically and effectively in a green direction. (2) We need to revisit the past, borrowing and modifying its best elements. The Clean Air Act and the creation of the world's first Department of the Environment were pioneering, for all their flaws. Since the 1980s policymakers have become far more aware of how damaging pollution is to health; LA21 provided a rare oasis with the potential to bring social and ecological thinking together at the local level; green taxes have now been on the agenda for years, though usually as a ball to be kicked around the political pitch; and, though detached from its ephemeral 'quality of life' agenda, New Labour was making progress on solar and wind power, demonstrating some admirable leadership within the EU and legislated to require all new houses to be zero-carbon. (3) And we need to think creatively about the future, not just in terms of innovative proposals (Basic Income, local currencies, personal carbon trading, transition towns, community energy schemes, etc.) but vis the overall conceptual framework, e.g. the respective merits of ascetic, industrious and restorative systems.

In short, developing a green welfare state requires us to *redirect, reinvent and reimagine*. Unfortunately, what has not evolved in the field of social policy is an ecosocial politics, which connects the dots and enables us to plot and manoeuvre a way forward.

This book has hopefully illustrated why Stern was only partly right when he characterised climate change as the greatest market failure ever. First, climate change failures have repeated a pattern of failures on environmental issues that stretch back further over several decades. Second, markets do not exist in isolation but are always shaped in and through social and political contexts. Ongoing environmental problems therefore represent not just the greatest *market failure* ever but perhaps also *the greatest social policy failure* ever. With one qualification.

We still have a narrowing window of opportunity. The greatest social policy successes may lie ahead of us. But that window will not remain open indefinitely. It may be that what lies ahead of us will be the greatest social policy failure yet.

Notes

1 Note my comments in Chapter 8 re 'welfare hybridity'.
2 But recall my comment in the Introduction, such that the nineteenth century was characterised by many reforms that can in retrospect be termed ecosocial.
3 Recall the definition of sustainability in the Introduction: not exceeding the regenerative and absorptive capacities of natural ecosystems.
4 The ecological burden created by welfare systems could conceivably be higher or lower than this but, for illustrative purposes, let's bypass this consideration.

References

Abel-Smith, B. (1980) 'The Welfare State: Breaking the post-war consensus', *Political Quarterly*, 51: 17–34.

Adams, J. (2011) *Tony Benn: A Biography*, 2nd edn, London: Biteback.

Addison, P. (1985) *Now the War is Over*, London: BBC and Jonathan Cape.

Addison, P. (1994) *The Road to 1945*, London: Pimlico.

Addison, P. (2005) 'The Impact of the Second World War', in Addison, P. & Jones, H. (eds) *A Companion to Contemporary Britain 1939–2000*, Oxford: Blackwell.

Addison, P. (2010) *No Turning Back*, Oxford: Oxford University Press.

Alcock, P. (2006) *Understanding Poverty*, 3rd edn, Basingstoke: Palgrave Macmillan.

Andersen, S. (1993) *The Struggle over North Sea Oil and Gas*, Oxford: Oxford University Press.

Andersen, T. & Leal, D. (2015) *Free Market Environmentalism for the Next Generation*, New York: Palgrave Macmillan.

Arnold, G. (1978) *Britain's Oil*, London: Hamish Hamilton.

Atkinson, A. (2000) 'Distribution of Income and Wealth', in Halsey, A. H. with Webb, J. (eds) *Twentieth-Century British Social Trends*, Basingstoke: Macmillan.

Atteridge, A. (2013) 'The Evolution of Climate Policy in India: Poverty and global ambition in tension', in Held, D., Roger, C. & Nag, E.-M. (eds) *Climate Governance in the Developing World*, Cambridge: Polity.

Bäckstrand, K. & Elgström, O. (2013) 'The EU's role in Climate Change Negotiations: From leader to "leadiator"', *Journal of European Public Policy*, 20(10): 1369–86.

Bacon, R. & Eltis, W. (1976) *Britain's Economic Problem*, London: Macmillan.

Baggott, R. (1997) 'Evaluating Health Care Reform: The case of the NHS internal market', *Public Administration*, 75(2): 283–306.

Baker, D., Gamble, A. & Seawright, D. (2002) 'Sovereign Nations and Global Markets: Modern British Conservatism and hyperglobalism', *British Journal of Politics and International Relations*, 4(3): 399–428.

Baldwin, S. (1927) *On England and Other Addresses*, London: Philip Allan.

Bale, T. (2010) *The Conservative Party from Thatcher to Cameron*, Cambridge: Polity.

Bale, T. (2012) *The Conservative since 1945*, Oxford: Oxford University Press.

Ball, S. (2008) *The Education Debate*, Bristol: Policy Press.

Balls, E., Ussher, K., Brooks, R. with Vance, R. (2007) 'Beyond Stability: Labour's economic story', in Pearce, N. & Margo, J. (eds) *Politics for a New Generation*, Basingstoke: Palgrave Macmillan.

Barnard, C., Deakin, S. & Hobbs, R. (2003) '"Fog in the Channel, Continent Isolated":

Britain as a model for EU social and economic policy?', *Industrial Relations Journal*, 34(5): 461–76.

Barnett, C. (1995) *The Lost Victory*, London & Basingstoke: Macmillan.

Barry, B. (1999) 'Sustainability and Intergenerationaal Justice', in Dobson, A. (ed.) *Fairness and Futurity*, Oxford: Oxford University Press.

Barry, J. (1994) 'The Limits of the Shallow and the Deep: Green politics, philosophy, and praxis', *Environmental Politics*, 3(3): 369–94.

Barry, J. (2005) 'Ecological Modernisation', in Dryzek, J. & Scholsberg, D. (eds) *Debating the Earth*, 2nd edn, Oxford: Oxford University Press.

Barry, N. (1987) *The New Right*, London: Routledge.

Bartle, I. (2002) 'When Institutions No Longer Matter: Reform of telecommunications and electricity in Germany, France and Britain', *Journal of Public Policy*, 22: 1–27.

Baxter, P. (2005) 'The East Coast Big Flood, 31st January–1 February 1953: A summary of the human disaster', *Philosophical Transactions of the Royal Society A*, 363(1831): 1293–312.

Beckett, A. (2009) *When the Lights Went Out*, London: Faber & Faber.

Beckett, F. & Hencke, D. (2009) *Marching to the Fault Line*, London: Constable.

Beder, S. (1996) 'Charging the Earth: The Promotion of Price Based Measures for Pollution Control', *Ecological Economics*, 16: 51–63.

Bell, M., Davis, D. & Fletcher, T. (2004) 'A Retrospective Assessment of Mortality from the London Smog Episode of 1952: The role of influenza and pollution', *Environmental Health Perspectives*, 112(1): 6–8.

Benedick, R. (1998) *Ozone Diplomacy*, 2nd edn, Cambridge, Mass: Harvard University Press.

Benn, M. (2011) *School Wars*, London: Verso.

Benn, T. (1974) *Speeches*, Nottingham: Spokesman Books.

Benn, T. (1990) *Conflicts of Interest: Diaries, 1977–80*, London: Arrow Books.

Benn, T., Morrell, F. & Cripps, F. (1974) *A Ten-Year Industrial Strategy for Britain*, Nottingham: Institute for Workers' Control.

Benson, J. (1994) *The Rise of Consumer Society in Britain*, London: Longman.

Bernstein, S. (2001) *The Compromise of Liberal Environmentalism*, Chichester: Columbia University Press.

Bevan, A. (1978) *In Place of Fear*, London: Quartet Books.

Beynon, H. (2014) '"Still Too Much Socialism in Britain": The legacy of Margaret Thatcher', *Industrial Relations Journal*, 45(3): 214–33.

Biehl, J. (ed.) (1997) *The Murray Bookchin Reader*, London: Cassell.

Blair, A., Leopold, J. & Karsten, L. (2001) 'An Awkward Partner? Britain's Implementation of the Working Time Directive', *Time & Society*, 10(1): 63–76.

Blair, T. (2010) *A Journey*, London: Hutchinson.

Blanden, J. & Gregg, P. (2004) 'Family Income and Educational Attainment: A review of approaches and evidence for Britain', *Oxford Review of Economic Policy*, 20(2): 245–63.

Blundell, V. H. (1994) 'Flawed Land Acts, 1947–76', in Tideman, N. (ed.) *Land and Taxation*, London: Shepheard Walwyn.

Boardman, B. (2007) 'Home Truths', ECI Research Report 34, Environmental Change Institute, University of Oxford.

Boardman, B. (2010) *Fixing Fuel Poverty*, London: Earthscan.

Bogdanor, V. (2004) '1974: The crisis of Old Labour', in Seldon, A. (Anthony) & Hickson, K. (eds) *New Labour, Old Labour*, London: Routledge.

Bogdanor, V. (2011) 'Britain in the Twentieth Century: The Conservative reaction, 1951–65', lecture given at Gresham College, 13 December.

Bond, A., Mortimer, K. & Cherry, J. (1998) 'The Focus of Local Agenda 21 in the United Kingdom', *Journal of Environmental Planning and Management*, 41(6): 767–76.

Bonefeld, W., Brown, A. & Burnham, P. (1995) *A Major Crisis?* Aldershot: Dartmouth.

Bonoli, G., George, V. & Taylor-Gooby, P. (2000) *European Welfare Futures*, Cambridge: Polity Press.

Bosanquet, N. (1983) *After the New Right*, London: Heinemann Educational Books.

Boughton, J. (2002) 'Why White, not Keynes? Investing the postwar international monetary system', IMF Working Paper, WP/02/52.

Boulding, K. (1949) 'Income or Welfare?', *Review of Economic Studies*, 17: 79.

Boulding, K. (1966) 'The Economics of the Coming Spaceship Earth', in Jarrett, H. (ed.) *Environmental Quality in a Growing Economy*, Baltimore, John Hopkins Press.

Bourguignon, F. (2015) *The Globalization of Inequality*, Princeton: Princeton University Press.

Bové, J. (2004) 'A Farmers' International?', in Mertes, T. (ed.) *A Movement of Movements*, London: Verso.

Brehony, K. & Deem, R. (2003) Education Policy', in Ellison, N. & Pierson, C. (eds) *Developments in British Social Policy 2*, Basingstoke: Palgrave Macmillan.

Bridgen, P. (2006) 'A Straightjacket with Wriggle Room: The Beveridge Report, the Treasury and the Exchequer's Pension Liability, 1942–59', *Twentieth Century British History*, 17(1): 1–25.

Britton, A. (1993) 'The Economy in the 1980s – A review of the decade', in Healey, N. (ed.) *Britain's Economic Miracle: Myth or reality?*, London: Routledge.

Brivati, B. (1997) *Hugh Gaitskell*, London: Richard Cohen Books.

Brown, C. (2005) *Prescott*, London: Politico's.

Brown, G. (2011) *Beyond the Crash*, London: Simon & Schuster.

BSR (2014) *Climate Change: Implications for extractive and primary industries*, Cambridge: Cambridge University Press.

Bulpitt, J. & Burnham, P. (1999) 'Operation Robot and the British Political Economy in the early 1950s: The politics of market strategies', *Contemporary British History*, 13(1): 1–31.

Burchardt, T. & Holder, H. (2009) 'Inequality and the Devolved Administrations: Scotland, Wales and Northern Ireland', in Hills, J., Sefton, T. & Stewart, K. (eds) *Towards a More Equal Society?* Bristol: Policy Press.

Burk, K. & Cairncross, A (1992) *Goodbye, Great Britain*, New Haven & London: Yale University Press.

Burke, E. (1960) *The Correspondence of Edmund Burke: Volume 2, July 1768 – June 1774*, edited by Lucy S. Sutherland, Cambridge: Cambridge University Press.

Burnell, P. (1998) 'Britain's New Government. New White Paper, New Aid? Eliminating world poverty: a challenge for the twenty-first century', *Third World Quarterly*, 19(4): 787–802.

Burns, C., Carter, N., Davies, G. & Worsfold, N. (2013) 'Still Saving the Earth? The European Parliament's environmental record', *Environmental Politics*, 22(6): 935–54.

Burrows, R. & Loader, B. (eds) (1994) *Towards a Post-Fordist Welfare State?*, London: Routledge.

Buttle, G. (2008) *A Signal Failure?*, Durham Theses, Durham University. Available at: http://etheses.dur.ac.uk/2469/

Byatt, I. (2013) 'The Regulation of Water Services in the UK', *Utilities Policy*, 24: 3–10.

Byrne, P. (1997) *Social Movements in Britain*, London: Routledge.

Cahill, M. (2002a) *The Environment and Social Policy*, London: Routledge.

Cahill, M. (2002b) 'The Implications of Consumerism for the Transition to a Sustainable Society', in Cahill, M. & Fitzpatrick, T. (eds) *Environmental Issues and Social Welfare*, Oxford: Blackwell.

Cahill, M. (2011) 'Transport', in Fitzpatrick, T. (ed.) *Understanding the Environment and Social Policy*, Bristol: Policy Press.

Cairncross, A. (1996) 'The Heath Government and the British Economy', in Ball, S. & Seldon, A. (Anthony) (eds) *The Heath Government 1970–74: A Reappraisal*, London: Routledge.

Callaghan, J. (John) (1990) *Socialism in Britain*, Oxford: Basil Blackwell.

Callaghan, J. (John) (2000) *The Retreat of Social Democracy*, London: Routledge.

Callaghan, J. (James) (2006) *Time and Chance*, London: Politico's.

Callinicos, A. (2001) *Against the Third Way*, Cambridge: Polity.

Callinicos, A. (2010) *Bonfire of Illusions*, Cambridge: Polity.

Campbell, J. (1987) *Nye Bevan and the Mirage of British Socialism*, London: Weidenfeld & Nicolson.

Campbell, J. (2000) *Margaret Thatcher, Volume One: The grocer's daughter*, London: Jonathan Cape.

Campbell, J. (2003) *Margaret Thatcher, Volume Two: The iron lady*, London: Jonathan Cape.

Carson, R. (2000) *Silent Spring*, Middlesex: Penguin.

Carter, N. (2006) 'Party Politicization of the Environment in Britain', *Party Politics*, 12(6): 747–67.

Carter, N. (2008) 'Combatting Climate Change in the UK: Challenges and obstacles', *The Political Quarterly*, 79(2): 194–205.

Carter, N. (2009) 'Vote Blue, Go Green? Cameron's Conservatives and the Environment', *The Political Quarterly*, 80: 233–42.

Carter, N. & Jacobs, M. (2014) 'Explaining Radical Policy Change: The case of climate change and energy policy under the British Labour Government 2006–10', *Public Administration*, 92(1): 125–41.

Carter, N. & Lowe, P. (2000) 'The Conservative Government and Sustainable Development in the UK, 1988–97', in Young, S. (ed.) *The Emergence of Ecological Modernisation*, London: Routledge.

Carter, N. & Ockwell, D. (2007) *New Labour, New Environment? An analysis of the Labour Government's policy on climate change and biodiversity loss*, London: Friends of the Earth.

Cashman, A. & Lewis, L. (2007) 'Topping Up or Watering Down? Sustainable development in the privatized UK water industry', *Business Strategy and the Environment*, 16: 93–105.

Castle, B. (1993) *Fighting All the Way*, London: Macmillan.

Charmley, J. (2008) *A History of Conservative Politics since 1830*, 2nd edn, Basingstoke: Palgrave Macmillan.

Chasek, P., Downie, D. & Brown, J. (2010) *Global Environmental Politics*, 5th edn, Philadelphia: Westview.

Childs, D. (2001) *Britain since 1945: A political history*, 5th edn, London: Routledge.

Chitty, C. (2002) 'The Role and Status of LEAs: Post-war pride and fin de siècle uncertainty', *Oxford Review of Education*, 28(2–3): 261–73.

Chitty, C. (2009) *Education Policy in Britain*, 2nd edn, Basingstoke: Palgrave Macmillan.

Choonara, J. (2009) 'Marxist Accounts of the Current Crisis', *International Socialism*, No. 123, http://isj.org.uk/marxist-accounts-of-the-current-crisis/

Chote, R., Crawford, R., Emmerson, C. & Tetlow, G. (2010) *Public Spending Under Labour*, London: IFS.

Christoff, P. (1996) 'Ecological Modernisation, Ecological Modernities', *Environmental Politics*, 5(3): 476–500.

Christoff, P. & Eckersley, R. (2013) *Globalization and the Environment*, Lanham, Maryland: Rowman & Littlefield.

Clapp, B. W. (1994) *An Environmental History of Britain*, London: Longman.

Clapson, M. (2005) 'Cities, Suburbs, Countryside' in Addison, P. & Jones, H. (eds) *A Companion to Contemporary Britain 1939–2000*, Oxford: Blackwell.

Clark, T. with Heath, A. (2014) *Hard Times*, New Haven & London: Yale University Press.

Clark, T. & Dilnot, A. (2002) *Long-Term Trends in British Taxation and Spending*, IFS Briefing Note, no. 25.

Clarke, J., Gewirtz, S., Hughes, G. & Humphrey, J. (2000) 'Guarding the Public Interest? Auditing public services', in Clarke, J., Gewirtz, S. & McLaughlin, E. (eds) *New Managerialism, New Welfare?* London: Sage.

Clarke, M. (2010) *Challenging Choices*, Bristol: Policy Press.

Clarke, P. (1998) 'The Rise and Fall of Thatcherism', *London Review of Books*, 20(24): 14–20.

Cleveland, C. & Ruth, M. (1999) 'Indicators of Dematerialization and the Materials Intensity of Use', *Journal of Industrial Ecology*, 2(3) 15–50.

Common, M. & Stagl, S. (2005) *Ecological Economics*, Cambridge: Cambridge University Press.

Commoner, B. (1972) *The Closing Circle*, London: Jonathan Cape.

Commoner, B. (1976) *The Poverty of Power*, New York: Alfred A. Knopf.

Congdon, T. (1989) *Monetarism Lost and Why it Must be Regained*, Policy Study no. 106, London: Centre for Policy Studies.

Connell, A. (2011) *Welfare Policy under New Labour*, London: I. B. Taurus.

Connolly, C., Martin, G. & Wall, A. (2008) 'Education, Education, Education: The third way and PFI', *Public Administration*, 86(4): 951–68.

Connelly, J., Smith, G. & Benson, D. & Saunders, C. (2012) *Politics and the Environment*, 3rd edn, London: Routledge.

Convery, F. (2009) 'Origins and Development of the EU ETS', *Environ Resource Econ*, 43: 391–412.

Corkindale, J. (2001) *Reforming Land Use Planning*, London: IEA.

Costanza, R., Cumberland, J., Daly, H., Goodland, R., Norgaard, R., Kubiszewski, I. & Franco, C. (2015) *An Introduction to Ecological Economics*, 2nd edn, Boco Raton, Florida: CRC Press.

Cox, C. & Dyson, A. (1969) *Fight for Education*, London: Critical Quarterly Society.

Crafts, N. (2013) 'Returning to Growth: Policy Lessons from History', *Fiscal Studies*, 34(2): 255–82.

Craig, D. (2006) *Plundering the Public Sector*, London: Constable.

Crosland, T. (1956) *The Future of Socialism*, London: Jonathan Cape.

Crosland, T. (1974) *Socialism Now*, London: Jonathan Cape.

Crowson, N. (2012) 'Revisiting the 1977 Housing (Homeless Persons) Act: Westminster, Whitehall, and the Homelessness Lobby', *Twentieth Century British History*, 24(3): 424–47.

Cullingworth, B. & Nadin, V. (2006) *Town and Country Planning in the UK*, 14th edn, Abingdon: Routledge.

Cullingworth, B., Nadin, V., Hart, T., Davoudi, S., Pendlebury, J., Vigar, G., Webb, D. & Townshend, T. (2015) *Town and Country Planning in the UK*, 15th edn, London: Routledge.

Curtice, J. & Steed, M. (1986) 'Proportionality and Exaggeration in the British Electoral System', *Electoral Studies*, 5(3): 209–28.

Dagdeviren, H. (2009) 'Limits to Competition and Regulation in Privatized Electricity Markets', *Annals of Public and Cooperative Economics*, 80(4): 641–64.

Dalal-Clayton, B., Bass, S., Sadler, B., Thomson, K., Sandbrook, R., Robins, N. & Hughes, R. (1994) *National Sustainable Development Strategies: Experience and dilemmas*, Environmental Planning Group, London: The International Institute for Environment and Development.

Dalton, H. (1962) *High Tide and After: Memoirs, 1945–60*, London: Frederick Muller Ltd.

Daly, H. (2007) *Ecological Economics and Sustainable Development*, Cheltenham: Edward Elgar.

Darley, G. (1990) *Octavia Hill*, London: Constable.

Darling, A. (2011) *Back from the Brink*, London: Atlantic Books.

Davies, J. (2012) 'Active Citizenship: Navigating the Conservative heartlands of the New Labour project', *Policy & Politics*, 40(1): 3–19.

de las Heras, B. P. (2013) Beyond Kyoto: The EU's contribution to a more sustainable world economy, *European Law Journal*, 19(4): 577–93.

Deacon, B. (2001) 'International Organisations, the EU and Global Social Policy', in Sykes, R., Palier, B. & Prior, P. (eds) *Globalization and European Welfare States*, Basingstoke: Palgrave.

Dean, H. (1999) 'Citizenship', in Powell, M. (ed.) *New Labour, New Welfare State?* Bristol: Policy Press.

Dean, H. (2014) 'Social Rights and Natural Resources', in Fitzpatrick, T. (ed.) *The International Handbook on Social Policy and the Environment*, Cheltenham: Edward Elgar.

Dean, M. (2013) *Democracy under Attack*, Bristol: Policy Press.

DEFRA (2004) *Quality of Life Counts: Indicators for a strategy for sustainable development for the United Kingdom, 2004 Update, Updating the baseline assessments made in 1999*, London: DEFRA.

DEFRA (2006) *The Development of the Water Industry in England and Wales*, London: DEFRA.

Dekkers, C. & Oudenes, M. (2007) 'EU ETS in the Post-2012 Regime: Lessons learned', in Douma, W., Massai, L. & Mantini, M. (eds) *The Kyoto Protocol and Beyond*, The Hague; T M C Asser Press.

Dell, E. (2000) *A Strange Eventful History*, London: HarperCollins.

Della Porta, D. & Diani, M. (1999) *Social Movements: An introduction*, Oxford: Blackwell.

Denham, A. & Garnett, M. (2001a) 'From "Guru" to "Godfather": Keith Joseph, "New" Labour and the British Conservative tradition', *Political Quarterly*, 72(1): 97–106.

Denham, A. & Garnett, M. (2001b) *Keith Joseph*, Cheltenham: Acumen.

Department for Transport (2011) *Transport Statistics Great Britain: 2011*, London: Department for Transport.

Department of Social Security (1998) *A New Contract for Welfare*, London: HMSO.

Department of the Environment (1992) *Think Globally, Act Locally: Putting the '92 Earth Summit into practice*, London: Department of the Environment.

Department of the Environment, Transport and the Regions (2000a) *Transport 2010: The ten year plan*, London: TSO.

Department of the Environment, Transport and the Regions (2000b) *Climate Change: the UK Programme*, London: DETR.

Department of the Environment, Transport and the Regions (2001) *Achieving a Better Quality of Life: Review of progress towards sustainable development*, Government annual report 2000, London: DETR.

Dirix, J., Peeters, W. & Sterckx, S. (2015) 'Is the EU ETS a Just Climate Policy?', *New Political Economy*, 20(5): 702–24.

Disney, R. (2015) *The Right to Buy Public Housing in Britain: A Welfare Analysis*, IFS Briefing Note BN162, London: IFS.

Disraeli, B. (1981) *Sybil*, Oxford: Oxford University Press.

Dobson, A. (2003) *Citizenship and the Environment*, Oxford: Oxford University Press.

Doherty, B. (1992) 'The Fundi-Realo Controversy: An analysis of four European green parties', *Environmental Politics*, 1(1): 95–120.

Dore, M., Kushner, J. & Zumer, K. (2004) 'Privatization of Water in the UK and France – What can we learn?', *Utilities Policy*, 12: 41–50.

Dorey, P. (1999a) 'Despair and Disillusion Abound: The Major Premiership in Perspective', in Dorey, P. (ed.) *The Major Premiership*, Basingstoke: Macmillan.

Dorey, P. (1999b) 'The 3 Rs – Reform, Reproach and Rancour: Education policies under John Major', in Dorey, P. (ed.) *The Major Premiership*, Basingstoke: Macmillan.

Dorey, P. (2006a) 'Industrial Relations Imbroglio', in Dorey, P. (ed.) *The Labour Governments, 1964–70*, London: Routledge.

Dorey, P. (2006b) 'From a "Policy for Incomes" to Income Policies', in Dorey, P. (ed.) *The Labour Governments, 1964–70*, London: Routledge.

Dorey, P. (2006c) 'Conclusion', in Dorey, P. (ed.) *The Labour* Governments, 1964–70, London: Routledge.

Dorey, P. (2006d) 'Education, Education, Education', in Dorey, P. (ed.) *The Labour Governments, 1964–70*, London: Routledge.

Dorey, P. (2011) *British Conservatism*, London: I. B. Tauris.

Dorey, P. (2014) 'The Legacy of Thatcherism for Education Policies: Markets, managerialism and malice (towards teachers)', in Farrall, S. & Hay, C. (eds) *The Legacy of Thatcherism*, Oxford: Oxford University Press.

Dorling, D. (2010) 'New Labour and Inequality: Thatcherism Continued?', *Local Economy*, 25(5–6): 397–413.

Dorling, D. (2014) 'Mapping the Thatcherite Legacy: The human geography social inequality in Britain since the 1970s', in Farrall, S. & Hay, C. (eds) *The Legacy of Thatcherism*, Oxford: Oxford University Press.

Drake, F. (2009) 'Black Gold to Green Gold: Regional energy policy and the rehabilitation of coal in response to climate change', *Area*, 41(1): 43–54.

Driver, S. (2009) 'Work to be done? Welfare reform from Blair to Brown', *Policy Studies*, 30(1): 69–84.

Driver, S. & Martell, L. (2002) *Blair's Britain*, Cambridge: Polity.

Duffy, S., Waters, J. & Glasby, J. (2010) *Personalisation and the Social Care 'Revolution': Future options for the reform of public services*, Health Services Management Centre, Policy Paper 3, University of Birmingham.

Durucan, S., Jozefowicz, R. & Brenkley, D. (2010) 'Coal Mining Research in the United Kingdom: A historical review', in Brune, J. (ed.) *Extracting the Science*, Colorado: Society for Mining Metallurgy.

Dwyer, P. (2008) 'The Conditional Welfare State', in Powell, M. (ed.) *Modernising the Welfare State*, Bristol: Policy Press.

Ehrich, P. (1975) *The Population Bomb*, New York: Ballantine Books.

Eichengreen, B. (2008) *The European Economy since 1945*, Princeton: Princeton University Press.

Elliott, L. (2012) 'Britain's Richest 5 Gained Most from Quantitative Easing – Bank of England', *Guardian*, 23 August.

Ellis, C. (2010) 'Letting it Slip: The Labour Party and the "mystical halo" of nationalization, 1951–1964', *Contemporary British History*, 26(1): 47–71.

Ellison, N. (2011) 'Public Expenditure and the Mixed Economy of Welfare', in Bochel, H. (ed.) *The Conservative Party and Social Policy*, Bristol: Policy Press.

Etzioni, A. (1995) *The Spirit of Community*, London: Fontana.

European Commission (2013) *Progress towards Achieving the Kyoto and EU 2020 Objectives*, Report from the Commission to the European Parliament and the Council, COM(2013) 698 final.

Evandrou, M. & Falkingham, J. (2009) 'Pensions and Income Security in Later Life', in Hills, J., Sefton, T. & Stewart, K. (eds) *Towards a More Equal Society?* Bristol: Policy Press.

Evans, B. & Theobold, K. (2003) 'LASALA: Evaluating Local Agenda 21 in Europe', *Journal of Environmental Planning and Management*, 46(5): 781–94.

Evans, E. (1997) *Thatcher and Thatcherism*, London: Routledge.

Evans, M. & Cerny, P. (2003) 'Globalization and Social Policy', in Ellison, N. & Pierson, C. (eds) *Developments in British Social Policy 2*, Basingstoke: Palgrave Macmillan.

Fairclough, N. (2000) *New Labour, New Language?*, London: Routledge.

Farlow, A. (2013) *Crash and Beyond*, Oxford: Oxford University Press.

Farnsworth, N. (2007) 'The EU Emissions Trading Directive: Time for revision?', in Douma, W., Massai, L. & Mantini, M. (eds) *The Kyoto Protocol and Beyond*, The Hague: T M C Asser Press.

Farrall, S. & Hay, C. (2014) 'Locating "Thatcherism" in the "Here and Now"', in Farrall, S. & Hay, C. (eds) *The Legacy of Thatcherism*, Oxford: Oxford University Press.

Fella, S. (2006) 'New Labour, Same Old Britain? The Blair Government and European Treaty Reform', *Parliamentary Affairs*, 59(4): 621–37.

Ferguson, N. (2008) *The Ascent of Money*, Middlesex: Penguin.

Ferguson, N. (2014) *The Great Degeneration*, Middlesex: Penguin.

Field, F. (1989) *Losing Out*, Oxford: Blackwell.

Finlayson, A. (2003) *Making Sense of New Labour*, London: Lawrence & Wishart.

Finlayson, A. (2007) 'Making Labour Safe: Globalisation and the aftermath of the social democratic retreat', in Hassan, G. (ed.) *After Blair*, London: Lawrence & Wishart.

Fischer, D. (1970) *Historians' Fallacies*, London: Routledge & Kegan Paul.

Fitzpatrick, R. & Chandola, T. (2000) 'Health', in Halsey, A. H. with Webb, J. (eds) *Twentieth-Century British Social Trends*, Basingstoke: Macmillan.

Fitzpatrick, T. (2003) *After the New Social Democracy*, Manchester: Manchester University Press.

Fitzpatrick, T. (2005) *New Theories of Welfare*, Basingstoke: Palgrave.

Fitzpatrick, T. (2011a) 'Environmental Policy' in Fitzpatrick, T. (ed.) *Understanding the Environment and Social Policy*, Bristol: Policy Press.

Fitzpatrick, T. (2011b) 'Challenges to Social Policy', in Fitzpatrick, T. (ed.) *Understanding the Environment and Social Policy*, Bristol: Policy Press.

Fitzpatrick, T. (2012) 'Cash Transfers', in Baldock, J., Mitton, L., Manning, N. & Vickerstaff, S. (eds.) *Social Policy*, 4th edition, Oxford: Oxford University Press.

Fitzpatrick, T. (2014a) *Climate Change and Poverty*, Bristol: Policy Press.

Fitzpatrick, T. (2014b) 'An Ecosocial Understanding of Poverty', in Fitzpatrick, T. (ed.) *International Handbook on Social Policy & the Environment*, Cheltenham: Edward Elgar.

Fitzpatrick, T. (2016) 'The Sixth Giant? Environmental Policy and the Labour Government, 1945–51', *Journal of Social Policy*, 45(1): 65–82.

Fleming, M. (1980) 'Industrial Policy', in Maunder, W. (ed.) *The British Economy in the 1970s*, London: Heinemann.

Foot, M. (1975) *Aneurin Bevan: Volume 2*, London: Paladin.

Ford, J. (2003) 'Housing Policy', in Ellison, N. & Pierson, C. (eds) *Developments in British Social Policy 2*, Basingstoke: Palgrave Macmillan.

Forrest, R. & Murie, A. (2011) *Selling the Welfare State: The privatisation of public housing*, London: Routledge.

Forster, A. (2002) 'Anti-Europeans, Anti-Marketeers and Eurosceptics: The evolution and influence of Labour and Conservative opposition to Europe', *Political Quarterly*, 73: 299–308.

Foster, J., Clark, B. & York, R. (2010) *The Ecological Rift*, New York: Monthly Review Press.

Fotaki, M. (2014) 'Can Consumer Choice Replace Trust in the National Health Service in England? Towards developing an affective psychosocial conception of trust in health care', *Sociology of Health & Illness*, 36(8): 1276–94.

Fraser, I. (2014) *Shredded*, Edinburgh: Birlinn Ltd.

Friedman, M. & Friedman, R. (1980) *Free to Choose*, Boston, Mass.: Thomson Learning.

Fukuyama, F. (1992) *The End of History and the Last Man*, New York: Free Press.

Galbraith, J. K. (1984) *The Affluent Society*, 4th edn, Middlesex: Penguin.

Gamble, A. (2009) *The Spectre at the Feast*, Basingstoke: Palgrave Macmillan.

Gannon, P. (2015) 'Between America and Europe: Transatlantic influences on the policies of Gordon Brown', *Journal of Transatlantic Studies*, 13(1): 1–19.

Gao, F. (2007) 'The International Climate Regime: Where do we stand?', in Douma, W., Massai, L. & Mantini, M. (eds) *The Kyoto Protocol and Beyond*, The Hague: T M C Asser Press.

Garcia-Sanchez, I. & Prado-Lorenzo, J.-M. (2008) 'Determinant Factors in the Degree of Implementation of Local Agenda 21 in the European Union', *Sustainable Development*, 16: 17–34.

Gareau, B. & DuPuis, E. (2009) 'From Public to Private Global Environmental Governance: Lessons from the Montreal Protocol's stalled methyl bromide phase-out', *Environment and Planning A*, 41: 2305–23.

Garfield, S. (2005) *Our Hidden Lives*, London: Ebury Press.

Garnett, M. & Hickson, K. (2009) *Conservative Thinkers*, Manchester: Manchester University Press.

George, S. (2004) *Another World is Possible if…*, London: Verso.

Geyer, R. (2000) 'The State of European Union Social Policy', *Policy Studies*, 21(3): 245–61.

Giddens, A. & Pierson, C. (1998) *Conversations with Anthony Giddens*, Cambridge: Polity.

Giddens, A. (1994) *Beyond Left and Right*, Cambridge: Polity.

Giddens, A. (1998) *The Third Way*, Cambridge: Polity.

Giddens, A. (2000) *The Third Way and Its Critics*, Cambridge: Polity.

Giddens, A. (ed.) (2001) *The Global Third Way Debate*, Cambridge: Polity.

Giddens, A. (2002) *Where Now for New Labour?*, Cambridge: Polity.

Giddens, A. (2007) *Over to You, Mr. Brown*, Cambridge: Polity.

Giddens, A. (2009) *The Politics of Climate Change*, Cambridge: Polity.

Gilbert, M. (1992) *Churchill: A life*, London: Minerva.

Gilbertson, T. & Reyes, O. (2009) *Carbon Trading: How it works and why it fails*, Critical Currents no. 7, Occasional Papers series, Dag Hammarskjöld Foundation, Uppsala.

Gilmour, I. (1992) *Dancing with Dogma*, London: Simon & Schuster.

Gilmour, I. & Garnett, M. (1997) *Whatever Happened to the Tories*, London: Fourth Estate.

Ginsburg, N. (2001) 'Globalization and the Liberal Welfare States', in Sykes, R., Palier, B. & Prior, P. (eds) *Globalization and European Welfare States*, Basingstoke: Palgrave.

Glendinning, C. (2003) 'Health Policies', in Ellison, N. & Pierson, C. (eds) *Developments in British Social Policy 2*, Basingstoke: Palgrave Macmillan.

Glennerster, H. (1995) *British Social Policy Since 1945*, Oxford: Blackwell.

Glennerster, H. (2007) *British Social Policy since 1945*, 3rd edn, Oxford: Wiley-Blackwell.

Gordon, G. (2012) *Environmental Justice*, London: Routledge.

Gore, A. (1992) *Earth in the Balance*, Boston, MA: Houghton Mifflin.

Gourvish, T. (1986) *British Railways, 1948–73*, Cambridge: Cambridge University Press.

Graham, C. (2006) 'The Politics of Necessity: Electricity and water in Great Britain', *Journal of Consumer Policy*, 29: 435–48.

Green, D. (1993) *Reinventing Civil Society*, London: Civitas.

Green, E. H. H. (2002) *Ideologies of Conservatism*, Oxford: Oxford University Press.

Green, R. (2006) 'Market Power Mitigation in the UK Power Market', *Utilities Policy*, 14: 76–89.

Greener, I. (2002) 'Understanding NHS Reform: The policy-transfer, social learning, and path-dependency perspectives', *Governance*, 15(2): 161–84.

Grieve Smith, J. (1997) *Full Employment: A pledge betrayed*, Basingstoke: Macmillan.

Griffiths, S. (2009) 'The Public Services under Gordon Brown – Similar reforms, less money', *Policy Analysis*, 30(1): 53–67.

Gummer, J. & Moreland, R. (2000) *The European Union and Global Climate Change: A review of five national programmes*, London: Sancroft International Ltd.

Hall, P. A. (2007) 'The Evolution of Varieties of Capitalism in Europe', in Hancké, B., Rhodes, M. & Thatcher, M. (eds) *Beyond Varieties of Capitalism*, Oxford: Oxford University Press.

Hall, S. (1998) 'The Great Moving Nowhere Show', *Marxism Today*, November/December, 9–14.

Hall, T. (1986) *Nuclear Politics*, Middlesex: Penguin Books.

Halliday, S. (2007) *The Great Filth*, Port Stroud: The History Press.

Hamel, P., Lustiger-Thaler, H., Pieterse, J. & Rosenwil, S. (eds) (2001) *Globalization and Social Movements*, Basingstoke: Palgrave.

Hanley, N., Shogren, J. & White, B. (2007) *Environmental Economics in Theory and Practice*, 2nd edn, Basingstoke: Palgrave Macmillan.

Hann, D. (1986) *Government and North Sea Oil*, Basingstoke: Macmillan.

Hannigan, J. (2011) 'Social Challenges: Causes, explanations, solutions', in Fitzpatrick, T. (ed.) (2011) *Understanding the Environment and Social Policy*, Bristol: Policy Press.

Hansen, J. (2009) *Storms of My Grandchildren*, London: Bloomsbury.

Hantrais, L. (1995) *Social Policy in the European Union*, Basingstoke: Macmillan.

Hardin, G. (1998) 'The Tragedy of the Commons' in Dryzek, J. & Schlosberg, D. (eds) *Debating the Earth*, Oxford: Oxford University Press.

Hardt, M. & Negri, A. (2000) *Empire*, Cambridge, Mass.: Harvard University Press.

Harrington, M. (1993) *Socialism: Past and future*, London: Pluto Press.

Harris, B. (1995) 'The Battle of Brightlingsea', *Independent*, 20 January.

Harris, J. (1997) *William Beveridge*, revised edition, Oxford: Clarendon.

Harris, K. (1995) *Attlee*, revised edition, London: Orion.

Harris, P. (2008) 'Implementing Climate Equity: The case of Europe', *Journal of Global Ethics*, 4(2): 121–40.

Harrison, K. & Sundstrom, L. (2010) 'Conclusion', in Harrison, K. & Sundstrom, L. (eds) *Global Commons, Domestic Decisions*, Cambridge, Mass.: MIT Press.

Harvey, D. (2005) *A Brief History of Neoliberalism*, Oxford: Oxford University Press.

Hasegawa, J. (1999) 'The Rise and Fall of Radical Reconstruction in 1940s Britain', *Twentieth Century British History*, 10(2): 137–61.

Hastings, S. (2002) *Evelyn Waugh*, London: Vintage.

Hattersley, R. (2001) 'It's No Longer My Party', *Observer*, 24 June.

Hattersley, R. (2004) 'The Case against Selection', in Benn, M. & Chitty, C. (eds) *A Tribute to Caroline Benn*, London: Continuum.

Havardi, J. (2010) *Greatest Briton: Essays on Winston Churchill's life and political philosophy*, London: Shepheard-Walwyn.

Hay, C. (1999) *The Political Economy of New Labour*, Manchester: Manchester University Press.

Hay, P. (2002) *A Companion to Environmental Thought*, Edinburgh: Edinburgh University Press.

Hayden, A. (2014) 'Stopping Heathrow Airport Expansion (For Now): Lessons from a victory for the politics of sufficiency', *Journal of Environmental Policy & Planning*, 16(4): 539–58.

Hayek, F. (1982) *Law, Legislation and Liberty*, London: Routledge.

Healey, D. (1989) *The Time of My Life*, London: Michael Joseph.

Healey, N. (1993) 'The North-South Divide: Has regional policy failed?', in Healey, N. (ed.) *Britain's Economic Miracle: Myth or reality?*, London: Routledge.

Heath, A. & Payne, C. (2000) 'Social Mobility', in Halsey, A. H. with Webb, J. (eds) *Twentieth-Century British Social Trends*, Basingstoke: Macmillan.

Heffernan, R. (2000) *New Labour and Thatcherism*, Basingstoke: Palgrave.

Helm, D. (2004) *Energy, the State, and the Market*, revised edition, Oxford: Oxford University Press.

Henderson, H. (1981) *The Politics of the Solar Age*, New York: Doubleday.

Hennessy, P. (1993) *Never Again*, London: Vintage.

Hennessy, P. (2007) *Having It So Good*, Middlesex: Penguin.

Herring, H. (2001) 'The Conservation Society: Harbinger of the 1970s environment movement in the UK', *Environment and History*, 7(4): 381–401.

Hewitt, M. (2002) 'New Labour and the Redefinition of Social Security', in Powell, M. (ed.) *Evaluating New Labour's Welfare Reforms*, Bristol: Policy Press.

Hey, C. (2005) 'EU Environmental Policies: A short history of the policy strategies', in Scheuer, S. (ed.) *EU Environmental Policy Handbook*, European Environmental Bureau.

Hickson, K. (2004a) 'Equality' in Plant, R., Beach, M. & Hickson, K. (eds) *The Struggle for Labour's Soul*, London: Routledge.

Hickson, K. (2004b) 'Economic Thought', in Seldon, A. (Anthony) & Hickson, K. (eds) *New Labour, Old Labour*, London: Routledge.

Hickson, K. (2005a) 'Inequality', in Hickson, K. (ed.) *The Political Thought of the Conservative Party since 1945*, Basingstoke: Palgrave Macmillan.

Hickson, K. (2005b) *The IMF Crisis of 1976 and British Politics*, London: I. B. Tauris.

Hill, M. (1999) 'Rolling Back the (Welfare) State: The Major governments and social security reform', in Dorey. P. (ed.) *The Major Premiership*, Basingstoke, Macmillan.

Hills, J. (1998) *Thatcherism, New Labour and the Welfare State*, CASE/13, London School of Economics.

Hills, J. (2005) 'Introduction', in Hills, J. & Stewart, K. (eds) *A More Equal Society?*, Bristol: Policy Press.

Hills, J. (2009) 'Future Pressures: Intergenerational links, wealth, demographyand sustainability', in Hills, J., Sefton, T. & Stewart, K. (eds) *Towards a More Equal Society?* Bristol: Policy Press.

Hills, J., Sefton, T. & Stewart, K. (2009) 'Conclusions: Climbing every mountain or retreating from the foothills?', in Hills, J., Sefton, T. & Stewart, K. (eds) *Towards a More Equal Society?* Bristol: Policy Press.

Hobsbawn, E. (1994) *Age of Extremes*, London: Abacus.

Hogg, Q. (1947) *The Case for Conservatism*, Middlesex: Penguin.

Hoggart, R. (2009) *The Uses of Literacy*, Middlesex: Penguin.

Holland, S. (1975) *The Socialist Challenge*, London: Quartet Books Ltd.

Holland, S. (2004a) 'Ownership, Planning and Markets', in Plant, R., Bech, M. & Hickson, K. (eds) *The Struggle for Labour's Soul*, London: Routledge.

Holland, S. (2004b) 'The Industrial Strategy', in Seldon, A. (Anthony) & Hickson, K. (eds) *New Labour, Old Labour*, London: Routledge.

Honderich, T. (2005) *Conservatism*, revised ed., London: Pluto Press.

Hopkin, J. & Wincott, D. (2006) 'New Labour, Economic Reform and the European Social Model', *The British Journal of Politics and International Relations*, 8: 50–68.

Hovi, J. & Sprinz, D. (2010) 'Why the United States did not become a party to the Kyoto Protocol: German, Norwegian, and US perspectives', *European Journal of International Relations*, 18(1): 129–50.

Howard, M., Garnham, A., Fimister, G. & Veit-Wilson, J. (2001) *Poverty the Facts*, 4th edn, London: CPAG.

Huang, P. (2009) 'Over-breeders and the Population Bomb', in Mazur, L. (ed.) *A Pivotal Moment*, Washington DC: Island Press.

Huckle, J. (2008) 'An Analysis of New Labour's Policy on Education for Sustainable Development (ESD) with Particular Reference to Socially Critical Approaches', *Environmental Education Research*, 14(1): 65–75.

Hudson, R. (2013) 'Thatcherism and its Geographical Legacies: The new map of socio-spatial inequality in the divided kingdom, *The Geographical Journal*, 179(4): 377–81.

Hughes, D. (2006) *What is Environmental History?*, Cambridge: Polity Press.

Hutton, W. (1995) *The State We're In*, London: Vintage.

Hutton, W. (2010) *Them and Us*, London: Little, Brown.

Irvine, S. & Ponton, A. (1991) 'Population Explosion', in Dobson, A. (ed.) *The Green Reader*, London: Andre Deutsch.

Iversen, T. & Stephens, J. (2008) 'Partisan Politics, the Welfare State, and Three Worlds of Human Capital Formation', *Comparative Political Studies*, 41: 600–37.

Jacobs, M. (1999) *Ecological Modernization*, London: Fabian Society.

Jameson, C. (2012) *Silent Spring Revisited*, London: Bloomsbury.

Jay, D. (1962) *Socialism in the New Society*, London: Longmans.

Jefferies, M. & Tyldesley, M. (2011) 'Rolf Gardiner: *Eminence Vert?*', in Jefferies, M. & Tyldesley, M. (eds) *Rolf Gardiner: Folk nature and culture in interwar Britain*, Farnham: Ashgate.

Jeffreys, K. (1998) 'Winston Churchill and the Wartime Coalition: 1940–45', *History Review*, December, 44–9.

Jeffreys, K. (2000) *Anthony Crosland*, London: Politico's.

Jeffreys, K. (2004) 'The Old Right', in Plant, R., Bech, M. & Hickson, K. (eds) *The Struggle for Labour's Soul*, London: Routledge.

Jenkins, S. (2006) *Thatcher and Sons*, London: Allen Lane.

Jessop, B., Bonnett, K. & Bromley, S. (1990) 'Farewell to Thatcherism? Neo-liberalism and "New Times"', *New Left Review*, 179: 81–102.

Johnson, P. (2001) 'New Labour: A distinctive vision of welfare policy?', in White, S. (ed.) *New Labour*, Basingstoke: Palgrave.

Jollands, N., Waide, P., Ellis, M., Onoda, T., Laustsen, J., Tanaka, K., de T'Serclaes, P., Barnsley, I., Bradley, R. & Meier, A. (2010) 'The 25 IEA Energy Efficiency Policy Recommendations to the G8 Gleneagles Plan of Action', *Energy Policy*, 38: 6409–18.

Jones, C. & Murie, A. (2006) *Right to Buy*, Oxford: Blackwell.

Jones, H. (2000) '"This is Magnificent!": 300,000 houses a year and the Tory revival after 1945', *Contemporary British History*, 14(1): 99–121.

Jones, K. & Tymms, P. (2014) 'Ofsted's Role in Promoting School Improvement: The mechanisms of the school inspection system in England', *Oxford Review of Education*, 40(3): 315–30.

Jordan, A. (2000) 'Environmental Policy', in Dunleavy, P., Gamble, A., Holliday, I. & Peele, G. (eds) *Developments in British Politics 6*, Basingstoke: Macmillan.

Jordan, A. (2002) *The Europeanization of British Environmental Policy*, Basingstoke: Palgrave Macmillan.

Jordan, A. (2006a) 'The Environmental Case for Europe: Britain's European environmental policy', CSERGE Working Paper EDM 06–11, University of East Anglia.

Jordan, A. (2006b) 'The United Kingdom: From "policy taking" to "policy shaping"', in Jordan, A. & Liefferink, D. (eds) *Environmental Policy in Europe*, London: Routledge.

Jordan, A. (2006c) 'Environmental Policy', in Bache, I. & Jordan, A. (eds) *The Europeanization of British Politics*, Basingstoke: Palgrave Macmillan.

Jordan, A., Wurzel, R., Zito, A. & Brückner, L. (2003a) 'European Governance and the Transfer of 'New' Environmental Policy Instruments (NEPIS) in the European Union', *Public Administration*, 81(3): 555–74.

Jordan, A., Wurzel, R., Zito, R. & Brückner, L. (2003b) 'Policy Innovation or "Muddling Through"? "New" environmental policy instruments in the United Kingdom', *Environmental Politics*, 12(1): 179–200.

Joseph, K. & Sumption, J. (1979) *Equality*, London: John Murray.

Joyce, R. & Sibieta, L. (2013) 'An Assessment of Labour's Record on Income Inequality and Poverty', *Oxford Review of Economic Policy*, 29(1): 178–202.

Judge, K. (2004) 'The British Welfare State in Transition', in Deakin, N., Jones-Finer, C. & Mathews, B. (eds) *Welfare and the State: Crisis of the Welfare States*, London: Routledge.

Judt, T. (2005) *Postwar*, London: Vintage Books.

Judt, T. (2010) *Ill Fares the Land*, London: Allen Lane.

Kalman, L. (2010) *Right Star Rising: A new politics, 1974–1980*, London: W. W. Norton & Co.

Keegan, W. (2003) *The Prudence of Mr. Gordon Brown*, Chichester: John Wiley & Sons.

Keegan, W. (2012) *Saving the World? Gordon Brown reconsidered*, Searching Finance Ltd.

Kelly, M. (2008) *Public Attitudes to Child Poverty*, DWP Research Summary, London: DWP.

Kelly, R. (2001) 'Family Policy: Opening up choice', in Lawson, N. & Sherlock, N. (eds) *The Progressive Century*, Basingstoke: Palgrave.

Kenny, M. (1995) *The First New Left*, London: Lawrence & Wishart.

Kesicki, F. (2010) 'The Third Oil Price Surge – what's different this time?', *Energy Policy*, 38(3): 1596–606.

Keynes, J. M. (1954) *The General Theory of Employment, Interest and Money*, London: Macmillan.

Keynes, J. M. (2009) *Essays in Persuasion*, New York: Classic House Books.

King, A. & Crewe, I. (2013) *The Blunders of our Governments*, London: Oneworld.

King, D. & Wickham-Jones, M. (1999) 'Bridging the Atlantic: The Democratic (Party) origins of welfare to work', in Powell, M. (ed.) *New Labour, New Welfare State?* Bristol: Policy Press.

King's Fund (2014) *The UK Private Health Market*, London: King's Fund.

Kirk, R. (1985) *The Conservative Mind*, 7th edn, Washington: Regnery Publishing.

Klein, N. (2000) *No Logo*, London: Flamingo.

Klein, N. (2004) 'Reclaiming the Commons', in Mertes, T. (ed.) *A Movement of Movements*, London: Verso.

Klein, N. (2014) *This Changes Everything*, London: Allen Lane.

Knill, C. & Liefferink, D. (2007) *Environmental Politics in the European Union*, Manchester: Manchester University Press.

Krugman, P. (2008) *The Return of Depression Economics and the Crisis of 2008*, London: Penguin.

Kus, B. (2006) 'Neoliberalism, Institutional Change and the Welfare State: The case of Britain and France', *International Journal of Comparative Sociology*, 47(6): 488–525.

Kymlicka, W. (2002) *Contemporary Political Philosophy*, 2nd edn, Oxford: Oxford University Press.

Kynaston, D. (2007) *Austerity Britain: 1945–51*, London: Bloomsbury.

Kynaston, D. (2009) *Family Britain: 1951–57*, London: Bloomsbury.

Kynaston, D. (2015) *Modernity Britain: 1957–62*, London: Bloomsbury.

Lansley, S. (2012) *The Cost of Inequality*, London: Gibson Square.

Lansley, S. & Mack, J. (2015) *Breadline Britain*, London: Oneworld Publications.

Lansley, S. & Reed, H. (2013) *How to Boost the Wage Share*, London: TUC.

Larkham P. & Lilley, K. (2012) 'Exhibiting the City: planning ideas and public involvement in wartime and post-war Britain', *Town Planning Review*, 83(6): 647–68.

Last, N. (2008) *Nella Last's Peace*, edited by Malcolmson, P. & Malcomson, R., London: Profile Books.

Lawson, N. (1989) 'Energy Policy', in Helm, D., Jay, J. & Thompson, D. (eds) *The Market for Energy*, Oxford: Clarendon.

Lawson, N. (1992) *The View from No. 11*, London: Bantam Press.

Le Grand, J. (1982) *The Strategy of Equality*, London: George Allen & Unwin.

Le Grand, J. (2003) *From Knight to Knave and From Pawn to Queen*, Oxford: Oxford University Press.

Legge, K. (2012) *Tackling Poverty at Home and Abroad: New Labour's public politics of poverty*, PhD thesis, University of Nottingham.

Leibfried, S. & Pierson, P. (eds) (1995) *European Social Policy*, Washington DC: The Brookings Institute.

Leontitsis, V. (2011) 'Environmental Policy', in Bache, I., George, S. & Bulmer, S. (eds) *Politics in the European Union*, Oxford: Oxford University Press.

Leopold, A. (1949) *A Sand County Almanac*, Oxford: Oxford University Press.

Letwin, S. (1993) *The Anatomy of Thatcherism*, New Brunswick, NJ: Transaction Publishers.

Levett, R. (2001) 'Sustaining Development', in Lawson, N. & Sherlock, N. (eds) *The Progressive Century*, Basingstoke: Palgrave.

Levitas, R. (2005) *The Inclusive Society?*, 2nd edn, Basingstoke: Palgrave Macmillan.

Levitas, R. (2006) 'The Concept and Measurement of Social Exclusion', in Pantazis, C., Gordon, D. & Levitas, R. (eds) *Poverty and Social Exclusion in Britain*, Bristol: Policy Press.

Leys, C. (1985) 'Thatcherism and British Manufacturing: A question of hegemony', *New Left Review*, 151: 5–25.

L'Hôte, E. (2010) 'New Labour and Globalization: Globalist discourse with a twist?', *Discourse and Society*, 21(4): 355–76.

Lindsay, T. & Harrington, M. (1979) *The Conservative Party, 1918–79*, London & Basingstoke: Macmillan.

Linklater, A. (2014) *Owning the Earth*, London: Bloomsbury.

Lister, R. (1998) 'From Equality to Social Inclusion: New Labour and the welfare state', *Critical Social Policy*, 18: 215–25.

Lister, R. (2007) 'The Real Egalitarianism? Social justice after Blair', in Hassan, G. (ed.) *After Blair*, London: Lawrence & Wishart.

Lister, R. & Bennett, F. (2010) 'The new "champion of progressive ideals"?', *Renewal*, 18(1/2). www.renewal.org.uk/articles/the-new-champion-of-progressive-ideals

Lloyd, E. (2006) 'Children, Poverty and Social Exclusion', in Pantazis, C., Gordon, D. & Levitas, R. (eds) *Poverty and Social Exclusion in Britain*, Bristol: Policy Press.

Lodge, G. (2013) 'Thatcher and North Sea Oil – A failure to invest in Britain's future', *New Statesman*, 15 April. www.newstatesman.com/politics/2013/04/thatcher-and-north-sea-oil-%E2%80%93-failure-invest-britain%E2%80%99s-future

Loft, C. (2001) 'Reappraisal and Reshaping: Government and the railway problem', *Contemporary British History*, 15(4): 71–92.

Lombroso, D. & Vinet, F. (2011) 'A Comparison of the Causes, Effects and Aftermaths of the Coastal Flooding of England in 1953 and France in 2010', *Natural Hazards and Earth Systems Sciences*, 11: 2321–33.

Lowe, P. & Ward, S. (1998) 'Lessons and Prospects: The prospects for the UK environment in Europe', in Lowe, P. & Ward, S. (eds) *British Environmental Policy and Europe*, London: Routledge.

Lowe, R. (1996) 'The Social Policy of the Heath Government', in Ball, S. & Seldon, A. (Anthony) (eds) *The Heath Government 1970–74: A Reappraisal*, London: Routledge.

Lowe, R. (2004) 'Education Policy', in Seldon, A. (Anthony) & Hickson, K. (eds) *New Labour, Old Labour*, London: Routledge.

Lowe, R. (2005) *The Welfare State in Britain since 1945*, 3rd edn, Basingstoke: Palgrave Macmillan.

Lowe, S. (2011) *The Housing Debate*, Bristol: Policy Press.

Lupton, R., Heath, N. & Salter, E. (2009) 'Education: New Labour's Top Priority', in Hills, J., Sefton, T. & Stewart, K. (eds) *Towards a More Equal Society?* Bristol: Policy Press.

Lynch, P. & Whitaker, R. (2013) 'Where there is Discord, Can they Bring Harmony? Managing intra-party dissent on European integration in the Conservative Party', *British Journal of Politics and International Relations*, 15(3): 317–39.

Lynk, E. (1993) 'Privatisation, Joint Production and the Comparative Efficiencies of Private and Public Ownership: The UK water industry case', *Fiscal Studies*, 14(2): 98–116.

Lytle, M. (2007) *Gentle Subversive: Rachel Carson, Silent Spring, and the rise of the environmental movement*, Oxford: Oxford University Press.

Macekura, S. (2011) 'The Limits of the Global Community: The Nixon administration and global environmental politics', *Cold War History*, 11(4): 489–518.

MacGregor, S. (2003) 'Social Exclusion', in Ellison, N. & Pierson, C. (eds) *Developments in British Social Policy 2*, Basingstoke: Palgrave Macmillan.

MacKay, D. & MacKay, G. (1975) *The Political Economy of North Sea Oil*, London: Martin Robertson.

Macmillan, H. (1969) *Tides of Fortune: 1945–55*, London: Macmillan.

Macmillan, H. (2003a) *The Macmillan Diaries: The cabinet years, 1950–57*, edited by Peter Caterrall, London: Macmillan.

Macmillan, H. (2003b) *The Macmillan Diaries, Vol. II: Prime Minister and after, 1957–66*, edited by Peter Caterrall, London: Macmillan.

Macrory, R. (2011) 'Weighing Up the Performance', *Journal of Environmental Law*, 23(2): 311–17.

Margo, J., Dodha, S. & Vance, R. (2007) 'State of the Nation: Audit of Britain', in Pearce, N. & Margo, J. (eds) *Politics for a New Generation*, Basingstoke: Palgrave Macmillan.

Marquand, D. (1988) *The Unprincipled Society*, London: Fontana Press.

Marquand, D. (1991) *The Progressive Dilemma*, London: Heinemann.

Marquand, D. (2004) *Decline of the Public*, Cambridge: Polity.

Marquand, D. (2009) *Britain Since 1918*, London: Pheonix.

Marquand, D. (2013) *Mammon's Kingdom*, London: Allen Lane.

Marwick, A. (1999) *The Sixties*, Oxford: Oxford University Press.

Marwick, A. (2003) *British Society Since 1945*, 4th edn, London: Penguin.

Mattausch, J. (1989) *A Commitment to Campaign*, Manchester: Manchester University Press.

Matthews, R., Feinstein, C. & Odling-Smee, J. (1982) *British Economic Growth, 1856–1973*, Stanford: Stanford University Press.

Matthijs, M. (2012) *Ideas and Economic Crises in Britain from Attlee to Blair (1945–2005)*, London: Routledge.

Mayor of London (2002) *Fifty Years On: The struggle for air quality in London since the great smog of December 1952*, London: Greater London Authority.

Mazur, L. & Saperstein, S. (2009) 'Afterword: Work for justice', in Mazur, L. (ed.) *A Pivotal Moment*, Washington DC: Island Press.

McAllister, I. & Studlar, D. (2000) 'Conservative Euroscepticism and the Referendum Party in the 1997 British General Election', *Party Politics*, 6(3): 359–71.

McCormick, J. (1989) *Acid Earth: The Global Threat of Acid Pollution*, 2nd edn, London: Routledge.

McCormick, J. (1995) *The Global Environmental Movement*, 2nd edn, Chichester: John Wiley & Sons.

McCulloch, G. (1994) *Educational Reconstruction: The 1944 Education Act and the Twenty-first Century*, Abingdon: Woburn Press.

McGowan, F. (2001) 'Social Democracy and the European Union: Who's changing whom?', in Martell, L. (ed.) *Social Democracy*, Basingstoke: Palgrave.

McGrew, A. (2004) 'Globalisation' in Plant, R., Bech, M. & Hickson, K. (eds) *The Struggle for Labour's Soul*, London: Routledge.

McKibbin, R. (1998) *Classes and Cultures*, Oxford: Oxford University Press.

McKie, R. (2015) 'Thirty years on, scientist who discovered ozone layer hole warns: "it will still take years to heal"', *Observer*, 19 April.

McManus, M. (2016) *Edward Heath*, London: Elliott & Thompson.

McQuail, P. (1994) *Origins of the DoE*, London: Department of the Environment.

McSmith, A. (2011) *No Such Thing as Society*, London: Constable.

Medhurst, J. (2014) *That Option No Longer Exists: Britain, 1974–76*, London: Zero Books.

Meek, J. (2014) *Private Island*, London: Verso.

Metcalf, D. (2005) *British Unions: Resurgence or perdition?*, London: The Work Foundation.

Mill, J. S. (1970) *Principles of Political Economy*, Middlesex: Penguin.

Milne, S. (2014) *The Enemy Within*, 4th edn, London: Verso.

Mishan, E. J. (1967) *The Costs of Economic Growth*, London: Staples Press.

Mishra, R. (1990) *Welfare State Capitalist Society*, London: Routledge.

Monbiot, G. (2003) *The Age of Consent*, London: Flamingo.

Morgan, K. (2001) *Britain Since 1945*, new edition, Oxford: Oxford University Press.

Morgan, K. (2007) *Michael Foot: A life*, London: Harper Perennial.

Morgan, K. (2011) *Ages of Reform*, London: I. B. Tauris.

Morphet, J. (2013) *How Europe Shapes British Public Policy*, Bristol: Policy Press.

Mort, F. (1989) 'The Politics of Consumption', in Hall, S. & Jacques, M. (eds) *New Times*, London: Lawrence & Wishart.

Mudd, G. (2013) 'The Limits to Growth and "Finite" Mineral Resources: Re-visiting the assumptions and drinking from that half-capacity glass', *International Journal of Sustainable Development*, 16(3–4): 204–20.

Mullainathan, S. & Shafir, E. (2013) *Scarcity*, London: Allen Lane.

Mullard, M. & Swaray, R. (2010) 'New Labour Legacy: Comparing the Labour Governments of Blair and Brown to Labour Governments since 1945', *The Political Quarterly*, 81(4): 511–21.

Murie, A. (2014) 'The Housing Legacy of Thatcherism', in Farrall, S. & Hay, C. (eds) *The Legacy of Thatcherism*, Oxford: Oxford University Press.

Murray, C. (1984) *Losing Ground*, New York: Basic Books.

Muschamp, Y., Jamieson, I. & Lauder, H. (1999) 'Education, Education, Education', in Powell, M. (ed.) *New Labour, New Welfare State?* Bristol: Policy Press.

Nehring, H. (2005) 'The Growth of Social Movements' in Addison, P. & Jones, H. (eds) *A Companion to Contemporary Britain 1939–2000*, Oxford: Blackwell.

Nelson, G. with Campbell, S. & Wozniak, P. (2002) *Beyond Earth Day*, Madison: University of Wisconsin Press.

Newman, J. & Clarke, J. (2009) *Publics, Politics and Power*, London: Sage.

Nickell, S., Redding, S. & Swaffield, J. (2008) 'The Uneven Pace of Deindustrialisation in the OECD', *The World Economy*, 31(9): 1154–84.

O'Hara, G. (2012) *Governing Post-War Britain: The Paradoxes of Progress, 1951–1973*, London: Palgrave Macmillan.

O'Mahony, M. & Vecchi, M. (2001) *The Electricity Supply Industry: A study of an industry in transition*, National Institute Economic Review, No. 177.

Oakeshott, M. (1991) *Rationalism in Politics and Other Essays*, Indianapolis: Liberty Fund.

Oberthür, S. (2011) 'The European Union's Performance in the International Climate Change Regime', *Journal of European Integration*, 33(6): 667–82.

Office for National Statistics (2013) *170 Years of Industrial Change across England and Wales* www.ons.gov.uk/ons/rel/census/2011-census-analysis/170-years-of-industry/170-years-of-industrial-changeponent.html

Oppenheim, C. (2001) 'Enabling Participation? New Labour's welfare-to-work policies', in White, S. (ed.) *New Labour*, Basingstoke: Palgrave.

Oreskes, N. & Conway, E. (2011) *Merchants of Doubt*, London: Bloomsbury.

O'Riordan, T. & Cameron, J. (1994) *Interpreting the Precautionary Principle*, London: Routledge.

Orton, M. & Rowlingson, K. (2007) *Public Attitudes to Economic Inequality*, York: JRF.

Orwell, G. (1962) *The Road to Wigan Pier*, Middlesex: Penguin.

Orwell, G. (1998) *Smothered Under Journalism*, London: Secker & Warburg.

Ostrom, E. (2012) *The Future of the Commons: Beyond market failure and government regulation*, London: IEA.

Page, M. (2003) 'Transport and Social Policy', in Ellison, N. & Pierson, C. (eds) *Developments in British Social Policy 2*, Basingstoke: Palgrave Macmillan.

Page, R. (2015) *Clear Blue Water?* Bristol: Policy Press.

Panitch, L. & Leys, C. (1997) *The End of Parliamentary Socialism*, London: Verso.

Park, A., Bryson, C., Clery, E., Curtice, J. & Phillips, M. (eds) (2013) *British Social Attitudes: the 30th Report*, London: NatCen Social Research.

Parker, C. & Karlsson, C. (2010) 'Climate Change and the European Union's Leadership Moment: An inconvenient Truth.' *Journal of Common Market Studies*, 48(4): 923–43.

Parker, M. (2000) *Thatcherism and the Fall of Coal*, Oxford: Oxford University Press.

Paton, C. (2002) 'Cheques and Checks: New Labour's Record on the NHS', in Powell, M. (ed.) *Evaluating New Labour's Welfare Reforms*, Bristol: Policy Press.

Payne, A. (2006) 'Blair, Brown and the Gleneagles agenda: Making poverty history, or confronting the global politics of unequal development?', *International Affairs*, 82(5): 917–35.

Pearce, D. (1991) 'Introduction', in Pearce, D. (ed.) *Blueprint 2*, London: Earthscan.

Pearce, D. & Barbier, E. (2000) *Blueprint for a Sustainable Economy*, London: Earthscan.

Pearson, P. & Watson, J. (2012) *UK Energy Policy, 1980–2010*, London: The Parliamentary Group for Energy Studies.

Pemberton, H. (2012) 'The Failure of "Nationalization by Attraction": Britain's cross-class alliance against earnings-related pensions in the 1950s', *Economic History Review*, 65(4): 1428–49.

Pierson, P. (ed.) (2001) *The New Politics of the Welfare State*, Oxford: Oxford University Press.

Pimlott, B. (1985) *Hugh Dalton*, Jonathan Cape.

Pimlott, B. (1992) *Harold Wilson*, London: HarperCollins.

Plachciak, A. (2013) 'The Issue of International Development within Tony Blair's Policy of New Labour Party', *Economics & Sociology*, 6(2): 171–9.

Plant, R. (2004a) 'End, Means and Political Identity' in Plant, R., Bech, M. & Hickson, K. (eds) *The Struggle for Labour's Soul*, London: Routledge.

Plant, R. (2004b) 'Political Thought: Socialism in a cold climate', in Seldon, A. (Anthony) & Hickson, K. (eds) *New Labour, Old Labour*, London: Routledge.

Pollard, M. (1978) *North Sea Surge*, Lavenham: Lavenham Press.

Pollock, A. (2004) *NHS plc*, London: Verso.

Porteous, T. (2005) 'British Government Policy in Sub-Saharan Africa under New Labour', *International Affairs*, 81(2): 281–97.

Powell, M. (1999) 'Introduction', in Powell, M. (ed.) *New Labour, New Welfare State?* Bristol: Policy Press.

Power, A. (2009) 'New Labour and Unequal Neighbourhoods', in Hills, J., Sefton, T. & Stewart, K. (eds) *Towards a More Equal Society?* Bristol: Policy Press.

Prabhakar, R. (2003) *Stakeholding and New Labour*, Basingstoke: Palgrave Macmillan.

Prescott, J. (2009) *Docks to Downing Street*, London: Headline.

Pugh, M. (2010) *Speak for Britain!* London: The Bodley Head.

Radice, G. (2008) *The Tortoise and the Hares*, London: Politico's.

Raison, T. (1990) *Tories and the Welfare State*, Basingstoke: Macmillan.

Ramsden, J. (1995) *The Age of Churchill and Eden, 1940–57*, London: Longman.

Rawnsley, A. (2000) *Servants of the People*, London: Hamish Hamilton.

Rawnsley, A. (2010) *The End of the Party*, London: Penguin.

Rayner, T., Russel, D. & Lorenzoni, I. (2008) '"It's Demand, Stupid": The failure and future of integrating climate change concerns into UK transport policy', *British Politics*, 3: 373–89.

Reich, R. (1991) *The Work of Nations*, New York: Alfred A. Knopf.

Rhodes, C. (2014) *Manufacturing: Statistics and policy*, SN/EP/1942, London: House of Commons Library.

Rhodes, M. (2007) 'The European Project Renewed', in Pearce, N. & Margo, J. (eds) *Politics for a New Generation*, Basingstoke: Palgrave Macmillan.

Rhodes, R. (1988) *The Making of the Atomic Bomb*, Middlesex: Penguin.

Richards, K. (1993) 'Redistribution under Conservatism: Past and future', in Healey, N. (ed.) *Britain's Economic Miracle: Myth or reality?*, London: Routledge.

Richards, S. (2010) *Whatever it Takes*, London: Fourth Estate.

Ritschel, D. (1995) 'Macmillan', in George, V. & Page, R. (eds) *Modern Thinkers in Welfare*, Hemel Hempstead: Prentice Hall/Harvester Wheatsheaf.

Ritzer, G. (2010) *Globalization*, London: Wiley-Blackwell.

Roberts, I. (2000) 'Leicester Environment City: Learning how to make Local Agenda 21, partnerships and participation deliver', *Environment and Urbanization*, 12(2): 9–26.

Robinson, C. (1981) 'North Sea Oil: A Chance to Change?', in Gaskin, M. (ed.) *The Political Economy of Tolerable Survival*, London: Croom Helm.

Robinson, E. (2015) 'History, Nostalgia and the Re-writing of Clause IV', paper presented to the PSA Annual International Conference, 30 March–1 April 2015, City Hall and Town Hall, Sheffield.

Robinson, N. (2005) 'Transport Policy', in Dorey, P. (ed.) *Developments in British Public Policy*, London: Sage.

Rogers, A. (1993) *The Earth Summit*, Los Angeles: Global View Press.

Rome, A. (2003) '"Give Earth a Chance": The Environmental Movement and the Sixties', *The Journal of American History*, 90(2): 525–54.

Root, A. (2000) 'Transport and Communications', in Halsey, A. H. with Webb, J. (eds) *Twentieth-Century British Social Trends*, Basingstoke: Macmillan.

Rootes, C. (2003a) 'The Transformation of Environmental Activism: An introduction', in Rootes, C. (ed.) *Environmental Protest in Western Europe*, Oxford: Oxford University Press.

Rootes, C. (2003b) 'Britain', in Rootes, C. (ed.) *Environmental Protest in Western Europe*, Oxford: Oxford University Press.

Rose, C. (1990) *The Dirty Man of Europe*, London: Simon & Schuster.

Ross, G. (1995) 'Assessing the Delors Era and Social Policy', in Leibfried, S. & Pierson, P. (eds) *European Social Policy*, Washington DC: The Brookings Institute.

Rowbotham, S. (1997) *A Century of Women*, London: Viking.

Rowe, J. (2000) 'The Local Agenda 21 Issue Commission in Bath and North-East Somerset: Review of a community consultation exercise towards sustainability', *Local Government Studies*, 26(2): 71–92.

Rowntree, S. & Lavers, G. (1951) *Poverty and the Welfare State*, London: Longmans Green & Co.

Rutledge, I. (2007) 'New Labour, Energy Policy and "Competitive Markets"', *Cambridge Journal of Economics*, 31: 901–25.

Rydin, Y. (2003) *Urban and Environmental Planning in the UK*, 2nd edn, Basingstoke: Palgrave.

Sainsbury, R. (2003) 'Understanding Social Security Fraud', in Millar, J. (ed.) *Understanding Social Security*, Bristol: Policy Press.

Sandbrook, D. (2005) *Never Had It So Good*, London: Little, Brown.

Sandbrook, D. (2006) *White Heat: 1964–70*, London: Little, Brown.

Sandbrook, D. (2011) *State of Emergency*, London: Penguin.

Sandbrook, D. (2013) *Seasons in the Sun*, London: Penguin.

Sandel, M. (2012) *What Money Can't Buy*, London: Allen Lane.

Sanderson, J. B. (1961) 'The National Smoke Abatement Society and the Clean Air Act (1956)', *Political Studies*, 9(3): 236–53.

Sapsford, D., Johnes, G., Harvey, A. & de Kervenoael, R. (1997) 'British Employers and the Social Chapter: Some survey evidence', *Industrial Relations Journal*, 28(3): 236–42.

Sassi, F. (2009) 'Health Inequalities: A persistent problem', in Hills, J., Sefton, T. & Stewart, K. (eds) *Towards a More Equal Society?* Bristol: Policy Press.

Sbragia, A. M. (2000) 'Environmental Policy', in Wallace, H. & Wallace, W. (eds) *Policy-Making in the European Union*, Oxford: Oxford University Press.

Schaefer, A. (2009) 'Corporate Greening and Changing Regulatory Regimes: the UK water industry', *Business Strategy and the Environment*, 18: 320–33.

Schlipphak, B. & Mause, K. (2015) 'Increasing Winners-Losers Gap? Increasing Euroscepticism? Exploring the Economic Crisis' Conflict Potential', in Krieger, T., Neumärker, B. & Panke, D. (eds) *Europe's Crisis*, Baden-Baden: Nomos.

Schreurs, M. & Tiberghien, Y. (2010) 'European Union Leadership in Climate Change', in Harrison, K. & Sundstrom, L. (eds) *Global Commons, Domestic Decisions*, Cambridge, Mass.: MIT Press.

Schumacher, E. F. (1973) *Small is Beautiful*, New York: Harper & Row.

Scott Cato, M. (2009) *Green Economics*, London: Earthscan.

Scruton, R. (2006) *A Political Philosophy*, London: Continuum.

Scruton, R. (2013) *Green Philosophy*, London: Atlantic Books.

Seawright, D. (2005) 'One Nation', in Hickson, K. (ed.) *The Political Thought of the Conservative Party since 1945*, Basingstoke: Palgrave Macmillan.

Sefton, T., Hills, J. & Sutherland, H. (2009) 'Poverty, Inequality and Redistribution', in Hills, J., Sefton, T. & Stewart, K. (eds) *Towards a More Equal Society?*, Bristol: Policy Press.

Seldon. A. (Anthony) (2004) *Blair*, London: Simon & Schuster.

Seldon, A. (Anthony) (2007) *Blair Unbound*, London: Pocket Books.

Seldon, A. (Anthony) (2010) *An End to Factory Schools: An education manifesto, 2010–2020*, London: Centre for Policy Studies.

Seldon, A. (Anthony) with Baston, l. (1997) *Major: A political life*, London: Weidenfeld & Nicolson.

Seldon, A. (Anthony) & Lodge, G. (2010) *Brown at 10*, London: Biteback Publishing.

Seldon, A. (Arthur) (1968) *After the N.H.S.*, London: IEA.

Selman, P. (1998) 'Local Agenda 21: Substance or spin?', *Journal of Environmental Planning and Management*, 41(5): 533–53.

Shabecoff, P. (1988) 'Global Warming Has Begun, Expert Tells Senate', *New York Times*, June 24.

Shaw, R., Attree, M. & Jackson, T. (2010) 'Developing Electricity Distribution Networks and their Regulation to Support Sustainable Energy', *Energy Policy*, 38: 5927–37.

Sheail, J. (2002) *An Environmental History of Twentieth Century Britain*, Palgrave Macmillan.

Sheail, J. (2007) '"Torrey Canyon": The political dimension', *Journal of Contemporary History*, 42(3): 485–504.

Shepard, B. & Hayduk, R. (eds) (2002) *From ACT UP to the WTO*, London: Verso.

Simon, J. & Kahn, H. (1998) 'Introduction to *The Resourceful Earth*', in Dryzek, J. & Schlosberg, D. (eds) *Debating the Earth*, Oxford: Oxford University Press.

Skidelsky, R. (2003) *John Maynard Keynes*, London: Macmillan.

Skidelsky, R. & Skidelsky, E. (2012) *How Much is Enough?*, London: Allen Lane.

Skovgaard, J. (2014) 'EU Climate Policy after the Crisis', *Environmental Politics*, 23(1): 1–17.

Smith, C. (2013) 'Adam Smith and the New Right', in Berry, C., Paganelli, M. & Smith, C. (eds) *The Oxford Handbook of Adam Smith*, Oxford: Oxford University Press.

Smith, G. (2000) 'Schools', in Halsey, A. H. with Webb, J. (eds) *Twentieth-Century British Social Trends*, Basingstoke: Macmillan.

Smith, J. (2005) 'A Missed Opportunity? New Labour's European policy 1997–2005', *International Affairs*, 81: 703–21.

Smith Wilson, D. (2005) 'Gender: Change and continuity', in Addison, P. & Jones, H. (eds) *A Companion to Contemporary Britain 1939–2000*, Oxford: Blackwell.

Snowdon, C. (2015) *Selfishness, Greed and Capitalism*, London: IEA.

Social Mobility and Child Poverty Commission (2014) *Elitist Britain*. www.gov.uk/government/uploads/.../Elitist_Britain_-_Final.pdf

Sorkin, A. R. (2009) *Too Big to Fail*, London: Allen Lane.

Spencer, N. & Dowler, E. (2007) 'Introduction', in Dowler, E. & Spencer, N. (eds) *Challenging Health Inequalities*, Bristol: Policy Press.

Stephens, J. C., Hansson, A., Lui, Y., de Coninck, H. & Vajjhala, S. (2011) 'Characterising the International Carbon Capture and Storage Community', *Global Environmental Change*, 21(2): 379–90.

Stern, N. (2007) *The Economics of Climate Change*, Cambridge: Cambridge University Press.

Stern, N. (2009) *A Blueprint for a Safer Planet*, London: The Bodley Head.

Stevenson, J. (2003) 'The Countryside, Planning, and Civil Society in Britain, 1926–1947', in Harris, J. (ed.) *Civil Society in British History: Ideas, Identities, Institutions*, Oxford: Oxford University Press.

Stewart, K. (2009a) '"A Scar on the Soul of Britain": Child poverty and disadvantage under New labour', in Hills, J., Sefton, T. & Stewart, K. (eds) *Towards a More Equal Society?* Bristol: Policy Press.

Stewart, K. (2009b) 'Poverty, Inequality and Child Well-Being in International Context: Still bottom of the pack?', in Hills, J., Sefton, T. & Stewart, K. (eds) *Towards a More Equal Society?* Bristol: Policy Press.

Stewart, K. (2012) 'Child Poverty: What have we really achieved?' in CPAG (ed.) *Ending Child Poverty by 2020: Progress made and lessons learned*, London: CPAG.

Stiglitz, J. (2010) *Freefall*, London: Allen Lane.

Streeck, W. (1995) 'From Market Making to State Building? Reflections on the political economy of European social policy', in Leibfried, S. & Pierson, P. (eds) *European Social Policy*, Washington DC: The Brookings Institute.

Tawney, R. H. (1952) *Equality*, 4th edn, Totowa, New Jersey: Barnes and Noble.

Tawney, R. H. (2004) *The Acquisitive Society*, New York: Dover Publications.

Taylor, H. (1997) *A Claim on the Countryside*, Edinburgh: Keele University Press.

Taylor, N. (1998) *Urban Planning Theory since 1945*, London: Sage.

Taylor, R. (2004) 'The Rise and Fall of the Social Contract', in Seldon, A. (Anthony) & Hickson, K. (eds) *New Labour, Old Labour*, London: Routledge.

Taylor, R. (2006) *Major*, London: Haus Publishing.

Taylor, R. K. (1991) 'Environment, Economics, and Ethics', in Pearce, D. (ed.) *Blueprint 2*, London: Earthscan.

Taylor-Gooby, P. (1996) 'The United Kingdon: Radical departures and political consensus', in George, V. & Taylor-Gooby, P. (eds) *European Welfare Policy*, Basingstoke: Macmillan.

Taylor-Gooby, P. (2005) 'UK Pension Reform: A Test Case for a Liberal Welfare State?', in Bonoli, G. and Shinkawa, T. (eds) (2005) *Ageing and Pension Reform Around the World*, Aldershot: Edward Elgar.

Thatcher, M. (1990) *Our Threatened Environment*, London: Conservative Political Centre.

The Economist (2008) 'Cheap or Green? When poverty and greenery collide', *The Economist*, 7 August.

Thomas, K. (1983) *Man and the Natural World*, London: Allen Lane.

Thompson, E. P. (1976) *William Morris*, rvd edition, London: Merlin Press.

Thompson, N. (2006) 'The Fabian Political Economy of Harold Wilson', in Dorey, P. (ed.) *The Labour Governments, 1964–70*, London: Routledge.

Thorpe, D. R. (2010) 'Lord Walker: Durable left-of-centre Conservative politician who served in government under Heath and Thatcher', *Independent*, 24 June.

Thorpe, D. R. (2011) *Supermac: The life of Harold Macmillan*, London: Pimlico.

Thorsheim, P. (2006) *Inventing Pollution*, Ohio University Press.

Tickell, O. (2008) *Kyoto2*, London: Zed Books.

Timmins, N. (2001) *The Five Giants*, revised edition, London: HarperCollins.

Titmuss, R. (1950) *Problems of Social Policy*, London: HMSO & Longmans.

Titmuss, R. (1970) *The Gift Relationship*, London: George Allen & Unwin.

Todd, S. (2014) *The People*, London: John Murray.

Tomlinson, J. (1997) *Democratic Socialism and Economic Policy*, Cambridge: Cambridge University Press.

Tomlinson, J. (2004) 'Economic Policy', in Seldon, A. (Anthony) & Hickson, K. (eds) *New Labour, Old Labour*, London: Routledge.

Tomlinson, J. (2005) 'Managing the Economy, Managing the People: Britain c.1931–70', *Economic History Review*, 58(3): 555–85.

Tomlinson, J. (2014) 'British Government and Popular Understanding of Inflation in the Mid-1970s', *Economic History Review*, 67(3): 750–68.

Toye, R. (2013) *The Roar of the Lion*, Oxford: Oxford University Press.

Toynbee, P. & Walker, D. (2001) *Did Things get Better?* Middlesex: Penguin.

Toynbee, P. & Walker, D. (2004) 'Social Policy and Inequality', in Seldon, A. (Anthony) & Hickson, K. (eds) *New Labour, Old Labour*, London: Routledge.

Toynbee, P. & Walker, D. (2005) *Better or Worse?*, London: Bloomsbury.

Toynbee, P. & Walker, D. (2009) *Unjust Rewards*, London: Granta Publications.

Toynbee, P. & Walker, D. (2010) *The Verdict*, London: Granta Publications.

Turner, G. & Alexander, C. (2014) 'Limits to Growth was Right. New research shows we're nearing collapse', *Guardian*, 2 September.

Turner, R. (1995a) 'Introduction', in Turner, R. (ed.) *British Economy in Transition*, London: Routledge.

Turner, R. (1995b) 'Conclusions', in Turner, R. (ed.) *British Economy in Transition*, London: Routledge.

Tuxworth, B. (1996) 'From Environment to Sustainability: Surveys and analysis of Local Agenda 21 process development in UK local authorities', *Local Environment*, 1(3): 277–97.

Uekötter, F. (2007) 'Green Nazis? Reassessing the environmental history of Nazi Germany', *German Studies Review*, 2: 267–87.

Unander, F., Karbuz, S., Schipper, L. Khrushch, M. & Ting, M. (1999) 'Manufacturing Energy Use in OECD countries: Decomposition of long-term trends', *Energy Policy*, 36: 769–78.

United Nations (2015) *The Millennium Development Goals Report 2015*, New York: United Nations.

Urry, J. (2011) *Climate Change and Society*, Cambridge: Polity.

Vandenbroucke, F. & Vleminckx, K. (2011) 'Disappointing Poverty Trends: Is the social investment state to blame?', *Journal of European Social Policy*, 21(5): 450–71.

Veith, S. (2010) *EU Emission Trading Scheme*, Bern: Peter Lang.

Verrinder, G. (2011) 'Health and Environment', in Fitzpatrick, T. (ed.) *Understanding the Environment and Social Policy*, Bristol: Policy Press.

Viereck, P. (2006) *Conservative Thinkers: From John Adams to Winston Churchill*, New Brunswick, NJ: Transaction Publishers.

Vlachou, A. (2014) 'The European Union's Emissions Trading System', *Cambridge Journal of Economics*, 38: 127–52.

Voisey, H. (1998) 'Local Agenda 21 in the UK', in O'Riordan, T. & Voisey, H. (eds) *The Transition to Sustainability*, London: Earthscan.

Voisey, H. & O'Riordan, T. (1998) 'Sustainable Development: The UK national approach', in O'Riordan, T. & Voisey, H. (eds) *The Transition to Sustainability*, London: Earthscan.

Waine, B. (1995) 'A Disaster Foretold? The case of personal pensions', *Social Policy & Administration*, 29(4): 317–34.

Waldfogel, J. (2010) *Britain's War on Poverty*, New York: Russell Sage Foundation.

Walker, A., Sinfield, A. & Walker, C. (eds) *Fighting Poverty, Inequality and Injustice*, Bristol: Policy Press.

Walker, C. (2014) '"Don't Cut Down the Tall Poppies": Thatcherism and the strategy of inequality', in Farrall, S. & Hay, C. (eds) *The Legacy of Thatcherism*, Oxford: Oxford University Press.

Walker, G. & King, D. (2008) *The Hot Topic*, London: Bloomsbury.

Wall, D. (1999) *Earth First! and the Anti-Roads Movement: Radical environmentalism and comparative social movements*, London: Routledge.

Wall, D. (2010) *Rise of the Green Left: Inside the worldwide ecosocialist movement*, London: Pluto Press.

Wallerstein, I. (2004) 'New Revolts against the System', in Mertes, T. (ed.) *A Movement of Movements*, London: Verso.

Walsh, M. & Wrigley, C. (2001) 'Womanpower: The transformation of the labour force in the UK and USA since 1945', *Refresh*, 30: 1–4.

Walsha, R. (2003) 'The One Nation Group and One Nation Conservatism', *Contemporary British History*, 17(2): 69–120.

Wapshott, N. (2012) *Keynes/Hayek: The clash that defined modern economics*, London: W. W. Norton & Co.

Ward, B. (1972) *Only One Earth*, Middlesex: Penguin.

Weale, A. (1992) *The New Politics of Pollution*, Manchester: Manchester University Press.

Webb, J. (Josephine) (2000) 'Social Security', in Halsey, A. H. with Webb, J. (eds) *Twentieth-Century British Social Trends*, Basingstoke: Macmillan.

Webb, J. (Janette) (2009) 'Gender and Occupation in Market Economies: Change and restructuring since the 1980s', *Social Politics*, 16(1): 82–110.

Webster, C. (2002) *National Health Service: A political history*, 2nd edn, Oxford: Oxford University Press.

Weight, R. (2003) *Patriots*, London: Pan Books.

Weiler, P. (2000) 'The Rise and Fall of the Conservatives' "Grand Design for Housing", 1951–64', *Contemporary British History*, 14(1): 122–50.

Wells, J. (1993) 'The Economy after Ten Years: Stringer or weaker?', in Healey, N. (ed.) *Britain's Economic Miracle: Myth or reality?*, London: Routledge.

West, P. (1998) 'Market – what Market? A review of health authority purchasing in the NHS internal market', *Health Policy*, 44(2): 167–83.

Westaway, T. (1980) 'Stabilisation Policy and Fiscal Reform', in Maunder, W. (ed.) *The British Economy in the 1970s*, London: Heinemann.

Wickham-Jones, M. (2004) 'The New Left', in Plant, R., Bech, M. & Hickson, K. (eds) *The Struggle for Labour's Soul*, London: Routledge.

Wilkinson, R. & Pickett, K. (2009) *The Spirit Level*, London: Allen Lane.

Williams, F. (1961) *A Prime Minister Remembers*, London: Heinemann.

Wincott, D., Buller, J. & Hay, C. (1999) 'Strategic Errors and/or Structiral Binds? Major and European integration', in Dorey. P. (ed.) *The Major Premiership*, Basingstoke, Macmillan.

Winskel, M. (2002) 'When Systems Are Overthrown: The "Dash for Gas" in the British electricity supply industry', *Social Studies of Science*, 32(4): 563–98.

Wise, W. (1968) *Killer Smog*, Chicago: Rand McNally.

Wolmar, C. (2007) *Fire and Steam*, London: Atlantic Books.

Wood, B. & Carter, J. (2000) 'Towns, Urban Change and Local Government', in Halsey, A. H. with Webb, J. (eds) *Twentieth-Century British Social Trends*, Basingstoke: Macmillan.

World Commission on Environment and Development (1987) *Our Common Future*, Oxford: Oxford University Press.

World Health Organisation (1997) *City Planning for Health and Sustainable Development*, Copenhagen: WHO Regional Office for Europe.

Wright, E. O. (2010) *Envisioning Real Utopias*, London: Verso.

Wynne, B. & Simmons, P. with Waterton, C., Hughes, P. & Shackley, S. (2001) 'Institutional Cultures and the Management of Global Environmental Risks in the United Kingdom', in The Social Learning Group, *Learning to Manage Global Environmental Risks, Volume 1: A Comparative History of Social Responses to Climate Change, Ozone Depletion and Acid Rain*, Cambridge, Mass.: The MIT Press.

Yearley, S. & Forrester, J. (2000) 'Shell, a Sure Target for Global Environmental Campaigning?' in Cohen, R. & Rai, S. (eds) *Global Social Movements*, London: Athlone Press.

Yorkshire Post (2013) 'Amateur Radio Fans Mark Flood Anniversary', *Yorkshire Post*, 25 November.

Young, H. (1990) *One of Us*, London: Pan Books.

Ziegler, P. (2010) *Edward Heath*, London: Harper Press.

Zijderveld, A. (1999) *The Waning of the Welfare State*, London: Transaction.

Zweiniger-Bargielowska, I. (2005) 'Living Standards and Consumption', in Addison, P. & Jones, H. (eds) *A Companion to Contemporary Britain 1939–2000*, Oxford: Blackwell.

Index

Page numbers in **bold** denote figures; those with 'n' refer to notes.

Aalborg Charter 160
acid rain 2, 107–8, 109, 110, 133
Addison, P. 11
Agenda 21 151–2
atomic bomb 53
Attlee, Clement 60
Austerity Britain (Kynaston) 10–11

Baggott, R. 140
Baldwin, Stanley 35
banks 222, 223–4
Baxter, P. 45, 47, 48
Beeching, Richard 56–7
Benn, Tony 95–6, 100, 105–6, 114
Better Quality of Life, A 183–5, 188
betterment levy 20–1, 36, 37–8
Bevan, Aneurin 17, 21, 62, 63
Beveridge Report 11, 23, 28, 63, 122
Blair, Tony 161, 169, 170, 171, 172, 194, 197
Blueprint for a Green Economy (Pearce) 136
Blundell, V. H. 20
Bond, A. 160
Boulding, Kenneth 70
Bourguignon, F. 194–5
Bretton Woods system 78
Brower, David 87
Brown, Gordon 171, 173, 194, 200, 210–13, 223–4
Brundtland Commission 132–3
Burke, Edmund 35
Burns, C. 200
Butler, R. A. 29, 32–3

Cahill, M. 39
Callaghan, James 97, 104, 111n3

Campaign for Nuclear Disarmament (CND) 54–5
capitalism 12, 105, 174, 235; deregulated capitalism 6–7; free market capitalism 30; Keynesian view of 13–15; welfare state capitalism 68, 91, 95–6
car ownership 55, 57, 135
Carson, Rachel 70–1
Carter, N. 150, 186, 206, 218–19
Castle, Barbara 65
Central Electricity Generating Board (CEGB) 108
Child Support Agency (CSA) 161–2
Child Trust Fund 204
chlorofluorocarbons 133
Church of England 123
Churchill, Winston 27–8, 31, 32, 36, 44–5, 50
Clean Air Act (1956) 46–7, 48, 49, 57, 58, 109, 110, 145, 231
Clean Development Mechanism (CDM) 201–2
climate change 2, 119–20, 132, 133–4, 134–5, 137, 147, 151, 159, 193, 232; Climate Change Levy 182; connection with poverty 197; EU policy 197–9, 220–1; Stern's report on, 2007 217
Climate Change Act (2008) 217–18
Climate Change: the UK Programme (DETR) 186
Club of Rome 88–9
coal industry 15, 118–20
Commoner, B. 85, 105
Conservation Society 86
Conservative government (1951–55) 27–41; conservative welfare state 33–4; consumerism 38–40; environmental

Conservative government (1951–55)
  continued
  policy 36–8; nature and the
  Conservatives 35–8; 'one-nation
  conservatism' 29, 91; social reforms
  32–5; two conservatisms 30–1
Conservative government (1979–87)
  113–30; coal industry, decline of
  118–20; environmental policy 126–8;
  inequality 122–5; miners' strike
  (1984–85) 118–19; new parties 125–6; a
  new philosophy 114–16; social reforms
  120–2; state and economy, refashioning
  of 116–20
Conservative Party 11, 28–9; market voice
  30–1; middle way conservatism 29, 32,
  33, 50; Selsdon agenda 79–80; social
  voice 30–1
Conservative policies (1990–97) 149–68;
  'Back to Basics' rhetoric 162–3;
  environmental policy 157–9;
  environmentalism in the 1990s 150–2;
  EU Social Chapter 163–4, 166; Europe
  united 155–9; globalisation 152–3, 164,
  165; green movements 153–5; local
  agendas 159–61; politics of the globe
  150–2; relationship between social and
  environmental policy agendas 165–7;
  social Europe 164–5; social reforms 161–4
consumerism 6, 38–40, 70, 71, 126
Control of Pollution Act (1974) 90, 127
Convention on Long-Range
  Transboundary Air Pollution 108
Copenhagen Summit (2009) 220–1
Council for the Preservation of Rural
  England 22
countryside, access to 21–2, 73
Countryside Alliance 181
Craig, D. 212
Crewe, I. 19
Criminal Justice and Public Order Act
  (1994) 154
Crosland, Tony 18, 62, 66, 91, 104–5, 106
Cullingworth, B. 37, 38
currency problems 78, 98, 144, 149–50

Daly, H. 13, 15
Dancing with Dogma (Gilmour) 113–14
Darling, Alistair 224–5
DEFRA 187
Dekkers, C. 200
democracy 123, 153
Department of the Environment (DoE)
  89–91, 92, 108, 157, 159, 231

Department of the Environment,
  Transport and the Regions (DETR)
  182, 183, 187
Disability Discrimination Act (1995) 162
disasters: Chernobyl 132; cleaning the air
  46–7; environment and government
  48–9; flood prevention 47–8; flooding
  44–5, 57, 110; Macmillan's response to
  52–3; media reports 45; nuclear
  accidents 54; smog 2, 24, 42–3, 45, 46,
  57, 110; *Torrey Canyon* 69, 73–4, 75
Disraeli, Benjamin 28–9
Dobson, A. 201
Dorling, D. 123

Earth Day 77
Earth Summit (1992) 150–2
Ecologist, The 87–8
'Economic Consequences for Our
  Grandchildren' (Keynes) 12
economic policy 64–5, 81–2, 84;
  Conservative government (1979–87)
  116–20; environmental economics 84,
  136–7; Labour government (1974–79)
  96–9
education 29, 33–4, 51, 66–7, 82–3,
  103–4, 179–80, 205, 214; National
  Curriculum and league tables 137–9
Education Act (1944) 16, 29
Ehrlich, Paul 71–2, 86
electricity 143–4, 186
Emissions Trading Scheme (ETS) 193,
  199–201, 208, 234
Employment Relations Act (1999) 172
Energy Act (2008) 219
energy production 84, 85, 118, 218–19;
  electricity privatisation 143; energy
  markets 193–4; North Sea gas and oil
  99–101; renewables 186
Environment Act (1995) 159
Environment Agency 159, 182
Environmental Action Programmes
  (EAPs) 155–6, 193
environmental policy: Conservative
  government (1951–55) 36–8;
  Conservative government (1970–74)
  84–91; Conservative government
  (1979–87) 126–8; Conservative policies
  (1990–97) 157–9; ecosocial system,
  building of 236, **237**; election
  manifestoes 150; environmentalism in
  the 1990s 150–2; EU influence 156–7;
  future policy-making 232–41; global
  politics 88–9; Labour government

(1964–70) 69–74; Labour government (1997–2001) 180–7; Labour government (1997–2005) 206–7; Labour government (2005–10) 216–21; marketisation 231–2; political philosophy of the ecosocial 234–5; relationship with social policy agenda 1–3, 8, 24–5, 48–9, 57–8, 74–5, 92–3, 109–11, 145–7, 165–7, 187–8, 208–9, 226–7, 229–41, **230**; residual and weak sectoral integration 231; weak modernisation 232
Equality (Joseph and Sumption) 123, 125
Etzioni, A. 173
European Economic Community (EEC) 65, 96, 144, 146
European Union (EU) 155–9, 165–6; and climate policy 197–9, 220–1; environmental policy 166; and New Labour 191–4; Social Chapter 163–4, 166, 172, 191; social policy 164–5
Euroscepticism 164
Evans, B. 161
exchange rate mechanism (ERM) 144, 149–50
externalities 7, 56, 120, 136

Faith in the City (Church of England) 123
Family Allowances Act (1945) 16
Farlow, A. 223, 224
financial crash (2008) 221–5
Financial Services Authority (FSA) 224–5
flooding 2, 44–5, 57, 110; prevention 47–8
Fowler, Norman 122
free markets 6–8, 115, 125, 137, 166, 232, 234
Friends of The Earth (FoE) 87, 154
Future of Socialism, The (Crosland) 62

G8 197
Gaitskell, Hugh 62, 63
Galbraith, J. K. 70, 124
General Theory of Employment, Interest and Money, The (Keynes) 14
Geyer, R. 165
Giddens, Tony 173–4, 175, 180, 226
gift exchange notion 235
Gilbertson, T. 200–1
Gilmour, Ian 113–14
Gleneagles Summit 197, 206
global warming 132, 146–7
globalisation 152–3, 164, 165, 171–3, 190, 192
Goldsmith, Edward 87–8

Gordon, G. 47–8
green belts 19, 37
green movements 86–8, 91, 109, 153–5, 206
Green Party 87
greenhouse effect 2, 131–2
Greenpeace 87, 154

Hansen, James 131–2, 133, 202
Hardin, G. 71
Harris, P. 198
Hattersley, Roy 66–7, 174
Hayek, Friedrich 50, 123
Healey, Denis 96, 98, 99
Heath, Edward 79, 80–2, 89
Helm, D. 118
Hill, Octavia 22
Hogg, Q. 31
Holland, Stuart 105–6
Housing (Homeless Persons) Act (1977) 103
housing policy 19, 21, 83, 205–6, 215; council house sales 121; homelessness 103, 122; rent controls 51, 66; slum clearance 38
Hutton, Will 170

In Place of Fear (Bevan) 62
In Place of Strife (Wilson and Castle) 65, 96
individualism 115, 122, 126, 203
industrial relations 117; miners' strike (1984–85) 118–19
industry 117–18; coal industry 118–20; deindustrialisation 100, 118, 119, 120–1; voluntary agreements with regulators 158
inequality 122–5, 170, 187, 195, 215–16
inflation 52, 81, 84, 96–8, 116, 144
international development 194–5
International Monetary Fund (IMF) 98

Jacobs, M. 218–19
Joseph, Keith 80, 82, 83, 123, 125
Joyce, R. 215, 216

Kahn, H. 71
Keegan, W. 224
Keep Left group 61, 62
Keynes, John Maynard 12–13, 31, 84, 191; and nature 13–15
King, A. 19
Kinnock, Neil 125–6, 169

Klein, N. 236
Knill, C. 157
Kyoto Protocol 181, 191, 193, 195–6, 198, 208; emissions trading 199–201; offsets trading 201–2

Labour government (1945–51) 10–26; countryside policy 21–4; forgotten environmentalism 18–19; Keynes and nature 13–15; Keynes's revolution 12–13; nationalisation 15–16; planning and housing policy 19–21; relationship between social and environmental policy agendas 24–5; social reform 16–18
Labour government (1974–79) 95–112; air pollution and acid rain 107–8, 109, 110; economic policy 96–9; Labour politicians, new ideas of 104–7; North Sea gas and oil 99–101, 109; public expenditure 102; relationship between social and environmental policy agendas 109–11; social reforms 101–4
Labour government (1997–2001) 169–89; *A Better Quality of Life* strategy 183–5, 188; Climate Change Levy 182; ecosocial agenda 186–7; emissions 186; globalisation 171–3; health and education 179–80; modernising the environment 180–7; planning policy 181–2; relationship between social and environmental policy agendas 187–8; social security policy 175–9; 'Third Way' 173–5; transport policy 185–6; workfare 177
Labour Party 11, 17–18, 21, 23, 29, 96, 169–70; 1951 election defeat 60–1; divisions 62–4, 114, 171, 210–11
Labour's international agenda (1997–2005) 190–209; emissions trading 199–201; energy markets 193–4; environmental policy 206–7; Europe and the world 197–202; health, education and housing policies 204–6; international development 194–5; Kyoto Protocol 195–6; New Labour in Europe 191–4; poverty and society 202–6; relationship between social and environmental policy agendas 208–9; social reforms 203–4; trading offsets 201–2; unities 197
land: nationalisation 23; ownership 35–6; planning policy 19–21; value 14–15, 20–1, 37–8, 105
Last, Nella 33

Lavers, G. 17
Lawson, Nigel 118
Legge, K. 202
lend-lease 12
Liefferink, C. 157
Limits to Growth (Club of Rome) 88–9
Lisbon Treaty 192
Local Agenda 21 152, 158, 159–61, 166–7
London smog 2, 24, 42–3, 45, 57, 110
Low Carbon Transition Plan 2009 218–19
Lowe, R. 140

Macmillan, Harold 49–53, 54, 57
McQuail, P. 90
Major, John 149, 157–8, 232
Mandelson, Peter 178
Marwick, A. 69, 70
Marx, Karl 14
Mattausch, J. 55
media 45
Middle Way, The (Macmillan) 50
Miliband, David 217, 220
Mill, John Stuart 14
Millennium Developments Goals (MDGs) 191, 194–5
Mishan, E. J. 70
Monbiot, G. 191
Montreal Protocol 133, 134, 152
Morgan, K. 91

Nadin, V. 37, 38
National Assistance Act (1948) 17
National Health Act (1946) 17
National Health Service (NHS) 33, 51, 66, 82, 179, 214–15; internal market 139–40; patients' rights 213; pay beds 103; preventive health 204–5
National Insurance Act (1946) 17
National Insurance Act (1959) 51
national parks 19
National Smoke Abatement Society 46
'National Strategy for Neighbourhood Renewal' (New Labour) 161
National Trust 22, 23
National Union of Mineworkers (NUM) 118–19
nationalisation 15–16, 61; of land 23
nature 71; and the Conservatives 35–8; ecological burden on 236, **238**; and Keynes 13–15; raw materials 15–16, 110
New Deal for Transport, A (white paper) 185
New Labour 161, 170, 171, 187–8, 232; and the EU 191–4; and globalisation

171–3; social policy mantras 175; 'Third Way' 173–5, 225
New Left 68
New Right 113, 114–16, 121, 124–5, 126, 135
New Towns Act (1946) 19
Norway 101, 111n7
nuclear programme 52–4

Oberthür, S. 198
Ockwell, D. 186
oil production 78; North Sea gas and oil 99–101, 109
Organisation of Petroleum Exporting Countries (OPEC) 78
Orwell, George 10, 15
Oudenes, M. 200
Our Common Future (Brundtland Commission) 132–3
ozone layer 133

Passport to Pimlico (film) 11
Payne, A. 197
Pearce, D. 136–7
Pearson, P. 120
pensions 51, 122, 178–9; Pension Credit 203–4; state-earnings-related pension 102
Pensions Act (1975) 102
personalisation 212–13
Pimlott, B. 69
planning policy 19–21, 24–5, 36–8, 64, 73, 128, 181–2
pollution 2, 24, 77; air pollution 2, 24, 42–3, 45, 57, 58, 107–8, 109, 110, 119; cleaning the air 46–7; emissions 186, 195–6, 198–9, 206, 219; emissions trading 199–201, 208; government failures 127–8; grandfathering 199; offsets trading 201–2; *Torrey Canyon* 69, 73–4, 75; transboundary problems 110–11; water pollution 90
Poor and the Poorest, The (Townshend and Abel-Smith) 67
population 71–3, 73, 110, 135
Population Bomb, The (Ehrlich) 71–2
Porritt, Jonathan 195–6
poverty 63, 67, 68, 83, 123–4, 141, 160, 194, 215–16; child poverty 178, 203; connection with climate change 197; and society 202–6
power crises (1970–74) 77–94; boom and bust economic policy 81–2, 84; currency problems 78; economic

problems 78–80; environmental policy 84–91; environmentalism as a social malaise 91–2; global politics 88–9; green movements 86–8, 91; oil production 78; poverty 83; relationship between social and environmental policy agendas 92–3; social reforms 82–3
Prescott, John 182, 185, 188, 194, 226
pressure groups 21–2
Private Finance Initiative (PFI) 172–3
privatisation 116–17, 120, 141–3, 154–5, 192
protest groups 68–9, 154
public goods 6, 120, 141–3
public sector: perception of inefficiency 140–1; privatisation 141–3
Pugh, M. 18

Rachman, Percy 66
railways 55–7, 155, 185
Rating Act (1966) 66
Reclaim the Streets 154
Rent Act (1957) 51
Reyes, O. 200–1
Rio Declaration on Environment and Development 151
risk 180
Rose, C. 127
Rowntree, S. 17
Rutledge, I. 193

Sandbrook, D. 68, 69–70
Scargill, Arthur 118–19
Schumacher, E. F. 14, 15
Scott Report (1942) 22–3
Sex Discrimination Act (1975) 103
shared public spaces 38, 233, 234
Shaw, R. 219
Sheail, J. 73–4
Sibieta, L. 215, 216
Silent Spring (Carson) 70–1
Simmons, P. 107–8, 127
Simon, J. 71
Single European Act (SEA) 144, 156, 163
Skidelsky, R. 15
Social Democratic Party (SDP) 114
social exclusion 177, 187
social policy: ecosocial system, building of 236, **237**; European Union (EU) 164–5; future policy-making 232–41; marketisation 231–2; relationship with environmental policy agenda 1–3, 8, 24–5, 48–9, 57–8, 74–5, 92–3, 109–11,

social policy *continued*
145–7, 165–7, 187–8, 208–9, 226–7,
229–41, **230**; residual and weak sectoral
integration 231; weak modernisation
232
social reforms: Conservative government
(1951–55) 32–5; Conservative
government (1970–74) 82–3;
Conservative policies (1987–90)
137–41; Conservative policies
(1990–97) 161–4; Labour government
(1945–51) 16–18; Labour government
(1964–70) 66–7; Labour government
(1974–79) 101–4; Labour government
(1997–2001) 175–80; Labour
government (1997–2005) 203–4;
Labour governments (1997–2010)
214–17
social security benefits 34, 67, 82, 103,
122, 162, 213, 215; tax credits 176, 203
Socialism Now (Crosland) 104–5
Socialist Challenge, The (Holland) 105–6
Society for the Protection of Ancient
Buildings 22
spaceship Earth notion 69
stakeholding 170
State We're In, The (Hutton) 170
Stern, Nicholas 137, 196, 201, 217, 240
Stevenson, J. 21, 22
subsidiarity 158
Sumption, Jonathan 123, 125
sustainability 39, 132–3, 156, 160–1,
183–5

Tawney, R. H. 234
taxation 23, 33, 116, 123, 159, 213; Poll
Tax 144; tax credits 176, 203, 215
Taylor, R. K. 137
Thatcher, Margaret 82–3, 95–6, 98,
118–19, 163, 231–2; and environmental
issues 134–6; Thatcherism 113, 124–5,
144–5
Theobold, K. 161
This Common Inheritance (white paper)
150, 158
Thorsheim, P. 45
Tickell, O. 196, 200
Titmuss, R. 23–4, 235
Town and Country Planning Act (1947)
19–21, 23, 36, 37
Town and Country Planning Act (1959)
37

Town and Country Planning Act (1968)
73
Town and Country Planning Acts (1953
and 1954) 37
Town Development Act (1952) 36–7
Townsend, Peter 67
trade unions 65, 68, 79, 80, 82, 97–8, 172;
miners' strike (1984–85) 118–19;
Thatcher's reform of 117
Transport Act (1968) 73
transport policy 55–7, 73, 105, 154–5,
185–6, 206–7; air travel 206, 220

United Nations Conference on the
Human Environment (1972) 88, 107
United Nations Framework Convention
on Climate Change 151

Vietnam War 68

wages 97, 120, 175, 176, 215, 222;
minimum wage legislation 172
Walker, Peter 89, 90
Wall, D. 87
Ward, Barbara 85
Water Act (1973) 90
water supply and sewage 142–3
Watson, J. 120
Welfare Reform Act (2007) 213
welfare state 11, 68, 121–2; Conservative
attitude to (1970–74) 83–4; diminution
239; effectiveness at dealing with
environmental problems 3; free-riding
welfare state 236, **238**; green welfare
state 235–6, **238**, 239–40; hyper-
productivity 239; post-productivism
239–40; relationship with the economy
101–2; retrenchment of 7
West, P. 140
Williston, Brian 43
Wilson, Harold 63–4, 65, 69, 96; National
Plan 64; speech at 1969 Labour Party
conference 74, 75
women 121
Wood, Kingsley 28
Working Time Directive (1993) 164,
191–2
World Commission on Environment and
Development *see* Brundtland
Commission
World3 88–9
Wynne, B. 107–8, 127

For Product Safety Concerns and Information please contact our EU
representative GPSR@taylorandfrancis.com
Taylor & Francis Verlag GmbH, Kaufingerstraße 24, 80331 München, Germany

www.ingramcontent.com/pod-product-compliance
Ingram Content Group UK Ltd.
Pitfield, Milton Keynes, MK11 3LW, UK
UKHW021618240425
457818UK00018B/631